THE ATTACK ON HIGHER EDUCATION

American higher education is under attack today as never before. A growing right-wing narrative portrays academia as corrupt, irrelevant, costly, and dangerous to both students and the nation. Budget cuts, attacks on liberal arts and humanities disciplines, faculty lay-offs and retrenchments, technology displacements, corporatization, and campus closings have accelerated over the past decade. In this timely volume, Ronald G. Musto draws on historical precedent – Henry VIII's dissolution of British monasteries in the 1530s – for his study of the current threats to American higher education. He shows how a triad of forces – authority, separateness, and innovation – enabled monasteries to succeed, and then suddenly and unexpectedly to fail. Musto applies this analogy to contemporary academia. Despite higher education's vital centrality to American culture and economy, a powerful, anti-liberal narrative is severely damaging its reputation among parents, voters, and politicians. Musto offers a comprehensive account of this narrative from the mid twentieth century to the present, as well as a new set of arguments to counter criticisms and rebuild the image of higher education.

Award-winning historian Ronald G. Musto has taught at three universities and served at ACLS Humanities E-Book (co-director), the Medieval Academy of America (co-executive director, co-editor of *Speculum*), and Italica Press (co-publisher). He is Honorary Research Fellow at the University of Bristol. He is co-author, with Eileen Gardiner, of *The Digital Humanities*.

Advance Praise for *Attack on Higher Education*

Employing ample historical knowledge, a fine eye for current trends, and a razor-sharp analytical prose, Ronald Musto has offered a bracing and necessary examination of the current plight of higher education. Though his focus is U.S. higher education, the book has global implications. As a history, a landscape analysis, and a font of suggestions for a way forward, Musto's book will be essential reading for all those who care about the future of higher education.

Christopher Celenza, James B. Knapp Dean, Krieger School of Arts
and Sciences, Johns Hopkins University

When Ronald Musto was writing this wise, well-informed, and alarming book, even he could not have known how trenchant his analyses would appear by the date of publication or how quickly his prophecies would begin to come true. As institutions of higher education struggle to find a "new normal" in the midst of pandemic and authoritarian uproar, they risk failing to see how powerful are the forces arrayed against them. Musto can tell them.

James O'Donnell, University Librarian, Arizona State University

Ron Musto's *Attack on Higher Education* is a profoundly timely and transformative work – a must read for anyone who cares about higher education – where we are now and how we got here. Shakespearean in scope and depth, this book tells an extraordinarily powerful and complex story, at times exhilarating and painful, that impacts each of us today. Indeed, it is one of the most moving, important, engaging, and significant books I have read in a long time. I simply could not put it down.

Suzanne P. Blier, Allen Whitehill Clowes Professor of Fine Arts
and Professor of African and African American Studies,
Harvard University

Of the many books out there about the crisis of American higher education, read Musto's first. Even readers who disagree with his point of view will learn from his nuanced portrait of the university's uncomfortable multiple allegiances – to knowledge, democratic education, and elitism – that have left it so vulnerable to the changes wrought by new media and technology. Musto's existential questions and suggested strategies should be required reading for chairs and deans.

Joy Connolly, President, American Council of Learned Societies

The Attack on Higher Education

The Dissolution of the American University

Ronald G. Musto

CAMBRIDGE
UNIVERSITY PRESS

CAMBRIDGE
UNIVERSITY PRESS

University Printing House, Cambridge CB2 8BS, United Kingdom

One Liberty Plaza, 20th Floor, New York, NY 10006, USA

477 Williamstown Road, Port Melbourne, VIC 3207, Australia

314–321, 3rd Floor, Plot 3, Splendor Forum, Jasola District Centre, New Delhi – 110025, India

103 Penang Road, #05–06/07, Visioncrest Commercial, Singapore 238467

Cambridge University Press is part of the University of Cambridge.

It furthers the University's mission by disseminating knowledge in the pursuit of education, learning, and research at the highest international levels of excellence.

www.cambridge.org
Information on this title: www.cambridge.org/9781108471923
DOI: 10.1017/9781108559355

© Ronald G. Musto 2021

First published 2021

Printed in the United Kingdom by TJ Books Limited, Padstow, Cornwall

A catalogue record for this publication is available from the British Library.

ISBN 978-1-108-47192-3 Hardback

To Ann, Eileen, Michele, Nathalie, Phillip, and Sebastian

Epigraph

For the church was the first thing that was spoiled; then the abbot's lodging, the dormitory and refectory, with the cloister and all the buildings around, within the abbey walls. For nothing was spared except the ox-houses and swinecoates and other such houses or offices that stood outside the walls – these had greater favour shown to them than the church itself. ... Thirty years after the Suppression I asked my father ... if he thought well of the religious people and of the religion followed at that time? And he told me yes, for he saw no cause to the contrary. "Well," I said, "then how did it come to pass that you were so ready to destroy and spoil the thing that you thought so well of?" "What should I have done," he asked, "might not I as well as the others have had some profit from the spoils of the abbey? For I saw that everything would disappear and therefore I did as the others did."

— Conversation between Michael Sherbrook and his father on the latter's role in the sack of Roche Abbey, during the Dissolution. From British Library, Add. Ms 5813, quoted in Historic England, "A near contemporary account of the 'spoilation of Roche' Abbey, Yorkshire."[1]

---

[1] www.english-heritage.org.uk/visit/places/roche-abbey/history/suppression.

Contents

Preface: The Idea of This Book

The following book came out of a polemic I published in 2015 comparing the current crisis in American higher education to the period of Henry VIII's Dissolution of the English monasteries in the 1530s.[1] That polemic was essentially political and predated the ascendancy of the then Republican majorities in the US states, congress, judiciary, and White House. Formalized into a book proposal, it was generously accepted by Cambridge University Press. This was not a particularly novel or radical comparison. University of California President Clark Kerr had invoked the parallels between the university and the monastery as early as 1964,[2] and he had done so by recalling Cardinal Newman's earlier notion of humanist higher education. It was revived by anthropologist Margaret Meade in her analysis of events at Columbia University in 1968.[3] But to turn a brief article into a reflective book required more than simply expanding out narrative with details and examples.

Two major events have intervened between the time when I first conceived this book and when it reached its current form: one political and one personal. Though the 1960s taught us the essential unity of these forms, I will briefly try to disambiguate them here. The first, political, was the election of Donald Trump as president and the 2016 capture of the House, Senate, and Supreme Court by a right-wing movement embodied in the current Republican Party. Richard

---

[1] www.academia.edu/17629520/The_Dissolution_of_the_Universities.

[2] Clark Kerr, *The Uses of the University* (Cambridge, MA: Harvard University Press, 1964), 1–2.

[3] "The Wider Significance of the Columbia Upheaval," *Columbia University Forum* (Fall 1968), excerpted in Wallerstein and Starr, 423–29, at 423–24.

Hofstadter's *Anti-Intellectualism in American Life*[4] and *The Paranoid Style in American Politics*[5] long ago analyzed this movement as a constant challenge to our intellectual culture and consensus. Projected as a possible threat to American higher education in my essay of 2015, this movement became the dominant political force in the United States – much contested and resisted – but still dominant over many areas of policy-making and the American mindset. This reality has both confirmed my original forebodings and prompted me to assume a more analytical than polemical tone for this volume.

The second event has been my departure from the United States in early 2018, prompted only in part by politics and largely by the cultural and intellectual predilections of two semi-retired medievalists. From my perch in Clifton in Bristol, England and an honorary appointment as Research Fellow in the Centre for Medieval Studies at the University of Bristol, many of the heated issues of life in the United States – its materialism, its violence, its anti-intellectualism, and its chasms of inequality – now seem less personally threatening and confining and more objectively analyzable. This distance makes the following book more an attempt to describe, analyze, and hopefully suggest paths away from the brink.

I do not claim to be an expert in higher education, nor in politics or political economy. I do, however, approach this book from the perspective of a scholar of a certain age. I have published on various aspects of American culture: war, peace, social justice, the impact of the digital revolution on our daily lives and our habits of thought and social life, on urban history, space, and institutions. As senior staff at the American Council of Learned Societies and co-Executive Director of the Medieval Academy of America and co-editor of its journal *Speculum*, I have served an apprenticeship to experts in many aspects and issues of higher education. These have included its basic forms of communication; its organization and finance; its problems of hiring, tenure, and promotion; and its impact on American social, cultural, and intellectual life.

---

[4] Richard Hofstadter, *Anti-Intellectualism in American Life* (New York: Vintage Books, 1962).

[5] Richard Hofstadter, *The Paranoid Style in American Politics* (New York: Vintage Books, 1965; rev. ed., with new foreword by Sean Wilentz, 2008).

As a specialist in late medieval history, with some knowledge of the events surrounding the dissolution of that social and intellectual universe, I was naturally drawn to historical comparisons, analogies, and metaphors. As pioneers in the digital humanities, I and my partner Eileen Gardiner had become well familiar with the metaphors and analogies that accompanied the digital – the new iteration of the book from manuscript to print, then from print to digital; the new web of online relationships analogous to the thick social networks of communication among writers and readers found in the medieval textual communities built around the fluid manuscript cultures of late medieval Italy and Europe. To be clear, the early modern monarchy of sixteenth-century England cannot legitimately be compared to the democratic republic of the United States in the twenty-first in terms of its political structures, deployment of state power, structural checks and balances, and forms of resistance and civil society. But the convergence of various social, economic, and cultural forces that led to the Dissolution certainly can be taken as a model – either as a metaphor or an analogy – for the same types of convergences at work in twenty-first-century America. Such use of metaphor and analogy is in many ways part and parcel to all historical study – however scientific or literary its methodologies – and it seemed a natural extension to latch on to the metaphor of the Dissolution of the Monasteries under Henry VIII as a way of exploring the current crisis in American higher education.

*

This book is not an indictment of American higher education but a reflection on the growing narrative of those who would destroy it. *Chronicle of Higher Education* columnist Vimal Patel highlighted the process by which America's colleges and universities are losing control of this narrative and how it is exploited, and distorted, by media and politicians.[6] To present the components of this narrative, I will bring into play all the themes used by the critics of our system of higher

[6] "Colleges Are Losing Control of Their Story: The Banh-Mi Affair at Oberlin Shows How," CHE (Oct. 31, 2019), at www.chronicle.com/article/Colleges-Are-Losing-Control-of/247465.

education. Just as Thomas Cromwell's 1535 Act of Suppression of the monasteries contained many kernels of truth – amplified by a consistent and negative narrative – so too the argument against the university builds on acknowledged faults and internal contradictions long addressed by and in American higher education. My aims in this book are two: first to elucidate this developing narrative, to delineate its scope, and to identify its major elements; and second, to attempt to underscore the dangers posed by such a narrative and its related political gambits.

The following chapters bring together both advanced research and journalistic reporting on current trends. But this is not a journalistic coverage that balances reports and statistics against interviews with experts or the person-on-the-street. It seeks rather to take a step back from daily, journalistic coverage to attempt something more reflective, something that might be of value over and above reportage. In the sense that this book might be considered a polemic at all, it is as a portrayal of the rhetorical threat to higher education, primarily in the United States, secondarily in North America as a whole and for the United Kingdom and Australia, which all face similar ideological programs and challenges. In as much as it is based on a growing body of fact and evidence, it also attempts to summarize for both academics and the general public the danger posed to American culture, economy, and society by unexamined assumptions and attitudes toward higher ed.

This book is therefore about narratives: their bases, development, and use. It is also a book about vast economic resources and those who would control them. The two themes are inextricably linked. In FY 2013–14 the total spent in the US on higher education was $517 billion (3 percent of GDP): nearly $324 billion at public institutions, $173 billion at private nonprofit institutions, and $20 billion at private for-profit institutions. This is a vast treasure, larger in proportion than the value of all the lands and moveable wealth of the dissolved monasteries seized by Henry VIII in the 1530s. Control of these resources has become a vital public interest. The narrative about higher ed's nature, management, and benefits is therefore as important as the one that helped Henry VIII and Thomas Cromwell dissolve the monasteries.

*

A crisis is upon us, beyond a doubt. Over the past decade it has become apparent to all in American higher education – administrators, faculty, students, funders, and critics – that our system of learning is facing unprecedented threats to and transformations of its basic goals, institutions, and freedoms. Few today could claim that such statements are hyperbolic or memetic. Few, on the other hand, might agree – at this point – with the recent radio comment by a Tennessee lawmaker, which he himself later characterized as "hyperbole": "If there's one thing that we can do to save America today, it's to get rid of our institutions of higher education right now and cut the liberal breeding ground off!"[7]

Few, however, have attempted – as we will do here – to join together the various strains of contention over higher education today into a single narrative. This has its dangers, of course. Oversimplification and rigidity are chief among them. Yet, as the following book seeks to demonstrate, higher ed in the US has been subjected to just such an increasingly multifaceted, if largely simplified and mistaken, narrative by its enemies. In the following pages we therefore seek to unravel and analyze the elements of its construction, and to make our readers aware of how they do fit into a master narrative of decline, abuse, and societal in-utility, a narrative that must first be acknowledged before it can be usefully met and countered. Will this attempt stand as consistent, timely, and convincing? We hope that by constructing it we will serve less to discourage or condemn than to provide a useful frame for further analysis, discussion, and action.

This volume seeks to provide a historical perspective on the changes that have affected higher education from the beginnings of the Western university system in the twelfth century. It does so by synthesizing a great deal of historical and contemporary research and analysis. This book thus hopes to present enough evidence to convince readers of the plausibility of the demise of the historical humanities, liberal arts and sciences in the current system of American higher education and of the destruction of the fabric that once housed these core disciplines and

---

[7] Dillon Thompson, "Tennessee Lawmaker Kerry Roberts Says Abolishing Higher Education Would 'Save America'," AOL.com (Sept. 10, 2019), at news.yahoo.com/tennessee-lawmaker-kerry-roberts-says-145522610.html.

their values. Beyond that, it seeks to pose questions to academics across the disciplines: what do we do now, and where do we go? what can we preserve of the old system? what do we build anew?

*

The methodology of this book is largely a historical one. In chapters 1–3 we lay out the deep historical antecedents of modern institutional issues. These antecedents include essential background, such as a brief history of monasticism and its contributions to Western culture and institutions, the nature of the humanities and liberal arts, their intended audiences and social purposes, their organization and dissemination. Within the latter we examine the origins of the universities in both medieval monastic and cathedral schools, the birth and development of early modern humanism and its pedagogy, and its impact on higher education in Europe, in Britain, and then in America. Once in America we trace the history of the American college and university system into the 1960s and the crisis symbolized by "1968." Chapters 4–9 then provide historical background, current developments, and modern examples of a variety of issues both affecting American higher education and forming part of a cohering narrative being formed by the right-wing about higher ed's failings. Our conclusions attempt both to reiterate these themes and findings and to look forward to some possible futures.

Each chapter follows roughly the same structure: deep historical origins, presentation of data, analysis derived from both monographs and journal literature, and then case studies to illustrate the major themes of the chapter and section. Such examples have had to be selective: the current literature is flooded with cases reflecting every aspect of the current crisis in higher education. In the later chapters of this book, where we discuss the most pressing issues facing higher education today, most of the examples are from journalistic sources but are at least two or three years old. Our research into most of these case studies was completed at the end of 2019. We have updated it only selectively as necessary to provide as accurate an account of our examples as possible. We have taken this approach to add necessary perspective and to avoid both the tone of journalism – as cogent as this can be – and its sense of constantly shifting ground.

We are attempting to point out general trends and to tie them to historical examples as well; and for this we have needed at least this small degree of perspective. In place of a journalistic approach we have drawn upon a wide variety of sources: historical and contemporary monographs and journal articles, collections of primary-source documents, letters, speeches, and treatises on the wide range of themes discussed in the following chapters, statistical reports, and surveys drawn from Department of Education, Humanities Indicators, and other quantitative sources, and a wide range of current media coverage ranging from the *Chronicle of Higher Education* and *Inside Higher Ed*, to *USA Today*, the *New York Times*, the *Washington Post*, the *Atlantic*, the *Huffington Post*, the *New York Post*, and many others, from the right and left. Such outlets include everything from reportage to interviews, to analysis and criticism. The range of this material has helped us avoid one-sided analysis; but it also reflects the heightened interest in and scrutiny of higher ed among Americans today. There are also many fine examples of grand overviews of higher education, written by leading practitioners and experts, that take comprehensive account of many of these themes. We have used the work of David Knowles, Eamon Duffy, Diarmaid MacCulloch, G. W. Bernard, and Paul Grendler for early chapters; of Richard Hofstadter, Wilson Smith, and John Thelin for later chapters; and we have summarized the thinking of several others, including Derek Bok, William Bowen, and Michael Crow in our final conclusions.

Acknowledgments

I would like to thank those who helped with advice, expertise, and questions during the research and writing of this book: C. David Burak of Santa Monica College; Christopher Cronin of Columbia University Libraries; Joseph J. Esposito of Clarke & Esposito, LLC and of Ithaka S+R; George Ferzoco of the University of Bristol; F. Donald Logan of Emmanuel College, Boston; Carolyn Meussig of the University of Calgary; James Neal of Columbia University Libraries; James O'Donnell of Arizona State University; Ann Okerson of the Center for Research Libraries; Benjamin Pohl of the University of Bristol; and Robert B. Townsend of the American Academy of Arts and Sciences.

At Cambridge University Press my thanks to Beatrice Rehl, Humanities Publishing Director and sponsoring editor for this book who trusted in the promise of a brief polemic to become a book and who has guided it through from concept to publication; to Katherine Tengco Barbaro, Senior Content Manager for Humanities; and to Sarah Turner for her close and professional attention to the final copy-editing of this book.

I dedicate this book to our New York friends – Nathalie Altman, Phillip Baldwin, Michele Beck, Sebastian Currier, and Ann McCoy – who listened to early versions of this idea at our monthly gatherings and whose questions and comments helped me make it more formal and rigorous. My special thanks, as ever, to Eileen Gardiner, life friend, partner, and collaborator in all I have done and do, for advice, ideas, guidance, and encouragement in the development and completion of this project. Livy wrote that one of the purposes of writing history was so that one could remain remote but still record – with mixed interest and anxiety – events unfolding all around. In many senses Dr. Gardiner and I have remained close to – and remote from – the developments affecting American higher education that this book traces and analyzes. We both continue to share our interest and anxiety, and hope to see favorable omens over these events.

Abbreviations

CHE   *The Chronicle of Higher Education*

Hofstadter & Smith   *American Higher Education: A Documentary History.* Richard Hofstadter and Wilson Smith, eds. 2 vols. (Chicago: University of Chicago Press, 1961).

IHE   *Inside Higher Education*

Ridder-Symoens   Ridder-Symoens, Hilde, ed. *A History of the European University* I: *Universities in the Middle Ages* (Cambridge: Cambridge University Press, 1991).

Smith & Bender   *American Higher Education Transformed, 1940–2005: Documenting the National Discourse.* Wilson Smith and Thomas Bender, eds. (Baltimore: Johns Hopkins University Press, 2008).

Thelin   Thelin, John R. *A History of American Higher Education*, 2nd ed. (Baltimore: Johns Hopkins University Press, 2011).

Wallerstein & Starr   *The University Crisis Reader: The Liberal University under Attack.* Immanuel Wallerstein and Paul Starr, eds., vol. I (New York: Vintage Books, 1971).

Part I
Background

CHAPTER 1

Introduction

THE METAPHOR

THIS BOOK STARTED WITH A HYPOTHESIS that I first published online in 2015: that the "Dissolution of the Monasteries" under Henry VIII in England in the 1530s provides a working metaphor for current challenges to higher education in the United States, and by extension to other Anglophone systems.[1] Why has this book adopted such a historical metaphor? Centuries, political systems and economies, social systems, and universes of belief divide our world from that of late medieval and early modern England and Europe. Skeptics will be quick to point out that – unlike the medieval monastery – the modern American university is secular, devoted to the pursuit of reason and knowledge, open to all, and forged around the values of this, not the next, world. They will add that, unlike the medieval monastery that emerged from a hatred of the world and civil society and was the tap root of all "medieval" obscurantism, the modern university was born of Renaissance and Enlightenment. It freed minds and bodies from the bonds of authority and blind tradition. It unchained and opened books and knowledge for all. Excellence and the free exchange of ideas were and are its inspirations and guiding principles. How can any valid comparisons – positive or negative – be made between the two institutions? This book seeks to answer these objections by demonstrating the clear affinities between the institutional life cycles of the monastery and the university.

---

[1] www.academia.edu/17629520/The_Dissolution_of_the_Universities.

DISSOLUTION: DEFINITIONS

Before we begin, we should look at what we, and the English of the 1530s, mean by "dissolution" and its root term "to dissolve." According to the *Oxford English Dictionaries*, "dissolution" might have four main and subsidiary meanings: 1. the action of formally ending or dismissing an assembly, partnership, or official body; 2. the action or process of dissolving or being dissolved; 3. disintegration, decomposition, or from this "death"; and 4. debauched living, dissipation.[2] In Parliament's Dissolution legislation, the word clearly refers to the first form. The first act of February 4, 1535 used the words "suppressed or dissolved,"[3] as did the second Act of May 23, 1539.[4] Yet in any social and cultural context multiple meanings of words always come into play, intentionally or not adding further dimension and context to strict definition. Thus the very notion of dissolution carried with it connotations of dissolving, disintegration, and decomposition, that is, less an official action imposed on a body or decided by some authority than a natural process of aging and decay.

If we examine the meanings of the verb "to dissolve," we derive the following six main and subsidiary definitions: 1. (with reference to a solid): to become or cause to become incorporated into a liquid so as to form a solution; 2. to disappear; 3. to subside uncontrollably into (an expression of strong feelings); 4. to dissolve an image or scene in a film, or to change gradually to (another) scene; 5. to close down or dismiss (an assembly or official body); and 6. to annul or end (a partnership or marriage). The idea and the actions that derived from the parliamentary acts of 1535 and 1539 carry over for us most of these meanings of the word "dissolve." Reviewing these meanings for our modern eye and ear

---

[2] See https://en.oxforddictionaries.com/definition/dissolution.

[3] Statutes of the Realm, III, 575, 27 Henry VIII, c. 28, reprinted in J. R. Tanner, *Tudor Constitutional Documents* (Cambridge: Cambridge University Press, 1922), 59–63, at 60.

[4] The Second Act of Dissolution, also known as the Act for the Dissolution of the Greater Monasteries, 31 Hen. VIII c. 13, Tanner, *Tudor Constitutional Documents*, 64–67. See the British National Archives, at www.nationalarchives.gov.uk/help-with-your-research/ research-guides/dissolution-monasteries-1536-1540/#4-the-dissolution-and-the-build-up-to-it-1524-1540-key-records.

will help us understand why this historical metaphor may be appropriate to the current condition of higher education in the United States.

The first meaning of "to dissolve," to "become or cause to become incorporated into a liquid," is what most modern readers will bring to mind and is the most useful for the modern processes that we hope to examine. In a very real sense the monasteries did dissolve: materially their bricks, stones, glass, lead, wood, their books, vestments, liturgical objects, fields, crops, granges were all dispersed into the local societies and economies of their dioceses and parishes. Their men and women melted away: into hospitals, colleges, parishes, and other religious institutions or more directly integrated into secular society. Like the walls of a cell in biology, the walls of the monasteries dissolved to discharge the mitochondrial materials that they had formerly kept protected and intact. What dissolved, then melted into the culture around it.

The second meaning, "to disappear," is also important: what had been a crowning achievement of Western culture for a thousand years disappeared in Britain within five years, leaving behind only contested records in parchment and stone. The monasteries' daily routines, chants, liturgical hours, processions, rituals, instructions, and labors concentrated in particular places simply ceased to exist. These places most often survived in name, but what had given them meaning suddenly ceased to be. The third meaning, focusing on human emotion, finds much evidence from the reign of Henry VIII: in protests, in pleadings, in accusations, in self-abasing excuse and attempts to ingratiate, in the agony of expulsion and punishment, in later recriminations and narratives up to our own century. The fourth meaning, borrowed from film practice and theory, uses the "dissolve" as the punctuation point of a narrative. We have all seen the "dissolve" countless times in film, video, and television, perhaps without taking too much notice, especially because it has become part of our everyday visual language. As one act or scene finishes and the screen goes dark – even only for a second or two – the "dissolve" calls an end to the action and prepares the viewer for whatever new is to come. A "dissolve" marks the transition from old to new. Again, the fifth and sixth meanings, "to close down" or "to annul" – institutional or contractual – come closest to the historical situation discussed here. All these meanings and connotations, of both "dissolution" and "dissolve," carry significant weight for us today, and we will refer to them again as our narrative and analysis of higher education in America unfolds.

THE INSTITUTIONAL TRIAD

Throughout this book we will also frame our narrative and analysis with a historical dynamic among three important factors crucial to the medieval monastery, to American higher education, or to any vibrant institution. This is the triad formed by three nodes: authority, separateness, and innovation. By "authority" we use all three meanings laid out by sociologist Max Weber.[5] These include the traditional authority of long-established cultural patterns, the charismatic authority of individuals, and the legal authority embodied in bureaucracies. All three forms of authority are characteristic of higher education: in its venerable traditions of teaching, learning, research, and expertise; in the accomplishments and personalities of individual teachers and leaders; and in its long history of embodied hierarchies, ranks, and degrees. Our usage of "authority," when not historical, can also be lateral. That is, it can derive from collaboration and consensus as well as the hierarchical authority of tradition, charisma, or law defined by Weber or invoked by John Henry Newman.[6] Authority lies at the heart of many modern debates over the university: the charismatic authority of the professorate either to pass on tradition (Allan Bloom)[7], or to challenge it (Henry A. Giroux)[8] the authority of the canon to encapsulate an idea or an ideology of culture and civilization; the authority of the university within society as a focus of accumulated knowledge and expertise; and the rigid professional

---

[5] Max Weber, "Politics as a Vocation," in *Weber's Rationalism and Modern Society*, Tony Waters and Dagmar Waters, eds. and trans. (New York: Palgrave Macmillan, 2015), 129–98.

[6] John Henry Newman, *The Idea of a University Defined and Illustrated: In Nine Discourses Delivered to the Catholics of Dublin* (Dublin: J. Duffy, 1852), Preface; in Project Gutenberg, 2008, at www.gutenberg.org/files/24526/24526-pdf.pdf.

[7] Allan Bloom, *The Closing of the American Mind: How Higher Education Has Failed Democracy and Impoverished the Souls of Today's Students* (New York: Simon and Schuster, 1987).

[8] Henry A. Giroux, "Liberal Arts Education and the Struggle for Public Life: Dreaming about Democracy," in Darryl J. Gless and Barbara Hernstein Smith, eds., *The Politics of Liberal Education*, (Durham, NC: Duke University Press, 1992), 119–44.

hierarchies of hiring, tenure, promotion, and their accompanying critical assessments.

The second node, "separateness," includes first, the physical separation that allows the college and university campus to exist (if so desired) physically apart from its surrounding environment, whether urban or rural; and second, the intellectual separateness that allows faculty and students to engage in teaching and learning around the entire range of accumulated knowledge, to question and to probe without the pressures of external social, cultural, economic, or political demands. As Tudor educator Roger Ascham (*c*.1515–68) put it, the classroom is "a sanctuary from fear."[9] As Erik Erikson phrased it four centuries later, the university is a "psycho-social moratorium" from the outside world.[10] In addition to spatial separation there is also a temporal one, a time set aside for students – whether three, four, or six years – to learn and explore, to match subjects that they have learned with their own spiritual and physical make-up and goals before entering the world of economy and profession. Such separation is embodied in the classic American campus: a green and leafy space apart, with clear boundaries, a distinct architecture recalling deep cultural roots and projecting authority, and a physical plan quite distinct from urban, suburban, and rural environments. So too the campus' sense of time: a system of semesters or terms distinct from the world of career and commerce, one not bound by rigid work days but by schedules and rhythms of its own.

In 1992, Gerald Graff reflected on the popular image of American higher education that inextricably links separateness with authority in a way that recalls medieval monasticism and religious life:

> Consider our most familiar image of the college, graphically depicted in the photographs of virtually every catalog: an oasis of pastoral serenity, removed from everything that is conflictual or dissonant in adult urban experience. Small intimate groups of students and professors gather

---

[9] Quoted in Rebecca W. Bushnell, *A Culture of Teaching: Early Modern Humanism in Theory and Practice* (Ithaca, NY: Cornell University Press, 1996), 186.

[10] Quoted by Daniel Bell in 1966, in Wilson Smith and Thomas Bender, eds., *American Higher Education Transformed, 1940–2005: Documenting the National Discourse.* (Baltimore: Johns Hopkins University Press, 2008), 170.

under shady trees on the smooth, sloping campus green. The professors are a benevolent lot, formidably learned and strict, of course, if colorfully ineffectual in the real practical world. For like ministers of the church, they presumably live removed from the harsh demands of commercial getting and spending that "real people" must reluctantly graduate into after their college days are over. It is just this otherworldliness that makes the professor's lessons so valuable in retrospect. ... These lessons exemplify that realm of "value" that the commercial and industrial world has so little respect for.[11]

The third node of this triad is "innovation." Research, creativity, knowledge creation, currency, or any number of other terms can also signify an institution's ability to advance cultural, intellectual, even economic knowledge, understanding, and application. Here the university has long stood out as an incubator of new ideas and their practical applications. The word has become standard in discussions of higher education and is a basso continuo for coverage in the *Chronicle of Higher Education*.[12] Pedagogy itself should be considered another key element in this formula, but it both underlies – and rests upon – all the three key elements we have already outlined and cannot be distinguished from them.

American higher ed has long recognized this triad. Writing in 1894, George Santayana noted: "Harvard was scientific ... it was complex, and ... it was reserved."[13] But this tripartite dynamic is both active and fragile. None of these three nodes are static, nor do they exist in themselves. Each will draw from and build upon the other two: authority deriving from a tradition of innovation, fostered by separation; innovation deriving from an ability to draw on institutional authority and the separate time and space to create; separateness protected both by the authority of an institution and by its reputation to create and innovate.

---

[11] Gerald Graff, "Teach the Conflicts," in Darryl J. Gless and Barbara Herrnstein Smith, *The Politics of Liberal Education* (Durham, NC: Duke University Press, 1992), 61.

[12] See, for example, its "The Innovation Imperative" report, at https://store.chronicle .com/collections/reports-guides/products/the-innovation-imperative.

[13] John R. Thelin, *A History of American Higher Education*, 2nd ed. (Baltimore: Johns Hopkins University Press, 2011), 162.

Not all institutions of higher education can claim an equal balance among all three of these nodes. One might, for example, surrender separateness for a stronger role in projecting authority or in adopting its culture to society's need for innovation. Conversely, it might surrender innovation for an enhanced position of separation and of the authority that comes from established knowledge and expertise. Such was the position of Cardinal Newman. For conservative thinker Allan Bloom, separateness went hand-in-hand with the absolute authority of the professorate but seems to have excluded innovation.[14] For critics on the left, such as Giroux and Michael Ryan, such separateness is a myth, the classroom never divorced from politics and "real life," and whatever authority traditionalists claim accompany it is really the product of individual charisma of teachers.[15] Thus the academy might surrender institutional authority in favor of a full immersion in the processes of social change and innovation. But the results of breaking down walls are two-edged. A university might trade off its authority or its separateness to some larger entity like the government or a corporate alliance in exchange for financial support or the prestige that comes from innovation.

In 1980, literary scholar Geoffrey Hartman equated "innovation" with "currency":

> Since the academy is, despite everything, a good place, one that protects the scholar's freedom to work on any topic that does not make him rich, we accept the trade-off that substitutes leisure for influence, and shape our lives accordingly. ... The isolation of the humanist may be a blessing in disguise. Yet there are signs at present that humanists, because of their isolation, have lost their currency, which is about all that was left after they had lost their authority.[16]

In the best of all possible worlds, the university will offer all three nodes of this dynamic triad in equal measure and will achieve what has

---

[14] In Bloom, *The Closing of the American Mind*, 244–5.

[15] See Bushnell, *Culture of Teaching*, 188–93.

[16] From Geoffrey Hartman, *Criticism in the Wilderness: The Study of Literature Today* (New Haven: Yale University Press, 1980), 289.

become the classic image of American higher education. In the worst, it might surrender any two of these elements and cease to function as a viable institution on any level. Losing authority and innovation, for example, it might become what Hartman feared: the stultified refuge of outdated traditions and disciplines. Losing authority and separateness, it might focus on innovation alone and become merely another business, a corporate university that exists solely for monetary reward; or it might surrender innovation and separateness, becoming nothing but a little-heeded voice of outworn authority and tradition, merely tolerated if not respected.

Using this dynamic, the history laid out in the following pages will also remind readers that the liberal arts, and humanists in particular, have been marginalized, ignored, and then reintroduced into systems of higher education repeatedly over the centuries. The current tensions between "career" and "arts" education is nothing new, nor is it particularly malevolent. But to insure that it is not, humanists must reimagine their place yet again. Deserts, mountaintops, isolated studies, and campuses all figure as major images of the scholar – whether the scientist or the humanist – at work. They encourage both innovation and separation and thus enhance authority. But then so too do over-flowing lecture rooms, brilliant publications well received and long-cherished, cultural capital, power, and influence. But the how and why of the humanities – and the broader liberal arts and sciences – change with each age. How that is now changing is the subject of this book.

THE MONASTERY

To explain this historical metaphor of dissolution, the following pages provide a brief review of medieval monasticism and highlight its cultural, political, and social significance. Why and how did monasteries provide the driving force of Western civilization for a millennium? What elements contributed to this?

First, from its origins among the hermits of third-century Roman Egypt, the authority of the monastery was based on the archetypal sacredness of the holy man and woman.[17] Over the next centuries the holy man and woman, separated from society and leading a new kind of spiritual and material life, developed a charismatic authority that challenged and transformed the inherited cultural and material life of antiquity. Second, their separateness underlay both an intellectual and a moral authority. Appeals by popes, emperors, and kings to monastic leaders to provide intellectual and spiritual leadership and to settle disputed issues became a major element of medieval political and cultural life. Third, monasticism's life of "work and prayer" enshrined in the Rule of Benedict of Nursia (d.*c*.547), became the driving force of medieval innovation.

"Prayer" (*ora*) and the inner life of the mind and spirit it symbolized, was now organized not by state cults of external ritual or even by the increasingly hierarchical structures of the early Church. "Work" (*labora*) meant a stark break with the lifestyle of the Roman ruling class, from which most early monks came. Manual labor in working the soil and growing one's own crops, building one's own monastery and maintaining it, even in copying one's own books and silently reading them took the role of the slave and transformed it into the life of the new monastic citizen. Self-governing groups of men or women now organized themselves around the basic principles of successive versions of Benedict's Rule. The very separateness of the monasteries from the affairs of the world thus made them a place apart that existed to benefit society as a whole. Benedict himself likened the monastery to what James Clark has called a "tabernacle retreat."[18]

Key elements of monastic life became physical manifestations of these ideals. Foremost was the monastery itself as a place apart. Several idealized plans for medieval monasteries survive. The best is that of St Gall in

---

[17] Peter Brown, *The Cult of Saints: Its Rise and Function in Latin Christianity* (Chicago: University of Chicago, 1980). Brown's work has been challenged by Ramsey MacMullen, "The Place of the Holy Man in the Later Roman Empire," *Harvard Theological Review* 112.1 (January 2019): 1–32.

[18] James Clark, *The Benedictines in the Middle Ages* (Woodbridge: Boydell, 2014), 131–32. On the Rule, see Clark, *Benedictines*, 5–30.

Switzerland,[19] dating from *c.*825 but based on an even earlier but now-lost manuscript original.[20] The ideas embodied in the plan date back to Roman city planning and architectural theory. Not a detail is random, and no space is left undefined or devoid of function or a specific relationship to the whole. It is urban and institutional planning at its best. Health and medicine; harnessing water supplies for mills, drinking, sanitation, and waste removal; education, hospitality and reception; ample accommodations for the rich and housing for the poor; places of worship and liturgy, craft and support facilities that included gardens, granaries, workshops, water-powered grindstones and mortars, and livestock barns, workshops for saddlers and shoemakers, curriers and turners, fullers, blacksmiths, and goldsmiths, coopers and wheelwrights, drying kilns and mortars for grain, are all laid out in a rational and interdependent system.[21] The plan of the abbey of Canterbury,[22] or the ruins of Fountains Abbey[23] in Yorkshire offer other examples.

Unlike the aristocratic Roman estate, the addition of the monastic chapter house physically embodied the shared governance of monastic life, for here the community regularly discussed and often openly debated aspects of their communal life and rule.[24] All of these innovations in the arts, architecture, technology, and the protocols of public life created a vast network of spiritual intercession and charismatic authority. Powerful abbots and abbesses became leaders to match and challenge the power and authority of princes and emperors.

As monasticism spread and its organization became more complex, agriculture, horticulture, and husbandry became major activities of monastic life. Forest, waste, and swamp clearance, better and more

---

[19] See Walter Horn and Ernest Born, *The Plan of St Gall*, 3 vols. (Berkeley: University of California Press, 1979); and Lorna Price, *The Plan of St Gall in Brief* (Berkeley: University of California Press, 1982).

[20] For the plan, see www.stgallplan.org/en/index_plan.html.

[21] See Diagram III: Organization of Service Facilities, in Price, *The Plan of St Gall*, 18–19.

[22] Canterbury Psalter, University of Cambridge, Trinity College Library, MS R.17.1. For the plan, see https://commons.wikimedia.org/wiki/File:Eadwine_psalter_-_Waterworks_in_Canterbury.jpg.

[23] For the plan, see George Hodges, *The Project Gutenberg EBook of Fountains Abbey* (Project Gutenberg, 2016), at www.gutenberg.org/files/52581/52581-h/52581-h.htm.

[24] For what follows, see Clark, *Benedictines*, 102–5, 131–65.

sophisticated methods of raising crops, sheep, and cattle were a mainstay of monastic theoretical knowledge and sustainable skill sets that soon spread to lay society both through local land-management arrangements and through deliberate imitation. When such intense activity was multiplied many-fold both by extensive land-holdings and the common interests and methods of monastic orders, new scientific forms and economic models developed to keep pace with the European-wide increase in output. Monastic innovations were adopted by lay landholders, but the higher levels of literacy and organization enjoyed by the monasteries insured that they would remain the avant-garde of economic growth and culture into the fourteenth century.

Work could often be combined with prayer in monastic advances in architecture, sculpture, painting, and decorative arts. But the monastery's most important application of this new understanding of work was in the development of the book.[25] It is well known that one of the major revolutions in reading and writing technology was the move away from the ancient scroll to the medieval codex: pages bound within two rigid covers, a technological innovation that made both reading and reference far easier and standardized. Scripture, then writings of late ancient Christian theologians, Roman historians, poets, rhetoricians, philosophers, architects, military theorists, composers, astronomers, and physicists all underwent a process of transformation from the scroll to the codex with their inclusion in monastic libraries.

Over the centuries such works were copied again and again in tens of thousands of codex manuscripts. Their survival – despite the ravages of war, fire and flood, looting and theft – was the major intellectual accomplishment of the monastery. St Gall's plan clearly shows both the scriptorium and the monastic library. The well-worn clichés of monasteries' chaining dusty old books and preventing their dissemination was as much a fiction of self-promoting humanists of the fifteenth century as of lightly informed celebrity scholars of the twenty-first. They are no more indicative of intellectual oppression than that of pens chained in twentieth-century banks: both were designed to guarantee continued

---

[25] See Clark, *Benedictines*, 238–47.

access to multiple users. Up until the use of new computer technologies in the past three decades, the survival of practically the entire corpus of ancient learning in the West – both Greek and Roman – was the accomplishment of the medieval monastery.

Such texts were soon overshadowed by new, innovative work undertaken within the cloister. Books of liturgy, prayer and ritual, biblical texts and commentaries, but also works of philosophy, of biology, agriculture and other day-to-day skills, of law, history, biography (sacred and secular), poetry, literature, music, astronomy, and mathematics – of all the ancient and new liberal arts and sciences – were written and disseminated by the monastery. Greek and Roman works were supplemented, refined, and sometimes superceded by the new philosophical, mathematical, and scientific thinking of the Muslim world, transmitted to the Latin West largely through translation centers in Iberia and spread through monastic circles.

The millennium between 500 CE and 1500 CE saw monasticism spread furiously.[26] The estimated 1,193 monastic houses of all types and sizes in c.500 grew to an estimated 20,369 by 1500. With a total population in Europe of about 62 million in 1500, this represented a per-capita ratio of about 1 monastery per 3000 people. In Britain the total estimated number of monasteries by 1500 was 1,333 for a population of 2.75 million,[27] or about 1 per 2,000. By contrast, in the United States in the year 2010 there existed 4,600 colleges and universities out of a total population of 309 million, or 1 per 67,174. Comparing these numbers, one cannot overestimate how deeply monasticism had penetrated and affected medieval life and society.

---

[26] David Knowles, *Christian Monasticism* (New York: McGraw Hill, 1969); C. H. Lawrence, *Medieval Monasticism*, 4th ed. (London: Routledge, 2015); Gert Melville, *The World of Medieval Monasticism* (Athens, OH: Cistercian Publications, 2016); Clark, *Benedictines*; and Alison I. Beach and Isabelle Cochelin, eds., *The Cambridge History of Medieval Monasticism in the Latin World*, 2 vols. (Cambridge: Cambridge University Press, 2020).

[27] David Knowles and R. N. Hadcock, *Medieval Religious Houses: England and Wales* (London: Longman, 1971), 494–95, put the number in England and Wales alone at about 925 by 1500. They note there, and on pp. 45–47, the difficulties and variations in deriving final, accurate numbers.

DISSOLUTION

By the 1530s, humanists like Desiderius Erasmus and Thomas More had formed a coherent critique of monasticism as a life with little or no direct benefit to society. In 1517 Martin Luther, himself an Augustinian Friar, began the Protestant Reformation in Wittenberg, Saxony. Among the Protestants' first impulses was to dissolve monastic communities as having no biblical authority and to reintroduce their communities and members into more secular life. Having lost their authority and reputation for innovation within society, the monasteries stood as increasingly meaningless hoarders and squanderers of both material and spiritual wealth, as glaring examples of a Christianity in dire need of reform. Their only remaining attribute, their very separateness, was characterized as scandal and offense to Reformation society. Monastic suppression followed in the Protestant Swiss Confederation starting in 1523, in Sweden in 1527, and in Denmark in 1528.[28]

By the later 1520s, it was becoming clear that Henry VIII's own realm was being seriously divided by these religious differences, and that the reformers were becoming an important spiritual, social, and economic force. Reform spirit ran high in Catholic England as well, fueled by both humanist thought and royal and religious concerns. Cardinal Thomas Wolsey, archbishop of York, Henry VIII's chancellor, and England's highest-ranking prelate, had already planned a major consolidation and reform of religious houses in the 1520s. His chief lieutenant in that work was a young Thomas Cromwell.

Henry himself thus had various reasons to embrace the reform, which he did in the 1520s. His own extravagant expenditures on domestic projects, his expanding government, the lavish court display of his and competing Renaissance courts, and his military and diplomatic ambitions on the Continent, soon left him looking for new sources of income as well. He ultimately found some of them in the monasteries.[29] By 1500,

---

[28] For what follows, see David Knowles, *The Religious Orders in England* III. *The Tudor Age* (Cambridge: Cambridge University Press, 1959, repr. 2004), 157–72.

[29] Knowles, *Religious Orders*, III:195–205; Knowles and Hadcock, *Medieval Religious Houses*; G. W. O. Woodward, *The Dissolution of the Monasteries* (London: Pitkin, 1974); Eamon Duffy, *The Stripping of the Altars: Traditional Religion in England, 1400–1580* (New Haven,

the 1,330 religious houses in Britain owned 25 percent of all Britain's lands but housed only about 12,000 monks and nuns, or less than .05 percent of the total British population.[30]

One still cannot say with any certitude what the motives for Henry and his chief minister, Thomas Cromwell, may have been in the Dissolution of the Monasteries that followed the Suppression Acts of 1535 and 1539. But some analysis is important here, since our goal in setting out this background is to attempt, by historical analogy, to gain some insight into current political and social attitudes toward US universities. Henry's insatiable need for funds certainly contributed, but so did centuries of criticism of monastic abuse and more recent Protestant calls to purify the Church by eliminating many of England's oldest religious institutions and practices. Catholic reformers like Erasmus and More joined in a humanist critique of medieval religious habits, including pilgrimage and monasticism. Many bishops were convinced that sequestered monastic incomes were better spent on more public diocesan needs, education, and pastoral care. Wolsey implemented a papal reform bull in 1518 but met with limited success; and in 1529 the Crown and Parliament agreed on widespread reforms. Cromwell himself had been key to implementing Wolsey's program.

According to the most recent – and generally held authoritative – treatment of Cromwell,[31] as late as the winter of 1536, the king, his council, and Cromwell were all uncertain on a course of action concerning Church reform and monastic discipline. It seems that they initially

Yale University Press, 1992; 2nd, rev. ed., 2005); G. W. Bernard, *The King's Reformation: Henry VIII and the Remaking of the English Church* (New Haven: Yale University Press, 2005), esp. 225–474; G. W. Bernard, "The Dissolution of the Monasteries," *History* 96.324 (2011): 390–409; Diarmaid MacCulloch, *Thomas Cromwell: A Revolutionary Life* (London: Allen Lane, 2018). These events have been fictionalized by Hilary Mantel in her Cromwell trilogy: *Wolf Hall* (2009), *Bring Up the Bodies* (2012), and *The Mirror and the Light* (2020), all London, HarperCollins.

[30] E. Buringh and J. Van Zanden, "Charting the 'Rise of the West': Manuscripts and Printed Books in Europe, A Long-Term Perspective from the Sixth through Eighteenth Centuries," *Journal of Economic History* 69.2 (2009): 409–45, and 427, Table 5; Bernard, "Dissolution," 390.

[31] MacCulloch, *Thomas Cromwell*, 318–22, 430–35, 439–41, 487–92, 509–12. Bernard, *King's Reformation*, generally concurs with this analysis.

conceived of a nationwide reform of houses, a "thinning out" of lax and recalcitrant monks who had abused their separate privilege and position of authority, or of houses that simply could no longer support a dwindling community. No notion of dissolution was brought up at all in deliberations or bills for Parliament. At his most radical Cromwell had envisioned merely the closures of the most intractable or unsustainable houses and a series of open forums to convince monks to leave the cloistered life voluntarily.

Ideology, joined with practical goals, often builds an unstoppable and revolutionary momentum; and by 1534, Henry and Cromwell had decided on the Visitation of all monastic houses in the kingdom,[32] with the Crown's assessments of monastic holdings complete by May 1535. By early 1535, Parliament had passed the first Act of Suppression of Religious Houses for abbeys with total value of under £200 and communities of under twelve. Its stated goal was reform, not dissolution.[33] Cromwell had in fact, attempted on several occasions to prevent the king from ordering the dissolution of larger houses, with mixed results. But the anti-reform northern revolt known as the Pilgrimage of Grace in 1536 sealed the fate of many large houses, as their abbots were declared traitors. The Crown henceforth associated monastic resistance with active treason. By 1537 Henry appears to have decided on the total Dissolution, either by the surrender of monastic communities themselves or by their forced seizure. But as late as the Act for the Dissolution of Abbeys of 1539,[34] legal wording remained ambiguous, and England's grandest Benedictine houses stood intact.

Events soon got the best of all parties. An alliance of France and the Holy Roman Empire against England forced Henry VIII into a major national-defense effort: securing England's borders with an extensive – and vastly expensive – fortress-building campaign not matched until the later nineteenth century. This demanded an immediate infusion of cash:

---

[32] For these events, see Knowles, *Religious Orders*, III:268–349; Bernard, *King's Reformation*, 243–47, 433–74.

[33] Statutes of the Realm, III, 575, 27 Henry VIII, c. 28; in Tanner, *Tudor Constitutional Documents*, 59–63.

[34] Statutes of the Realm, III, 733, 31 Henry VIII, c. 13; in Tanner, *Tudor Constitutional Documents*, 64–67.

the last surviving monasteries and women's houses were targeted for confiscation using existing legal precedent. But as late as the executions of the abbots of Glastonbury, Reading, and Gloucester in autumn 1539 hope remained that some form of monastic life would survive.[35] No grand, centralized plan drove the final Dissolution, but numerous converging, if disparate, interests shaped it. Only the closing of Waltham Abbey in March 1540 completed the piecemeal, stop-and-go process.

Many monastic houses had cooperated enthusiastically in their dissolution, since by 1537 Cromwell had begun a policy of generous pensioning to encourage departures – with a looming alternative of execution for treason for recalcitrant religious. While mendicant friaries and monastic shrines had been dissolved, many Benedictine houses had voluntarily converted their monastic status into that of "collegial" houses: "colleges" or residential communities of regular clergy. These were more immersed into the communities around them. Some were even incorporated into universities or joined the colleges set up by religious orders. Bickingham College in Cambridge morphed into Magdalene College, for example. The dissolution of these houses was less a destruction than a spilling out into the wider cultural and political matrix around them.

According to Diarmaid MacCulloch, "The dissolution of the monasteries was not a certainty until it was complete. What it was not was a long-term scheme authored by Thomas Cromwell."[36] According to G. W. Bernard, "No 'smoking gun' has been found that would enable the historian to indicate a precise date or to see this as a policy for which particular individuals were responsible."[37] Again, no grand, centralized plan, no conspiracy at the topmost echelons of government and society, no deliberate acts of legislation, no unchallenged willfulness of heads of state, no ideological extremism ended English monasticism. Expert analyses indicate that a multitude of motivations and events produced a result that no one could have predicted or planned. Such are the processes of history. Not the actions of a few important men but a multipolar, multi-valanced unfolding of causations and a variety of human agencies that only in retrospect can be reassembled in narrative

---

[35] See Knowles, *Religious Orders*, III:376–417; Bernard, *King's Reformation*, 462–74.
[36] MacCulloch, *Thomas Cromwell*, 492.   [37] Bernard, *King's Reformation*, 440.

and interpreted as a "natural" outcome of personalities, ideas, and larger socio-economic and cultural forces at work. We must bear this in mind when approaching and understanding events very close to us in time and space.

*

Whatever Henry's and Cromwell's intent, the long-term effects of their actions are well known. A British landscape strewn with "bare ruined choirs" testifying to the wholesale disassembly of monastic buildings, the confiscation of their lands and moveables, and the transformation of remaining monastic buildings – whether church naves, choirs, cloisters, or other buildings into parish churches, lay manor houses, or school facilities. The monasteries' dissolution had a true, physical aspect, like the bursting of a seed pod and the dispersal of its contents, or the breakdown of a cell wall and the spread of its protoplasm. The old enclosed and separate institution of monasticism now dissolved into the secular, lay landscape of Britain. The dispersal of monks and nuns into the new Protestant lay world, the adaptation of buildings for parish uses, the wholesale dispersal of libraries to individuals or lay institutions, the conversion of monastic landed wealth to new royal or lay owners, the distribution of vestments, furnishings, liturgical vessels to either cash or use in private estates all produced a melting down of separation and of walls into society at large.

Much, however, did not survive: church buildings were stripped of their lead roofs, vaulting and timbering, their stonework, columns and capitals, and pavings. Wall paintings, sculptures in stone and wood, stained glass, all eventually met the same fate, despite efforts of local parishes to hide or reuse them. Nor was the destruction solely the work of local forces: Cromwell himself hired Italian architect Giovanni Portinari to dismantle Lewes Priory church and to enhance the surviving residential buildings for his son Gregory.

As Eamon Duffy has so well documented, many hands were at work. The defacing, painting over, breaking up, burning and burial of medieval devotional arts destroyed not only an artistic legacy but a vibrant link to the past and to Europe as a whole. The shared culture of a millennium now lay shattered in what may be seen as a deliberate destruction of cultural memory and spiritual meaning. In a matter of a few years, one thousand years of deeply embedded spiritual, cultural, and material customs, habits and beliefs, rituals and devotions, prayers, sacraments, and intellectual and physical disciplines had disappeared from the British physical and mental landscape. The process took decades to complete, but there was no return. What took the place of the monasteries? Reuse of abbey buildings as new cathedrals and diocesan schools, their incorporation into university infrastructure, and local parish uses certainly provided some continuity, but the world had irrevocably changed. Though voices rose in protest, they were too weak and divided to match that of a national state finally determined on their destruction and replacement. Many welcomed the break, whether from indifference to the old order or from zeal for the new. Revolutions may be inspired by the grand ideas or ambitions of the few, but they are carried out by the small hands of many. What may begin with a handful of personalities and ideas takes on a momentum of its own and develops in directions few might have envisioned. By 1550 the monastic life of separation, prayer, and works no longer served as the innovator of European culture or as its seat of authority. That role had been taken over first by the cathedral school and then by the university. Let us step backward a bit to examine these.

THE CATHEDRAL SCHOOL

In the Carolingian–Ottonian age, roughly from the eighth to the eleventh century, various imperial courts had sponsored a reform of monastic education to emphasize a functional literacy for court and Church. Both palace and religious schools aimed to create leaders for the "Christian Republic." By the eleventh and twelfth centuries and the rise of mercantile towns and cities, however, monasteries found themselves the neighbors of a new lay society eager to learn the literate skills of business and civic life. With the growth of towns as civic and ecclesiastical capitals, the cathedral became a new focus of administration and religious life and ritual. Part of this new mission of the cathedral was the creation of cathedral schools.[38]

---

[38] C. Stephen Jaeger, *The Envy of Angels: Cathedral Schools and Social Ideals in Medieval Europe, 950–1200* (Philadelphia: University of Pennsylvania Press, 1994).

At most cathedral schools, the ancient liberal arts were all part of an increasingly standardized curriculum that stressed *litterae et mores*: learning and ethics, with greatest emphasis on the development of wisdom.[39] For the most part this derived from ancient models that were less tied to the study of texts themselves than to the moral and civic examples that they conveyed. C. Stephen Jaeger has called this a "charismatic culture," as opposed to a strictly "intellectual" one. The distinction is important, for it focuses on the social functions of higher education, its place in the world, rather than its incubation of a set of standardized disciplines with their own internal logic and rules of behavior and reward.

Such schools found themselves increasingly absorbed into a pan-European church structure driven by reformers in Rome and other centers. The need for consistent theological, legal, and humanities education throughout Latin Europe drove pressures to upgrade cathedral schools. Faculties too changed rapidly at the turn of the twelfth century as the new disputational philosophers began to attract students away from the old moral educators. By the twelfth century the most successful cathedral school turned out to be that of Notre Dame in Paris. This school combined an excellent location – the capital of the French kings – and a string of brilliant and charismatic teachers. Peter Abelard's irreverent and egotistical methods exemplify Paris' shift toward what would become known as Scholasticism with its emphasis away from *mores* and rhetorical training and toward intellectual disputation (dialectic) and logic, from the authority of good men to the authority of good books. The Paris cathedral school at Notre Dame became a "university" when it received its first royal charter, which that school currently dates to 1200.

THE UNIVERSITY

The term "university" tells us much about how medieval society conceived this new institution and how these ideas have remained or

---

[39] See Sarah B. Lynch, *Medieval Pedagogical Writings: An Epitome* (Leeds: Kismet Press), 87–104.

developed with us today.[40] The Latin word *universitas* derived from the same root as "universe" and means a collective body. A guild, trade association, city government, political assembly, or burial association might be described as a *universitas*. In their origins, schools like Paris and Bologna were such trade associations – in Bologna (*c*.1100) of students, in Paris (*c*.1200) of faculty – who had banded together for mutual support, protection from economic, political, and social pressures. These two universities set the models for all later establishments.

The universities started as laicized versions of monastic self-regulation, with their own masters and organization, rules of conduct, and recognized levels of status. The difference here was that these groupings claimed no special space, no campus in any modern sense, and certainly no permanent buildings for lectures, offices, or housing. Their space was an intellectual one, a sharp break with the moral instruction of the cathedral schools and their masters toward a new form of learning and active debate distinguished by intense study of approved texts. The separateness of the university was its own self-awareness of a core mission and a core group of masters and students. Later additions of "colleges" (boarding houses), chapels, assembly and instruction halls, or land holdings were secondary to the essential activity of intellectual focus, research, writing, and teaching around a set curriculum by qualified teachers and students. Lacking walls, the university's separateness derived from its bonds of mutual interest, respect, process, and recognition among its masters and its students and the resulting authority that it exercised within the larger world.

Like monasticism, the university movement was pan-European and responded to new populations, means, and social and political values

---

[40] For what follows see Hilde Ridder-Symoens, ed., *A History of the European University* I. *Universities in the Middle Ages* (Cambridge: Cambridge University Press, 1991); H. Randall, *The Universities of Europe in the Middle Ages*, 3 vols. repr. (Oxford: Oxford University Press, 1988); Lawrence Stone, ed., *The University in Society* I. *Oxford and Cambridge from the 14th to the Early 19th Century* (Princeton: Princeton University Press, 1974, repr. 2019); A. B. Cobban, *The Medieval Universities: Their Development and Organization* (London: Methuen, 1975); J. M. Kittellson and P. J. Transue, eds., *Rebirth, Reform and Resilience: Universities in Transition, 1300–1700* (Columbus: Ohio State University Press, 1984); Paul F. Grendler, *The Universities of the Italian Renaissance* (Baltimore: Johns Hopkins University Press, 2002).

and ends. It was born to meet the needs of medieval society, both intellectual and practical. The main specialties of the universities were four: philosophy, theology, medicine, and law, depending on region, government and papal establishments, and period. They were what we today would call professional schools. Paris represented the religious and spiritual in its emphasis on theology and philosophy; Bologna and other Italian universities the secular emphasis on medicine and law.

While modern American universities are often characterized (and often criticized) for their various theoretical turns, whether French literary theory, feminist thought, or the digital humanities, medieval culture is often seen as static. Yet the rediscovery of ancient philosophical texts – largely of Aristotle, transmitted from the Greek through Arabic and Jewish translations and commentaries and then in direct Latin translations – produced just this sort of dramatic and unsettling new intellectual turn. During the twelfth century it provided the major intellectual basis for the university and its methods. Thomas Aquinas is the best known of the Scholastic teachers and writers on logic, philosophy, and theology. Dialectic provided a basis for methodology, analysis, and outlook. For five hundred years it dominated countless areas of intellectual, moral, legal, and political thought across regions, cultures, and political systems.

Unlike our modern, open university systems, however, the cohort of Latin literates during most of the Middle Ages and Renaissance was drastically smaller than any literate community today.[41] Extrapolating estimates of literacy across medieval and early modern populations remains an imperfect science.[42] Suffice it to say that the numbers

---

[41] See Franz H. Bäuml, "Varieties and Consequences of Medieval Literacy and Illiteracy," *Speculum* 55.2 (1980): 237–65; Charles F. Briggs, "Literacy, Reading, and Writing in the Medieval West," *Journal of Medieval History* 26:4 (2000): 397–420; Ian F. Moulton, ed., *Reading and Literacy in the Middle Ages and Renaissance* (Turnhout: Brepols, 2004); Robert Black, "Literacy in Florence, 1427," in Daniel E. Bornstein and David Spencer Peterson, eds., *Florence and Beyond: Culture, Society and Politics in Renaissance Italy* (Toronto: Centre for Reformation and Renaissance Studies, 2008), 195–210; Buringh and Van Zanden, "Charting the 'Rise of the West'"; Paul Grendler, *Schooling in Renaissance Italy: Literacy and Learning, 1300–1600* (Baltimore: Johns Hopkins University Press, 1989), 71–78.

[42] Jan De Vries, *European Urbanisation, 1500–1800* (London: Methuen, 1984, reprt., Routledge, 2013); and John Munro, "Medieval Population Dynamics to 1500" (University

attending university and then becoming faculty were a very small percentage of the European population, perhaps fewer than 2 to 3 percent.
Though university students came almost exclusively from the upper
merchant and aristocratic families, some clerics, especially in the mendicant orders (Franciscans, Dominicans, Augustinians, etc.) came from
many social backgrounds and could rise to the highest levels of skill,
governance, and international reputation. The mendicants' own special
schools at universities like Paris and Oxford aided this mobility. But the
university population remained a small elite.

*

The history of the medieval universities is full of violent confrontations
between the university masters and students and the authorities and
residents of their host cities. "Town and gown" meant more than social
tension in an age where weapons were ready at hand and riots, loss of
life, and destruction of property could erupt over any number of causes.
But if conflict proved too threatening to the university, it could simply
pick up and move to another town. So did a *universitas* of scholars move
to Oxford in 1165 when English members were expelled from Paris; as
did those of troubled Oxford, who moved to Cambridge in 1209.

This combination of separateness, authority, and innovation made
the universities the arbiters of European intellectual, religious, and
political life. Major European decisions ranging from the orthodoxy of
individuals to the legitimacy of kings and emperors were referred to the
faculty of Paris or some other leading university. Beyond this, however,
on a day-to-day level, we can see how the university permeated this late
medieval culture. It created an international intellectual and professional class that shared common language (Latin), methodology (scholastic or dialectic), subject matter (theology, law, medicine), and
infrastructure (faculties, degrees, colleges, etc.). National and regional
differences and specialties certainly existed, but these developed within
this commonly acknowledged matrix of intellectual authority and
longstanding tradition.

of Toronto, September 2013), at www.economics.utoronto.ca/munro5/
L02MedievalPopulationC.pdf.

THE HUMANIST UNIVERSITY

The history of higher education is one of continual change – and balance – between the practical and the theoretical, between creating citizens and teaching professional skills. With Francesco Petrarch (1304–74) and the Italian humanist movement the pendulum again swung away from professional training to creating the life and values of the free citizen. Petrarch's criticisms of the medieval schoolmen, like the later humanists' criticisms of monasticism, have come to be emblematic of humanist attitudes toward medieval culture.[43] He harkened back to the pursuit of the liberal arts in the classical tradition that medieval universities like Paris had marginalized. Like Petrarch, the early humanists also downplayed the study of Aristotle and the syllogisms of dialectic and embraced their own study of the ancient liberal arts, finding in these texts a renewed source of wisdom, virtue, and example in public life. Their classically inspired style soon graced the chancellories of Italy's city states and the courts of its princes. They created a new lay, civic culture that self-consciously broke with monastic devotion and university specialization.

Humanists soon became tutors to Italy's ruling elites and then to the *ancien regime* across Europe.[44] Giovanni Pontano's *The Prince* (1468), Machiavelli's *The Prince* (1513), Erasmus' *The Education of a Christian Prince* (1516), and Guillaume Budé's *Education of the Prince* (1516) all aimed to instill a new sense of Christian political reality, duty, and virtue in rulers. Humanists also developed a theory of education for young men and women in works like Pier Paolo Vergerio's *On Noble Manners and Liberal Studies for Young Men* (*c.*1403) and Aeneas Silvius Piccolomini's *On the Education of the Free* (1450). Baldassarre Castiglione's *The Book of the Courtier* (1516) attempted the same with the manners and outlook of court officials. Classic textbooks followed, including Juan Luis Vives' *An*

---

[43] See Ernst Cassirer, Paul Oskar Kristeller, and John Herman Randall, Jr., *The Renaissance Philosophy of Man* (Chicago: University of Chicago Press 1969), 47–139; and Petrarca, *Invectives*, David Marsh, trans. (Cambridge: Harvard University Press, 2003), 2–179.

[44] Anthony Grafton and Lisa Jardine, *From Humanism to the Humanities* (Cambridge, MA: Harvard University Press, 1986). For a recent survey, see Christopher S. Celenza, *The Intellectual World of the Italian Renaissance: Language, Philosophy, and the Search for Meaning* (New York: Cambridge University Press, 2020).

Introduction to Wisdom (1524), and Erasmus' *On the Education of Children* (1529) and *On Civility* (1530).[45]

*

By 1525, humanists had infiltrated such universities as Florence, Bologna, Padua, Pavia, Naples, and Rome, specializing in what came to be known as the *studia humanitatis*, the liberal arts of grammar, rhetoric, oratory, history and biography, literature, and moral and later natural philosophy (natural science).[46] By the 1470s, the humanists had also perfected a new form of critical discourse, carried out not in scholastic debate but in written and printed treatises that could be shared by a European "republic of letters." These "liberal arts and sciences" were not "liberal" in any sense of being politically progressive (or correct) but "liberal" in the sense that they aimed to create "free" (*liberi*) men who could both participate in civil society and who could assume leadership roles. Instead of the goals of the medieval universities – to create a specialized, professional class of doctors, lawyers, and speculative thinkers – the humanists' goal was to develop a new, self-conscious, and secular elite. Without too much of a stretch in translation, what we call "the liberal arts" might better be labeled for an American audience today as "freedom studies."

While many examples of humanist women writers and thinkers continue to be discovered through contemporary research, the humanists themselves were an elite club of men who shared the misogyny of their day. There were exceptions: Thomas More, Erasmus, and Juan Luis Vives promoted the equal education of women, even if social convention and law forbade most women from participating in civil society.

THE BRITISH SCHOOLS

With these last names, we arrive at the shores of Britain. Here several strands of both medieval and humanist intellectual culture came

---

[45] See Craig W. Kallendorf, trans., *Humanist Educational Treatises* (Cambridge, MA: Harvard University Press, 2002).

[46] For details, see Grendler, *Universities*, 199–248.

together in the late fifteenth and early sixteenth centuries to lay the foundations of the early modern British and early American university systems.[47] Oxford and Cambridge universities held an almost complete monopoly on English higher education throughout the medieval and early modern periods. Within a short time after Oxford's foundation, the liberal-arts faculty gained dominance over the others in terms of organization, student numbers, and control over the university's constitution and lecture schedules.[48] A long tradition of English natural science also contributed to Oxford's difference.

Another distinctive element of Oxford was its college system.[49] Our word "college" derives from the Latin *collegium* or a "gathering together." This could be any association: a guild, a burial society, or even a criminal gang. Medieval colleges originated in Paris as residential halls *c.*1180. The most famous was the Collège de Sorbonne, founded by royal chaplain Robert de Sorbon in 1257. These colleges began as common residence halls for scholars so that they could share expenses, food, order, and security. They grew into self-governing associations (*collegia*), often grouped around common faculties and hosting core lectures and masters.

At Oxford the colleges became central to the physical and institutional identity of the university. Merton College was first, in 1264, and there followed the foundation of a string of colleges whose names still resonate within the academic world: University, Balliol, Exeter, Oriel, Queens, New College, Lincoln, and then Magdalen, founded in 1458. These new colleges served the same purpose as the medieval monasteries: they both localized and made communal a form of life – intellectual,

---

[47] Joan Simon, *Education and Society in Tudor England* (Cambridge: Cambridge University Press, 1966); Fritz Caspari, *Humanism and the Social Order in Tudor England* (New York: Columbia University Teacher's College Press, 1968); Ian M. Green, *Humanism and Protestantism in Early Modern English Education* (Farnham: Ashgate, 2009, 2nd ed. New York: Routledge, 2016).

[48] See J. M. Fletcher, "The Faculty of Arts," in J. I. Catto and Ralph Evans, eds. *The History of the University of Oxford* I. *The Early Oxford Schools* (Oxford: Oxford University Press, 1984), 369–99; and P. Osmund Lewry, "Grammar, Logic and Rhetoric," in Catto and Evans, *The History*, 401–33.

[49] Cobban, *Medieval English Universities*, 111–60; J. R. L. Highfield, "The Early Colleges," in Catto and Evans, *The History*, 225–63.

social, and economic – that created and nurtured a new cultural institution. They formed identity and embodied separation from both other faculties and disciplines and from the world at large. New learning was institutionalized, and this "gathering together" fostered new energies, cross-fertilizations, and critical mass that brought both intellectual and social innovation. Our word "collegial" packs multiple levels of meaning, but chief among these is the sense of group identity, separateness, and the corporate authority that derives from them.

*

By 1209, students fleeing from troubles in Oxford had begun gathering at the *studium* in Cambridge,[50] and by 1229, King Henry III was inviting students from Paris to the emerging university, to which he granted a royal charter in 1231. But Cambridge remained in Oxford's shadow throughout the Middle Ages, closely imitating its system of colleges and governance. Only in the fifteenth century, with Oxford's scholasticism associated with heretical thought and disfavored by both students and the Crown, did Cambridge become a leading English institution, attracting the new humanists and natural scientists. Throughout this period, however, the two "Oxbridge" universities maintained close institutional and personal connections.

At Cambridge the early dissolution of two small religious houses resulted in their conversion into the new Jesus and Christ Colleges. St. John's College was founded in 1511 and soon became a center of the new humanism. Chancellor John Fisher, with the full support of Lady Margaret Beaufort, Henry VII's mother, changed Cambridge into an international leader of the new learning.[51] Fisher encouraged the activities of these English humanists, bolstered by his invitation to Continental thinkers like Erasmus, who lived and wrote there as early as 1499. By 1520, Fisher had transformed the curriculum of Cambridge

[50] See Christopher N. L. Brooke, ed., *A History of the University of Cambridge*, 4 vols. (Cambridge: Cambridge University Press, 1988–2004), especially vol. I: Damian Riehl Leader, *The University to 1546* (1988); and Cobban, *Medieval English Universities*.

[51] For what follows, see Riehl Leader, *University*, 264–348; Cobban, *Medieval English Universities*, 243–56; Green, *Humanism*, 191–265.

to the Erasmian model of reform based on a new understanding of both pagan and Christian antiquity. But as Lutheranism spread on the Continent, this model could not withstand the religious divisions from within and the pressures of King Henry's divorce from Catherine of Aragon and his Act of Supremacy from without. For his resistance Chancellor Fisher was executed in June 1535. He was replaced by Thomas Cromwell.

By the end of 1535, Henry VIII had appointed Cromwell visitor of the university to implement a series of injunctions against the teaching of canon law, which he followed with the prohibition of scholastic philosophy and methodology. He also endowed five new chairs in divinity, Hebrew, Greek, physical science, and civil law. This accelerated a dramatic shift in the university curriculum to new Protestant humanist models. In 1546, the king went on to found Trinity College on St. John's model, and the new Protestant university had come to stay. By the time of Parliament's statutes of 1570, Cambridge was legally bound to produce leaders for the Anglican Church, and the humanist curriculum for the preparation of a secular elite was entrenched.

In exchange for surrendering their separateness and self-governance, these new college foundations at Oxbridge innovated in their teaching methods, supplementing the tutorial system with lectureships. The impact of the Italian humanists and their insistence on the ancient Latin and Greek models of good style and historical exempla gave new – and different – life to this faculty on the university level.[52] Oxbridge also embraced the new technology of print. By 1478, Oxford had published its first printed work, a treatise of St. Jerome. There followed seventeen other print publications until 1487, more between 1517 and 1519, and a steady stream after 1585. By the 1520s Cambridge also boasted a new printing press; and a royal charter of 1534 gave the university the privilege of naming three official printers for what was becoming a steady outflow of new humanist scholarship, most especially around the Scriptures.

---

[52] See Green, *History*, 35–40; J. I. Catto, "Conclusion: Scholars and Studies in Renaissance Oxford," in Catto and Evans, *The History*, 769–83; Laurence W. B. Brockliss, *The University of Oxford: A History* (Oxford: Oxford University Press, 2016), 56–85.

THE GENTLEMAN SCHOLAR

Not all cultural authority or innovation came solely from closed university circles. As early as the 1420s, Humphrey, duke of Gloucester and brother of King Henry V, had begun assembling his library of medieval, classical, and contemporary humanist learning that would evolve into Duke Humphrey's Library at the Bodleian in Oxford.[53] Some monasteries, such as Evesham, continued to have a vibrant intellectual climate, open to the new humanist movement as an aid to spiritual life.[54] The broadening English middle classes – a propertied elite that formed the majority of members of parliament and of civil magistracies, drawn from the gentry, merchants, professionals, and wealthy farmers – also formed a cultural group that combined interest in both the new Protestant reforms and the heady influence of Italian humanism.[55]

Over the next two generations, many English scholars traveled to Italy. From their contacts, teachers, and readings they absorbed the ideals of the humanists, most especially their use of the Roman and Greek classics, and developed a new sense of secular political leadership, duty, and virtue. Humanism also flowed in the opposite direction, from the Continent. Duke Humphrey employed several Italian scholars residing in England. Henry VII began hiring Italian and French humanists, such as Giovanni Gigli, Pietro Carmeliano, and André Bernard as diplomats, secretaries, teachers, poets, and historians.[56] Far better known is Desiderius Erasmus's friendship with and frequent stays at the household of Thomas More, during which appeared Erasmus' *Praise of Folly* (1511) and More's *Utopia* (1516). At Cambridge Erasmus completed or worked on several of his most important works, including translations of Greek classical and early Christian works, and his *Novum Instrumentum*, or

---

[53] Green, *History*, 33–39; Catto, "Conclusion"; Elisabeth Leedham-Green and Teresa Webber, *The Cambridge History of Libraries in Britain and Ireland* I. *To 1640* (Cambridge: Cambridge University Press, 2013), 265–485.

[54] See Knowles, *Religious Orders*, III:100–107; Green, *History*, 36.

[55] Riehl Leader, *History*, 314–19.

[56] MacCulloch, *Thomas Cromwell*, 22–28, 56–59, et passim; Bernard André, *The Life of Henry VII*, Daniel Hobbins, ed. and trans. (New York: Italica Press, 2011), xi–xl.

edition of the Greek New Testament (1516).[57] Henry VIII himself was heavily influenced by Erasmus' reform ideas.[58] But other strains of humanism, heavily influenced by Protestant thinkers like John Calvin and Philip Melanchthon, eventually won the day.[59]

*

By the early sixteenth century both Castiglione's realistic *Book of the Courtier* and the ideals of Erasmus' writing had come together in England to create a vibrant humanist literature of education.[60] Thomas Elyot's *The Governor* (1531), the anonymous *Institution of a Gentleman* (1555), and Sir Humphrey Gilbert's *Queen Elizabeth's Academy* (1572) are among the best-known examples. These influences had many outlets – in public office, at the Inns of Court, at the royal palace, among influential churchmen, such as John Colet at St. Paul's Cathedral and School in London, on the university level, and also in the new medium of print, which vastly expanded the literature of this Christian "courtesy theory."[61]

Then, as now, there was an anti-intellectual backlash that involved more than ideas. Richard Pace, humanist secretary of state to Henry VIII, recalled a heated discussion at a banquet, during which a conservative reacted angrily to the new humanist education of young men: "All learned men are beggars," he blurted, "even Erasmus, that most learned

---

[57] See E. E. Reynolds, *Thomas More and Erasmus* (New York: Fordham University Press, 1965); Riehl Leader, *History*, 291–319; Erasmus, "A Pilgrimage for Religion's Sake," in his *Ten Colloquies*, Craig R. Thompson, ed. and trans. (Indianapolis: Bobs-Merrill, 1957), 56–91; Knowles, *Religious Orders* III:141–56.

[58] Bernard, *King's Reformation*, 232–38 et passim.   [59] Green, *Humanism*, 9–15.

[60] See William Harrison Woodward, *Vittorino da Feltre and Other Humanist Educators* (1963); William Harrison Woodward, *Desiderius Erasmus Concerning the Aim and Method of Education* (1964); William Harrison Woodward, *Studies in Education during the Age of the Renaissance, 1400–1600* (1967); Marian Leona Tobriner, *Vives' Introduction to Wisdom* (1968); all New York: Columbia University Teacher's College Press, with reprints. See also Grafton and Jardine, *From Humanism to the Humanities*; Douglas Bush, *The Renaissance and English Humanism* (Toronto: University of Toronto Press, 1939, repr., 2016); Bushnell, *Culture of Teaching*; Kallendorf, *Humanist Educational Treatises*; and Green, *Humanism*, 127–90.

[61] Bushnell, *Culture of Teaching*, 117–43; Green, *Humanism*, 33–52, 78–93, 249–65, 334–57; Caspari, *Humanism and the Social Order*, 276–87; David R. Carlson, *English Humanist Books: Writers and Patrons, Manuscript and Print, 1475–1525* (Toronto: University of Toronto Press, 1993).

man, is poor, I am told." He would rather see his own son hang than study humanist letters: "Gentlemen's sons ought to be able to blow their horn skillfully, to hunt well, and to carry and train a hawk elegantly; but the study of letters is to be left to the sons of peasants." Pace replied that if the king were receiving foreign dignitaries for high affairs of state, "your son would but blow into his horn, if he were educated according to your wishes, and the learned sons of peasants would be called upon to reply."[62] Pace's anecdote certainly hit the mark: not all of English society was swept away by the new (or old) learning.

Nor was the new humanism aimed at social equality. It reflected the hierarchical structures and values of its time. But those who embraced the new liberal arts were certainly being prepared to govern those who didn't. Those who did came increasingly from the gentry and nobility. The humanist curricula created a British elite capable of leading and ruling.[63] These trends are encapsulated in the education and career of Sir Philip Sidney (1554–86), ardent Protestant, courtier, diplomat, poet, and soldier who died fighting against Catholic Spain.[64] He was also among the few Elizabethans to support English exploration and colonization of America. He funded the explorations of Sir Martin Frobisher to find the Northwest Passage and planned an expedition with Sir Francis Drake. In 1582 Richard Hakluyt dedicated his *Divers Voyages Touching the Discoverie of America* to him. The legacy of such English humanists and reformers in founding the American system of higher education will form the basis of our next chapter.

---

[62] Caspari, *Humanism and the Social Order*, 257–58.

[63] Caspari, *Humanism and the Social Order*, 1–44, 251–94; Green, *Humanism*, 18–25.

[64] See Caspari, *Humanism and the Social Order*, 295–331; Bushnell, *Culture of Teaching*, 147–58.

CHAPTER 2

The American University to 1968

INTRODUCTION

C HAPTER 2 WILL EXAMINE THE ORIGINS AND DEVELOPMENT of higher education in the United States in the seventeenth and eighteenth centuries from humanist colleges like Harvard, Yale, and William & Mary to the beginnings of the American university system in Thomas Jefferson's University of Virginia and others. It will then discuss how Enlightenment traditions of higher education evolved in nineteenth-century Germany. Its basic components were the lecture hall, the advanced seminar, the research paper, and the monograph, all held together by a hierarchical system of professional training, appointment, and promotion. These were bolstered by professional societies with strict membership requirements and benefits, journals, conferences, honors, and their concomitant prestige and authority. By the late nineteenth century this system was being imported into North America. As American life in general became more industrialized and professionalized, this German model made gradual headway, resulting in the American university model of the twentieth century. This valued long apprenticeship, deep research, focused expertise, and the modes of authority that derived from them. This model was enshrined in Vannevar Bush's 1945 report, *Science, the Endless Frontier* and in the 1964 report of the Commission on the Humanities.

This chapter will then trace the increase in university and college numbers and will quickly track the changing American economy and shifting demands for different forms and levels of education. It will next discuss the impact of the New Deal and World War II on the development of the American college and the consequent postwar boom in higher ed with the rise of the American research university and public state systems. The chapter will conclude with the great watershed of the 1960s and 1970s, with their rapidly increasing enrollments – and demographic changes within these numbers – disciplines, faculties, and physical plants; the increased involvement of the university with business and government; and the place of the university in the social, cultural, and political changes of the 1960s.

THE AMERICAN COLLEGE

In 1606, King James I of England granted a charter for two colonies in North America. When the Massachusetts Bay Colony was finally established in 1628, the tensions in English society between Puritans and Anglicans, between Parliamentary and Royalist parties were already developing. The English Civil Wars that followed between 1642 and 1651 led to the victory of Parliament and the creation of the Commonwealth, then to the Protectorate of Oliver Cromwell and the subsequent restoration of the monarchy. Men on both sides of the conflict had been educated in the humanist tradition. Both sides could summon up Greek and Roman exemplars for their parliamentary and royalist ideologies of civic duty, governance, and action because England had for two hundred years been absorbing the humanism born in Italy and by then the mark of all educated elites in Europe, whether Catholic or Protestant.[1] Oxford walked warily through the early years of the Reformation, largely due to its damaging association with earlier Lollard heresy and its opposition to Henry VIII's divorce. Meanwhile, Cambridge had become a haven for dissident, Puritan Protestants during Elizabeth I's reign; and Emmanuel College itself was established as a Puritan house. After the Parliamentary victory in the Civil War, many Anglican masters at Cambridge were ousted in favor of Puritans.[2]

---

[1] Caspari, *Humanism and the Social Order*, 392–94. See Green, *Humanism*, 16–18, for a summary of the scholarship, and 191–265 on the teaching of classical and biblical languages.

[2] Christopher Brooke, "Cambridge in the Age of the Puritan Revolution," in Victor Morgan, *History of the University of Cambridge* II. *1546–1750* (Cambridge: Cambridge University Press, 2004), 464–82.

Of the first 132 university-educated members of the Massachusetts Bay Colony, about 100 were graduates of Cambridge, 35 from Emmanuel College alone, and an early proposal was to name the colony "Emmanuel." New England luminaries, such as William Brewster, John Cotton, Thomas Hooker, Richard Saltstone, Samuel Stone, Nathaniel Ward, Roger Williams, and John Winthrop I, were all Cambridge graduates. In 1636, a college was founded in the village of Newtowne across the Charles River from Boston, by vote of the colony's Great and General Court. When the governors of Massachusetts determined to set up this first college, their model was that of their alma mater. The curriculum was that of the humanists and the liberal arts as reformed through both the Protestant and Puritan movements, heavily influenced by St. Augustine, with a heavy emphasis on the correct readings of Scripture via a knowledge of ancient languages and humanist philology.[3] The college named Nathaniel Eaton (1610–74) as its first master. Eaton had attended Trinity College, Cambridge before going off to Italy to receive his doctorate at the University of Padua. At Trinity he had become the friend of John Harvard of Emmanuel College, Cambridge. By 1639, however, Eaton had been fired as political and religious controversies swirled around the young colony. He was succeeded by the college's first president, Henry Dunster (1609–59), a graduate of Magdalene College, Cambridge, a specialist in Hebrew and other "oriental" languages. Soon after, the college was named after John Harvard, who on his death in 1638 bequeathed his library and half his monetary estate to it.

The authority conferred on the new Harvard College by its lineage, faculty, and mission combined with two other institutional roles important for the development of American higher education. Its new "college" was, on the medieval European model, both a building and a corporate entity, guaranteeing its separate identity. In this regard Harvard College became the first American corporation, a key element in later developments.[4] Cambridge, MA was also home to innovation and the creation of

---

[3] For early American education, see Philo A. Hutcheson, *A People's History of American Higher Education* (New York: Routledge, 2019), 19–43; Thelin, 1–40; Lynch, *Medieval Pedagogical Writings*, 12–16, 87–104; Green, *Humanism*, 123–24 for the example of Cotton Mather.

[4] Thelin, 1.

new knowledge, hosting the first printing press in British North America, imported in 1638 to serve both the new Harvard College and the Bay Colony. Appropriately, the first book printed in British North America was the *Bay Psalm Book* of 1640 edited by John Cotton, Richard Mather, and others. In 1661, the Indian College, in the village now renamed Cambridge, published John Eliot's *Indian Bible*, a translation of Scripture into Algonquin.[5] From the start, American publishing was inextricably linked to the dynamic between higher education and widespread dissemination.

*

All the major eastern liberal-arts colleges and universities had been founded before the American Revolution: Harvard (1636), William & Mary (1693), Yale (Collegiate School of Connecticut, 1701), University of Pennsylvania (Benjamin Franklin's College of Philadelphia, 1740), Princeton (College of New Jersey, 1746), Columbia (King's College, 1754), Brown (College of Rhode Island, 1764/5), Rutgers (Queens College, 1766), and Dartmouth (Moor's Indian School, 1769).[6] But John Thelin reminds us of three essential facts about American higher education. First, these schools were not the first in the Americas. The University of Santo Domingo was established in 1538 directly along the humanist model adopted in Renaissance Spain. Universities followed in both Mexico and Peru (San Marco, 1551). In French Canada, the Université Laval (Séminaire du Québec) was established in 1663. The Colegio de San Nicolás Hidalgo in Morelia, Mexico, founded in 1540, remains the oldest continuously operating university in North America.[7]

Secondly, Thelin cautions us against drawing too close a comparison between the British American and Oxbridge models.[8] Most of the Bay

---

[5] Joseph Blumenthal, *The Printed Book in America* (Boston: David R. Godine and Dartmouth College Library, 1977), 1–4; Scott E. Caspar and Joan Shelly Rubin, "The History of the Book in America," in Michael F. Suarez, S. J. and H. R. Woudhuysen, eds., *The Book: A Global History* (Oxford: Oxford University Press, 2013), 682–709, at 683–84; David D. Hall, *A History of the Book in America*, 5 vols. (Chapel Hill: University of North Carolina Press, 2000–2010), I:1–151.

[6] Hutcheson, *A People's History*, 20–35 et passim; Thelin, 1–2.   [7] Thelin, 38–39.

[8] Thelin, 8–11.

Colony founders of Harvard were Cambridge graduates, and the first universities to this day prize their "Englishness" in everything from campus-Gothic architecture, to their seals, their academic robes and processions, to their administrative titles. But the governing structure of Harvard and almost all the British North American schools followed not Oxbridge but the Scottish Presbyterian model of Edinburgh and Glasgow. Not a faculty *universitas*, but a strong external board of trustees (often including local civil magistrates) and a powerful president governed the new American schools and set the precedent for American higher education. American colleges were legally American corporations well before the American commercial revolution made the corporate model the norm. The differences also arose in a variety of other areas: in the college system itself, in their student bodies, in their physical plant, in their sense of identity and separateness, in their curricula and authority – whether religious or secular – and in their paths to innovation.

There were other differences from the Oxbridge model, brought about as much by ideology as by the conditions of the early colonies. Schools were rarely able to imitate the fully developed college and quad system of the English universities, and campuses hardly existed. Like the very first universities of Europe, American schools were essentially based on their faculties. They owned few buildings and little land to set them apart from their surroundings. When they were constructed they were the most expensive of colonial buildings, and thus rare and often incomplete. "Colleges" in the sense of identifiable residential buildings were relatively late in coming, and only the Anglophile nostalgia of the late nineteenth and early twentieth century produced those Gothic and Georgian campuses we associate with the earliest American schools.[9] Wren Building (1695) at William & Mary and Massachusetts Hall (1720) at Harvard were rarities. More usual was King's (Columbia) College's use of the Trinity Church schoolhouse for instruction. Even schools like William & Mary encouraged students to take lodgings wherever they could find them, including with their parents.

---

[9] Thelin, 115–16 et passim.

Student bodies also differed in significant ways. In the northern colonies most students came from the relatively wealthy mercantile classes of the growing seaboard cities. As colleges developed in the south, their students were, by and large, the sons of the Tidewater plantation aristocracy. Few children of the tradesmen class or below were granted entry into these schools, and only the later denominational colleges and scholarship funds of the nineteenth century brought them into the higher-education system. Those students who did matriculate were clearly defined by the Oxford model: ranked and listed by social class. In 1769, the College of Rhode Island's (Brown's) decision to list students by surname was considered a radical departure. Overall, however, the student population in colonial America was small. Few early schools had enrollments of over 100 students, and the total remained less than 1 percent of the American population; and up to the mid nineteenth century constituted less than 2 percent, numbers that match the overall percentage in medieval English universities.[10] Again, the university in America was not the collective of faculty, self-governing and selective, but a corporate body governed by a board of trustees and administered by a president answerable to that board. Faculty were generally low-paid, and their careers were contingent on inconsistent finance and political winds.

Third, these colleges were generally established in growing mercantile cities and served these centers by providing intellectual leaders (both clerical and secular) and administrators and as magnets for a new governing class. Fully one quarter of the Bay Colony's tax revenues (about £400) went to found Harvard, and William & Mary's foundation in 1693 received generous royal support of about £2,000. All these colonial colleges remained closely tied to their urban and colonial governments, and all depended on philanthropy and constant fundraising from external sources. In the colonial period at least, separateness was not a major distinguishing factor in American university life; but the two other essential factors – authority and innovation – were only enhanced by this closeness to the developing social and economic world of the colonies.

[10] Thelin, 20, 68–69.

While early archival evidence is scarce, the humanist liberal arts –
filtered through the Protestant Reformation and American Puritanism –
remained central to this curriculum and mission.[11] Latin grammar,
philology, and the ability to understand the word of holy Scripture,
oratory and the rhetorical tradition, law and political philosophy based
on the examples of virtue and vice found in the ancient historians and
philosophers, all remained central. So too did English humanism's mission of educating "Christian gentlemen," a class of civic and religious
leaders who would take the lessons of the past as guides to proper
behavior and governance. New York's King's College prospectus
declared that it would "enlarge the Mind, improve the Understanding,
polish the whole Man, and qualify them to support the brightest
Characters in all the elevated stations in life."[12] John Witherspoon's
1772 prospectus for the college of New Jersey (Princeton University)
stressed that "Experience shows the use of a liberal education ... to
those who do not wish to live for themselves alone, but would apply their
talents to the service of the public and the good of mankind."[13] Brown
University's charter begins with a similar statement:

> Institutions for liberal Education are highly beneficial to Society, by
> forming the rising Generation to Virtue, Knowledge and useful literature
> and thus preserving in the Community a Succession of Men duly qualified
> for discharging the Offices of Life with usefulness and reputation.[14]

In the southern Tidewater colonies, several colleges and small acad-
emies had been established before the Revolution. These included King
William's School in Annapolis (1696, St. John's College, chartered 1784),
Augusta Academy (1749, chartered 1782, later Washington & Lee
University), and the College of Charleston (1770, chartered 1785).
After the Revolution, and once British royal control over charters was
ended, the scene expanded rapidly. Southern states saw the foundation
of many more colleges – public, private, and sectarian – among them
Transylvania University in Lexington, Virginia, soon to be Kentucky

---

[11] A good introduction is Andrew Fitzmaurice, *Humanism and America: An Intellectual History of English Colonisation, 1500–1625* (Cambridge: Cambridge University Press, 2004).

[12] Quoted in Thelin, 26.   [13] Quoted in Thelin, 26.   [14] Quoted in Thelin, 37.

(1780), the University of Georgia (Franklin College, 1785), the University of North Carolina (1789), the University of South Carolina (South Carolina College, 1801), and many others in the next two decades. After his early failure to expand the curriculum of William & Mary in 1779, Thomas Jefferson founded the University of Virginia (1819) as a model school, with its highly selective faculty from America and Europe, student self-governance, new curriculum, a separate campus, university buildings, college dormitories, eating halls, and spacious grounds. In his plans Jefferson shared with the southern schools a true disposition for innovation, breaking with the strictly liberal-arts curricula of the older northern schools.

Further south, the first prospectus of the University of North Carolina advertised:

> The subjects to which it is contemplated by the Board to turn the attention of the students on the first establishment are – the study of languages, particularly the English – History, ancient and modern – the Belles Lettres and Moral Philosophy – the knowledge of the mathematics and Natural Philosophy [Science] – Agriculture and Botany, with the principles of Architecture. ... Gentlemen conversant in these branches of Science and Literature, and who can be well recommended, will receive very handsome encouragement by the Board.[15]

Several things are clear: the ancient liberal arts and natural sciences remained core, as did the historical perspective of the core curriculum. As suited the education of a wealthy, rural elite, however, southern schools innovated in the addition of subject matter that would guide students in the creation and maintenance of their plantation wealth and society: agriculture, botany, and architecture. Also clear is the south's exclusive focus on elite, white males, the "well recommended" gentlemen. Women, workers (including slaves), populations of color were excluded from these early foundations. Yet women of the same class were afforded higher education, and between 1800 and 1860 there existed fourteen degree-granting schools for women in both the south and the new Northwest Territories. Back in New England Mary Lyon's

---

[15] Quoted in Thelin, 58–59.

Mount Holyoke College (1837) became the paragon of women's institutions. These schools – many termed "female seminaries" – equaled those for males in their curricula and rigor. Exceptional was Oberlin Collegiate Institute, which stressed equal education both by gender and by race. Like their medieval ancestors, however, female graduates of these schools learned in the vernacular languages (including English) and not in Latin. In a tradition that went back to Quintilian's advice on the education of women, they were not expected to enter public life but to wisely and virtuously support their husbands and families in their leadership positions.[16]

The early Republic and the shift from restrictive royal charters to ambitious new state laws witnessed an explosion of college foundations. In 1800 there were twenty-five degree-granting colleges in the United States. By 1820 that number had risen to fifty-two, and by 1860 it had soared to 281, of which about forty failed.[17] Overall, however, new statistical models point to a survival rate of about 80 percent.[18] New foundations were largely in the south, the "west," and the northwest, but the east and New England also saw their fair share. While 175 medical schools had been founded by 1840, only about three dozen law schools existed before the Civil War. Even though Transylvania University in Kentucky included both medicine and law departments, medicine was not considered central to American university education, and, like law, practical experience counted far more than a degree for professional careers.

The older northern schools shared in these experiments in expanding curricula and student demographics. New England's "hilltop colleges" excelled in attracting the sons of upwardly mobile families of modest background and those headed for the ministry, teaching, and other professions. The two US military academies, West Point (1802) and Annapolis (1845), also made prestigious the study of applied science and engineering and set a precedent for many publicly funded institutions. There still existed little to differentiate the public from the private school and its purposes, however. The 1819 Supreme Court decision in

---

[16] Thelin, 55–56; Lynch, *Medieval Pedagogical Writings*, 115–28.   [17] Thelin, 41–42.
[18] Thelin, 44–45.

Dartmouth College v. Woodward set the legal precedent for protecting college charters from state interference and started on the road to the creation of the American university as a place apart.

*

With the 1860s, the Civil War, and the Morrill Land Grant Act of 1862, American higher education embarked on a new phase.[19] Almost all southern schools had been shut down during the war, but with Reconstruction and the nation's westward expansion, colleges and universities of all types were founded in large numbers. Though liberal arts remained key to attracting students, maintaining prestige and authority, and to long-term survival, new curricula were eagerly embraced as experimentation and innovation became a keystone of American education. The liberal arts remained the chief attraction for students and their parents, either as a means of social and professional advancement or as the best preparation for already-existing elites. Educating for character, whether of the northern "gentleman scholar" or the southern "Christian gentleman," remained the ideal. Many new, innovative fields either failed to attract students or were actively opposed by practitioners in everything from agriculture to medicine.

Between 1796 and 1861 the Federal and state governments had made numerous grants and provided subsidies to a host of schools; but the Federal Morrill Act formalized this process by giving incentives to the states to develop and fund a variety of schools that would foster the "useful arts." These included agriculture, mining, engineering, military training, and mechanics. Many "A&M" schools were thus founded throughout the country, but the liberal arts were also encouraged and funded. Schools like Texas A&M, the California College of Oakland (University of California), New York Agricultural College (Cornell University), and MIT were a direct result of these policies. Existing schools, like the University of North Carolina, added schools of applied science.

---

[19] Thelin, 74–109. For excerpts, see Richard Hofstadter and Wilson Smith, *American Higher Education: A Documentary History*, 2 vols. (Chicago: University of Chicago Press, 1961), II:568–69.

Women's education also expanded during this period. So too did "normal" or education schools designed to educate teachers for budding primary and secondary school systems that, ironically, lagged behind the creation of universities. Religious schools also proliferated, either because local denominations resisted sending their children to larger urban schools or because of their special appeal to ethnic minorities. By 1890, a variety of groups had founded numerous schools for African-Americans, either to specifically educate a new elite in the liberal arts – W. E. B. Dubois' "talented tenth" – or to provide education and training in an array of skilled occupations. Hampton Institute of Virginia and Tuskegee in Alabama are prominent examples. Only with the founding of the Wharton School in Philadelphia in 1881 was business considered worthy of a college curriculum. Ironically, it was the Wharton School that preserved the teaching of history, government, and economics that the University of Pennsylvania had discarded.

*

By the 1850s, many leading intellectuals and their publications had begun to form a growing critique of the old colonial model of the liberal arts and religious college. Both internal social and economic developments in the United States and a new awareness of European innovations spurred a re-evaluation and a search for new models that would both enhance higher education's authority and its ability to attract students and financial support. The call for the modern university coalesced first in theory, and then more slowly in practice. Brown University's Francis Wayland criticized the liberal-arts college,[20] while James Morgan Hart and Lincoln Steffen praised the new German university.[21] In the 1870s and 1880s publications, such as *The Nation, Atlantic Monthly,* and *Harper's* took up the critique. In 1861, Yale University granted the first Ph.D. in the United States. In 1876, Johns Hopkins University became the first US university founded on the German model. In 1884, John Burgess, president of Columbia University, defined the three major elements of any major American university: an urban setting, private control, and

---

[20] Hofstadter & Smith, II:478–87.   [21] Hofstadter & Smith, II:569–83; Thelin, 87.

granting advanced degrees in the liberal arts and sciences. Unlike the German model of European university, however, most American schools with that designation achieved growth by simply adding new schools to existing ones – for medicine or law, for example – and by offering Ph.D.s in existing fields. Thus the "comprehensive" American research university took a unique path that was only realized in full in the mid twentieth century.

First, however, we should look more closely at what exactly the "German model" meant and how it applied to the United States.[22] In 1810, the University of Berlin was founded along the theoretical lines laid out by Wilhelm von Humboldt, brother of Alexander, the famous naturalist. An essential part of Prussian national revival, Berlin's university became the basis of the Humboldtian or German model. This ascription to Humboldt is now disputed, but most scholars still agree on its essential elements. These included an urban setting, a unity of research and teaching (*Wissenschaft*) "for their own sake," higher degrees in the faculty of philosophy (the Ph.D.), a freedom from French prescriptive curricula, the revival of ancient Greek civilization through the professionalized philological study of its texts and a proper understanding of its artistic legacy (neo-humanism), the individual pursuit of truth through this education (*Bildung*), the a-political separateness of the university from state interference (*Einsamkeit*), and the new idea of academic freedom (*Freiheit*) to pursue whatever line of research and teaching the faculty considered apt and valuable.[23] Only at the beginning of the twentieth century, however, did this constellation of features come together to form a recognizable ideological model. In addition, most students remained focused on professional advancement, not ideal engagement with Truth. What remains true, however, was that Humboldt's theories offered a path out of the historical decline of the European university that was losing all three of its major features: authority, innovation, and a sense of separate identity. For Humboldt and his contemporary German idealists like Fichte, the university was a "sacred institution" that bridged

---

[22] See Robert D. Anderson, *European Universities from the Enlightenment to 1914* (Oxford: Oxford University Press, 2010), esp. 51–65.

[23] Anderson, *European Universities*, 55–56.

the human and the divine in the pursuit not of mere facts or professional careers, but of knowledge.

Added to this model was a systematized credentialing, a new division into departments, new curricula and scholarly communication, regular lecture schedules, and the advanced seminar guided by the new empiricism and scientific method championed by the German historian Leopold von Ranke.[24] The model included the doctoral thesis, the scholarly article and journal, the monograph, the process of peer review, the laboratory, the research institute and learned society distinguished according to discipline, the regular scholarly conference, the award system of academic hiring, rank, and promotion, of salaries and perquisites, of graduate assistantships and office allocations, the distinguished service and book awards, and the positions on editorial and promotion boards. Many saw this development as enshrining the ideals of research and knowledge, independent of external interference. Yet other critics have seen it as the intellectual aspect of a high-bourgeois reaction to the era of revolution and as the subordination of the intellectual classes to the needs of bureaucracy and the neo-absolutist state.[25] However interpreted in Europe, however, its impact on American higher education was formative and profound.

ANTI-INTELLECTUALISM

Other cultural forces were also at work in America throughout the nineteenth century. In two seminal works the Pulitzer-Prize winning historian Richard Hofstadter traced what he identified as the long and deeply engrained strain of anti-intellectualism in American life.[26] Writing in the 1950s and 1960s during, and in the wake of, the McCarthy hearings and its scapegoating of academics and intellectuals, Hofstadter attempted to trace these attitudes not simply to individual,

[24] See Leonard Krieger, *Ranke: The Meaning of History* (Chicago: University of Chicago Press 1977); Rens Bod, *A New History of the Humanities* (Oxford: Oxford University Press, 2013), 250–58.

[25] Anderson, *European Universities*, 61–65, 103–6.

[26] Richard Hofstadter, *Anti-Intellectualism in American Life* (New York: Vintage Books, 1962); and Richard Hofstadter, *The Paranoid Style in American Politics* (New York: Vintage Books, 1965).

political motives and ambitions but to deep strains in American life, from which these attacks drew much of their force. As he laid out in his highly influential analyses, much of this tradition was transmitted directly with the English settlement of America and developed during the process of colonization and western expansion of the frontier. It was reinforced by both American populism and anti-elitism and by successive waves of religious revivalism. According to Hofstadter, these are "the ideal assumptions of anti-intellectualism":

> Intellectuals, it may be held, are pretentious, conceited, effeminate, and snobbish; and very likely immoral, dangerous and subversive. The plain sense of the common man, especially if tested by success in some demanding line of practical work, is an altogether adequate substitute for, if not actually superior to, formal knowledge and expertise acquired in the schools. Not surprisingly, institutions in which intellectuals tend to be influential, like universities and colleges, are rotten to the core.[27]

To be fair, Hofstadter stressed that this anti-intellectualism did not define American society but was only one strain of its cultural life. On the other hand, he exalted the "respective residues of the aristocratic and priestly backgrounds of the intellectual function,"[28] "as the highest human activity."[29] Hofstadter was explicit in tracing this anti-intellectual strain to the Anglo-Saxon heritage of the first American colonies,[30] and we have already seen this at work, for example, in Tudor England in Richard Pace's account above.[31] Hofstadter highlighted two essential elements of American culture that contribute to this attitude. The first, a basic egalitarian strain inherited again from English Puritanism and other dissenting groups who, rightly, associated university knowledge with power and privilege; and second, the closely related strain of American Evangelism, which at its core, in the interpretation of Scripture, rejected authority in favor of the individual's ability to discern the truth. This was a strain of Renaissance thought that one can also trace to Erasmus and then to English Puritans' "godly" unease or

---

[27] Hofstadter, *Anti-Intellectualism*, 18–19.   [28] Hofstadter, *Anti-Intellectualism*, 33.
[29] Hofstadter, *Anti-Intellectualism*, 28.   [30] Hofstadter, *Anti-Intellectualism*, 20.
[31] Chapter 1, 31–32.

outright hostility to humanist moral, philosophical, and theological positions.[32] These two elements merged in American life in what became the class-based character of American Protestant denominations, ranging from the high Anglicanism of the elite classes to more popular congregations of Baptists and Methodists, which tended to stress the internal emotional experience of religion over established Church ritual, institutions, and authority. By the 1850s, 70 percent of all American Protestants were nominally either Methodists or Baptists.[33] The later immigrant Catholic culture also tended to disparage intellectual endeavors in favor of more working-class occupations and lifestyles. It is important to remember, however, that the great majority of college foundations in the East, Midwest, and South had religious affiliations and missions – whether Protestant or Catholic – well into the twentieth century.

If the original Puritanism of Massachusetts Bay and other colonies reflected the Protestant humanism of Oxbridge, by 1700 there had already emerged a rift between an urban, lay humanism and a rural evangelical culture.[34] This was starkly revealed in the Great Awakening of c.1720–50, led by such luminaries as Jonathan Edwards and George Whitefield, who brought the message of John Wellesley to North America. Part and parcel to this revival was a distrust of the educated and what was perceived as their top-down authority, especially in regard to biblical interpretation. Even when the evangelicals did found colleges – and from the 1830s the long tradition of Wesleyan colleges is testimony to this – they at first rejected the Oxbridge tradition in favor of a more direct piety and practical training; and both Edwards and Whitefield attacked Harvard and Yale for their alleged departure from Christian piety.[35]

By 1790, nearly 90 percent of the pioneer population in the western states and territories were unchurched; and they shared a radical American Protestant rejection of the European past. By the mid nineteenth century, itinerant preachers like John Mason Peck and Peter Cartwright found the local populations in the Mississippi basin almost

---

[32] See Green, *Humanism*, 115–25. [33] Hofstadter, *Anti-Intellectualism*, 90–91.
[34] Hofstadter, *Anti-Intellectualism*, 55–80. [35] Hofstadter, *Anti-Intellectualism*, 72–73.

completely illiterate and without any secular or religious education at all. What seemed to unite these settlements culturally was an intense dislike of any establishment, an antipathy to authority, elites, education, and the East Coast.[36] Even educated preachers like Charles Finney, a key figure of American Revivalism in the 1820s and 1830s, declared in his *Memoirs* that "I found myself utterly unable to accept doctrine on the ground of authority ... I had no where to go but directly to the Bible, and to the philosophy or workings of my own mind." Education, especially of the Eastern humanist kind, was the enemy of Christian virtue: "four years at classical studies and no God in them ... Learned men may understand their *hic, haec, hoc*, very well and may laugh at the humble Christian and call him ignorant, although he may know how to win more souls than five hundred of them." Setting the stage for later political stances, he noted that, "It is more difficult to labour with educated men, with cultivated minds and moreover predisposed to skepticism, than with the uneducated."[37]

After the Civil War, the United States saw a new breed of popular preacher typified by Dwight L. Moody, well known for his hostility to education. Learned ministers, for example, "are often educated away from the people," and in general "the educated rascal is the meanest kind of rascal." Moody's anti-intellectualism melded with political populism into a pro-corporate gospel: "I say to the rich men of Chicago, their money will not be worth much if communism and infidelity sweep the land. ... There can be no better investment for the capitalists of Chicago than to put the saving salt of the Gospel into these dark homes and desperate centers [of American working-class poverty]."[38] Businessmen responded well to Moody because he spoke their language. As one contributor remarked, he and other fundraisers "are one of us."[39] Moody's approach was brought to high pitch by Billy Sunday, whose career reached from the 1890s to 1935. A sports figure turned preacher, Sunday used a raw, straightforward language of masculine virtues and ready anger that won the support of both conservative politicians and the

[36] Hofstadter, *Anti-Intellectualism*, 76–80.

[37] Hofstadter, *Anti-Intellectualism*, 92–95, 103–4.

[38] Hofstadter, *Anti-Intellectualism*, 106–16.   [39] Thelin, 125.

robber barons. While Jesus himself was a "scrapper," "thousands of college graduates are going as fast as they can straight to hell. If I had a million dollars, I'd give $999,999 to the church and $1 to education. . . . When the word of God says one thing and scholarship says another, scholarship can go to hell!"[40] By the 1920s, and in the hands of men like Sunday and William Jennings Bryan, these strains had come together to oppose many key elements of modern life and scientific knowledge. This biblical fundamentalism and hostility to secular learning culminated in the landmark Scopes Trial of 1925, in the wake of which intellectuals of all types were denounced as enemies of American values. Only the sweeping changes of the New Deal of the 1930s and 1940s pushed these trends to the sidelines – for a time.

THE MODERN RESEARCH UNIVERSITY

In the year 1900 the model of the modern research university was solidified with the first meeting of the Association of American Universities.[41] By 1910, Edward Slosson, editor of the *Independent,* claimed that one could identify the traits of "great American universities" as well as the majority of other schools, which he designated the "standard American university." According to Thelin's analysis of these designations, the "great universities" offered the following characteristics: schools like Harvard, Stanford, Chicago, and Columbia were generally endowed heavily by major philanthropists, the likes of Stanford, Vanderbilt, or Carnegie, who accepted the new "gospel of wealth" and its public obligations.[42] They were led by strong presidents who combined first-rate scholarship with an easy manner among the donor class, vastly expanding endowments and programs in both the sciences and liberal arts. These universities were housed in vast and complex campuses, with a variety of standard classroom, dormitory, commons, and athletic facilities, clearly separated from their urban or rural

---

[40] Hofstadter, *Anti-Intellectualism,* 114–41.

[41] The list of members included: Harvard, Hopkins, Columbia, Chicago, California, Clark, Cornell, Catholic, Michigan, Stanford, Wisconsin, Pennsylvania, Princeton, and Yale. See Thelin, 110.

[42] Thelin, 127–45.

surroundings both by a distinctive architecture and by broad, green expanses of walled or fenced grounds. They generally adhered to the German model set by Humboldt and his followers, with a clear-cut, professionalized faculty who prized expertise in particular fields, taught through lectures, advanced seminars, and dissertation direction. They could rely on a stable and standard scholarly infrastructure of sophisticated libraries and laboratories, campus museums, and observatories. They belonged to scholarly societies, published in journals and through monographs, participated in strict peer-review processes, advanced through clear-cut academic ranks, and made decisions on granting a hierarchy of advanced degrees in standardized professional schools. The German model of academic freedom and separation also predominated, as in the American business climate of the time, allowing almost unregulated experimentation and innovation.

But the imagined Anglo-Saxon origin myth remained fixed and strong. As Cornell's co-founder and president, Andrew Dickson White (1832–1918), put it:

> Every feature of the little American college seemed all the more sordid. But gradually I began consoling myself by building air-castles. These took the form of structures suited to a great university – with distinguished professors in every field, with libraries as rich as the Bodleian, halls as lordly as that of Christ Church or Trinity, chapels as inspiring as that of King's, towers as dignified as those of Magdalene and Merton, quadrangles as beautiful as those of Jesus and St. John's ... dreaming of a university worthy of the commonwealth and of the nation.[43]

In reality, most universities, even the greatest, found it difficult to live up to such standards throughout the first half of the twentieth century. Philanthropists delighted in funding vast, new, all-inclusive (and exclusive) campuses in the historicist architectural fashion of the day, whether Oxbridge Gothic, Classical Revival, Neo-Romanesque, or Georgian Colonial. But they were ready to move on to other pursuits when it came to actually paying for operating costs or making up for tuition shortfalls. Programs and professional schools lagged behind standards and

[43] Thelin, 117.

expectations. Princeton resisted granting the Ph.D. for years; while Hopkins' fortunes waxed and waned dramatically. Most schools had few graduate students to speak of, and granted even fewer Ph.D.s, and most failed to align their undergraduate and graduate curricula. The great private universities were often matched or outstripped by expanded land-grant and state schools like California, Michigan, or Wisconsin, whose missions clearly joined learning with "useful" occupations and civic responsibility.[44]

Foundations, such as the ones founded by Carnegie, Rockefeller, and Rosenwald, stepped in to make up shortfalls, but with clear-cut agendas for educational policy changes directed by powerful new boards and presidents, often drawn from, and constantly in alliance with, new corporate interests and organizational models.[45] The resulting growth of university administrations – pressed by the funding foundations – reduced both faculty self-governance and authority. Such changes came at a time when "college" was still restricted to less than 5 percent of eighteen- to twenty-two-year-olds for whom the experience was becoming synonymous with easy lifestyles, collegiate sports, and the new mobility of the white, commercial middle classes. At the turn of the century the "Christian gentleman" was already far along the way toward becoming the "Arrow Shirt Man;" and the educated woman was becoming the "swell" and "swank" of the Seven Sisters, both the objects of fascination from a newly aspirational American public.[46]

It was only the New Deal of the 1930s and 1940s, and its call for expertise in many fields vital to economic recovery and the war effort, that restored a great deal of authority both to individual faculty members and to the university scene in general. As the professorate became increasingly self-conscious of their nearly "priestly" status, the campus became synonymous with a new meritocracy.[47] Under pressure from foundations a new hierarchy of American universities emerged as funding increasingly went to three dozen of the nearly 1,000 US institutions of

[44] Thelin, 131–45.   [45] Thelin, 238–45.   [46] See Thelin, 155–259.

[47] Edward Shils, recollections of the 1930s at the University of Pennsylvania. See Thelin, 222.

higher learning.[48] Vastly expanded physical campuses became the focus of national attention as centers of innovation and authority. From 1918 levels, enrollments shot up nearly five-fold to 1.3 million students by 1941, or upwards of 15 percent of the college-age population. As *Life Magazine* proclaimed in 1937, the new university:

> has changed the campus from a scholarly retreat to a new and fabulous design for four years' living. . . . Behind this vast investment [in brick and stone] is tremendous faith in the benefits of higher education. This faith is a cornerstone of any democratic philosophy, the pith and kernel of what writers since Jefferson have called the American Dream. . . . [Current students] will in twenty years occupy the seats of authority.[49]

With World War II came dramatic but temporary drops in enrollment as enlistment and draft siphoned off many college-age men and women. Meanwhile, the college campus became a training ground for officers and home to a wide variety of war-related research projects. The leading research universities that emerged from war emergency and its funding had undergone a sudden revolution in organization and resources that joined a new corporate administrative structure to a civil-service model of the professorate. Strictly imposed levels of status began the process of downplaying the collective authority of the faculty in favor of the charismatic authority of a few well-funded and publicized campus stars who brought the university attention and additional funding for their research. In this sense again the university traded some of its separateness for an increase in authority and innovation.

The postwar boom that lasted from 1945 to about 1970 was fueled by several factors. The 1945 report, *Science, the Endless Frontier* by Carnegie Institution president Vannevar Bush saw the role of the university as innovation and the independent, elite research university as its vehicle. In Bush's lexicon "Best Science" was "Big Science," and government spending on a select few universities was the way to achieve it. Writing as World War II came to a close, Bush declared:

---

[48] Thelin, 238–39.   [49] June 7, 1937, p. 23, quoted in Thelin, 205–6.

Progress in the war against disease depends upon a flow of new scientific knowledge. New products, new industries, and more jobs require continuous additions to knowledge of the laws of nature, and the application of that knowledge to practical purposes. Similarly, our defense against aggression demands new knowledge so that we can develop new and improved weapons. This essential, new knowledge can be obtained only through basic scientific research. . . . How do we increase this scientific capital? First we must have plenty of men and women trained in science, for upon them depends both the creation of new knowledge and its application to practical purposes. Second we must strengthen the centers of basic research which are principally the colleges, universities and research institutes. These institutions provide the environment which is most conducive to the creation of new scientific knowledge and least under pressure for immediate, tangible results.[50]

Federal funding flowed freely from a handful of agencies, including the National Institutes of Health, the National Science Foundation, and most especially the Department of Defense, which funded research in both traditional major universities and the newly expanding state-university systems, most especially in California. The goal was less pure research than its applications in defense, infrastructure, industry, and agriculture. The 1957 launch of the Soviet satellite Sputnik and the emerging "space race" capped nearly two decades of a Federal push to make the university its research arm. These goals were encapsulated in the National Defense Education Act of 1958.[51]

The second factor was the great increase in enrollments. These came first from beneficiaries of the GI Bill (Serviceman's Readjustment Act of 1944) that by 1950 had sent two million veterans to colleges and universities of every kind with portable Federal finance and generous time limits. President Truman's Commission on Higher Education of 1946 saw it as central to democracy and national defense and called for reforms ranging from increased racial integration to vast new

---

[50] Excerpted in Smith & Bender, 20–21.   [51] Excerpted in Smith & Bender, 398–402.

investments.[52] There followed the projected and then the real baby-boom population explosion. College enrollments soared from 1.5 million nationwide in 1940 to nearly 8 million in 1970, rising in the 1960s alone from 3.6 to 7.9 million. The demand for higher education was such that even the greatly expanded public state systems could not meet it. The junior or community, two-year college found such new appeal that by the 1960s one new community college was being founded each week.[53]

The third major factor was the central role that higher education played in American culture after World War II. State legislatures almost universally approved generous spending for new or expanded campuses, curricula, and faculty. Riding on its reputation for patriotic service and expertise, academia became central to public policy in any number of fields. As Columbia sociologist Daniel Bell put it in 1966,

> The university now occupies a central position in the society. Formerly its
> chief function was that of conserving and transmitting the intellectual
> traditions and cultural values of society. Now the university serves more
> as the center for research and innovation. Though the university once
> reflected the status system of the society, it now determines status.[54]

Academic experts in everything from astrophysics to Herodotus appeared regularly in newspapers and magazines and in the newly exploding medium of television, all aimed at an expanding and aspirational new middle class hungry for both material success and the cultural credentials that accompanied it. As tax-generated government investment in all forms of American life continued, inequality fell to its lowest levels in the history of the globe, and the doors of opportunity started opening for anyone with any type of college education. For those with post-graduate degrees the highest levels of America's new administrative society lay open. So long as the graduates were white and male, class and ethnic differences began to disappear, at least from public discussion and display. "College" was both the key and the door.

---

[52] For the text, see Hofstadter & Smith, II:970–90.   [53] Thelin, 300.

[54] From Daniel Bell, *The Reforming of General Education: The Columbia College Experience in its National Setting* (New York: Columbia University Press, 1966), 277.

But several elements of American life remained constant reminders of the fragile structure – and artificially unified identity – of an American system that combined heavily funded elite university research with broad-based and leveling universal higher education. As early as 1955, Douglas Bush, distinguished professor of the classical tradition in English literature at Harvard, voiced the disdain of many academics for this egalitarian strain of American higher ed:

> In schools, colleges and universities today, the results of the huge increase in the student body suggests a rather painful thought: the principle of education for all, however fine in theory, in practice ultimately leads to education for none. In other words, the ideal of education for all forces acceptance of the principle that the function of education is primarily social and political rather than purely intellectual; if school standards are geared to an almost invisibly low average there is not much real education available for anyone, even for the gifted.[55]

The legacy of American higher education's foundation as religious schools to educate a learned, devoted, and civically engaged elite also cannot be overstated. Predating the Culture Wars – and laying the groundwork for them – conservative intellectual William F. Buckley Jr. reiterated this tradition as it applied to his alma mater in his widely read *God and Man at Yale: The Superstitions of "Academic Freedom"*:

> But we can ... raise the question whether Yale fortifies or shatters the average student's respect for Christianity. There are, of course, some students who will emerge stronger Christians from any institution, and others who will reject religion wherever they are sent. But if the atmosphere of a college is overwhelmingly secular, if the influential members of the faculty tend to discourage religious inclinations, or to persuade the student that Christianity is nothing more than "ghost-fear," or "twentieth-century witchcraft," university policy quite properly becomes

---

[55] William F. Buckley Jr. "Education for All Is Education for None," *New York Times* (January 9, 1955): 13, 30–31; (January 23, 1955): 63.

a matter of concern to those parents and alumni who deem active Christian faith a powerful force for good and for personal happiness.[56]

Given this history, we cannot easily dismiss the religious right's harsh reaction to changes in American higher ed in the late twentieth and the twenty-first century, expressed through the Culture Wars. New religious foundations, even in the extreme example of Bob Jones University, are not radical departures from – but a new embrace of – this long American tradition. Leaders of higher education and its analysts must bear this in mind before harsh and sweeping condemnations are in order, or, if in order, to clearly distinguish how such schools might differ from the American norm.

A second factor as potent as America's evangelical foundations was its anti-intellectual and anti-elitist strains that carried with them what Richard Hofstadter called the "paranoid style" in American politics. We have already seen the anti-elitists and anti-intellectual strains of American disdain for much of higher education, but with the late 1940s and early 1950s these combined with a virulent anti-Communism to make the university and the education foundation particular targets of the American right wing. Senator Joseph McCarthy's House Un-American Activities Committee held high-profile hearings targeting State Department and other government officials, Hollywood actors, directors, and writers for their affiliations with the Communist Party and other left-wing activities. But other, more local initiatives joined with Washington's investigations. Elite schools like Harvard and Yale became especial targets of right-wing polemicists like William F. Buckley, while states and heads of university systems and individual schools demanded loyalty oaths from faculty and launched investigations into the activities of individuals that at times exceeded even McCarthy's zeal. The purges of faculty at the University of California were only the most prominent of hundreds of similar actions by trustees and presidents of colleges and universities across the United States during these years.[57]

---

[56] William F. Buckley Jr. *God and Man at Yale: The Superstitions of "Academic Freedom"* (Washington, DC: Regnery, 1951), 3–4.

[57] See the 1952 court record surrounding the UC loyalty oath in *Tolman v. Underhill*, excerpted in Smith & Bender, 462–63.

Poorly organized and culturally adverse to political resistance, both well-placed individuals and organizations like the American Association of University Professors failed to resist the initial pressures aimed at dissolving decades-old bonds of authority and separation that had marked the golden era of American intellectual life.[58]

*

Even with the demise of radical right-wing witch hunts by the late 1950s, the American university was developing its own culture of discontent. The 1962 anthology edited by Berkeley psychologist Nevitt Sanford entitled, *The American College: A Psychological and Social Interpretation of Higher Learning* attempted to alert university and college administrators to several unsettling strains that demonstrated the internal contradictions of elite aspiration built upon the broadened base of large-scale enrollments. The large-scale takeover of university research agendas by Federal agencies – mostly channeling them to defense research – was beginning to have its impact. In 1963, UC President Clark Kerr could take his cue from business and government to describe – if not altogether approve of – the new "multiversity" as a divergence from the humanist Oxbridge model and as a "knowledge industry":[59]

> The multiversity in America is perhaps best seen at work, adapting and growing, as it responded to the massive impact of federal programs beginning with World War II. A vast transformation has taken place without a revolution, for a time almost without notice being taken. The multiversity has demonstrated how adaptive it can be to new opportunities for creativity; how responsive to money; how eagerly it can play a new and useful role; how fast it can change while pretending that nothing has happened at all; how fast it can neglect some of its ancient virtues ... Basic to this transformation is the growth of the "knowledge industry," which is coming to permeate government and business and to draw into it more and more people raised to higher and higher levels of skill.

---

[58] See Thelin, 274–77; Ellen Schrecker, *No Ivory Tower: McCarthyism and the Universities* (New York: Oxford University Press, 1986).

[59] In Kerr, *The Uses of the University*, 34, 66.

The production, distribution, and consumption of "knowledge" in all its forms is said to account for 29 percent of gross national product, according to Fritz Machlup's calculations; and "knowledge production" is growing at about twice the rate of the rest of the economy. Knowledge has certainly never in history been so central to the conduct of an entire society. What the railroads did for the second half of the last century and the automobile for the first half of this century may be done for the second half of this century by the knowledge industry: that is, to serve as the focal point for national growth. And the university is at the center of the knowledge process.

As reflected in Harold Orlans' 1962 survey, however, many faculty voiced discomfort with the increasing Federal role in this transform-ation.[60] At the same time, the anonymity of large state systems in which students often felt lost gave rise to the widespread trope on the computer punch-card: "do not fold, spindle or mutilate." By the early 1960s strict controls over student activities and expression had given rise to the Free Speech Movement at Berkeley and other campuses.[61] Among the faculty, a chasm began opening between science research stars, charismatic media magnets, and the majority of their colleagues. The purges and betrayals of the McCarthy era had also left a lingering legacy of personal animosities and amnesias. Meanwhile, new cultural criticisms from an emerging counterculture and the continued exclusion of racial minor-ities and women from the centers of university life invigorated new calls for transformation that brought academic life and debates to an increas-ingly alarmed American public. It took only the slowly emerging shadow of what was first referred to as "Indochina" and then as "Vietnam" to bring all these issues to a head. By the end of the 1960s both the left and the right were beginning to question whether the United States had a recognizable "system" of higher education and, if so, whether that system embodied any values other than its own perpetuation and expansion.

---

[60] *The Effects of Federal Programs on Higher Education: A Study of 36 Universities and Colleges* (Washington, DC: Brookings Institute, 1962), excerpted in Smith & Bender, 402–5. For broader critiques on the 1960s, see Smith & Bender, 405–12.

[61] See Smith & Bender, 345–47; Thelin, 307–8.

CHAPTER 3

The Retreat from 1968

INTRODUCTION

WE CANNOT HERE SURVEY THE RECORD of university protest, compromise, retrenchment, and innovation during what has come to be known as the "student movement" of the 1960s. Media and politicians continue to focus on its most famous episodes: the student revolts at Columbia in 1968, Cornell and Harvard in 1969, and at Kent State and Jackson State in 1970, decried by both right and left for violent upheaval and its suppression. Yet for those who were there, who saw and remember, the 1960s are best remembered for their nonviolent organizing, petitioning, political engagement, silent witness, marches, sit-ins and teach-ins on hundreds of campuses, involving hundreds of thousands of students in support of civil rights and women's rights and for an end to the military draft and the war in Vietnam. Memories, official pronouncements, and histories did, and will continue to, diverge.[1] Here, however, we will focus on two incidents. The first is the 1968 student occupation at Columbia University and the ensuing reaction. The second includes two incidents at Cornell University.[2] All were real events, involving the aspirations and actions of real protagonists. They fit into a far larger historical context and interpretive schema, but I hope that their uses here will be seen again as apt and useful metaphors, humanist *exempla* of larger historical forces and personalities at work.

---

[1] See Wallerstein & Starr; Barbara Ehrenreich, *Fear of Falling: The Inner Life of the Middle Class* (New York: HarperCollins, 1989); Smith & Bender.

[2] See Ehrenreich, *Fear of Falling*, 57–96.

COLUMBIA '68

Columbia University in the 1950s and 1960s shared in the rise of the research university across a broad array of fields and individual disciplines in both the sciences and the humanities. Its students on both the undergraduate and graduate levels were among the most desired and accomplished in the nation. Its faculty achieved a prominence enjoyed by few other institutions. It consistently ranked among the top ten in the world, often among the top half-dozen universities in the nation. Its status eclipsed that of any other of the dozens of colleges and universities in the greater New York City area. Its administration and endowment were among the best in the nation. Its main campus in the heart of Manhattan's Upper West Side was an array of imposing Beaux-Arts buildings designed by McKim, Meade and White on thirty-two acres that housed dormitories, libraries, laboratories, offices, and classrooms.

In 1968 Columbia's main campus was literally separated and protected from its surroundings by a continuous line of buildings and high iron gates, often joined by brick and granite walls several stories high that stared blankly over neighboring streets.[3] It was also perched high above its urban surroundings by Morningside Heights' natural topography: the Manhattan's Rift valley to the north, the slopes of Riverside Drive to the west, and the precipitous cliffs of Morningside Park to the east, which separate it from the Harlem community. Inside its walls Columbia's main lawns are bracketed on the north by the Pantheon-like Low Library administration building and on the south by its Butler Library, into whose granite entablatures are carved the names of great male thinkers of the European past.

Columbia, like most of its fellow Ivy League universities, had grown rich, "gilt by association,"[4] through its endowments, research and defense contracts with the US government. Innovation here meant high-level research that dissolved its metaphorical walls of separation from the external world. But by 1968, that outside world was in ferment. The apparent calm and consensus of late 1950s America had been

---

[3] See https://undergrad.admissions.columbia.edu/photo/campus-aerial.

[4] The phrase is Thelin's to characterize the golden age of American university life in the postwar era to 1970. See Thelin, 260–316.

replaced by the civil rights, women's, and what would become the LGBTQ movements. Youth and "hippie" culture dominated media attention. Political assassinations and their aftermaths in urban uprisings, suppression, and white flight joined soaring urban poverty, neglect, and crime, accelerating the already rapid decay of major portions of the city. Morningside Heights suddenly felt less an aloof academic enclave and more a small island battered by successive storms.

Since the mid 1950s, Columbia University had also been expanding beyond its neoclassical enclave into the surrounding neighborhood. One particular plan called for the construction of a new gymnasium to be built on the slopes of neighboring Morningside Park, which overlooked Harlem and that – though neglected and underused, like most city parks at the time – was still prized by neighborhood residents. The plan was to build on a field already lend-leased to the university by the city. Despite continued protests from the community, in which over two dozen residents were arrested, despite a December 1967 Faculty Civil Rights Group report urging Columbia to abandon the plan, and despite NYC Parks Commissioner Hoving's call for a project review, the Columbia administration and board went ahead with construction plans. In this they broke an uneasy truce between a literally walled-in Columbia campus and the local Harlem community.

As Columbia planned to breach the wall of physical separation, internally students' intellectual and moral appeals were calling on academia – both faculty as a corporate body and as individuals – to exercise its authority to offer an intellectual and moral critique of the Vietnam War and racial injustice. In the eyes of many, American academia failed to do so when it most mattered. Columbia became the tinder-box of these tensions. Beginning in 1967 and continuing through the spring of 1968, Columbia's Students for Democratic Society (SDS) had staged nonviolent protests and sit-ins against the university's participation in the Institute for Defense Analyses (IDA), the escalating Vietnam War, military recruiting on campus, and the school's provision of student academic records to the Selective Service (military conscription) System. The protests led to more vocal confrontations with pro-military students; and following a sit-in in the Low Library administration building, several SDS leaders were subsequently placed on disciplinary probation.

In April 1968,[5] a group of Columbia's black undergraduates from the Society for African American Students seized and occupied Hamilton Hall, a center of undergraduate education on campus. Their stated goal was to "dramatize Columbia University's attempt to control the Harlem community and therefore hinder Black self-determination."[6] They demanded the end of construction of the Harlem's Morningside Park gym and amnesty for those arrested in demonstrations opposing the construction, Columbia's severing all institutional and individual ties to the IDA, and amnesty for all Columbia students involved in the protests. They were soon joined by the SDS in the occupation of several more buildings, including Low Library and the president's office, classroom, office, and laboratory facilities. The occupation became a cause célèbre on campuses across the country. Within Columbia debate raged over the proper response to the student takeover. As lines hardened, student demands became more rigid. Columbia's administration soon bowed to pressure to end the strike quickly. One week after the initial occupation, President Grayson Kirk gave campus access to NYC Police who "brutally" ended the occupation, arresting 524 students alone that first day.

The police action, which attacked and seized student occupiers, mediating faculty, and onlookers alike, provoked widespread disgust across the city and nation. Combined with the administration's hard line on student discipline, suspensions, and criminal charges, it provoked a student strike that resulted in the nearly complete shutdown of the university that lasted into the June commencement. It forced university President Kirk's resignation, the abandonment of the gym project, Columbia's break with the IDA, greater faculty power, and the beginnings of student participation in campus governance. In his report from the independent committee of inquiry established to review the Columbia "disturbance," distinguished jurist Archibald Cox cited the long-growing student discontent with Columbia life, brought to the

---

[5] For an informative timeline, with documents, see Jocelyn Wilk, curator, "1968: Columbia in Crisis," Columbia University Libraries, at https://exhibitions.library.columbia.edu/ exhibits/show/1968.

[6] "Our Demands," in Wallerstein & Starr, 161–62.

tipping point by the violence of the Vietnam War that underlay all the events. The university – "essentially a free community of scholars dedicated to the pursuit of truth and knowledge solely through reason and civility" – coalesced around the brutality of the police reaction. While condemning the disruptions and violence of the student occupiers, the report placed the burden of blame squarely on the university's administration and its "ways of an *ancien regime*."[7] Two years later, in 1970, William Scranton, head of the US President's Commission on Campus Unrest, laid out the same chain of causalities at Berkeley as at Columbia: "the rising tide of student opposition to war and racial injustice."[8]

In her "On the Steps of Low Library," Diana Trilling encapsulated the response of the left-liberal, Ivy League faculty to the events of 1968.[9] She was a Harvard (Radcliffe) graduate, brilliant essayist, and along with her husband, Columbia professor Lionel Trilling, a key member of the New York intellectuals centered on the Marxist *Partisan Review*, which stressed the political and social context of intellectual labor. From the distance of fifty years, when progressive discourse has moved on and developed in new and explicit turns, Trilling's "Steps" is often difficult to parse at face value. Her committed leftist politics, genuine critique of racial inequality, of the Vietnam War, and of the university administration's indifference and "arrogance of power" is undercut by a certain literary distance, an ironic and often satiric tone endemic to academic literary studies at mid-century. On first reading, one is never certain whether her revelations reflect her own thoughts, those of her colleagues, or those of her class. Her tone is often gently but sometimes bitterly mocking of these thoughts and ideas, of the student uprising, of the New Left, the anti-war movement, and of New York politics. In the end – and as she makes clear in a published exchange with Poet Laureate Robert Lowell – her essay deeply reflects both a tension between American egalitarianism and its elite culture and the dismay of the academic elite at a world

---

[7] Archibald Cox, et al., *Crisis at Columbia: Report of the Fact-Finding Commission Appointed to Investigate the Disturbance at Columbia University in April and May 1968* (New York: Vintage Books, 1968), 194.

[8] Excerpted in Smith & Bender, 373–79.

[9] In Diana Trilling, "On the Steps of Low Library," in *We Must March My Darlings: A Critical Decade* (New York: Harcourt Brace Jovanovich, 1977), 76–153.

collapsing around them. This observation is not to set elitism against egalitarianism in any larger context but to remind us that as late as the 1960s, in the United States, in New York City, the original, ancient ideal of a liberal-arts education remained "still sacred" to create "the educated classes," an elite, however defined.

For Trilling, Morningside Heights was "a constantly shrinking white island." Columbia itself remained a "white institution" beset by the constant fear of black Harlem just outside and below the campus, a fearsome place of the external other, "of possibly yet-unleashed black furies." The student takeover, initiated by black students, was such a force of unbridled nature, a "natural upheaval," a "catastrophe of nature." It resembled the hurricane she and her children had once experienced on the genteel coast of Connecticut: nature symbolism for a world out of order, where all natural boundaries are upset, an irrational force that leaves only destruction in its wake. Trilling would not be ignorant of the long tradition of nature symbolism and its uses, from Pliny's descriptions of Vesuvius, to Petrarch's description of the earthquake and tsunami that struck Naples in 1345 – the symbol of nature turned upside down by a woman sitting on Naples' royal throne – to the Romantic poets, uprooting reason and dissolving borders between realms, to the late paintings of Turner, of raw power without apparent order, with boundaries of separation dissolved in a world turned from the modern, enlightened, and liberal to the chaotic and atavistic. Trilling remarked that events at Columbia resembled the "demented world" portrayed in the 1963 Peter Weiss production, and Peter Brook's 1967 unsettling film version, of the play *Marat/Sade*. It marked the collapse of the liberal cultural establishment. As she recalled,

> all through the last week of April and throughout the month of May this was the potential horror which hung over our island. At night my husband on the campus, I, like (I suppose) all wives of faculty, obeyed our instruction to stay behind bolted doors ... an unopened book on my lap, the unceasing campus radio at my side, straining for the unfamiliar sound of the street beneath my shaded windows, the tramp or rush or scuffle of invasion ... for the sound of Harlem rushing upon our white island.[10]

[10] Trilling, "Steps," 87, 139.

The essay sets up constant parallels to Trilling's then-current reading: Norman Mailer's 1968 account of the 1967 anti-war march on the Pentagon in his *Armies of the Night*. Comparing this to the "existential" risks faced by Columbia faculty, she called this march a "nervous foray . . . free of involvement." Its "notables," including intellectuals like Lowell, Dwight Macdonald, and Paul Goodman, were "white tourists." She claimed that the action (which faced bayonet-wielding, massed army units) was safe and noncommittal to its participants. Throughout her essay Trilling failed to acknowledge the role the Vietnam War played in student discontent. In her correspondence with Lowell, she explicitly refused to see the connection between intellectual critique and the outside world of context and relevance that might involve personal risk.

Poet Robert Lowell's rebuttal summarizes the contemporaneous critique of Trilling's outrage and of the Enlightenment ideals of detached intellect and reformist authority that underlay it. Unlike the Trillings, Lowell was born into a Boston Brahmin family that traced its ancestry to the original Pilgrims on the *Mayflower*. Yet he was imprisoned during World War II as a conscientious objector and later strongly opposed the war in Vietnam. Replying, reluctantly, to Trilling's goading challenge of his activism, he retorted,

> On the great day, when she meets her Maker, John Stuart Mill on his right hand and Diderot on his left, they will say, "Liberalism gave you a standard; what have you done for liberalism?" Then she will answer that her record is clear of agitation about the Vietnam War, clear of a feverish concern for the drafting of reluctant young men to fight it, free of a nervous fear about the militarization of our country. Terror of the nuclear bombs never forced her to lose hope. She seems more preoccupied with the little violence of the unarmed student uprisings than with the great violence of the nation at war. She implied that we who are so horrified by napalm on human flesh are somehow indifferent to the piss on President Kirk's carpet.[11]

But Trilling was correct in her heart of hearts and in her analysis that consciously portrayed the end of the liberal romance of the American

[11] Trilling, "Steps," 148.

university. In her measured indictment, the academic world typified by Columbia in 1968 – aloof, unquestioned, hierarchical, and backward looking – was to lose every compass direction that had so marked American higher education only a decade earlier. "Columbia '68" symbolized the breaching of the two essential characteristics of the university: separateness and authority. The Columbia occupation and its suppression caught the attention of the nation for both sides' extreme attitudes and measures. But Columbia was neither isolated nor particularly characteristic of the many nonviolent actions taken by students in protests against the Vietnam War, university complicity in the war effort, student alienation and lack of self-determination, and the newly corporate university's expansion at the expense of local communities. Whatever the rights or wrongs of individuals or groups, the events left a trail of bitterness and defensiveness that marked Columbia's spirit well into the next decade. For America as a whole, "Columbia '68" marked the end of its idyllic image of the university as a tranquil space and time apart. It also discredited the lofty authority that academia held in US society and symbolically, at least, emphasized the end of university separateness.

CORNELL

The second case can be noted more briefly. It is essentially iconic and was broadcast widely by two Associated Press photos. Protests at Cornell had grown from general discontent over what many students felt was the university's complicity – or at least its silence – in the Vietnam War effort. In April 1969 a cross-burning on campus was answered by protestations from the campus' Afro-American Society. When these appeals went unmet by Cornell's administration and student protestors were arrested, black students occupied the university's Willard Straight Hall, calling for amnesty and university reforms. After being physically attacked by a white fraternity, they took up rifles as a symbol of self-defense and defiance. The action was met by the white students' burning down of the Afro-American Center, attempted reconciliation on the part of university President James A. Perkins – himself an advocate of civil rights and social justice – and by faculty condemnation of the escalating confrontation. In the weeks that followed, Perkins resigned his position, the faculty split over the action and reaction, and the campus followed the lead of others in reassessing its authority, its role in society, and its place in intellectual progress. As at Columbia and many other campuses across the nation, bitter feelings lingered.

"The Picture" of a young black man emerging from a campus building carrying a rifle and ammunition belts won a Pulitzer Prize but also sent shock waves across both academic circles and the American public at large.[12] To some it represented a bold revolutionary gesture, to most a dangerous attack on both academic and American values. According to conservative commentator David Horowitz, it was "the most disgraceful occurrence in the history of American higher education."[13] Allan Bloom claimed that that image shocked him into writing *The Closing of the American Mind.*

The second event was equally iconic, but its impact was far less shocking within both academia and broader American culture. During the faculty procession at Cornell's 1970 commencement, then-university-marshal Morris Bishop used the university's mace – the medieval symbol of both its separateness and its authority – to "jab" and forcefully fend off a protestor attempting to commandeer the ceremony microphone. The alleged jabee was reported as C. David Burak, "a well-known Cornell radical,"[14] a graduate in 1967, former head of the local chapter of SDS, and later a professor at Santa Monica College. According to news reports, he had attempted to expand the action of black students into a wider university action, much like what had happened at Columbia. Due to the university's interventions and student skepticism, the attempt failed, and the SDS was sidelined by subsequent events. Despite the media's selective memory, Burak's reputation for both radical politics

---

[12] See George Lowery, "A Campus Takeover That Symbolized an Era of Change," *Cornell Chronicle* (April 16, 2009), at https://news.cornell.edu/stories/2009/04/campus-takeover-symbolized-era-change.

[13] For what follows, see Jane Mayer, "How Right-Wing Billionaires Infiltrated Higher Education," *Chronicle Review*, CHE (Feb. 12, 2016), at www.chronicle.com/article/How-Right-Wing-Billionaires/235286.

[14] Joel Rudin, "Morris Bishop Dead at 80," *Cornell Daily Sun* 90.61 (Nov. 26, 1973), at https://cdsun.library.cornell.edu/cgi-bin/cornell?a=d&d=CDS19731126.2.3.

and its symbolic gestures remained strong.[15] Bishop was a well-known biographer of Petrarch, curator of the Fiske Petrarch Collection at the university's Olin Library, and a major popularizer of medieval and Renaissance culture. On Bishop's death in 1973, Cornell President Dale R. Corson reminisced that "the jab was given in typical Bishop style: with spontaneity, grace and effectiveness."[16]

REACTION

Events at Cornell – especially the icon of armed black activism – shocked conservative Cornell alumnus, donor, and former trustee John M. Olin, an arms manufacturer. An internal memo from his charitable foundation, which to that point had funded cultural institutions like museums, colleges, and universities, stated that he then "saw very clearly that students at Cornell, like those at most major universities, were hostile to businessmen and to business enterprise, and indeed had begun to question the ideals of the nation itself." In response he shifted his foundation's energies away from culture and toward politics, turning the atmosphere and thinking on America's campuses to the right. Inverting the Ford Foundation's social activism, Olin and his senior advisors planned an "advocacy philanthropy" for the right wing that specifically targeted academia as its chief battleground. But this battle was to be waged by stealth.

Olin and his foundation decided to engage in battle by underwriting research for graduate students and faculty, endowing fellowships, providing book subsidies, funding annual awards, and by gradually founding research institutes and academic programs at Harvard, Princeton, Chicago, Cornell, Dartmouth, Georgetown, MIT, Penn, Yale, and other elite schools. According to Olin Foundation President William Simon, former Treasury Secretary and energy tsar in the Republican Nixon and Ford administrations,

---

[15] According to private correspondence from Prof. Burak (March 1, 2020), he was prevented from getting close to the line of march or podium by campus police, and Bishop's jab was aimed at another student.

[16] Rudin, "Morris Bishop Dead."

What we need is a counter-intelligentsia . . . [It] can be organized to challenge our ruling "new class" – opinion makers . . . Ideas are weapons – indeed the only weapons with which other ideas can be fought. . . . Capitalism has no duty to subsidize its enemies . . . the mindless subsidizing of colleges and universities whose departments of politics, economics and history are hostile to capitalism . . . [Instead, they] must take pains to funnel desperately needed funds to scholars, social scientists and writers who understand the relationship between political and economic liberty. . . . They must be given grants, grants, and more grants in exchange for books, books, and more books.

By the time the Olin Foundation had spent down its last dollars in 2005, it would devote almost $180 million toward fostering right-wing agendas and faculty across the nation's elite schools. Their subsidies underwrote, helped publish, and spread the influence of such right-wing spokesmen in and out of academia as William F. Buckley Jr., Allan Bloom, John R. Lott Jr., Charles Murray, David Brock, Dinesh D'Souza, George Will, Robert George, William Kristol, Harvey Mansfield, Roger Ailes, Edward Meese, and Edward Feulner. Olin's legacy would be far broader, and we will discuss its impact in later chapters.

The Olin Foundation was not alone in funding a right-wing academic class and in attacking what it considered a leftist university culture. Horrified by student unrest, the Angela Davis case, and the shooting of black militants on campus, James Buchanan, then of UCLA's Economics Department and later Nobel Laureate for Economic Sciences, soon left the school for Virginia Tech, later claiming in his *Academia in Anarchy* that American higher ed was allowing "a handful of revolutionary terrorists to undo the heritage of centuries."[17] He set about developing a theory of "public choice," including public higher education as a pure business proposition badly run:

(1) those who consume its products [students] do not purchase it [at full-cost price]; (2) those who produce it [faculty] do not sell it; and (3) those who finance it [taxpayers] do not control it.[18]

---

[17] James M. Buchanan and Nicos E. Devletoglou, *Academia in Anarchy: An Economic Diagnosis* (New York: Basic Books, 1979), x–xi; quoted in Nancy MacLean, *Democracy in Chains: The Deep History of the Radical Right's Stealth Plan for America* (New York: Viking, 2017), 103.

[18] MacLean, *Democracy in Chains*, 104.

According to Duke University historian Nancy MacLean, Buchanan's thought formed the basis of the theory underpinning all the right-wing's subsequent efforts to roll back public education, to substitute public funding with family money and student loans so that students would become more critical and focused consumers, and to cut back or eliminate departments that encourage critical thinking about capitalism, including sociology, history, and literature. Privatization of all levels of education was to be the goal. Buchanan and his associate Gordon Tullock began discussing plans to deny humanities and liberal-arts education to public university students: to avoid producing a discerning working class likely to challenge the nation's elite.[19] Buchanan joined forces with Charles Koch's Institute for Humane Studies for "building a critical mass of freedom-friendly professors" and with the John M. Olin Foundation.[20]

ACADEME IN RETREAT

The use of violence by university officials – justified in the eyes of many – symbolized for many others the university's misuse of authority while continuing to maintain an illusion of separateness from larger social issues of war, violence, and injustice. The mixed, and often confused, reaction of the Columbia and Cornell faculties and administrations typified the response of much of American academe. Rejecting the call to use its authority to benefit society at large – or at the very least to make expressions of concern for its students unwillingly drafted into the horrors of Vietnam – it mustered the only authority left in the equation: that of force and power to preserve its institutional integrity and separateness. The wake of the student uprisings and activism of the 1960s saw the American university grasping for cohesion, meaning, and an essential role in American society. In order to reassess and reconfirm these, academia as a whole retreated from the dominance over the culture that it had exerted throughout the first half of the twentieth century.

This retreat took two forms: internally the retreat spread within universities, their administrations, alums, faculties, disciplines, and

---

[19] MacLean, *Democracy in Chains*, 106.   [20] Quoted in MacLean, *Democracy in Chains*, 138.

teaching, and among the student bodies. Externally the retreat was marked by a disenchantment with higher education among Americans: at first a dismay at the events of the 1960s, and then the growing chorus of criticism that had already developed in the late 1950s against large class sizes, impersonal teaching, and multiplication of fields, elitism, and corporatization. Criticisms came from left, middle, and right, from intellectuals and business leaders, from working, middle, and upper classes. The 1970 Scranton *Report of the President's Commission on Campus Unrest* probed this issue more explicitly:

> The great majority of Americans were outraged by violence on American campuses. Such reactions against campus unrest were often intensified by a more general revulsion against the distinctive dress, life style, behavior, or speech adopted by some young people. Concerned over what they saw as an erosion of standards, a loss of morality, and a turn toward violence, many Americans came to believe that only harsh measures could quell campus disturbances. Many failed to distinguish between peaceful dissent and violent protest and called for the elimination of all campus unrest. Such public backlash made events on campus – in particular protests, disruptions, and violence – a major political issue, both rationally discussed and irresponsibly exploited.[21]

Among those who took up the political issue were candidate and then-President Richard Nixon, Vice-President Spiro Agnew, and California Governor Ronald Reagan: all Republicans. While Nixon continued to speak in positive terms of higher education, his administration revived the rhetoric of 1950s McCarthyism with a growing political and media campaign against what his vice-president and political surrogate Spiro Agnew termed an "effete corps of impudent snobs who characterize themselves as intellectuals"[22] Nixon himself adopted a less confrontational, yet still critical, stance toward the university. In a speech at General Beadle State College in Madison, South Dakota, on June 3,

[21] Excerpted from Smith & Bender, 377.
[22] In a speech in New Orleans on October 19, 1969, quoted in Peter B. Levy, "Spiro Agnew, the Forgotten Americans and the Rise of the New Right," *Historian* 75 (Winter 2013): 719.

1969, he conflated student unrest with faculty weakness and the university's loss of authority, innovation (progress), and of separateness from society at large:

> Lately ... a great many people have become impatient with the democratic process. Some of the more extreme even argue, with curious logic, that there is no majority, because the majority has no right to hold opinions that they disagree with. Scorning persuasion, they prefer coercion. Awarding themselves what they call a higher morality, they try to bully authority into yielding to their "demands." On college campuses, they draw support from faculty members who should know better; in the larger community, they find the usual apologists ready to excuse any tactic in the name of "progress.". . . We have long considered our colleges and universities citadels of freedom, where the rule of reason prevails. Now both the process of freedom and the rule of reason are under attack. . . . No group, as a group, should be more zealous defenders of the integrity of academic standards and the rule of reason in academic life than the faculties of our great institutions. If they simply follow the loudest voices, parrot the latest slogan, yield to unreasonable demands, they will have won not the respect but the contempt of their students.[23]

Only a few days later, in a speech to the Commonwealth Club of San Francisco on June 13, 1969, then-California-Governor Ronald Reagan also used widespread student and public discontent against the "knowledge factory" as means of criticizing the current directions of American higher education. In so doing he struck at the heart of the post-war American research university's innovation, its authority, and its separateness:

> Is there a revolutionary movement involving a tiny minority of faculty and students finding concealment and shelter in the disappointment and resentment of an entire college generation that finds itself fed into a knowledge factory with no regard for their individuality, aspirations or their dreams? The answer is an obvious "yes," and the challenge to us is to establish contact with these frustrated young people and join in finding

---

[23] Wallerstein & Starr, 50–56 at 53–54.

answers before they fall to the mob by default ... Their legitimate grievances must be understood and solutions must be forthcoming. "Publish or perish" as a university policy must be secondary to teaching. Research, a vital and essential part of the process, must not be the standard by which the university rates itself. Its function is to teach, and its record must be established on the quality of graduates it offers to the world – not in the collecting of scholarly names in its catalog.[24]

Reagan's criticisms of student unrest built on widespread acknowledgment that the university was failing in its duty to most Americans. But it also marked the beginning of a general critique of higher education reaching into US political discourse on the highest levels that not even the McCarthy era had dared. One of Reagan's first interventions was to push the UCLA administration into firing one of the best-known symbols of the sixties. Angela Davis was a Sorbonne-educated assistant professor of philosophy, radical feminist, member of the Communist Party, supporter of the Black Panthers, and opponent of the Vietnam War. UCLA fired her despite protest from nearly every department and widespread demonstrations on campus. The courts later found the firing illegal, and UCLA reinstated her. The Regents again fired her in 1970.[25]

But not all intellectual criticism came from the right. Berkeley philosopher Richard Lichtman's "The University: Mask for Privilege" appeared in January 1968.[26] Lichtman set up a contrast between the traditional liberal-arts concept of the university expounded by John Stuart Mill and the California model of the multiversity described only a decade earlier by UC President Clark Kerr as the epitome of modern American higher ed:[27]

In the middle of the nineteenth century one of its astutest critics [Mills] noted: "The proper function of the University in national education is tolerably well understood. At least there is a tolerably general agreement

[24] Wallerstein & Starr, 130–32.
[25] Angela Davis, *An Autobiography* (New York: Random House, 1974).
[26] In *Center Magazine*, excerpted in Wallerstein & Starr, 101–20.
[27] In Kerr, *The Uses of the University* and other works. See also Chapter 2, 57–58.

of what a University is not. It is not a place of professional education. Universities are not intended to teach the knowledge required to fit men for some special mode of gaining their livelihood. Their object is not to make skillful lawyers, or physicians, or engineers, but capable and cultivated human beings." ... The pronouncements of Mill and Clark Kerr differ in several significant ways. The first stresses coherence, the second fragmentation; the first is exclusionary, the second is ready to incorporate any interest that society urges upon it; the first distinguishes between higher and lower knowledge, while the second distributes its emphasis in accordance with available financial support. Of greatest importance, perhaps, is that the older view regards itself as bound by intrinsic canons of culture, while the current conception accommodates and molds itself to prevailing trends. The first view holds to an ideal of transcendence, while the second is grossly imminent in its time. For contemporary doctrine, the ancient tension between what the world is and what it might become has all but vanished. The current perspective is an apologia, a celebration, an ideological consecration of this most lovely of all possible worlds – in short a consenting academy. ... That ideology is generally an inversion of reality is borne out by the current educational situation, for the University is in the process of intellectual dissolution at that precise moment of history in which the development of centralized, bureaucratic corporate power has been dominating progressively larger areas of national and international life and drawing the world's economy and destiny into an increasingly seamless whole.

In 1969 came a booklet published by the Cambridge, MA-based Africa Research Group, which focused on the structures of power it saw as embodied in Harvard University:

American universities – including their historic and elite quintessence, Harvard – are no ethereal communities of scholars. The proverbial absent-minded professors, the archive rats, the bohemians, and the assorted academic odd-balls who are still found on numerous campuses are only the sad but noble remnants of an utterly shattered classical bourgeois ideal of *Universitas*. Today, far from being cut off from the "real world outside," American universities are absolutely central components of the social system of technological warfare-welfare capitalism. The functions, goals, structures, and organization of the universities are directly and indirectly determined by the needs and perspectives of that social system.[28]

Such discourse reflected widespread left-wing criticism and paralleled that from the political right in its assertions that the university no longer held either authority or separateness from American society at large. If Nixon or Reagan could call for the universities to return to public service, as they defined it, the left asserted that the collapse of the medieval *universitas* tradition had already been accomplished and that American higher education did little more than serve the interests of society as defined by its corporate elites. Ironically, it was the left who expressed a nostalgic, if sometimes condescending, sense of loss for the separateness of the humanistic *universitas*, just as the right called for further political oversight and service to business and technology. Whatever the direction of critique, however, the result was the same. By 1970 the university had ceased to be revered in America as authoritative or separate, and its innovations were seen either to already serve perceived American corporate goals or to be in need of conforming to the political expression of these goals.

ACADEME'S GRAND BARGAIN

Internally to higher education, especially at the elite universities most affected by student activism of the 1960s, a grand bargain was struck in the wake of the student unrest: in exchange for abandoning societal authority, the universities would be left to themselves to develop a separateness from all external issues, which were thereafter caricatured as "relevance." As early as June 15, 1962, "The Port Huron Statement," the founding document of the Students for a Democratic Society (SDS), a chief instigator of university student protest, had issued the call for higher education to become "relevant":

> Social relevance, the accessibility to knowledge, and internal openness – these together make the university a potential base and agency in a movement of social change.[29]

---

[28] "How Harvard Rules," in Wallerstein & Starr, 99–101, at 100.

[29] Online at www2.iath.virginia.edu/sixties/HTML_docs/Resources/Primary/Manifestos/ SDS_Port_Huron.html.

In the humanities this flight from "relevance" was justified within increasingly arcane structures of hierarchical authority as "pure research." The execution by armed and ranked National Guard soldiers of four unarmed students and the wounding of nine protesting the Vietnam War on May 4, 1970 at Kent State University did little to reverse this retrenchment. In fact, faculty at Columbia seem to have adopted an even colder stance toward the activities of the Spring Moratorium that followed these deaths.

The 1969 article by Robert Brustein, dean of Yale's drama school, "Whose University: The Case for Professionalism," summed up the rapid reaction of faculties across the country who were attempting to regain authority by again shoring up the crumbling walls of separateness and within them reinforcing hierarchical distinctions of status and expertise:

> Among the many valuable things on the verge of disintegration in contemporary America is the concept of professionalism – by which I mean to suggest a condition determined by training, experience, skill, and achievement. ... The issue of authority is a crucial one here, and once again we can see how the concept of professionalism is being vitiated by false analogies. ... The problem is exacerbated in the humanities and social sciences with their more subjective criteria of judgement.[30]

Valid concerns over pedagogy and accumulated, factual standards soon morphed into a generalized reaction against any wider concerns than those of professionalism, summed up across the country by hostility to student demands for "relevance." As Marvin Levich, then professor of Philosophy at Reed College, put it in a speech to the Association of American Colleges in 1969:

> The question is ... "What should be the impact of the ideology of relevance on humanistic studies?" I will proceed as follows: First I will provide what will have to be a crude statement of some traits of the ideology that bear directly on the content and intellectual role of humanistic studies in higher education. I will say of these traits that at bottom they are clearly and dangerously anti-intellectual and, on the assumption that the humanistic

---

[30] *Bulletin of the Midwest Modern Language Association* 2.2 (Autumn, 1969): 31–36.

studies are not, that they pose a threat to them. Then I will refer to some features of humanistic studies that make them special targets, and likely victims, of the threat. I will finally maintain, unfashionably, that there is nothing much to be done in the face of the threat than to stand firm ... to the question of what is to be done about this, ... the answer is "Nothing."[31]

Levich qualified his grand "nothing" by admitting that changes could and should be made to syllabi and canons, to course offerings, and to forms of pedagogy. Yet he remained convinced that the general structures of liberal-arts education should remain untouched and unchanged. His call for "nothing" rang louder than his calls for limited reforms, his confidence in the historical edifices of higher learning echoing those of leading humanists and churchmen around the year 1500 in the face of similar critiques.

In historical studies such a steadfastness manifested itself in a resurgence of philological over contextual approaches to again dominate many humanities disciplines, while those who strayed beyond such narrow focus risked losing acceptance and career opportunities. One example, which touched at the core of humanistic studies themselves, reflected this reaction. One of the core concepts of Renaissance or early modern studies of the 1940s and of the post-war era was that of "civic humanism" developed by Hans Baron, himself a refugee from Nazi Germany. The "Baron Thesis" had stated that the development of humanism in fifteenth-century Florence came about as an active and self-conscious reaction of the republican commune to the growth of tyranny in Italy, most aggressively represented by Milan under the Visconti dukes. The theory gained widespread support – not despite, but because, of its relevance to contemporary twentieth-century issues – into the 1960s. At that point criticisms, largely based on close examination of the sources, began to challenge this reading.

In the post-1968 environment, however, these criticisms rapidly became the new orthodoxy. "Humanism," especially at centers hard hit by student discontent like Columbia, now took on a new meaning, long advocated by renowned scholars like Paul Oskar Kristeller, Baron's fellow German

---

[31] Wallerstein & Starr, 530, 533.

refugee. Kristeller's "humanism" was a closed, narrow set of professional disciplines and skills, with little if any larger contexts in politics or religion. Thus a series of models ranging from "civic humanism" to "religious humanism" to more specifically "Christian humanism" had become obsolete by the mid 1970s. Meanwhile, interpretations of humanism as a professional field, disengaged from any larger contexts, won the day rapidly and nearly absolutely. This is not to say that Kristeller's model was faulty or itself politically motivated. Nor do we suggest that scholarship into more and more sources, with new critical methods, could not have achieved this turnaround. But we do note the rapidity of the change in scholarly acceptance and suggest that its nearly unquestionable status was facilitated by this period of strong reaction to the events of "1968." Our explanation thus explicitly suggests larger contexts for intellectual change rather than intrinsic developments within research agendas and disciplines.

In testimony to the US House of Representatives, Jacques Barzun, University Professor at Columbia and perhaps the best-known academic intellectual of his day, summed up the growing academic disdain for relevance and the public role of the university by reemphasizing the fragile authority that comes from separation and again turning inward:

> How did the deterioration [of the university's role] take place? It was very rapid and very surprising to everybody. I think in the first place the university was partly responsible. It indulged a mistaken desire to enlarge its role through what it called public service, as if it had not performed public service before. . . . Under the new and multiplying "services" teaching was neglected, and a sort of buzzing activity replaced quiet thought. On the other hand, the result of these new activities out in the world brought forth the normal criticism that the public has a right to level at any of its service centers. So the university became a common target, an object of complaint, pressure, abuse, and further demand. By its very nature, it couldn't fight back. It had no press of its own, it has no party behind it. It is vulnerable, and it fell. So we ask, what is the true idea of the university, how does it best serve society? My answer is simple. . . . Students learn, teachers teach, and learn some more. The idea of the university in one word, is "study."[32]

[32] Special Subcommittee on Education, May 9, 1969.

This narrowing joined other increasingly professional constraints, such as publication, service requirements, and the privileging of individualistic charisma and authority. These changes coincided with an increasingly corporate model of employees competing for position, resources, salaries, and recognition. In 1971, these trends were summarized for the US Department of Health, Education and Welfare in the advisory commission's *Report on Higher Education* headed by Frank Newman, president-emeritus of the University of Rhode Island and president of the Education Commission of the States:[33]

> The professionalization of academic faculties has shaped the character of higher education in many ways. Increasingly, being a teacher has become part of a broader role centering around one's professional colleagues – attending professional conferences, writing and reviewing articles, sponsoring and recruiting apprentices into the discipline. Faculties at universities and the more prestigious colleges have come to view themselves as independent professionals responsible to their guilds rather than to the institutions which pay their salaries. They have established at their institutions a system of tenure and promotion designed to preserve their professional objectives. Those who slight the academic obligations of specialization, research, and publication are themselves slighted in promotion, esteem, and influence.

William Bousma, Harvard historian, president of the American Historical Association, and a leading expert on the very Renaissance humanist tradition that underlay the historic English and American university, reviewed the same situation from the point of view of students, the general American public, and the growing political opposition voiced by Ronald Reagan and others:

> Higher education, it seems to me, is experiencing a crisis of the most fundamental and dangerous kind – a crisis of public confidence that involves all elements of our diverse constituencies and threatens private and public universities alike. In spite of the conviction that learning in its various forms has never been more important and more urgently required

---

[33] Issued in Washington in March 1971.

in the modern world, in spite of the ease with which we can demonstrate this and the frequency with which it is asserted, universities have never been so unpopular or under such broad attack. Let me emphasize that criticism of us comes from every direction, some of it from places where we would least have expected it. Thus even our best students often insist that we are "irrelevant"; and if they frequently seem vague about the meaning of the word, this only suggests that it expresses discontents almost too deep and general for articulation.[34]

THE PUBLIC WEIGHS IN

While faculties called for more and more "professionalism," condemned "relevance," and insisted anew on hermetic enclosure, academic hierarchies, and scholarly specialties, politicians and the general public pushed in the opposite direction. They demanded accountability to society at large, the downgrading of research in favor of teaching, and increasing the very "relevance" that faculties were in the process of rejecting. For the first time in American history, the university itself was being identified as hostile to American values not by radical religious or political fringes but by the very centers of power and opinion.

President Richard Nixon's Special Message to the Congress on Higher Education of March 19, 1970 announcing the Higher Education Opportunity Act was a milestone in the relationship of government to academia.[35] Praising American higher education in terms that would appear almost left-wing to America in 2021, Nixon attempted to balance increasingly divergent visions of academic separateness and social utility. In some ways – along with his signing the Higher Education Act of June 23, 1972, which incorporated Title IX – the president signaled the continuation of post-war Federal policy to expand educational opportunities by class, race, and gender. Nixon praised higher

[34] William Bousma, "Learning and the Problem of Undergraduate Education," in John Voss and Paul L. Ward, eds., *Confrontation and Learned Societies* (New York: New York University Press, 1970), 70–103.

[35] Archives of the *New York Times,* at www.nytimes.com/1970/03/20/archives/text-of-nixon-message-to-congress-proposing-higher-education.html.

education's contributions to American culture, innovation, and economic growth, and for its alliance with the Federal government in serving the national purpose. At the same time, however, he joined the left in his critique of the academy for its retreat from social relevance and innovation:

> Something is wrong with higher education itself when curricula are often irrelevant, structure is often outmoded, when there is an imbalance between teaching and research and too often an indifference to innovation. ... The impressive record compiled by a dedicated educational community stands in contrast to some grave shortcomings in our post-secondary educational system in general and to the Federal share of it in particular. ... Too many people have fallen prey to the myth that a four-year liberal-arts diploma is essential to a full and rewarding life, whereas in fact other forms of post-secondary education – such as a two-year community college or technical training course – are far better suited to the interests of many young people. The turmoil on the nation's campuses is a symbol of the urgent need for reform in curriculum, teaching, student participation, discipline and governance in our post-secondary institutions.

Though speaking in terms that in general supported American higher education, Nixon announced the end of the national consensus for a college-educated middle class that had dominated the years leading to and following World War II. He directly linked this need for government intervention to the "turmoil" of the 1960s. While still using the language of the New Deal, the direction of the 1970s was becoming clear: higher ed had failed to live up to the expectations of authority and innovation that separation had enabled. It had lost much of its authority both internally and externally, and its current model had ceased to serve the public both in its failure to innovate and in its faculty's flight from "relevance." As John Thelin summarized the turbulent events of the time,

> By 1970, one piece of conventional wisdom was that the prototypical American university was under duress because "its center had failed to hold." A more discerning variation of this observation was the reminder by

81

academic critics that the essential source of malaise had been misunderstood, and hence misstated. The problem was not that the center had failed, but rather that the modern American university had no center at all.[36]

---

[36] Thelin, 316.

Part II
Dissolution?

CHAPTER 4

Introduction

I N THE SECOND PART OF THIS BOOK we will look at the current state of higher education in the United States, both in terms of its history, statistics, economics, and accomplishments and in terms of its image among the American public in the wake of developments since 1968. This part of the book will examine public opinion and focus on issues of governance, budgets, and subject matter, academic and campus controversies and scandals, the state of the profession, and developing political agendas and narratives. Such narratives and perceptions are all important. As the 2018 report, *Public Confidence in Higher Education* of the Association of Governing Boards of Universities and Colleges (AGB) phrases it:

> Public confidence, or trust, in higher education measures the general public's perception of whether colleges and universities fulfill their missions. Does the public trust the knowledge that the institutions impart and the research that they conduct? Does the public believe graduates have learned to think critically and independently, or does it think graduates were ideologically indoctrinated? The U.S. higher education system, which is composed of institutions that depend on government funding yet traditionally enjoy considerable independence, relies on public trust.[1]

Measured in objective statistics, by 1970 the American university and college had reached a level of unprecedented success: 2,573 institutions

---

[1] https://agb.org/sites/default/files/report_2018_guardians_public_confidence.pdf, at 2.

granted 1.07 million BA degrees out of a total enrollment of 8.65 million students, taught by 383,000 full-time faculty. With adjuncts included, the count came to nearly half a million university faculty. In 1970, American universities granted 29,872 doctorates. Higher education generated revenues of $21.5 trillion in 1970 ($133 trillion in 2016) dollars; placing it among the most important components of the US economy.[2] Yet, measured in intangibles – along the triad of authority, separateness, and innovation – American higher education had entered a period of crisis that, despite ups and downs and continuing measurable upward cycles, was to remain the constant into the 2020s.

By 1970, the university had experienced an unexpected fall from grace. Students, parents, politicians, and the general public now viewed the university with skepticism, suspicion, and often with outright hostility as the symbol and focus of all that had supposedly gone wrong with America in the 1960s. The recession of the 1970s also brought unforeseen retrenchment across American society that had a deep impact on higher education. With that recession and the end of the Vietnam War and the military draft, the academic year 1975–1976 saw the first decline in enrollments (by 175,000) since the end of the GI Bill's surge in 1951.[3]

As early as 1971, the Newman *Report on Higher Education* had issued a damning indictment for an institution that clearly needed the support of the public at large:[4]

> As we have examined the growth of higher education in the postwar period, we have seen disturbing trends toward uniformity in our institutions, growing bureaucracy, overemphasis on academic credentials, isolation of students and faculty from the world – a growing rigidity and uniformity of structure that makes higher education reflect less and less the interests of society.[5]

All the points of the triangle had been called into question on the highest levels: authority, separateness, and the ability to innovate were seen as compromised.

---

[2] See Thelin, 317.   [3] Thelin, 321.
[4] Issued in Washington in March 1971, excerpted in Smith & Bender, 40–41.
[5] vii, cited in Thelin, 430.

In the next part of this book we will attempt to outline the forms of this fall from grace, the components of the current critique, developments in higher ed and society at large that reinforce a growing opposition, the construction of a powerful narrative against academia, and some trends that point to future developments. Our intent is neither prophesy nor polemic but an attempt to pinpoint salient elements of this critique of American higher education through both historical analogy and current analysis.

*

A Pew Research Center poll dated July 10, 2017[6] – much debated, interpreted, and revised – revealed that 58 percent of Republicans thought that colleges and universities had a "negative effect on the way things are going in the country." Only 36 percent of Republicans maintained that they are good for the country. By comparison, Republicans gave favorable ratings to churches (73 percent) and to banks and other financial institutions (46 percent), while labor unions (33 percent) and the national media (10 percent) scored similarly low favorables. When polled on the same questions, 72 percent of Democrats or Democratic-leaning voters still saw higher education as a value to American society.

These were not isolated results. In a Gallup poll released on August 16, 2017, only 33 percent of Republicans, but 56 percent of Democrats, expressed confidence in American higher ed.[7] Republicans' chief objections focused on campus politics, cultural agendas, and subject matters taught. On the other hand, most Democrats' worries about higher education centered on its escalating costs. As disturbing was the sharp decline in Republican support for higher education from only two years before. According to Gallup,

> This divide has now crept into views of higher education, likely exacerbated by several high-profile student protests that have spurred debates about free speech and contentious choices for speakers on

---

[6] www.people-press.org/2017/07/10/sharp-partisan-divisions-in-views-of-national-institutions.

[7] https://news.gallup.com/poll/216278/why-republicans-down-higher.aspx.

campus. It could be the case that the frequency and coverage of these issues have contributed to the partisan divide, or that they have helped expose a divide that may have already been present.

Even more importantly, the greatest percentage of those polled by Pew who had negative views of higher education came from college-educated, upper-income families ($75,000+/yr.), and from older age brackets (50+).

One year later, a highly detailed and nuanced survey released by New America, a Washington, DC think-tank focused on issues of technology, security, and war, presented a somewhat different picture that showed general support among both Democrats and Republicans for the goals of American higher education for mobility and career opportunity (80 percent) and for public funding. Yet even within these more favorable findings, 61 percent of Republicans felt that the primary goal of education – job placement – did not require a college education on any level (compared to 40 percent of Democrats). Furthermore, 75 percent of those polled from both parties felt that the American university system needed major overhauls to meet vocational goals. The largest segment of negative views (nearly 50 percent) focused on high costs. As the executive summary states:

> New America's own survey data this year show that only one in four Americans thinks higher education is fine the way it is, indicating that higher education, for a variety of reasons – from concerns about affordability to quality of education to employment outcomes – is not delivering on its promise.[8]

Most intriguingly, the vast majority of respondents supported higher education's role in society and wanted more – not less – government involvement in its funding. But this again diverged by party affiliation:

> Perhaps as indication of the fact that a majority of Americans think that higher education is good for society, over three-quarters of them (77 percent) are comfortable with their own tax dollars going to support

---

[8] www.newamerica.org/education-policy/reports/varying-degrees-2018/executive-summary.

it. Over three-quarters also agree that state (78 percent) and federal (77 percent) government should spend more tax revenue on higher education to make it more affordable. ... There is a notable divergence in views between Democrats and Republicans on whether government should fund higher education because it is good for society or whether individuals should fund it because it is a personal benefit. A solid majority of Democrats (76 percent) sees it as a good for society, worthy of government investment, whereas about half of Republicans (52 percent) see it as a personal benefit that should be financed with individual investments.[9]

These results were further refined by surveys conducted by Civis Analytics and by Echelon later that same year. They show findings similar to those of New America but focus on the issues most important to Americans: a general support for higher education but grave concerns about its costs and effectiveness, regardless of party affiliation and other demographic factors. "The point at which 'big shifts' in polling numbers occur ... like those in the Pew survey, is 'when you embed other questions about cultural and political issues' into perceptions of higher education."[10] The AGB's *Public Confidence in Higher Education*'s summary report qualified many of these findings and stressed that:[11]

A number of recent reports – some from partisan sources, others from well-regarded independent surveyors such as the Pew and Gallup organizations – suggest that public trust in colleges and universities has declined. In today's politically fraught climate, such reports understandably alarm college and university board members and other higher education leaders. On closer inspection, however, public attitudes on higher education are more complex, nuanced, and, in some respects, positive than many reports say. There is indeed evidence of diminished

---

[9] www.newamerica.org/education-policy/reports/varying-degrees-2018/americans-believe-higher-education-is-a-public-benefit-and-that-the-government-should-do-more-to-make-it-affordable.

[10] IHE (December 15, 2017), at www.insidehighered.com/news/2017/12/15/public-really-losing-faith-higher-education.

[11] AGB, *Public Confidence in Higher Education*, https://agb.org/sites/default/files/report_2018_guardians_public_confidence.pdf.

public trust in higher education, but the evidence is mixed, its reliability unclear, and its interpretation debatable. Still, many thought leaders sense a decline in public trust in higher education and point to developments such as the first federal tax on some university endowments and continued declines in state funding of public universities as worrisome signs.

Alongside its picture of general support for higher education among Americans, the AGB report confirmed the large partisan divide in areas of perception and criticism, repeating the Gallup figures that show that the largest segment of Democrats polled (36 percent) felt college was too expensive; while the largest segment of Republicans (32 percent) felt it was too liberal and political. It repeated findings that:

only 13 percent of Americans strongly agree that "college graduates in this country are well-prepared for success in the workforce" ... and that seventy-nine percent of Americans do not think education beyond high school is affordable for everyone who needs it.[12]

As the report's conclusions stress:

Despite ongoing debate, confidence in the ability of colleges to fulfill their missions remains high when compared with most other American institutions. Nonetheless, recent evidence suggests that public trust is increasingly viewed through a partisan lens. Other survey evidence suggests that public confidence is threatened by continuing concerns about the cost of and access to higher education.[13]

The divide appears to have grown wider over a short time. A Pew Research poll conducted in August 2019 found that

only half of American adults think colleges and universities are having a positive effect on the way things are going in the country these days. About four-in-ten (38%) say they are having a negative impact – up from 26% in 2012.[14]

---

[12] AGB, *Public Confidence*, 10.   [13] AGB, *Public Confidence*, 12.

[14] Kim Parker, "The Growing Partisan Divide in Views of Higher Education," Pew Research Center: Social and Demographic Trends (Aug. 19, 2019), at www.pewsocialtrends.org/ essay/the-growing-partisan-divide-in-views-of-higher-education. See also Steven Johnson, "Conservatives Say Professors' Politics Ruins College. Students Say It's More

Of those polled, 59 percent of Republicans believe that higher education is harming the country, up from 37 percent in 2015. The main factor now, as then, for Republicans was "what is taught," with 79 percent of Republicans believing that professors' ideology was to blame, compared with just 17 percent of Democrats, who continue to focus on high costs and quality as the chief problems. The shift also comes from those most likely to vote, with 96 percent of Republicans over age 65 believing that professors' political and social views were at fault, compared with 58 percent of Republicans aged 18 to 34 who believe this. A Gallup poll conducted in 2018 found similar divides. A poll published in June 2019 by Third Way, a center-left think tank, had more nuanced results, however.[15] It found that 50 percent of Republicans had favorable views of higher ed, and 44 percent had negative ones. However, the survey pointed to the important factor of public perception as guided by partisan politics.

At the same time, students polled overwhelmingly believe that there is relatively little bias among university faculty. There are cases where students hesitate to express their views, but these are largely self-censorship, out of discomfort of what fellow students will think, not what faculty teach, say, or might believe. Nevertheless, the narrative has been fixed: higher education is harming the nation. We will return to these and later findings and their interpretations again in this book.

Democrats form a clear majority of voters in the United States, yet as of this writing the majority of state legislatures and governors' mansions are controlled by Republicans, as is the Supreme Court. Despite Democratic victories in 2020, workable majorities are slim. As the above polls indicate, emerging majorities have serious concerns about access

Complicated," CHE (Aug. 20, 2019), at www.chronicle.com/article/Conservatives-Say/246981; Andrew Kreighbaum, "Persistent Partisan Breakdown on Higher Ed," IHE (August 20, 2019), at www.insidehighered.com/news/2019/08/20/majority-republicans-have-negative-view-higher-ed-pew-finds.

[15] Tamara Hiler and Lanae Erickson, "Beyond Free College and Free Markets: Voters Want Greater Accountability in Higher Ed," at www.thirdway.org/polling/beyond-free-college-and-free-markets-voters-want-greater-accountability-in-higher-ed. See also Doug Lederman, "The Public's Support for (and Doubts About) Higher Ed," IHE (June 17, 2019), at www.insidehighered.com/news/2019/06/17/survey-shows-publics-support-and-qualms-about-higher-education.

and affordability; and within that majority, an empowered and vocal minority of well educated, upper-income Americans has recently emerged with a social, political, and economic outlook in which higher education's "cultural and political issues" have become a clear target of criticism.

The nature of these cultural and political issues will be the focus of the rest of this book. They include financial and budget concerns, related government policies, popular anti-intellectualism, political agendas, commercial interests, internal intellectual and political disputes among faculties, what we have termed the "scandals of academe," the loss of faculty positions and authority, dramatic shifts in curricula, and the rapidly increasing pace of campus closures, takeovers, and transformations. We will begin with issues of governance and public perception.

CHAPTER 5

Governance and Boards

INTRODUCTION

W RITING ON THE CHANGES IN TUDOR society that effected the rapid Dissolution of the Monasteries in the 1530s, historian David Knowles has written:

The age was, like our own, one of swift change in which the landmarks, social, intellectual, and economic, which had been familiar for centuries, suddenly shifted or vanished. . . . Something of the same change took place with the religious orders in the sixty years with which we are now to be concerned. In the past historians have often assumed that while all else remained steady, the monks fell rapidly into moral and pecuniary bankruptcy. It would be a truer view to see the world changing around them while they, for their part, were unable either to accompany that change or to adapt themselves to the demands and necessities of a different world. In that world both they and their neighbours round them were without any anchor save their ancestral and often now vestigial sense of spiritual realities, and a new sentiment of loyalty and obedience to the sovereign. They were to find every new influence a hostile one, in a grasping and acquisitive society which had as its characteristic quality a keen appreciation of the main chance.[1] . . . Monks and clergy alike were children of their age and country; it was this that made the Dissolution, and indeed many of the religious changes of the reign, not only possible but relatively easy of accomplishment.[2]

---

[1] Knowles, *Religious Orders*, III:7.   [2] Knowles, *Religious Orders*, III:198.

AMERICAN GOVERNANCE TRADITIONS

With the 1970s, Congress was the first to reflect the new popular coolness toward higher education. Lawmakers began to question the benefits and appropriation of almost limitless Federal spending on research. They also started doubting university administrators' ability to control student unrest and to produce innovation for dollar support. A new narrative of decline began to take hold of American perceptions of higher ed, as a large literature began to predict the demise of the system.[3] In 1957, Supreme Court Justice Felix Frankfurter had articulated "four essential freedoms" of a university: freedom to determine who may teach, what may be taught, how it should be taught, and who may be admitted to study.[4] By the late 1970s, these freedoms were in the process of being dismantled. In 1982, the Carnegie Foundation prefaced its report on campus governance with this statement:

> There remains in the control of higher education an inherent tension. Colleges and universities are expected to respond to the needs of society of which they are a part – while also being free to carry on, without undue interference, their essential work.[5]

In this chapter we will look at issues of governance by focusing on the roles of presidents and boards of trustees. After briefly summarizing the historical development of the American governance model, we will examine some of the more salient examples of conflict arising from this structure. We should stress at the outset that most boards operate responsibly, guiding their institutions – which are often the largest and richest corporate entities and employers in their regions – fairly and progressively. Whatever the backgrounds of board members, their selection is generally fair and well considered, and the vast majority of board members take their duties – both to their institutions and the public – seriously and responsibly. Board operating standards, structures, governance policies, shared governance with faculty, and transparency and accountability are remarkably high and subject to constant scrutiny and

---

[3] Thelin, 336–38.   [4] In Sweezy v. New Hampshire 354 US 234 (1957).
[5] Carnegie Foundation, *Control of the Campus: A Report on the Governance of Higher Education* (Princeton, NJ, 1982), 3–4.

self-evaluation. The Association of Governing Boards of Universities and Colleges (AGB), the nation's largest such organization – with a membership of 1,300 boards and 1,900 colleges, universities, and institutionally related foundations – provides a wide array of common standards and best practice. Its mission statement is clear:

> Governing boards must focus now more than ever on promoting central missions while running their institutions as effectively as possible. It is critical that they reinforce the value of higher education, innovate through the smart use of technology, and serve the needs of a shifting demographic.[6]

Our aim in this chapter, however, is neither praise nor blame of governance in higher education but to highlight some of the abuses of long-accepted standards that contribute to a growing narrative of the university as fallen from its ideals and as out of touch with American values.

*

From the very start, the American college system rejected the self-governing principles of Oxbridge. The Statutes of Harvard College of *c.*1646 implicitly gave final oversight of the institution to a board of "overseers" and explicitly established its governing principles in the very title of its statutes: The Laws Liberties and Orders of Harvard College Confirmed by the Overseers and President of the College.[7] The Harvard Charter of 1650 made this arrangement explicit by naming the "President and Fellows" of the "Corporation,"

> which said President and Fellows for the time being shall for ever hereafter in name and fact be one body politic and corporate in Law to all intents and purposes, and shall have perpetual succession, and shall be called by the name of President and Fellows of Harvard College.[8]

Overcoming early challenges that attempted to insert the role of resident faculty into governance, by 1723, the president, with the backing

---

[6] Association of Governing Boards of Universities and Colleges, https://agb.org/about-us.
[7] See Hofstadter & Smith, I:8–10.   [8] Hofstadter & Smith, I:10–12.

of Massachusetts Bay's governor, had firmly established governance in the hands of a board of non-resident Fellows.[9] Similarly, the charter of William & Mary College of 1693 specified governance by a "President" and a board of "Trustees, nominated and elected by the General Assembly."[10] The formula was repeated at Yale in 1745, whose charter established "an incorporate society, or body corporate and politik, and shall hereafter be called and known by the name of The President and Fellows of Yale College in New Haven."[11] The pattern thus set was repeated throughout the colonial and early republican period and became the norm of American higher education. Unlike the traditional Continental system or that of Oxbridge, faculty were granted little role in governance. As early as 1830, Prof. Benjamin Silliman of Yale remarked that "the faculty of Yale College have no voice in the appointment of Professors, by law – as the appointments are made by the board of Trustees called the 'President and Fellows.'"[12] The same observations were made in 1837 concerning relations between the faculty and the "corporate character of the board of trustees" across American colleges.[13]

By 1869, Charles William Elliot, in his inaugural address as the new president of Harvard, could call the board of trustees "the heart of the University."

> This board holds the funds, makes appointments, fixes salaries, and has, by right, the initiative in all changes of the organic law of the University. Such an executive board must be small to be efficient. It must always contain men of sound judgement in finance; and literature and the learned professions should be adequately represented in it. The Corporation should also be but slowly renewed.[14]

This combination of strong presidential power and independent board oversight, generally by non-academics from outside the university, made for the great innovations of American higher education. For the most part, the trustees maintained their distance from day-to-day faculty

---

[9] Hofstadter & Smith, I:21–32.   [10] Hofstadter & Smith, I:33–39.
[11] Hofstadter & Smith, I:49–53.   [12] Hofstadter & Smith, I:306–7.
[13] Hofstadter & Smith, I:311–28.   [14] Hofstadter & Smith, II:619.

instruction and relied on the president and faculty to set pedagogical policies.[15] The system allowed great new paths toward diversification, experimentation, and innovation that were precisely the benefits of corporate structure, making the university a nimble institution that responded well to the changing landscape of American culture, politics, and economics. Obvious prejudices against immigrant groups like Jews and Catholics, and racial and gender restrictions remained strong. But American colleges generally swept aside the Protestant sectarian preferences that once dominated many schools and opened faculty recruitment on the basis of merit. It allowed the rapid expansion of higher education in the late nineteenth and early twentieth century, its fulfillment of expectations in the world-war years, and its post-war boom. It enabled the university to become an active partner in national recovery, defense, and industrial and scientific innovation, capitalizing on its pools of expertise in a system where governing strategies and norms closely fit already existing corporate and government operating standards.

But such governance carried with it natural disadvantages, the most important of which was the very remoteness of the trustees from the core mission of the university. As early as 1902 John James Stevenson of New York University took up the issue[16]:

> Within the last thirty years, the relations between the teaching and the corporate boards have undergone a serious transformation ...within a generation, the small colleges have become large, many of them have expanded into true universities with numerous departments, hundreds of instructors and thousands of students; while the financial interests, expanding more rapidly than the institutions, have attained a magnitude in some cases as great as that of New York finances fifty years ago. No trustee in a large college today can know much of college work as such, can be acquainted with the faculties, can do much more than bear his share of the business responsibility. ... These patrons, if not college graduates, labor under a disadvantage in that they are unacquainted with the nature of the

---

[15] See, for example, the recollections of Johns Hopkins' early operations, in Hofstadter & Smith, II:752–56.

[16] John James Stevenson, "University Control," *Popular Science Monthly* 61 (September, 1902): 396–406.

work for which colleges have been founded ... the trustees' duties usually begin and end with labors on committees, so that naturally enough the business affairs with which they have to do become for them the all-important work of the institution. And this conception is strengthened by thoughtless assertions of men who ought to know better. Only recently this community was informed that the millionaires make the universities. With such flattery ringing in their ears, one is not surprised that some trustees forget the object for which the university exists and think of professors, when they think of them at all, as merely employees of the corporation, whose personality and opinions are as unimportant as those of a bank clerk.

As the "muckraking" social critic Thorstein Veblen wrote in 1918 in his *The Higher Learning in America:*

> The fact remains, the modern civilized community is reluctant to trust its serious interest to others than men of pecuniary substance, who have proved their fitness for the direction of academic affairs by acquiring, or by otherwise being possessed of, considerable wealth.[17]

Such critiques of the excessive power of university boards continued into the first two decades of the twentieth century.[18] John Thelin has again offered a good summary of the continued governance by boards of trustees with little knowledge or experience of academic life and goals:

> A peculiar consequence of this model was the inverse relation between the ultimate authority given to boards in marked contrast to their low profile and negligible accountability. Boards of trustees were silent partners who had been seldom analyzed – and only infrequently covered in the press ... boards of trustees of many universities were good candidates to be the "straight men" in the old vaudeville routine where a news reporter asked, "What do you think about ignorance and apathy in governance of higher education?" According to the script, their stock answer would be, "I don't know – and I don't care."[19]

---

[17] Thorstein Veblen, *A Memorandum on the Conduct of Universities by Business Men* (New York: Viking Press, 1918), excerpted in Hofstadter & Smith, II:818–32 at 820.

[18] See for example the record of the famous historian Charles A. Beard's resignation from Columbia University in Hofstadter & Smith, II:883–92.

[19] Thelin, 393–94.

Through the twentieth century "there were few (if any) checks and balances on board actions and decisions," with the result that presidents and their administrations exercised undue control over most university decision-making. By the late 1960s, however, as we have noted, fissures and gaps in university governance, missteps and miscalculations in policy and governance led to widespread discontent and serious disruptions among which UC Berkeley, Columbia, and Cornell are only the best-known examples of boards brought up short by events. By the late twentieth century, even the office of president was being affected by the ideology that the business community knew best, even if it knew little about higher education.[20] Presidents, especially in state systems, were drawn increasingly from corporate and military backgrounds, often with more or less successful political careers as their chief public credential. Yet even in the most heated days of the Columbia upheaval and the acknowledged missteps of its president and board, trustees found reasoned apologists for their role as defenders of university separateness (autonomy) and authority. Such advice is still worth bearing in mind:

> The powers of trustees are severely limited by custom and law, and by the realities of a university. In any well-established university, trustees normally leave educational decisions to the faculty. One of their primary educational functions, indeed, is simply to provide the educational community of the university – its students and faculty – with protective insulation. The trustees throw their mantle of influence and respectability around it, deflecting and absorbing criticisms and denunciations, and thus guarding the community's freedom. Indeed, it is doubtful that faculties and student bodies could by themselves, in many parts of the country, and without the help of trustees, successfully defend their autonomy.[21]

Whatever the interpretation of board culpability or virtue in the management of the university, however, by the beginning of the twenty-first century the board of trustees reigned supreme in university

---

[20] Thelin, 393–98.

[21] Charles Frankel, "The Trustees in Perspective," *Saturday Review* (Nov. 2, 1968), excerpted in Wallerstein & Starr, 497–500.

governance. This message continues to be repeated without question, for example, in this précis from Columbia University's Teacher's College:

> Boards of trustees at universities and colleges are generally made up of 30 to 45 members who operate collectively and through their committees that take on everything from reviewing academic programs to raising funds for the institution. Trustees and their boards uphold their fiduciary responsibility by working with the president and top administrators to approve major policies, make long range plans, and oversee the budget. The board must also work to preserve and protect the institution's reputation by helping define, support, and protect its mission. Here the board must make decisions as to the number and types of degrees offered, and the departments, divisions, and schools or colleges through which the curriculum is administered. Along with that, the board and the administration must have effective and efficient internal and external communications in place to insure transparency and that an accurate picture of their institution is being presented.[22]

Board Effect, another important source of policy advice, declared:

> As the final authority for college or university business, trustees make all legal and fiduciary decisions, although they delegate some specific powers and duties to others. The board of trustees is responsible for developing and approving the school's mission, strategic goals and objectives, and establishing policies related to programs and services.[23]

Even after the disruptions of the 1960s and the official statements and accommodations that followed, nowhere in these historical descriptions were the faculty or students mentioned, in any capacity, as having a significant role in university governance or in setting policy. How has this legacy affected the governance of the contemporary university, and as importantly, how has this continued concentration of power affected the perception of higher education at the beginning of this century?

[22] Mar. 10, 2009, at www.tc.columbia.edu/articles/2009/march/what-do-trustees-do.
[23] From Board Effect, Feb. 2, 2018, at www.boardeffect.com/blog/roles-responsibilities-board-directors-college-university.

BOARDS GONE WILD?

One outcome of the rapid upward shift in American wealth in the last quarter of the twentieth century was the disproportionate social and economic influence of what many term the new American oligarchy. Because so much of American cultural life is supported by private means, over the past generation the boards of directors and trustees overseeing the operations and missions of major US cultural and educational institutions have been colonized and transformed by members of this oligarchy. Individuals sometimes bring great expertise, sometimes guaranteeing sustainability and high standards. But the deeper structural transformation produced by this shift in wealth, power, and influence has had a more profound impact, reflecting the priorities and will of the 1 percent.

More pertinent but less broadly publicized is the "governing board overreach" that has become a byword in higher-education literature. This includes the actions of boards of trustees and institutional review boards ranging from Iowa, Illinois, UVA, Oregon, Texas, Penn State and Suffolk, to Sweet Briar, Brown, and Miami. Unchecked board decisions produce dramatic transformations of core mission goals; they interfere with research and publication; cover-up malfeasance and criminal activity; authorize over-ambitious spending and incur debt on stadiums, student centers, and presidential mansions. In the pages that follow we will provide several of the more prominent cases of board mismanagement. Our choices are necessarily limited and selective.

*

One of the most glaring examples of a university board's mishandling a crisis was the Pennsylvania State University (PSU) sex-abuse scandal. This emerged in November 2011 when assistant coach Jerry Sandusky was indicted on fifty-two counts of child molestation of students.[24] Among those involved in covering up the scandal, three Penn State officials – school president Graham Spanier, vice president Gary Schultz, and athletic director Tim Curley – were charged with perjury, obstruction

---

[24] For a compendium of coverage in the CHE, see www.chronicle.com/specialreport/Penn-State-Scandal/23.

of justice, failure to report suspected child abuse, and related charges. The court process and public debate over the allegations and eventual convictions continued for years. PSU's board of trustees commissioned an independent investigation by former FBI Director Louis J. Freeh, whose report stated that Penn State's longtime head football coach Joe Paterno – along with Spanier, Curley, and Schultz – had known about allegations of child abuse by Sandusky as early as 1998, had shown "total and consistent disregard . . . for the safety and welfare of Sandusky's child victims," and had "empowered" Sandusky. Even after the removal of Spanier and others, members of the administration, of the board of trustees, and many alums and members of the public downplayed the scandal or attempted to deny the investigative and court findings.

Could or should the PSU board be faulted for this scandal? Though individual members could honestly and reliably deny any knowledge or culpability, the long history of American governance practice and theory that we have just laid out underscores the board's sole responsibility for good governance and oversight. No board can escape praise or blame for events within their university. This seems to be borne out in the case of PSU. Five years after the initial indictments, on March 25, 2017, upon the conviction of former PSU President Spanier for child endangerment, Louis J. Freeh released a two-page statement that condemned the university's leaders and called for the resignation of then-President Eric J. Barron:

> The criminal conduct of these three men has cost the Commonwealth of Pennsylvania taxpayers over one quarter billion dollars, and the costs continue to escalate. Amazingly, Spanier was given a $6,000,000 "golden parachute" by PSU and continues to receive an annual PSU salary of $600,000, with his legal fees being paid by the same taxpayers. . . . Barron and a coterie of "Paterno denier" board members, alumni, cultlike groups such as Penn Staters for Responsible Stewardship, a former professional football player, and certain elected state political hacks have been nothing but apologists for Paterno, Spanier, Schultz, and Curley, more concerned about bringing back a bronze statue than worrying about the multiple child victims who have forever been so grievously harmed on the PSU campus.[25]

[25] www.scribd.com/document/342967406/32417-Louis-Freeh-Statement-Copy.

Other examples can be added from the almost weekly coverage in the *Chronicle of Higher Education* and other sources on every aspect of university governance. A prominent example that caught national attention was the June 2012 ouster of Teresa A. Sullivan, the popular and effective president of the University of Virginia, by its board of visitors and her reinstatement two weeks later after all segments of the school's population – faculty, students, alums – and the national media forced the trustees to reverse their decision. Subsequent investigations and news coverage revealed that the board had acted precipitously, without consulting the larger community, without a full vote, and through the secretive decision-making of its executive. It emerged that the board had grown impatient with Sullivan's academic approach and felt that she was hindering a more corporate pace for implementing curriculum changes, such as the adoption of MOOC's, favored by the board's rector.[26]

Over seven months from the end of 2015 through the spring of 2016, Suffolk University in Boston was rattled by an ongoing and very public battle between Suffolk's board and its new president, a former president of Leslie University in Cambridge, MA and the former president of the Walmart Foundation. The trustees, who operated without term limits and were openly split between an old guard and newer members – and who as a whole had many business ties that approached conflict of interest – attempted to actively interfere with day-to-day governance of the school. Only the promise of the president to step down half-way through her term, and the concurrent agreement for the board president to depart and the board to impose term limits on itself defused the damaging standoff.[27]

In July 2017, over objections from its chancellor, the board of governors of the University of North Carolina system voted to curtail UNC Law School's Center for Civil Rights from engaging in any litigation, thus unilaterally ending its well-regarded activity in fighting school

---

[26] Jack Stripling, Katherine Mangan, and Brock Read, "After 7 Tumultuous Years as President, Teresa Sullivan Plans to Leave UVa," CHE (Jan. 23, 2017), at www.chronicle.com/article/After-a-Tumultuous-7-Years/238977.

[27] For details: www.copleyraff.com/2016/03/04/board-overreach.

segregation. This followed the board's unexplained firing of university president Thomas Ross in January 2015. In 2015, the board had already voted to close UNC's Center on Poverty, Work, and Opportunity.[28] This action was taken after long lobbying by right-wing political forces in the state spearheaded by Jay Schalin, "director of policy analysis at the John William Pope Center for Higher Education, a right-wing think tank funded by discount-store magnate Art Pope, the conservative kingmaker who helped flip the state legislature to the Republicans in 2010 and bankrolled the 2012 election of Republican Governor Pat McCrory."[29] Such centers drew almost nothing from state coffers and relied on private grants for the most part. But Schalin and other members of Pope's circle were explicit in their attempts to wrest control of the university's board to further their agenda. When direct access failed, Pope was able to accomplish his purges through the state legislature itself, which was heavily indebted to his and UNC board members' campaign contributions and which, in turn, appoints the UNC board. According to Schalin, within the UNC system "the main problem has to do with the ideas that are being discussed and promoted, ... multiculturalism, collectivism, left-wing post-modernism." He would solve this problem by replacing the teaching of "French communist[s]" Derrida, Bourdieu, and Foucault [sic] with Ayn Rand. After the body voted in May 2017 to cut dozens of academic programs across the system, one member of the board of governors noted, "We're capitalists. ...We have to look at what the demand is, and we have to respond to the demand."

In February 2018, the faculty senate at Michigan State University voted sixty-one to four expressing no confidence in the school's board of trustees.[30] The vote was called as a protest of the board's

---

[28] J. Clara Chan, "U. of North Carolina Chancellor Criticizes Board's Proposal to Hamstring Civil-Rights Center," CHE (July 31, 2017), at www.chronicle.com/blogs/tickr/u-of-north-carolina-chancellor-criticizes-boards-proposal-to-hamstring-civil-rights-center/119483.

[29] Zoë Carpenter, "How a Right-Wing Political Machine Is Dismantling Higher Education in North Carolina," *Nation* (June 8, 2015), at www.thenation.com/article/how-right-wing-political-machine-dismantling-higher-education-north-carolina.

[30] Sarah Brown, "Michigan State's Faculty Senate Votes No Confidence in Embattled Trustees," CHE (Feb 13, 2018), at www.chronicle.com/article/Michigan-State-s-Faculty/242540.

decision to appoint John Engler, a former Michigan governor, to serve as interim president without consultation by faculty or student representatives. The entire selection process took only one week. Engler replaced President Lou Anna K. Simon, who resigned after strong criticism of her handling of the scandal surrounding university sports doctor Larry Nassar's sexual abuse of 265 young women and girls. Nassar was sentenced to up to 175 years in prison by two state courts. Although faculty have no power over board decisions, the symbolic vote sent a clear message about Michigan's lack of shared governance with faculty and the board's indifference to the student victims. We will discuss the Michigan State case further in Chapter 7.[31]

In May 2019, the board of trustees of the University of Southern California was rocked as internal disputes among the oversized board (fifty-six members, or over twice the national average of twenty-six) spilled out into the open. The scandal came in the wake of another sexual-abuse scandal in which the university president effectively protected a high-ranking faculty member who had the support and protection of the same board. Despite the president's removal over that scandal, USC's board chairman, a billionaire real-estate developer, continued a management style that outraged faculty, alums, and other trustees when he summarily fired a business school dean and personally headed up his replacement's search committee without further consultation. The board president also headed up an anonymous executive committee of the board, which was later revealed to consist of seventeen members, "almost as large as university boards in their entirety," according to the chair of Concerned Faculty of USC, a group representing about a third of the school's tenured faculty. In the wake of the admissions scandal, amid accusations of conflict of interest among trustees and board president, widespread calls for a complete restructuring of the board and for their resignation en masse were met with further opposition from the board president. According to *Inside Higher Education*, such revelations,

---

[31] Chapter 7, 165–66.

reinforced the image of the board as being the clubby bastion of rich and powerful, and sometimes famous, mostly white male donors … on a campus dotted with buildings and departments bearing the names of several trustees.

As another commentator wrote,

USC's leadership has long had a very defensive attitude – when bad things happen, the reflex seems to be to duck and wait for the storm to pass. A university that is confident of its place in the top tier would be more open to both its internal and external stakeholders about its failures. [32]

In response to a wave of successive scandals, in November 2019 USC moved to reform its board by drastically cutting its official numbers from sixty to thirty-five members, imposing three-year term and seventy-five-year-old age limits, reducing the number of its committees, diversifying membership, and limiting the ability of the university president and board chair to handpick members of its executive committee. Other measures included disclosures of committee memberships and the independent oversight of the university medical center. Regardless of the highly praised changes, faculty noted that they continued to be excluded from representation and shared governance.[33]

*

Sexual scandal, misuse of funds, conflicts of interest, board interference with day-to-day administration and with faculty hiring and firing have been matched by external political pressures on universities, often aided and abetted by politically appointed board members and chairs. In July 2019, revelations surfaced that the Republican governor of South

---

[32] See Marjorie Valbrun, "Does USC Need More Housecleaning?," IHE (May 21, 2019), at www.insidehighered.com/news/2019/05/21/usc-board-trustees-undergo-major-changes-wake-recent-scandals.

[33] Teresa Watanabe, "In Wake of Scandals, USC Radically Cuts Number of Trustees, Imposes Age Limits, Pledges More Diversity," *Los Angeles Times* (Nov. 5, 2019), at www.latimes.com/california/story/2019-11-05/scandals-usc-reforms-trustees-age-limits-diversity-rules; Jack Stripling, "Scandal-Ridden U. of Southern California Will Shrink Its Board. So What?," CHE (Nov. 6, 2019), at www.chronicle.com/article/Scandal-Ridden-U-of-Southern/247500.

Carolina had personally contacted members of the University of South Carolina's board to pressure them into hiring his pick for the next university system president. Ignoring student and faculty objections to the governor's choice – and to the closed method of selecting the field of candidates – the board reversed its previous decision to extend the search and acquiesced at its chair's urging. It was ready to appoint the governor's choice, Lt. Gen. Robert L. Caslen Jr., former superintendent of the United States Military Academy at West Point, until the process was temporarily halted by a court decision.[34] Later that month, however, the trustees voted eleven to eight to appoint Caslen.[35]

In October 2019, the board of trustees of the University of Mississippi secretly hired as its new chancellor an insider who had been appointed as a consultant to the search committee and who had not submitted a formal application.[36] The move confirmed publicly aired rumors circulating for weeks that the board would appoint one of its own circle in line with the wishes of powerful alums through a "back door" process that would circumvent an open and competitive search. The new chancellor, Glenn Boyce, has a doctorate in educational administration and decades of experience in higher ed. Nevertheless, faculty and students protested the breach of shared governance and transparency. Meanwhile, the appointment was lauded by conservative business interests concerned that "Ole Miss" had moved too far to the left. Trent Lott, a Mississippi alum who was forced out of his post as minority leader of the US Senate for praising Strom Thurmond's segregationist policies, told an interviewer that the new chancellor "appears to be a good ol' boy." James

---

[34] Nell Gluckman, "At the U. of South Carolina, Trustees Paused a Controversial Presidential Search. Then the Governor Stepped In," CHE (July 11, 2019), at www .chronicle.com/article/At-the-U-of-South-Carolina/246660.

[35] Nell Gluckman, "University of South Carolina Trustees Vote for Governor's Pick for President" CHE (July 19, 2019), at www.chronicle.com/article/University-of-South-Carolina/246736.

[36] Adam Ganucheau, "Glenn Boyce Appointed UM Chancellor as IHL Board Cuts Search Process Short," *Mississippi Today* (Oct. 3, 2019), at https://mississippitoday.org/2019/ 10/03/glenn-boyce-appointed-um-chancellor-as-ihl-board-cuts-search-process-short; Emma Pettit, "He Was a Consultant for the Search; Now He's the Chancellor. And the Faculty Is Furious," CHE (Oct. 4, 2019), at www.chronicle.com/article/He-Was-a-Consultant-for-the/247289.

H. Finkelstein, professor emeritus of public policy at George Mason University and an expert in campus leadership, summed up the situation:

> Governing boards just seem to be willing to do whatever they want to do ... governing boards seem to think that these rules are just advisory. ... [Board positions are] patronage positions. They see these presidencies, or chancellor of a university, as plums – these are big positions for lots of money.[37]

*

But not all criticism of boards comes from right-wing agendas or the pressures of external politics and economic interests. St. John's College of Annapolis, MD and Santa Fe, NM is known for its traditional liberal arts-only curriculum, its emphasis on the "great books," and its tutorial style of pedagogy. In June 2016, its board of visitors and governors waited until the end of the school year to approve and schedule the implementation of the college's administrative restructuring. According to conservative Roger Kimball, editor and publisher of *New Criterion* and former St. John's board member:[38]

> The pressure to be "relevant," to sign up for the usual academic roster of metrics, has been growing. Now, like a festering boil, it seems to have burst. The bureaucrats have supplanted the visionaries.

The plan called for the absorption of the Annapolis campus by Santa Fe under the direction of a new president who describes himself as a "change agent" on behalf of social-justice issues. While the board announced its planned meeting and asked for comments from all of the college's constituencies, faculty and alums have objected to the

---

[37] Sarah Brown, "Mississippi's Chancellor Search Provoked a Fury. Will It Change Anything?," CHE (Oct. 7, 2019), at www.chronicle.com/article/Mississippi-s-Chancellor/247298.

[38] Roger Kimball, "An Impending Coup at St. John's College," *RealClear Politics* (June 6, 2016), at www.realclearpolitics.com/articles/2016/06/06/an_impending_coup_at_st_johns_college_130786.html.

decision taken at a special board meeting in New York that appears to have ignored the college's tradition of faculty self-governance.[39]

*

Trustees' increased control of university life and policy has also been reflected in an uptick in presidential replacements, often of younger appointees not ready for retirement, and in the early or middle years of a presidential term.[40] In 2017, the American Council on Education reported that the tenure of college presidents had declined from 8.5 years in 2006 to 6.5 years in 2017.[41] Without full longitudinal data to track changes, various theories have revolved around largely anecdotal evidence. Factors include the increasing number of trustees drawn from the business world where short-term results – often measured by the quarter – are seen as the norm of performance, and a larger pool of college presidents drawn from an administrative class with managerial skill but no overall vision or theory of higher education. Ever conscious of perceptions, boards of trustees tend increasingly to make such firings and replacements effectively out of sight of students, faculty, and tuition payers – during summer recesses – and with far shorter review processes, again mirroring conditions in the business world.

Despite the increasing distrust of higher education discussed above, a 2018 poll of university trustees revealed that the majority remained out of touch with both the realities of campus life and with public perceptions of it. According to the Association of Governing Boards of Universities and Colleges, together with Gallup, 77 percent of college trustees said that the public has a somewhat or mostly positive view of higher education. Yet even this was an improvement over the 2017's

---

[39] Rick Seltzer, "Reorganization Feared at St. John's," IHE (June 7, 2016), at www
.insidehighered.com/news/2016/06/07/reorganization-st-johns-has-some-supporters-
worried-about-future-great-books.

[40] Rick Seltzer, "Swift and Silent Exits," IHE (June 7, 2017), at www.insidehighered.com/
news/2017/06/07/spate-presidents-fired-early-tenures-few-reasons-why.

[41] The American College President Study 2017, reported by Jack Stripling, "Behind a
Stagnant Portrait of College Leaders, an Opening for Change," CHE (June 20, 2017), at
www.chronicle.com/article/Behind-a-Stagnant-Portrait-of/240393.

poll, which found that 84 percent of trustees believed the public viewed higher education positively.[42]

*

One might legitimately ask whether these examples are typical, or merely sensational examples cherry-picked from the often gossipy reporting of the *Chronicle* and other media sources. The net effect of such scandals, however, is precisely to emphasize what is exceptional and high-profile. Our intent is not to condemn university and college boards but to point out the net effect on the public. Whether the audience is potential or current students, parents, alums, or the general voting public, such incidents cast doubt on the institutional integrity of the university. They abet calls for more public scrutiny and legislative oversight, and they reinforce the image of the university as having failed in its social mission. As such governance is scrutinized and called into question, the university appears to have lost both internal authority and separation from the outside world.

Our discussion of the triad of values surrounding academia – authority, separateness, and innovation – has noted that once any two of these elements have been compromised for any institution, the possibilities of its destruction grows larger as certain cohesive narratives take broader and broader hold. The overwhelming hostility to higher education among voting Republicans is not so much a confirmation that higher education is replete with mismanagement and scandal of governance as it is that a narrative portraying such failure as real and pressing has taken hold of a considerable – and highly motivated and empowered – segment of the American public.

---

[42] Eric Kelderman, "Most Trustees Believe that Public Approves of Higher Ed.," CHE (19 Dec., 2018), at www.chronicle.com/article/Most-Trustees-Believe-That/245361.

CHAPTER 6

Budget Wars

INTRODUCTION

I N MAY 2015, AT CHRISTIE'S in New York, nearly $1 billion in art was auctioned, $706 million on a single night.[1] The US alone accounted for $27.5 billion in art sales in 2015.[2] On November 15, 2017, one painting alone, the much-disputed Leonardo da Vinci *Salvator Mundi*, sold for over $400 million.[3] In February 2017, Republican majority lawmakers and administration officials planned to eliminate the National Endowments of the Humanities and Arts and their total annual budgets of $300 million (less than one-tenth of 1 percent of the total Federal budget FY 2017 of $3.85 trillion). The Trump administration later reiterated this call. A simple 1 percent transaction tax on annual US art auctions could generate enough funds to support both endowments' annual budgets. Why then is public support for the arts and humanities a special target of the right wing? The numbers make it clear that this is not a budget issue. Yet, eliminating these popular programs remains high on the right-wing's agenda because the endowments underscore a public commitment to authority, separateness, and innovation in the

---

[1] www.christies.com/results/?did=29&month=5&year=2015&locations=43.

[2] Eileen Kinsella, "What Does TEFAF 2016 Art Market Report Tell Us About The Global Art Trade?," *Artnet News* (March 9, 2016), at https://news.artnet.com/market/tefaf-2016-art-market-report-443615.

[3] Hannah Ellis-Petersen and Mark Brown, "How *Salvator Mundi* Became the Most Expensive Painting Ever Sold at Auction," *Guardian* (Nov. 17, 2017), at www.theguardian .com/artanddesign/2017/nov/16/salvator-mundi-leonardo-da-vinci-most-expensive-painting-ever-sold-auction.

liberal and performing arts. The NEH and NEA support and lend authority to a culture class outside the control and private patronage of a smaller and smaller group of corporate oligarchs.

How does a small group, a subset of the "1 percent" that Nobel-Prize economist Thomas Piketty has closely studied,[4] and that Citibank analysts have described as "the plutonomy,"[5] also manipulate the language and narrative of higher education? How does that impact both student populations and the endowments and budgets of private and public universities, private liberal-arts colleges, and community colleges? Many such plutocrats operate in good faith and with progressive goals for using their private fortunes toward the elimination of poverty, disease, and ignorance. Yet they also resist calls for the government and the public to set the public agenda and to control their philanthropy either through taxation or other legislation.[6] In this they are aided and enabled by wide cadres of middle-level administrators, media, and politicians, some directly on their payrolls through salaries and funding, others indirectly through common ideologies and interests. The conflict between private visions for the public good and the role of government and society is as old as Western society; and the conditions of the *ancien regime* to which Piketty so clearly drew comparisons in our own time seem again to have emerged as urgent social, economic, and political issues.

In this chapter we will attempt to synthesize these and other debates into an overall picture of changing attitudes and approaches to private and public resources. These debates necessarily address both the aspirations and needs of society and the nature of the educational system that embodies its ideals and practical goals. In turn, the allocation of

---

[4] Thomas Piketty, *Capital in the Twenty-First Century*, Arthur Goldhammer, trans. (Cambridge, MA: Harvard University Press, 2013).

[5] Ajay Kapur, Niall Macleod, and Narendra Singh, "Plutonomy: Buying Luxury, Explaining Global Imbalances," *Citigroup, Equity Strategy, Industry Note* (Oct. 16, 2005), at https://delong.typepad.com/plutonomy-1.pdf, 1.

[6] See, for example, Tim Haines, "Billionaire Leon Cooperman Cries over Prospect of Election between 'Polarizing' Trump and Warren's 'Idiocy': 'I Care,'" *RealClear Politics* (Nov. 5, 2019), at www.realclearpolitics.com/video/2019/11/05/billionaire_hedge-fund_manager_leon_cooperman_cries_over_prospect_of_trump-warren_election_i_care.html; or Jordan Weissman, "Bill Gates Was Right. Sort Of," *Slate* (Nov. 8, 2019), at https://slate.com/business/2019/11/bill-gates-elizabeth-warren-wealth-tax.html.

increasingly precious resources within higher education sends powerful messages to students, faculty, and the broad public about how we value advanced learning. These debates take place on several levels: within the university itself in its allocation of resources for programs, departments, faculties, administration, and facilities; on the private and public boards of these institutions; in the public forum of politics and legislation; and among the broader public in the debate over the costs and benefits of college and professional degrees and the system that produces them.

SOME DATA

With the financial recovery of the 1980s, American higher education entered a new phase of expansion. Externally, many colleges and universities were the largest corporations in their communities and regions, the largest employers, and the largest property holders. Their impact was both a welcome element of local economies and a source of growing contention as tax and other exemptions drew increasing scrutiny from state and local jurisdictions. University endowments also came under examination as well-publicized fundraising campaigns and soaring budgets called attention to the vast holdings of these institutions. As early as 1987 the then Secretary of Education William J. Bennett summarized the right-wing takeaway on higher education that had been forming since 1968:

> As I said on the occasion of Harvard's 350th anniversary, too many students fail to receive the education they deserve at our nation's universities. The real problem is not lack of money but failure of vision. Unfortunately, when it comes to higher education, this distinction is frequently lost. Stanford University's vague justification for increased charges – "new knowledge is inherently more expensive" – only underscores the lack of focus and purpose at some of our nation's most prestigious universities. Higher education is not underfunded. It is under-accountable and under-productive. Our students deserve better than this. They deserve an education commensurate with the large sums paid by parents and taxpayers and donors.[7]

[7] William J. Bennett, "Our Greedy Colleges," *New York Times* (Feb. 18, 1987), at www.nytimes.com/1987/02/18/opinion/our-greedy-colleges.html.

According to the National Center for Education Statistics (NCES) of the Department of Education, total fall 2016 enrollment in US colleges and universities was 20.2 million in 4,360 four-year colleges, universities, and two-year community colleges.[8] These numbers reflected a decline from peak numbers of 21.1 million students in 4,726 institutions in 2012–13. In 2017, total revenues for higher education were about $641 billion. Income from all public institutions of higher education (the Californias, Wisconsins, SUNYs, etc.) totaled $378.8 billion, those of private, not-for-profit schools (the Harvards, Stanfords, and Williamses) was about $243 billion, and the total for private for-profit colleges and universities (the University of Phoenixes) was about $19.4 billion. Since most controversy and debate centers around the finances of public colleges and universities, we will follow this thread for much of our analysis.

Total income for public higher-ed systems in 2017 included $75.8 billion in student tuition and fees; $142 billion in all forms of Federal, state, and local government aid and grants; $96 billion in all forms of campus income from such categories as hospitals, research income, copyrights, patents and the like; $27 billion in private grants, gifts, and other donations; and $38 billion in endowment revenues and other investment income. While government aid remained the largest source of funding (37.8 percent), the schools' own income-generating operations (25.3 percent) had become the second-largest source of revenue. Tuition and fees were becoming an increasingly larger component of income for public higher ed (19.9 percent), followed by endowment and other investment income (9.9 percent). External fundraising from private grants and donations still made up the smallest category of public education's income (7.1 percent).

Government aid has long been taken as the norm for public higher education, even though tuition and fee structures (for non-state residents, for example) have long been in place in state systems like

[8] S. A. Ginder, J. E. Kelly-Reid, and F. B. Mann, *Enrollment and Employees in Postsecondary Institutions, Fall 2017*; and *Financial Statistics and Academic Libraries, Fiscal Year 2017: First Look (Provisional Data) (NCES 2019-021rev)*, US Department of Education (Washington, DC: National Center for Education Statistics, 2019). Retrieved [29 Jul. 2019] from http://nces.ed.gov/pubsearch, 12–13, Table 5.

California or Louisiana from at least the 1930s.[9] State support expanded robustly across the nation after World War II and continued to increase through the 1960s.[10] Since the 1980s, however, tuition increases have garnered the most attention and scrutiny for public higher education. At the same time, campus income sources from hospitals, research initiatives, copyrights, patents and the like have often been seen as signs of corporatization and a certain drift from core missions.

*

In 2017, total expenditures for all colleges and universities was estimated at $576.3 billion. This includes $360.7 billion for public schools, $197.6 billion for private not-for-profit, and $17.98 billion for private, for-profit schools.[11] According to these figures, public higher education produced a surplus of about $18 billion after expenses, which could be interpreted to mean that public higher education was living comfortably within its means but at the expense of government subsidies and student tuitions. Private universities have also come under scrutiny from both government and segments of the public for the large surpluses in tax-exempt revenues ($45.3 billion in 2017 alone) that now accumulate in their endowment and other investment funds. Public college and university officials are quick to point out that new revenues from research-related endeavors, other campus activities, and fundraising were producing these surpluses. Nevertheless, the greatest shift in general public perception may be focused on the dollar amounts of state and federal aid to public systems and on tuition fees. It is here that the debate over funding and budgets has been the most visible and vocal. Such issues have brought both Republican- and Democratic-affiliated voters closer over their concerns for the condition of higher education.

*

In the fall of 2017, the total number of people employed in American higher education, including faculty, administrative, and campus staffs

---

[9] Thelin, 251–52.   [10] Thelin, 285–91.

[11] Ginder, Kelly-Reid, and Mann, *Enrollment and Employees*; and *Financial Statistics*, 15–16, Table 6.

numbered 3.98 million across all types of institutions.[12] Of this total 2.59 million were employed in public institutions; 1.21 million in private, not-for-profit schools; and 176,400 in private, for-profit schools. Of the total, faculty numbered 1.46 million in all institutions, or 36.6 percent of all those employed in American higher education: 908,649 in public colleges and universities; 443,962 in private, not-for-profit; and 104,577 in private, for-profit schools. Of the 1.46 million faculty, 741,111 were full-time (50.9 percent), and 716,077 part-time (49.1 percent). Average annual salaries ranged from $80,429 for public four-year schools to $89,229 for private, not-for-profit; to $47,603 for private for-profit schools. These averages reflected all types of schools from medical and law to humanities. Within these there were also large discrepancies. Public four-year college and university salaries ranged from $104,293 for a full professor to $57,235 for lecturers. Men averaged $93,235 and women $76,760. In private, not-for-profit schools men averaged $98,175 and women $79,637. On the low end of the scale, the 49.1 percent of part-time contingent faculty, the figures were most commonly calculated by the course, at an average of $2,700 per course with few if any benefits, for an annual average salary of $7,066.[13]

Faculty salaries – the one cost that the public sees – accounted for $62.3 billion across all types of private, not-for-profit schools, or only 31.5 percent of total expenses; and for $109.7 billion or only 30.4 percent for public schools. Despite the low percentages of expenditures devoted to faculty salary, faculty members are the face of higher education to most Americans. Nevertheless, a consistent narrative has developed that college and university faculty are paid too much, that they work too little, that they teach only a few courses a week, and that they take too much time off devoted to travel (a fraction of that of administrators) and

[12] Ginder, Kelly-Reid, and Mann, *Enrollment and Employees; and Financial Statistics*, 15–16, Table 6.

[13] American Association of University Professors, "Visualizing Change: The Annual Report on the Economic Status of the Profession, 2016–17," at www.aaup.org/file/FCS_2016-17 .pdf, 8 and 23, Table 13.

summer holidays. Public and government scrutiny has therefore focused on faculty as the major problem in rising college costs, the one unifying issue across party lines in the Pew and other surveys.

This is especially true as tuition climbs ever higher at both private and public institutions. In 2008–9, the US Department of Education's National Center for Education Statistics reported that the "average total tuition, fees, room and board rates charged for full-time undergraduate students in degree-granting institutions" ranged from $14,262 for in-state public university students to $31,273 for students at private, not-for-profit colleges.[14] For 2018–19, a decade later, the College Board reported that annual tuition for a four-year college ranged from $10,230 for in-state public university students, to $26,290 for out-of-state students, to $35,830 for students at private, not-for-profit colleges.[15] With room and board these average totals went up to $21,370, $37,430, and $48,510 respectively. Overall this represented a 2.86 percent increase from 2017–18, not adjusted for inflation. The 2018 inflation rate was 2.44 percent. When one compares the total tuition, fees, room and board for 2008–9 to those of 2018–19, these numbers represent an increase of 50 percent for in-state students at public universities and of 35 percent for those at private, not-for-profit schools. Meanwhile, the inflation rate for this decade, measured in constant 2000 dollars, was 45.82 percent.[16] This means that private colleges and universities fell behind inflation in their tuition increases. Tuition at public schools exceeded the inflation rate by about 4 percent, a real increase but hardly enough to justify skepticism about their high costs and well within a reasonable rate considering the decrease of public support from both state and Federal governments.

---

[14] US Department of Education, National Center for Education Statistics. (2018), *Digest of Education Statistics, 2016* (NCES 2017-094), Chapter 3, at https://nces.ed.gov/programs/digest/d16/ch_3.asp.

[15] College Board, "Trends in Higher Education: Average Published Undergraduate Charges by Sector and by Carnegie Classification, 2018–19," at https://trends.collegeboard.org/college-pricing/figures-tables/average-published-undergraduate-charges-sector-2018-19.

[16] Figures based on the US Bureau of Labor Statistics, Consumer Price Index, at www.in2013dollars.com/2000-dollars-in-2018.

Whatever the reality revealed by these figures, the Pew and Gallup surveys discussed in Chapter 4 indicated that Republican- and Democratic-leaning voters often differed sharply in their assessments of the merits and problems of higher education. But they shared the concern that it was becoming far too expensive and that its cost increases were far outpacing the general rate of inflation. As we also cautioned, the Pew and Gallup poll numbers were subjected to a great deal of scrutiny and some revision. The 2018 New America poll qualified much of the partisan-identified findings and drew some important, further conclusions:

> approximately three out of five Republicans are comfortable with their taxes going to support higher education. And although Pew data showed that Republicans believe higher education is having a negative impact on the way things are going in this country, New America's data show that 78 percent of Republicans feel positive about the colleges and universities located near them. ... Like last year, a majority of Americans say community colleges and public four-year colleges and universities are worth the cost (81 percent and 65 percent, respectively). They do not think this is the case for private nonprofit and for-profit colleges and universities (44 percent and 40 percent, respectively). ... Most Democrats and Republicans believe that public colleges and universities are worth the cost, though Republicans (59 percent) are less likely to believe this to be the case for four-year public colleges and universities than Democrats (69 percent). Less than half of Democrats and Republicans believe private nonprofit and for-profit institutions are worth the cost, though Democrats are more likely to believe that private nonprofit institutions are worth the cost (49 percent versus 36 percent of Republicans).[17]

On the specific issue of public support for student tuition, however, party affiliations reveal a dramatic difference. The vast majority (76 percent) of Democrats polled by New America believed that the Federal and state government should support tuition fees. A smaller majority of Republicans (52 percent) believed the opposite: that paying

---

[17] www.newamerica.org/education-policy/reports/varying-degrees-2018/introduction.

for college is the responsibility of students and their families. The main fault line appears to be the purpose of higher education, with the Democratic respondents believing it to be a social good and the majority of Republicans believing it to be a private, personal benefit.[18] Such beliefs are highly significant, again largely because of their impact on public policy toward higher education.[19] The large majority (70 percent) of Americans of whatever affiliation believe that students and their families pay for the costs of higher ed; whereas the reality, as we have seen above, is that students pay only 32.8 percent of costs at two-year colleges, 51.1 percent at public four-year colleges, and 74.5 percent only at private four-year colleges. These figures have remained fairly consistent since the mid 1990s. But if this belief is so prevalent, it translates into a demand for greater affordability as many American families feel the pinch of higher costs, reduced opportunity, and greater debt.

*

By 2006 student debt stood at an average of $17,000 for a senior in college. That included all enrollments for tuition-free, Federal and state-supported students.[20] In June 2018, *Forbes Magazine* reported that total US student debt was $1.52 trillion, owed by 44.2 million people.[21] Average student debt stood at $38,390. Median student debt was between $10,000 and $25,000, and 2 percent of borrowers owed $100,000 or more. California, Florida, Texas, and New York, traditionally states with some of the most robust university systems, were the four highest for total student-loan debt outstanding among resident borrowers.

As of July 2019, 34 million Americans over 25 – over ten percent of the US population – have some college credits but dropped out before

[18] www.newamerica.org/education-policy/reports/varying-degrees-2018/americans-believe-higher-education-is-a-public-benefit-and-that-the-government-should-do-more-to-make-it-affordable.

[19] www.newamerica.org/education-policy/reports/varying-degrees-2018/perception-versus-reality. For the origins of this ideology, see above, pp. 69–70.

[20] Thelin, 366–69.

[21] Zack Friedman, "Student Loan Debt Statistics in 2018: A $1.5 Trillion Crisis," *Forbes Magazine* (Jun. 13, 2018), at www.forbes.com/sites/zackfriedman/2018/06/13/student-loan-debt-statistics-2018.

receiving a diploma. In December 2018, the National Student Clearinghouse Research Center reported that in 2012 fewer than 60 percent of college freshmen graduated even in six years;[22] and the OECD puts the US nineteenth out of the twenty-eight countries whose college-graduation rates it studied. In one year alone the lost earnings for the 40 percent who do not graduate are an estimated $3.8 billion. The University of Pennsylvania's Pell Institute estimated that in 2017 students from families in the top income quartile were 4.8 times more likely to have earned a bachelor's degree by the age of 24 than were students whose families were in the bottom quartile. As David Kirp reports, at thirty-eight elite colleges, including five in the Ivy League – Dartmouth, Princeton, Yale, Penn, and Brown – more students come from the top 1 percent of the income scale than from the entire bottom 60 percent.[23]

*

In 2017, state university systems crossed an important threshold: overall income from tuition surpassed that of public tax support for the first time. Many state systems have rebounded from the Great Recession of 2008, have reversed education budget cuts, and in some cases have increased budgets. Yet the overall picture is one of a nation turning away from its mid-century commitment to universal higher education for all who sought it and for the creation of an aspirational middle class enabled by this publicly supported higher education. In addition, and perhaps more importantly, many Americans polled, especially Republicans, now see higher education far differently than they did a generation ago and as James Buchanan envisioned it. According to Arizona State University's executive vice president and treasurer, Morgan R. Olsen:

> Higher education in most parts of the country is moving from what is
> perceived as a public good, as economists would define the term, to a

---

[22] "Completing College: A National View of Student Completion Rates: Fall 2012 Cohort," at https://nscresearchcenter.org/wp-content/uploads/SignatureReport16.pdf.

[23] David Kirp, "The College Dropout Scandal," *Chronicle Review*, CHE (July 26, 2019), at www.chronicle.com/interactives/20190726-dropout-scandal.

private good. .... As that has happened, I think it has forced everyone to look at how they generate the resources.[24]

This thinking is echoed by William A. Herbert, executive director of the National Center for the Study of Collective Bargaining in Higher Education and the Professions, at the City University of New York's Hunter College: "So many forces are pushing for education [to be] viewed as a commodity, as an expectation with a return. It's devaluing education."[25]

But the picture is more complex – and troubling – than these statistics. Just as the student body is becoming more diverse racially and economically, the majority of states most affected by such changing demographics are seeing their worst budget cuts in real terms, despite nationwide economic recovery. These states are, almost without exception, controlled by Republican legislatures and governors. According to Ronald Brownstein:

> The latest annual survey of state spending by the State Higher Education Executive Officers found that, since 1992, spending per student – measured in inflation-adjusted dollars – has declined at public colleges and universities by about 8 percent (even after a recovery in spending after states' low point in 2012). In turn, per-student tuition revenue has increased by 96 percent. ... Since the recession in 2008, per-student appropriations for public higher education have declined by around one-sixth in Texas, Georgia, and North Carolina; by over one-fifth in Florida and Mississippi; by over one-fourth in South Carolina; by about one-third in Nevada and Alabama; and by over two-fifths in Arizona and Louisiana. ...But the biggest blue states present some notable exceptions to this pattern. New York, Illinois, and California have all increased per-student spending since 2008; and Oregon, Hawaii, and Maryland have held spending almost steady.[26]

[24] Lindsay Ellis, "How the Great Recession Reshaped American Higher Education," CHE (Sept. 14, 2018), at www.chronicle.com/article/How-the-Great-Recession/244527.

[25] Ellis, "Great Recession." See also pp. 69–70 above.

[26] Ronald Brownstein, "American Higher Education Hits a Dangerous Milestone," *Atlantic* (May 3, 2018), at www.theatlantic.com/politics/archive/2018/05/american-higher-education-hits-a-dangerous-milestone/559457.

Louisiana, Arizona, Alabama, Oklahoma, West Virginia, Georgia, and South Carolina top the list of Republican-controlled states that have made the largest shifts from state tax support to tuition fees, and this at a time when those most in need of support for higher education are women, people of color, and the poor. Some observers see this as more than coincidence and as a policy goal from a political party that has increasingly devoted itself to a zero-sum game of bolstering decreasing white, male power at the expense of all others.

*

Meanwhile, as students and their families find it increasingly difficult to pay for college themselves, the media has begun to focus on the increased wealth of both public and private colleges and universities. In the 2017–18 reporting year American colleges and universities raised $46.7 billion in contributions, the seventh consecutive year of increases in such donations.[27] Among the top ten were Harvard ($1.4 billion), Stanford ($1.1 billion) and Columbia ($1 billion), continuing to number ten, Yale ($586 million). Even state schools made the top ten. UCLA, for example, raised $787 million and UC San Francisco $730 million. The overall total was up 7.2 percent from the previous year. Analysts credit a very strong return on the donor class' investments (14 percent return from the S&P 500 Index) and continued uncertainty over tax laws for their charitable-contribution deductions. Such figures vastly increase the ability of many universities to expand campus facilities, launch and fund major research projects, hire and reward faculty and administrative staff, reduce student tuition and fees, and leverage their position within communities.

The largest endowments were startling. According to a report by the Congressional Research Service of May 4, 2018,[28] the top 25 US schools have 52 percent of all endowment wealth, and 11 percent of US

---

[27] Janet Lorin, "Colleges Raise $47 Billion in Ninth Straight Record Year," *Bloomberg* (Feb. 11, 2019), at www.bloomberg.com/news/articles/2019-02-11/u-s-colleges-raise-47-billion-in-ninth-straight-record-year.

[28] "College and University Endowments: Overview and Tax Policy Options," at https://fas.org/sgp/crs/misc/R44293.pdf.

universities hold roughly 75 percent of the $566.8 billion in endowment wealth. According to that report, the five wealthiest universities were Harvard University ($39.2 billion), Yale University ($29.4 billion), the University of Texas ($26.5 billion),[29] Stanford University ($26.5 billion), and Princeton University ($25.9 billion).[30] The average draw-down from these endowments was 4.4 percent. The average rate of return was 12.2 percent, resulting in an investment income of $64 billion in 2017 alone, a discrepancy in passive income that economists note has vastly increased endowment holdings and investment returns above and beyond those achieved by most families whose students attend these schools. Indeed, this discrepancy also characterized a widening inequality gap between the richest universities and those whose endowments were far smaller and whose alums' giving – based largely on their income brackets – was correspondingly also far smaller.[31]

Much of this income reflects a shift in traditional not-for-profit institutional investment strategies over the past decade away from fixed income and equity returns to higher-risk hedge funds and other "alternative" investments. In the wake of disclosures focusing on the "Paradise Papers" – and much to the public's shock – in 2017 it was disclosed that a large amount of these endowments was being invested offshore through "blocker" corporations to avoid taxes and public scrutiny.[32] So strong has the reaction been that for the first time Congress – lead by Republican Senators – has begun discussing the possibility of taxing endowments of over $1 billion at a rate of 1.4 percent.[33] Ironically, this is an idea very much in line with the progressive thinking of Thomas Piketty and other

---

[29] The Congressional report tracked private schools, since the consensus was that public institutions should not be held to the same standards for taxation purposes.

[30] www.investopedia.com/articles/markets/081616/top-5-largest-university-endowments.asp.

[31] Charles T. Clotfelter, "How Rich Universities Get Richer … and Leave Everyone Else Behind," CHE (Oct. 27, 2017), at www.chronicle.com/article/How-Rich-Universities-Get/241567.

[32] Stephanie Saul, "Endowments Boom as Colleges Bury Earnings Overseas," *New York Times* (Nov. 8, 2017), at www.nytimes.com/2017/11/08/world/universities-offshore-investments.html.

[33] Ben Myers and Brock Read, "If Republicans Get Their Way, These Colleges Would See Their Endowments Taxed," CHE (Nov. 2, 2017), at www.chronicle.com/article/if-republicans-get-their-way/241659.

economists as a means of tapping accumulating wealth to increase government revenues, to spur universities to draw down larger amounts in order to offset expenses and increase student aid, and to hold them more accountable to the public. The fate of such taxes and other changes to the tax code remains uncertain. But it is clear that government oversight of higher education – and its skepticism about the uses of university wealth – tracked increasingly negative public perceptions about the expenses of higher education at a time when the schools themselves continued to increase their unused wealth. In this scrutiny and its conclusions the narrative of the university's wealth began to resemble that of the monasteries as the English Crown began to scrutinize their assets and to construct its narrative for confiscation.

In addition, the accumulation of vast endowments and their concomitant fundraising often carry internal dangers that reflect negatively on public perceptions. According to the author of a study commissioned by Deloitte's Center for Higher Education Excellence, working in partnership with Georgia Tech's Center for 21st Century Universities,

> Despite its importance to their job, many presidents say they feel unprepared for the amount of fundraising they need to do on a regular basis. So when leaders are good at it ... the race for dollars begins to permeate the culture. Raising more than a million dollars a day takes leaders away from campus and doesn't allow them enough time to engage with faculty members and students and weave themselves into the fabric of the school they represent on a daily basis. It also changes the stakeholders of the university. Donors, often alumni, become just as important as students and faculty in making decisions on campus. This has been particularly true for many of the big issues that grab headlines about colleges: drinking, fraternities and athletics. Several college leaders have told me that they are reluctant to place restrictions on any of them because they don't want to offend alumni (read: donors) ... This is a problem especially for big public colleges and universities that increasingly depend more on alumni donations than they do on state taxpayer dollars.[34]

---

[34] Jeffrey J. Selingo, "The Blessing and Curse of Fundraising for Higher Education," *Washington Post* (Aug. 18, 2017), at www.washingtonpost.com/news/grade-point/wp/2017/08/18/the-blessing-and-curse-of-fundraising-for-higher-education.

Charles T. Clotfelter has summarized the impact of these great discrepancies:

> As a practical matter, colleges have performed much the same role in America that they have everywhere in modern societies: to educate the children of the ruling upper-middle class and, in effect, to reproduce those elites. One need not be a Marxist to acknowledge this fact. Writing almost a half a century ago, the sociologists Christopher Jencks and David Riesman reflected on the role of colleges in balancing the imperatives of reproduction and mobility. Higher education, they argued, serves this country's need "to prevent its elite from decaying into a hereditary aristocracy." To their credit, American colleges are more meritocratic than they were 50 years ago. Objective measures of academic merit have assumed a paramount role. Yet, rather than being a vehicle for social mobility, this system has worked instead to perpetuate the advantage of those in a financial position to do well on the tests.[35]

Much of this financial concentration has been justified by higher education officials due to the loss of federal and state funding. In August 2019, for example, legislators in California[36] – a liberal state – lambasted the state university chancellor for riding on a $1.5 billion surplus, accumulated over several years. The previous June California's state auditor had accused the system of hiding this as a secret slush fund at a time when tuition and student debt for both in-state and out-of-state students was rising dramatically. Similar accusations have been leveled in Ohio, Virginia, and Wisconsin. School administrators emphasize that such funds are a reserve against fluctuations in state aid and enrollment variations, and that much of the money has actually been set aside for capital and program projects and long-term maintenance. Nevertheless, the public perception – reinforced by criticisms by politicians and trade and faculty unions – was that of higher education joining in yet another club of extravagant wealth at the expense of taxpayers, students, and their families. John Thelin has attributed much of this disconnect to the

---

[35] Clotfelter, "How Rich Universities Get Richer."

[36] Dan Bauman, "A Public University with Too Much Money? Surpluses Are More Complicated than That," CHE (Aug. 28, 2019), at www.chronicle.com/article/A-Public-University-With-Too/247033.

catch-up involved between higher ed's long history of struggle and development and its current state of relative wealth. This has led in many cases, he argues, to continued pleas of poverty amid riches. He quotes a *Forbes Magazine*'s report on Harvard finances as an example of "fund-accounting" financial reports that gave the impression that:

> Harvard was managing its bottom line in such a way as to appear poorer than it really is. The university is in the midst of a plan to reportedly raise $2.5 billion on top of what is already the world's largest private endowment. Harvard is a bit like the rich man who wears scuffed shoes and a frayed collar when he visits his doctor.[37]

This is even more pronounced among the state university systems most in the public eye.[38] There is a body of evidence that state support of their own systems has decreased as a percentage of these systems' overall revenues. Nevertheless, many state systems have actually increased their revenues through the means outlined above: endowment growth, auxiliary revenues from campus facilities like hospitals, copyrights and patents, and the monetization of research. Thus, even as many states are increasing their net dollar amounts, these dollars are becoming a smaller percentage of overall state-system funding. This disconnect has created an increasingly negative perception in the public eye: public higher education's continued cries of poverty amid sparkling new laboratories, stadiums, and dormitories; tuition increases amid the escalating salaries of senior administrative cadres. At just one "flagship" state university of medium size (25,000 enrollment), the salaries of its top fifteen vice-presidents in 2010 totaled $4.75 million, plus an additional 15 percent in pension plan contributions for a total compensation to 15 people of $5.46 million. The president's chief-of-staff alone earned another $170,000 a year in salary and pension benefits.[39] In 2018, the American Association of University Professors[40] reported that average salary in

---

[37] Rhoula Khalaf, "Customized Accounting," *Forbes* (May 25, 1992): 50, quoted in Thelin, 359.

[38] See Thelin, 385–90.   [39] Thelin, 387–88.

[40] American Association of University Professors, "Visualizing Change: The Annual Report on the Economic Status of the Profession, 2016–17," at www.aaup.org/file/FCS_2016-17 .pdf, 21, tables 8–9.

2016–17 for college and university presidents was $334,617, a 4.3 percent increase from 2015–16, not adjusted for inflation. At private not-for-profit schools the average was $614,615, and the top pay was $1.5 million. At public institutions these figures were $448,614 with a maximum of just under $1 million. These salaries ranged from 3.6 to almost 4 times that of the most highly paid professors at these institutions.

*

We have discussed above the results of surveys conducted since 2017 in which the majority of Republicans oppose higher education or in which those who still support it – Republicans and Democrats alike – cite its high costs and decreasing value for dollar results in career and social advancement. In the 2017 series of surveys several trends were clear and common, whatever the political partisan takes on the overall value of higher education. These tended to focus – for both Republicans and Democrats – on the "value" of higher education in monetary terms. By 2019, this formula had become common wisdom: Americans now evaluate higher education based on value-for-dollar and return-on-investment (ROI) defined in terms of career success.[41] We will return to the issue of "value" in cultural terms, the other major factor in negative responses to higher education.

*

These realities have been exacerbated by the predicted crisis of student-loan debt characterized as a "higher-education bubble." How then has American society reacted to increased tuition and student debt, to reports of private universities reaping billions in passive income, to the perception that faculty salaries keep rising as faculty themselves do less and less; to reports that college administrators keep making more money

[41] "A First Try at ROI," Georgetown University Center on Education and the Workforce (November 2019), at https://cew.georgetown.edu/cew-reports/CollegeROI; Audrey Williams June, "A New Study Calculates Return on Investment — 40 Years After Enrollment. Here's What We Learned," CHE (Nov. 14, 2019), at www.chronicle.com/article/A-New-Study-Calculates-Return/247537; Beckie Supiano, "3 Key Findings From a New Study on What Graduates Get out of College," CHE (Nov. 14, 2019), at www.chronicle.com/article/3-Key-Findings-From-a-New/247546.

to produce more expensive results? As Thelin notes, despite large endowments, vigorous fundraising, and tuition increases, the reality of higher-ed finance has remained consistent over the past generation: cuts in state aid to public universities in the 1990s were only partially restored with the economy's recovery in the early 2000s.[42] But the financial crash of 2008 again wiped out this recovery. Hard-pressed state and local governments cut budgets across the board, and higher education was no exception. With the economic recovery of the Obama years, states did begin efforts to restore funding, but many never reached the levels of the early 1990s, or again, of those before 2008. As early as 2003, in the then-Democratically-controlled Michigan, polling showed higher education as the first priority for budget cuts, largely reflecting a widespread attitude that colleges and universities were wasting and misappropriating their resources, funds that the state needed to maintain "essential" over only "important" public services.[43]

As Fischer and Stripling put it as early as 2014:

> Behind these changes is a fundamental shift. Public colleges, once viewed as worthy of collective investment for the greater good, are increasingly treated as vehicles delivering a personal benefit to students, who ought to foot the bill themselves. The story of public higher education's transition from a key national priority to an increasingly neglected special interest is untidy. It cannot be traced to any single moment in time. It cannot be laid at the feet of any one individual or ideology. Rather, it is the story of dozens and dozens of consequential moves made by individual actors across the country. They are lobbyists and activists, anti-tax conservatives and big-government liberals, conflicted idealists and self-preservationists. Even college leaders themselves. They are the American public.[44]

According to a 2019 report from the National Bureau of Economic Research, these trends remain strong, and cuts to higher education exceed those of general state budget tightening. The authors noted that

---

[42] Thelin, 359–61.

[43] Karin Fischer and Jack Stripling, "An Era of Neglect: How Public Colleges Were Crowded out, Beaten up, and Failed to Fight back," CHE (March 2, 2014), at www.chronicle.com/article/An-Era-of-Neglect/145045.

[44] Fischer and Stripling, "An Era of Neglect." See also, pp. 69–70 above.

political considerations and attitudes toward higher education exacerbated these trends over the 2010s with outcomes that will both damage public higher education itself in the long term and produce a decline in higher education's economic impact for the broader economy and society.[45]

CASE STUDIES

Such statistics, their analyses, and their uses in the public forum have a concrete impact on both systems of higher education and on individual schools and their faculties and students. In the following pages we can provide only a few of the most salient examples of more general trends across the nation. Many more examples could be adduced. The examples provided come almost entirely from Republican-controlled statehouses and legislatures. While we also provide some examples from Democratic states, the reality is that current Republican ideology and the political message delivered to the public and reflected back in the public-opinion polls have been the driving forces behind most of these budget wars.

One of the most widely reported cases was that of the University of Wisconsin (UW) system under Republican governor Scott Walker. Wisconsin has a large state system with a spending total of over $6 billion annually. In 2013, Walker responded to the growing criticism of higher ed's costs by imposing a two-year tuition freeze. In 2014, upon news of a $1-billion surplus in the state system's budget, he proposed an additional two-year freeze. His 2015–17 budget then called for a 13 percent cut in the state's support for the system, or $250 million, with the largest cuts aimed at the system's flagship campus in Madison.[46] According to faculty sources, since Walker's election in 2011, budget cuts to the UW totaled $795 million by 2018. He defended his freezes by focusing on the key issue for most voters – affordability – noting in 2018 that tuition had gone

[45] John Bound, Breno Braga, Gaurav Khanna, and Sarah Turner, *Public Universities: The Supply Side of Building a Skilled Workforce*, National Bureau of Economic Research Working Paper No. 25945 (June 2019), at www.nber.org/papers/w25945.

[46] Scott Jaschik, "U of Wisconsin Board Approves Deep Cuts," IHE (July 10, 2015), at www .insidehighered.com/quicktakes/2015/07/10/u-wisconsin-board-approves-deep-cuts.

up by 118 percent in the decade before his freezes had gone into effect.[47] Nor were Walker and the Republicans alone in their pressure for cuts: the Great Recession of 2008 had also prompted Democrats to reduce the system's budget.

But Walker and his Republican majority's policies forced hard choices on the system's trustees: carrying out both the budget cuts and resorting to strategies that many state systems have adopted. These included shifting admissions policies to favor more out-of-state (and higher tuition-paying) enrollments. Students of most full-time, resident undergraduate programs at the flagship Madison campus paid $9,300 a year in 2017. Out-of-state and international students paid over $30,000 per year before factoring in fees. Thus systemwide, in-state resident undergraduate enrollments fell from 126,432 in 2012–13 to 117,613 in 2016–17. Over the same period, systemwide, non-resident undergraduate enrollments rose from 16,590 to 20,839. Even with this shift, by 2015 UW students were paying for nearly 50 percent of their college expenses, compared to 40 percent when Walker took office, according to data from the State Higher Education Executive Officers Association (SHEEO).[48] The system also cut about 20 percent of administrative positions and began studying the budgetary effects of implementing three-year bachelor's degrees across 60 percent of programs by 2020. Faculty also felt the brunt of higher productivity expectations, with pressure to impose new metrics on course hours taught and the weakening of tenure protections against layoffs and firings. As Walker declared on Milwaukee radio station WTMJ in defense of his 2015 budget, "Maybe it's time for faculty and staff to start thinking about teaching more classes and doing more work, and this authority frees up the [University of Wisconsin] administration to make those sorts of

[47] Rick Seltzer, "Scott Walker Loosens the Purse Strings," IHE (March 1, 2017), at www .insidehighered.com/news/2017/03/01/wisconsin-higher-ed-leaders-welcome- proposed-funding-worry-about-details.

[48] Danielle Douglas-Gabriel, "Scott Walker's Real Record on Higher Education in Wisconsin," *Washington Post* (August 13, 2015), at wapo.st/1DPWjnG?tid=ss_mail&utm_ term=.1acfe3ec38f3.

requests."[49] According to the American Association of University Professors' *Academe Blog*:

> In 2011, legislation curtailed the rights of faculty in the system to negotiate collectively. In 2015, the legislature severely weakened tenure, shared governance, and due process – and, by extension, academic freedom. Attacks underway this fall [2017] include the recent approval by the board of regents of an anti-free-speech proposal, a plan to merge the system's two- and four-year institutions, changes to procedures governing searches for chancellors and presidents, and a bill before the state legislature that would abolish a partnership with Planned Parenthood.[50]

Such cuts and policy changes were not value-free and the result of fiscal concerns alone. Nor were they merely reflecting political winds and opinion survey results but were implemented as the cutting edge of an ideological assault on the system's mission, embodied in the "Wisconsin Idea" since the earliest years of the twentieth century.[51] This idea holds that the university system was dedicated to service "to the government in the forms of serving in office, offering advice about public policy, providing information, and exercising technical skill, and to the citizens in the forms of doing research directed at solving problems that are important to the state and conducting outreach activities" that included the fostering of Wisconsin as a "laboratory for democracy."[52] In 2015, Walker proposed his controversial plan to change the university's mission statement to delete its mention of the "search for truth," with a directive "to meet the state's workforce needs." After initially defending the changes as a "drafting error," Walker was forced to drop the changes in his budget proposal after the public record revealed that he and his

[49] Lucy McCalmont, "Walker Urges Professors to Work Harder," *Politico* (29 Jan., 2015), at www.politico.com/story/2015/01/scott-walker-higher-education-university-professors-114716.

[50] Kelly Hand, "Academe Archives: Assaults on Higher Education in Wisconsin" (October 26, 2017) at https://academeblog.org/2017/10/26/academe-archives-assaults-on-higher-education-in-wisconsin.

[51] Thelin, 137.

[52] Jack Stark, "The Wisconsin Idea: The University's Service to the State," in Wisconsin Legislative Reference Bureau (ed.), *State of Wisconsin 1995–1996 Blue Book* (Madison: Wisconsin Legislature Joint Committee on Legislative Organization, 1995), 100–179.

inner circle had planned the changes for some time. Walker retreated from such positions and proposed increases to the university system's budget in time for his presidential and gubernatorial campaigns. His presidential bid was among the least successful of Republican candidates, however, and he was defeated for governor in the 2018 election. Walker's political losses were good news for his Democratic opponents, for unions, and for advocates of public education; and they reflected a growing concern over the dismantling of a popular and nationally renowned state system. Yet the impact of his budget cuts and his ideological assault remain to be reversed, and his model has had significant imitators.

*

At the University of North Carolina system, Republican-initiated austerity saw a cut in higher education funding by 25 percent between 2008 and 2015. In-state tuition rose by 35 percent over the same period. The system's board of trustees also imposed financial-aid limits that affect almost 22,000 low-income students. In August 2015, after less than ten minutes of discussion, the board voted to cap at 15 percent the amount of tuition revenue that universities could apply to need-based financial aid. Republican Governor McCrory called on schools to offset these cuts by limiting enrollment to "those who are ready for college," a statement that many observers saw as racially loaded. Meanwhile, the board had voted in April 2015 to increase the annual salaries of top administrators to as much as $1 million. In May 2015, Civitas, a right-wing think tank, described the North Carolina legislative budget that had already proposed another $26 million cut for UNC as "stuffed with pork barrel spending" and called for even further program eliminations.[53] Civitas, along with the John William Pope Center for Higher Education, is the creation of Art Pope, the discount-store magnate and former national chairman of the Tea Party's Americans for Prosperity.

*

---

[53] Quoted from Zoë Carpenter, "How a Right-Wing Political Machine is Dismantling Higher Education in North Carolina," *Nation* (June 8, 2015), at www.thenation.com/article/how-right-wing-political-machine-dismantling-higher-education-north-carolina.

In Louisiana, since becoming governor in 2008, Republican Governor Bobby Jindal, a former congressperson and president of the University of Louisiana System, had cut state support for higher education by $700 million, making Louisiana the state with the highest student per-capita cuts in the nation. In February 2015, however, Jindal called for an additional $400 million in cuts for the state university system, amid mounting warnings that such amounts would destroy the hurricane- and economy-damaged system beyond repair.[54] In response to criticisms, including stiff public pushback from LSU Chancellor F. King Alexander, the governor's office proposed a cut of $211 million that would offset the initial reductions by selling off parts of campuses and allowing individual campuses to raise their graduate students' tuition.[55] Even with Jindal's defeat and the election of Democratic Governor John Bel Edwards, the 2016 budget called for further cuts of $70 million on top of the system cuts of more than 40 percent since 2008, damage that could not easily be reversed even with a recovering economy. In 2015, the Louisiana Board of Regents reported that the public system had eliminated some 5,000 employees since 2009 and eliminated or consolidated nearly 600 academic programs. Meanwhile, online course and degree offerings increased by nearly 44 percent.[56] At Louisiana State, in-state tuition more than doubled since the 2008–9 academic year to $10,814 in 2017. The state funded about 70 percent of the university's budget in 2008 and only about 30 percent by 2017. Tuition charges make up for Louisiana's shortfalls, and they hit hardest those most served by public higher education: the poor and people of color.

*

[54] Katherine Mangan, "Louisiana's Governor Seeks Sharp Cuts at Already Cash-Strapped Colleges," CHE (February 17, 2015), at www.chronicle.com/article/Louisianas-Governor-Seeks/190077.

[55] Andy Thomason, "La. Governor's Proposed $211-Million Cut for Colleges is Smaller than Feared," CHE (March 2, 2015); Eric Kelderman, "LSU Chancellor Fights Budget Cuts with Candor and Swagger," CHE (May 13, 2015), at www.chronicle.com/article/LSU-Chancellor-Fights-Budget/230109.

[56] Eric Kelderman, "A Grim Budget Picture Means Even More Pain for Louisiana's Colleges," CHE (March 2, 2016), at www.chronicle.com/article/A-Grim-Budget-Picture-Means/235556.

In January 2017, the University of Illinois system entered its second year without funding from the state, as legislators fought with Governor Bruce Rauner, a Republican, over a budget, and the legislature entered a lame-duck session.[57] Local campuses began notifying the public that they had spent their final dollars, and that no relief from Illinois' government was in sight. The budget cut-off affected everything from administrators' ability to travel and perform daily tasks to slashes in enrollments. While the University of Illinois at Urbana-Champaign, the state's flagship campus, enrolled its largest-ever class, officials there worried aloud that it would not be able to operate through the new school year and that stop-gap spending measures made rational planning impossible. Even more significant was the impact on public perception. According to Fernanda Zamudio-Suaréz:

> every missed deadline creates a crisis of confidence among students and parents. Potential and current students are unsure what the stalemate means for their majors, tuition dollars, and grant funding ... And every semester, people are less confident that public colleges in Illinois can survive and cover the shortfall for much longer.

*

In April 2017, New Mexico's governor, Republican Susana Martinez, vetoed all funding for higher education, totaling $745 million, holding the state's colleges and universities hostage to her demand for spending slashes and no new taxes.[58] Even when restored, the 2018 budget would be 8.5 percent smaller than the previous year's and would cover only between 50 percent and 60 percent of total operating expenses. As the state's campus president wrote to the governor:

> The message the veto sent to our 133,505 registered students and their families, while unintended, leaves them confused and wondering whether

---

[57] Fernanda Zamudio-Suaréz, "Awaiting a State Budget, Illinois Colleges Adapt and Hope," CHE (January 6, 2017), at www.chronicle.com/article/Awaiting-a-State-Budget/238821.

[58] Chris Quintana, "The Next Higher-Ed Funding Battle to Watch May Be in New Mexico," CHE (April 19, 2017), at www.chronicle.com/article/The-Next-Higher-Ed-Funding/239826.

they should enroll in a New Mexico college or whether they'll be able to finish their degree and graduate.

Without state funding, tuition – which was $6,950 at the state's flagship – could almost triple to cover the lost revenue. Meanwhile, at state colleges and universities, enrollments dropped from about 153,000 in 2011 to about 133,500 in 2017.

*

Even in New York, a state with a Democratic governor, but with a then-Republican legislature, the cuts following the 2008 financial meltdown continued to impact higher education. In September 2017,[59] Samuel L. Stanley, Jr., president of the Stony Brook campus of the State University of New York, met with the faculty senate to lay out his plans for a $35-million budget cut that would eventually involve tenured faculty terminations and the end of many programs in the humanities, including theater arts, comparative literature, cinema and cultural studies, and graduate degree programs in cultural studies and comparative literature.[60] Disregarding student and faculty demonstrations and harsh criticism from faculty representatives over spending priorities (swimming pools, administrators' salaries), Stanley and his top administrators offered little explanation other than the ending of the state's 2011 challenge-grant program. Stanley spoke in the "not all things to all people" language of corporate decisions and markets:

> I think one thing that we know, that every educational institution knows, is that almost no place can be excellent in all areas. ... We really have to make decisions and set priorities of where we're going to invest. ... What are programs that are high quality, that have high demand from students, or are good and can become great? Those are programs we can be invested in. And there may be other programs we can no longer be

[59] Rebecca Liebson, "President Stanley's Plan to Address $35 Million Deficit Draws Ire of Faculty," *Statesman* (September 13, 2017), at www.sbstatesman.com/2017/09/13/president-stanleys-plan-to-address-35-million-deficit-draws-ire-of-faculty.

[60] Caroline Parker, "Students Respond to Controversial Humanities Cuts," *Statesman* (July 27, 2017), at www.sbstatesman.com/2017/07/27/students-respond-to-controversial-humanities-cuts.

invested in.... It's difficult when one gets down to the areas of teaching, to me, to say that we're going to keep one area and not another area just based purely on content. I think we really have to make decisions based on enrollment, based on scholarly impact. . . . The challenge when you invest in any situation is that you face the possibility that revenue will decline.

But as one faculty representative put it:

I moved my family here from Ohio and the only thing you have to tell me is that I'm not essential to the mission of the university? That I have no role to play, and you have no commitment to me, and your reputation will be fine? That is shameful.

As a graduate student remarked:

For us graduate students, we have already been decimated – psychologically, emotionally, mentally – by a tumultuous pedagogical environment. . . . The pressures of graduate school are immense, but when the institution doesn't support your work, and even actively attempts to eliminate your field of study, it's hard to keep up the fight.

As departments and programs were closed with little notice, faculty – many of them long-tenured – scrambled to find positions in other departments or programs in a situation that resembled the fate of sixteenth-century monks and nuns seeking safe homes away from their own dissolved monasteries.

*

Nowhere has this crisis been more apparent and alarming than in the state of Alaska. Elected governor in November 2018, Republican Michael Dunleavy, a former teacher, principal, and school-district superintendent, made it his number-one priority to slash Alaska's state budget deficit. This stood at $1.6 billion in a state that had refused to raise taxes for years. The governor announced in July 2019 that he would seek $444 million in cuts from the Republican controlled legislature, including $131 million from the state university system, or a 41 percent cut in the system's budget. This was on top of the $135 million in budget cuts that the system has already absorbed over the past five years. The cuts would apply to the 2019–20 school term, which had already begun. The savings accrued from his total budget, he declared, would finance the Alaska State Permanent Fund payout (based on declining natural-resource revenues) from $1,600 to $3,000 a year.[61] Dunleavy described the cuts to higher ed bluntly as "a policy choice."[62] Echoing the mantra of budget cutters in at least a dozen systems throughout the nation, Dunleavy remarked that "We can't continue to be all things for all people," and that the state could "turn the university into a smaller, leaner, but still very positive, productive university in the Northern Hemisphere."[63] He added that Alaska "can no longer afford to continue down the path of oversized spending, outsized government, and out-of-line priorities." The message was clear: higher education was a wasteful drain on public resources and energies.

Despite widespread media coverage and appeals from many constituencies, including the university board of regents, to reconsider the cuts, the legislature only quickened the schedule for the final vote in its special session. Conceding that the governor's cuts could eventually exceed $200 million, on July 22, 2019, the regents voted to implement them.[64] The plan included tuition hikes, program cuts, the possible closing of many satellite campuses that serve both Alaska Natives and other minority groups, and the summary lay-off of many faculty, including the long-tenured. The system began sending furlough notices to all staff members statewide, requiring them to take a specified number of

[61] Katherine Mangan, "'Unprecedented in Our History': One State Is on the Verge of Slashing Higher-Ed Funding, Leaving Public Colleges in a Panic," CHE (July 1, 2019), at www.chronicle.com/article/Unprecedented-in-Our/246596; and Katherine Mangan, "Budget Ax Looms for a University Facing Historic Cuts," CHE (July 8, 2019), at www .chronicle.com/article/Budget-Ax-Looms-for-a/246625.

[62] Cas Mudde, "Alaska's Governor is Trying to Destroy its Universities. The State May Never Recover," *Guardian* (July 6, 2019), at www.theguardian.com/commentisfree/2019/jul/06/mike-dunleavy-alaska-university-system-budget-cuts.

[63] Lindsay Ellis, "This 5-Word Phrase Has Become a Mantra for Slashing College Budgets," CHE (July 3, 2019), at www.chronicle.com/article/This-5-Word-Phrase-Has-Become/246616.

[64] Katherine Mangan, "University of Alaska Regents Vote to Declare Financial Exigency," CHE (July 22, 2019), at www.chronicle.com/article/University-of-Alaska-Regents/246746.

days off without pay. James R. Johnsen, president of the University of Alaska, said that the university would need to cut 1,300 faculty and staff positions systemwide. The move was so sudden and unprecedented, with little or no possibility of preparation or opposition, that it left students, faculty, and supporters in shock and without recourse. Infighting also began among the state's different campuses, with the faculty senate at Anchorage insisting that Fairbanks should shoulder most of the cuts, and well-placed senior faculty arguing for the dissolution of the statewide system into independent – and "competitive" – schools.[65] Cathy Sandeen, chancellor of the University of Alaska at Anchorage, warned that the cuts – which would hit the humanities the hardest – would turn the state system into a "collection of vocational schools." President Johnsen remarked that the cuts "will strike an institutional and reputational blow from which we may likely never recover."[66]

The state system, which already had the lowest college attendance rate in the nation, now saw the possibility of its degree completion rate falling to between 15 percent and 20 percent, with many students either completely dropping out of college or moving to other states to complete their degrees. If the plan materialized, faculty in the humanities would be left with few or no prospects. Simultaneously those in the sciences – especially in the state university's renowned climate-change programs – were being actively courted by other public and private universities. The net result was predicted to be the essential dismantling of higher education in the state in a process that lasted only six months to complete. Organized criticism from higher education – and a misstep by the governor in also planning slashes to benefits for senior citizens – caused widespread resistance to the budget plan. In August 2019, the governor and legislature announced that they had "listened" to the people of

[65] Nick Hazelrigg, "Faculty Fight in the Last Frontier," IHE (July 19, 2019), at www .insidehighered.com/news/2019/07/19/faculty-group-alaskas-anchorage-campus-says-fairbanks-should-bear-brunt-state-cuts.

[66] Mudde, "Alaska's Governor." See also Sheila Liming, "My University is Dying. And Soon Yours Will Be Too," *Chronicle Review*, CHE (Sept. 25, 2019), at www.chronicle.com/ interactives/20190925-my-university-is-dying.

Alaska and revised the planned cuts.[67] Higher education would now face only a $70-million cut, spread over three years, so that the system could plan for what was, nevertheless, a victory of the Republican ideologues in their plans to cut the system's budget. Later in August the board of regents voted to rescind its "exigency" declaration and to endorse the governor's smaller cuts.[68] Governor Dunleavy acknowledged this victory by claiming, "the budget vetoes in many respects got us to where we are today." Those budget cuts, of whatever size, have produced hiring freezes, travel reductions, and other cuts that are widely seen as hindering the system's ability to retain and hire faculty, and to attract students. There have also been fears that the system will now fail to meet its own state's accreditation standards.[69]

CONTINGENCY AND TENURE

These cuts have been felt more keenly – and obviously to the public – in the dwindling number of full professorships and tenured faculty lines across American higher education.[70] On the one hand, we can follow a trend toward the "charismatic" authority and inflated salaries and emoluments of the few superstar faculty, and on the other a trend toward a permanent underclass of "contingent faculty," variously estimated at between 50 percent and 75 percent of all current positions. With no voice or stake in their own curricula, governance or policy, the vast majority of faculty are now stripped of agency to develop professionally and of authority to mould their disciplines and pedagogy. They stand

---

[67] Katherine Mangan, "Amid Backlash, Alaska Governor Relents on Draconian Cuts for University System," CHE (August 13, 2019), at www.chronicle.com/article/Amid-Backlash-Alaska-Governor/246951.

[68] Katherine Mangan, "Alaska Regents Vote to Terminate Exigency Declaration," CHE (Aug. 20, 2019), at www.chronicle.com/article/Alaska-Regents-Vote-to/246980.

[69] Katherine Mangan, "Alaska's Accreditor Issues a Warning to the System," CHE (Sept. 10, 2019), at www.chronicle.com/article/Alaska-s-Accreditor-Issues-a/247256; Katherine Mangan, "Former Alaska Chancellors Express Alarm Over Accreditation Letter," CHE (Oct. 3, 2019), at www.chronicle.com/article/Former-Alaska-Chancellors/247281.

[70] For an overview, see Herb Childress, *The Adjunct Underclass: How America's Colleges Betrayed Their Faculty, Their Students, and Their Mission* (Chicago: University of Chicago Press, 2019).

incapable of defending their institutions from both internal realignment and external attack. The dynamics of this phenomenon are well known to those in higher ed. Some have called the situation the "gig academy."[71]

According to the American Association of University Professors,[72]

> "Contingent" faculty positions include both part- and full-time non-tenure-track appointments. Their common characteristic is that institutions make little or no long-term commitment to faculty holding these positions. Today, more than half of all faculty appointments are part-time. This includes positions that may be classified by the institution as adjuncts, part-time lecturers, or graduate assistantships. Many faculty in so-called "part-time" positions actually teach the equivalent of a full-time course load. Other part-time appointments are held by graduate student employees, whose chances of obtaining tenure-track positions in the future are increasingly uncertain. What is billed as a teaching apprenticeship often instead amounts to years of intensive, low-paid work that distracts from, rather than complementing, graduate studies. To support themselves, part-time faculty often commute between institutions and prepare courses on a grueling timetable, making enormous sacrifices to maintain interaction with their students. Since faculty classified as part-time are typically paid by the course, without benefits, many college teachers lack access to health insurance and retirement plans.

In 1975, according to the US Department of Education, 57 percent of university faculty members were tenured or on the tenure track. By 2007 that number had dropped to 31 percent.[73] Despite predictions of high demand for new PhDs,[74] between 1975 and 2015 the ratio of

---

[71] Adrianna Kezar, Tom DePaola, and Daniel T. Scott, *The Gig Academy: Mapping Labor in the Neoliberal University* (Baltimore: Johns Hopkins University Press, 2019).

[72] American Association of University Professors, "Background Facts on Contingent Faculty Positions [1975–2015]," at www.aaup.org/issues/contingency/background-facts.

[73] Daniel J. Ennis, "The Last of the Tenure Track," *Chronicle Review*, CHE (July 3, 2011), at www.chronicle.com/article/The-Last-of-the-Tenure-Track/128076.

[74] Vimal Patel, "How a Famous Academic Job-Market Study Got It All Wrong – and Why It Still Matters," CHE (Sept. 9, 2018), at www.chronicle.com/article/How-a-Famous-Academic/244458.

tenured to contingent faculty changed from 45 percent–55 percent to 30 percent–70 percent.[75] Department of Education 2017 figures[76] do not distinguish between tenure- and non-tenure track full-time. Its figures showed a total of 1.46 million faculty in public four-year institutions, of which roughly 741,000 were "full-time" and 716,000 were part-time. In private, nonprofit schools the total faculty numbered about 389,000, of which 191,000 were full-time and 198,000 were part-time. By November 2019 that number had readjusted slightly, with 51.5 percent categorized as full-time. But such figures came in the face of falling overall numbers of faculty, especially part-timers, as retrenchments and program cuts continued.[77]

The comparative 2017 figures for two-year colleges were 105,000 to 214,000, and for for-profit, two-year schools 8,200 to 11,600. Again, many full-time faculty were non-tenure track. According to the AAUP, "the percentage of instructional positions that is off the tenure track amounted to 73 percent in 2016, the latest year for which data are available."[78] TIAA, the faculty pension fund, reported data collected by Delta Cost Project from Department of Education data and targeted surveys. This data showed that contingent faculty represented the majority of all faculty positions in sixteen major state flagship institutions.[79] In 2017, over 905,000 faculty in the USA worked without a contract and with no hope of tenure.[80] In many ways this has created a class of free-floating culture workers, akin to the defrocked clergy of the twelfth and the sixteenth centuries, whose role in the broader society we will discuss later in this book.

---

[75] AAUP, "Trends in the Academic Labor Force, 1975–2015," at www.aaup.org/sites/default/files/Academic_Labor_Force_Trends_1975–2015.pdf.

[76] Ginder, Kelly-Reid, and Mann, *Enrollment and Employees*, 15, Table 6.

[77] Doug Lederman, "The Faculty Shrinks, but Tilts to Full-Time," IHE (Nov. 27. 2019), at www.insidehighered.com/news/2019/11/27/federal-data-show-proportion-instructors-who-work-full-time-rising.

[78] www.aaup.org/sites/default/files/2018-19_ARES_Final.pdf.

[79] Steven Hurlburt and Michael McGarrah, "The Shifting Academic Workforce: Where Are the Contingent Faculty?," TIAA-CREF Delta Cost Project (November 2016), at www.air.org/sites/default/files/downloads/report/Shifting-Academic-Workforce-November-2016.pdf, 14.

[80] www.chronicle.com/article/Contract-Lengths-of/246813.

That "contingent" status translates into low pay and lack of benefits. According to the *Chronicle of Higher Education*'s 2019 *Almanac*,[81] collected from faculty responses, the average compensation per course for 78 percent of contingent faculty in 2018 was under $4,000, with some adjuncts at religious-affiliated doctorate institutions being paid as high as $5,800 per course. Fifty-five percent of all adjuncts taught in the humanities, and 74 percent of them taught at a single institution, with an average of 65 percent teaching more than one course. Of these adjuncts 52 percent had attained a master's as their highest degree, and 32 percent held doctorates. Sixty-five percent of adjuncts relying on their academic income made less than $50,000 a year. Data collected by TIAA, however, indicates that in 2013, adjuncts teaching eight courses a year were earning a total average of $21,000.[82] According to the AAUP, on average women were paid 81.6 percent of the totals paid to men during academic year 2018–19.[83] In January 2014, the US House of Representatives published a report indicating that the majority of contingent faculty lived below the official US poverty line.[84] In 2015, one quarter of adjuncts relied on public assistance programs. Some had turned to sex work and sleeping in their cars.[85]

Statistics for contingent faculty by discipline are harder to come by. While a new report is nearing completion, the most recent figures from the Humanities Indicators Project of the American Academy of Arts and Sciences are from 2013–14.[86] After a modest rebound after the Great Recession,

---

[81] www.chronicle.com/article/Characteristics-of-Adjunct/246655.

[82] Hurlburt and McGarrah, *The Shifting Academic Workforce*, 5.

[83] American Association of University Professors, www.aaup.org/2018-19-faculty-compensation-survey-results.

[84] Elizabeth Segran, "The Adjunct Revolt: How Poor Professors Are Fighting Back," *Atlantic* (April 28, 2014), at www.theatlantic.com/business/archive/2014/04/the-adjunct-professor-crisis/361336.

[85] Alastair Gee, "Facing Poverty, Academics Turn to Sex Work and Sleeping in Cars," *Guardian* (Sept. 28, 2017), at www.theguardian.com/us-news/2017/sep/28/adjunct-professors-homeless-sex-work-academia-poverty; using statistics from UC Berkeley Labor Center, "The High Public Cost of Low Wages," at http://laborcenter.berkeley.edu/pdf/2015/the-high-public-cost-of-low-wages.pdf, 3.

[86] American Academy of Arts and Science, "Trends in the Demographics of Humanities Faculty: Key Findings from the 2012–13 Humanities Departmental Survey," at www.humanitiesindicators.org.

less than half of the faculty members were employed off the tenure track, but the percentages ranged from 19% of the faculty in history of science programs (which tended to be situated in specialized doctoral-level programs at research universities) to about 50% of the faculty in the communication discipline.

The percentage of non-tenure-track faculty of all status in the humanities ranged from about 55 percent in communications, languages and literatures, and English; through about 30 percent in history, art history, and religion; to about 20 percent in the history of science. These figures include upper-level undergraduate and graduate courses, however. The percentage of introductory courses taught to undergraduates across these disciplines was slightly larger in almost all cases; and it is here – on the typical "college" level – that students, parents, and the interested public garner their perceptions of the quality of instruction their dollars are buying. Recent trends appear to point to an even larger proportion of courses being taught by contingent and non-tenure-track faculty.

In addition to this rising inequality of outcome on the jobs side, academe also incorporates inequality in the production of Ph.D.s. A study published in 2015 found that the creation of future tenured faculty is disproportionately skewed toward elite schools:

> a new study published in *Science Advances* ... scrutinized more than 16,000 faculty members in the fields of business, computer science, and history at 242 schools. [Clauset] and his colleagues found, as the paper puts it, a "steeply hierarchical structure that reflects profound social inequality." The data revealed that just a quarter of all universities account for 71 to 86 percent of all tenure-track faculty in the U.S. and Canada in these three fields. Just 18 elite universities produce half of all computer science professors, 16 schools produce half of all business professors, and eight schools account for half of all history professors ... in history, the top 10 schools produce three times as many future professors as those ranked 11 through 20. .... It's not just young scholars who suffer under the current hiring hierarchy; innovation across all disciplines may be stifled. Because graduates from only a small number of universities account for the majority of faculty jobs, new ideas and discoveries from those elite institutions may be far more likely to gain traction in academia and in

the wider world than those from outside this group. (Not to mention that bad ideas coming out of this core group of schools may get more attention than they deserve.)[87]

Such numbers are unconsciously or not translated into the accepted wisdom of academe. At an ACLS annual meeting in the early 2000s, a distinguished senior professor, delegate of one of the nearly seventy-five ACLS learned societies present, declared to the assembly, "I know of no tenured faculty member in my field who does not deserve to be so. And I know of no one who does not have a tenured position who does deserve to have one." No one in the room raised an objection.[88]

*

Again, faculty are the most visible aspect of higher education for the public; and the quality of teaching, faculty engagement with students, and students' overall satisfaction are major elements in the public's attitudes toward college financing and independence from political interference. Even with the best efforts of contingent faculty, engagement with students on any level is difficult. Most adjuncts must contend with constrained schedules, lack of office hours or even offices, of regular connections with their colleagues or department, of support networks, and of access to campus services. With little guarantee of continuity or of permanent employment for contingent faculty, a sense of ad hoc, and often distracted, teaching is often the norm in many departments. Students find it difficult to develop trust in, or attribute authority to, individual teachers, who might be gone at the end of the semester. As early as the 1960s, this had translated into what many critics characterized as the faceless factory of higher education.[89] According to TIAA, colleges and universities with higher shares of students at risk of non-completion also have higher shares of contingent faculty,

---

[87] Joel Warner and Aaron Clauset, "The Academy's Dirty Secret," *Slate* (Feb. 23, 2015), at https://slate.com/human-interest/2015/02/university-hiring-if-you-didn-t-get-your-ph-d-at-an-elite-university-good-luck-finding-an-academic-job.html.

[88] Author's eyewitness account.   [89] See Chapter 3, 72.

particularly among private four-year and public two-year institutions.[90] As Aaron Hanlon succinctly put it:

> A professor who's forced to leave after one semester or one year can't be there to write recommendation letters, advise students on the job market, or just listen to what students have on their minds. Every student and parent needs to know this.[91]

FACULTY LAYOFFS AND TERMINATIONS

Reports of full-time positions being canceled and of tenured and non-tenured faculty alike being bought off or terminated continue to multiply. Examples could be drawn from any number of schools. In 2017 the University of Oregon began terminating non-tenure and contingent faculty positions in order to close a "$8.8-million budget shortfall in 2017–18 because of increasing salaries and retirement benefits" for tenured faculty and administrators.[92] By 2013, as it was preparing to make millions of dollars in payouts to cover legal settlements with victims of its teams' sexual harassment,[93] Penn State crossed the threshold of having more than 50 percent of its faculty as non-tenure track.[94] In April 2017, Wayne State University began a process of amending guidelines to enable administrators to strip tenure from "unproductive" senior faculty.[95] Although the cases involved the medical school, faculty representatives called it a breach of previous collective-bargaining agreements and a serious threat to all tenure. The school's president cited his motives as an

---

[90] Hurlburt and McGarrah, *The Shifting Academic Workforce*, 19, Fig. 8.

[91] Aaron Hanlon, "The University Is a Ticking Time Bomb: Treating Nearly 75 percent of the Professoriate as Disposable is Not Sustainable," *Chronicle Review*, CHE (April 16, 2019), at www.chronicle.com/article/The-University-Is-a-Ticking/246119.

[92] Lindsay McKenzie, "75 Non-tenure Jobs to Be Cut at U. of Oregon, Faculty Union Says," CHE (Feb. 28, 2017).

[93] See Chapter 5, 101–2.

[94] Nell Gluckman, "Universities Take Steps to Improve Working Conditions for Adjuncts," CHE (April 5, 2017), at www.chronicle.com/article/Universities-Take-Steps-to/239693.

[95] Sarah Brown, "Wayne State's Move to Strip 5 Professors of Tenure Sparks Unease about a Broader Threat," CHE (April 3, 2017), at www.chronicle.com/article/Wayne-State-s-Move-to-Strip/239678.

attempt to stave off adverse criticism from politicians and the public. In July 2017, Loyola University in New Orleans announced the elimination of sixty tenured faculty positions (thirty-nine faculty and staff buyouts, twenty-one positions unfilled). Despite higher enrollments and student retention rates, a university spokeswoman stated that "some cost efficiencies must be derived from changing our processes and structure" to close a budget gap of $25 million.[96]

In a closed-door meeting in June 2017, citing a "financial emergency," Mills College's board of trustees voted – over the objections of faculty – to close down five of eighteen departments and to lay off full-time tenured faculty.[97] In September 2017, SUNY at Stony Brook announced the elimination of non-tenure-track and some tenured faculty for what it claimed were budgetary reasons. The cuts were largely in the humanities. Meanwhile, the school opened up new tenure-track and tenured lines in the natural sciences.[98] In July 2017, the American Bar Association recommended the reduction of full-time, tenured faculty at its member law schools, a move opposed by the American Association of University Professors.[99] In October 2017, the University of Arkansas' board of trustees moved to change the terms under which tenured faculty might be fired, including such arbitrary norms as a "pattern of disruptive conduct or unwillingness to work productively with colleagues" and "fitness to serve the university."[100] In May 2018,

---

[96] Jessica Williams, "Loyola University to Cut 60 positions, Despite Expected Enrollment Boost this Fall," *New Orleans Advocate* (July 7, 2017), at www.nola.com/news/education/article_4a4f2686-a8ee-5512-bf15-3b29fe8aba4f.html.

[97] Hank Reichman, "Mills College Lays Off Five Tenured Professors," *AAUP Academe Blog* (July 4, 2017), at https://academeblog.org/2017/07/04/mills-college-lays-off-five-tenured-profesors.

[98] Colleen Flaherty, "Losing Tenure Bids to a Budget," IHE (September 21, 2017), at www.insidehighered.com/news/2017/09/21/stony-brook-professors-worry-budget-being-balanced-backs-junior-faculty-humanities; Colleen Flaherty, "Narrowing the Terms of Tenure," IHE (Dec. 13, 2017), at www.insidehighered.com/news/2017/12/13/university-arkansas-professors-want-stall-vote-changes-they-say-would-upend-tenure.

[99] Nick Roll, "Debating the Value of Full-Time Professors," IHE (July 14, 2017), at www.insidehighered.com/news/2017/07/14/american-bar-association-receives-pushback-tenure-proposal#.XW4ewM7W29g.link.

[100] Audrey Williams June, "U. of Arkansas System Considers Changes to Ease Tenured-Faculty Firings," CHE (Oct. 26. 2017), at www.chronicle.com/article/U-of-Arkansas-System/241571.

Catholic University's board of trustees, on the approval by a thirty-five to eight faculty senate vote, moved to give administrators authority to eliminate tenured positions to ease a \$3.5 million budget gap.[101] In September 2019, Marquette University announced that it was eliminating seventy-three staff positions (2.5 percent of total faculty and staff) either through terminations or leaving positions unfilled. President Michael Lovell noted that "the goal was to determine proactive solutions to remain financially strong, realizing we cannot continue to increase tuition at our recent pace because the burden is too great for our students and their families."[102] Dozens of other examples can be adduced, and we will return to issues of faculty layoffs and terminations in chapters 8 and 9.

*

More and more colleges and universities are terminating full-time and tenured faculty and hiring more contingent faculty. The majority of college administrators assert that this is for budgetary reasons. Where then are the generated savings being applied? Some analysis points less to the standard reasoning of economic "supply and demand" or budgetary explanations and more toward a consistent devaluation of the Ph.D. and the professional status of faculty itself, staffing increasing numbers of teaching posts with non-Ph.D.s.[103] The ultimate causes for such devaluations, however, remain "budgetary" in the board sense of higher education's priorities and power relationships: less money on faculty salaries, more on administration, facilities, and sports.

While sources from within academe could trace the year-by-year, discipline-by-discipline changes with some sangfroid, the world outside

[101] Jack Stripling, "Catholic U. Plan, Which Could Result in Layoffs of Tenured Profs, Moves Ahead," CHE (May 16, 2018), at www.chronicle.com/article/Catholic-U-Plan-Which-Could/243430.

[102] Devi Shastri, "Marquette University Announces 2.5% Staffing Cut Amid Demographic Changes," *Milwaukee Journal Sentinel* (Sept. 6, 2019), at https://eu.jsonline.com/story/news/education/2019/09/05/marquette-lays-off-24-faculty-and-staff-leaves-50-positions-unfilled/2225523001.

[103] Trevor Griffey, "The Decline of Faculty Tenure: Less from an Oversupply of PhDs, and More from the Systematic De-Valuation of the PhD as a Credential for College Teaching," *Labor Online* (Jan. 9, 2017), at www.lawcha.org/2017/01/09/decline-faculty-tenure-less-oversupply-phds-systematic-de-valuation-phd-credential-college-teaching.

higher ed was less sanguine and more willing to break down academe's wall of separateness. As early as 2009, noting what it reported as a shift in full-time faculty from 75 percent in 1960 to 27 percent in 2009, the *New York Times* was advising parents and students to examine the proportion of adjuncts to full-time and tenured faculty when selecting a college.[104] In May 2015, *Forbes Magazine* summarized the situation: "nearly three-quarters of American professors are contingent faculty. That's a problem for students."[105] *Forbes'* topic headers included "Rising Tuition and Falling Job Security," "Poor Teaching Conditions," "Effects on Student Outcomes (The Results Show)," "Diminished Future Prospects," before pointing readers to the *Chronicle of Higher Ed's* Adjunct Project to search salaries by college and system and advising readers that the American Federation of Teachers (AFT) provides a useful set of questions to ask of any school in which students and parents might be interested.

By June 2018, contingent faculty at over sixty schools had begun union organizing, largely with the Service Employees International Union (SEIU), the United Auto Workers, the AFT, and with Unite Here.[106] By that time, over 20 percent of postsecondary teachers had been unionized, according to Hunter College's National Center for the Study of Collective Bargaining in Higher Education and the Professions. Graduate student workers from at least fourteen different institutions had also voted to unionize. Some schools, like Penn and the University of Delaware, had actively taken steps to improve the professional status and salaries of contingent faculty. But many more schools faced labor actions as adjuncts began unionization drives only to be met with what one commentator has called "Trumpist opposition by university administrators" to avoid collective bargaining.[107] Administration opposition to

---

[104] Samantha Stainburn, "The Case of the Vanishing Full-Time Professor," *New York Times* (Dec. 30, 2009), at www.nytimes.com/2010/01/03/education/edlife/03strategy-t.html.

[105] Dan Edmonds, "More than Half of College Faculty Are Adjuncts: Should You Care?," *Forbes* (May 28, 2015), at www.forbes.com/sites/noodleeducation/2015/05/28/more-than-half-of-college-faculty-are-adjuncts-should-you-care.

[106] Kristen Edwards and Kim Tolley, "Do Unions Help Adjuncts? What Dozens of Collective-Bargaining Agreements Can Tell Us," CHE (June 3, 2018), at www.chronicle.com/article/Do-Unions-Help-Adjuncts-/243566.

[107] Segran, "The Adjunct Revolt."

unions was strong at many of the nation's top schools, including Harvard, UC Santa Cruz, Columbia, Yale, Boston College, the University of Chicago, Fordham, and Loyola of Chicago.[108] In every case where unionization has succeeded, however, adjunct faculty have gained salary and benefit increases, often as high as 68 percent, for their contract periods. They have also won increased job security, collegial benefits and support, and a role in shared governance.

Meanwhile the Trump administration had begun intervening to halt the spread of faculty and graduate student unionization. In September 2019 the National Labor Relations Board (NLRB) proposed a new regulation that would forbid graduate students at private colleges and universities from forming unions, a move that would also usurp Congress' power to alter the NLRB's enabling legislation.[109] Despite some successes, opposition grows difficult. The SUNY Stony Brook's graduate student's "hard to keep up the fight" might well be words spoken by a powerful abbot or a young monk in 1535. So too might be the words of one UNC law professor in the face of North Carolina's Republican budget- and program-slashing agenda,

> It's a right-wing Republican-controlled operation at this point, and no one
> can really stand in their way. But we're going to continue to speak out.
> I feel I've got no choice when things like this are happening.[110]

So too the response of the University of Michigan's then-president when faced with the reality of the state's abandoning its commitment to higher ed: "Of course I worry, but you know that old saying? You play with the hand you're dealt and move forward."[111] As often as not, budget wars and constraints have turned out to be less about real financial needs

[108] Andrew Goldstone, "The Uncounted: Jobs and Graduates" (Nov. 25, 2017), at https://andrewgoldstone.com/blog/job-market2017.

[109] Vimal Patel, "Grad Students at Private Colleges Could Lose the Right to Unionize," CHE (Sept. 20, 2019), at www.chronicle.com/article/Grad-Students-at-Private/247196; "US Seeks to Bar Graduate Students at Private Universities Who Get Paid for Work from Unionizing," *Physicsworld* (Sept. 27, 2019), at https://physicsworld.com/a/us-seeks-to-bar-graduate-students-at-private-universities-who-get-paid-for-work-from-unionizing.

[110] Carpenter, "Right-Wing Political Machine."

[111] Fischer and Stripling, "An Era of Neglect," at www.chronicle.com/article/An-Era-of-Neglect/145045.

on the part of colleges and universities and more about priorities – in instruction, disciplines, governance, and response to pressure from politicians and legislators, the donor class, media critics, and the public. What impact do these struggles have on higher ed's triad of authority, separateness, and innovation? We will examine some of these issues in subsequent chapters.

* * *

CHAPTER 7

The Scandals of Academe

INTRODUCTION

U NDERMINING HIGHER EDUCATION'S CLAIMS TO BOTH intellectual and civic authority – and breaking down its walls of separation from society at large – is a continuous narrative developed during the Culture Wars of the 1980s and 1990s of an academia awash in scandals. This narrative builds on a long tradition of real internal scandals of collegiate life and of American anti-intellectualism. These "scandals" have included athletic departments' overspending, overreach, and budgetary bloat; sexual politics, rape culture and faculty-student liaisons; political correctness, inhibition of free speech, and trigger warnings; and active and reverse discrimination. Changes in disciplinary approaches and curricula that are the necessary and natural result of intense research and innovation in the humanities deemphasize or actively challenge structures of dominance and hegemony that are narrated as "traditional values." Such decentering of outmoded curricula and approaches in turn give rise to the decades-old accusations of a left-leaning and disloyal academia. Isolated incidents, individual pronouncements, and mistaken administrative actions have joined verifiable trends in government regulation and campus codes.

Critics and commentators have pointed out that there loom far larger and more important scandals. These include the rising student debt discussed in Chapter 6, dropping rates of degree completion, continuing marginalization of women, people of color, and LGBTQ communities, and a widening gap between elite students attending elite schools and the rest of American society, who must increasingly fend for themselves even at public institutions. Since the theme of this book is an emerging narrative aimed against higher ed, this chapter will attempt to focus not on the justice or injustice, the truth or falsity of charges but on how such news has affected public discourse on the place of higher education, on parents' approaches toward their emotional and financial investment in their children's education, and on the use of such narratives by critics of higher education.[1] We cannot here discuss every controversy within the academy. Many of these are normal and professional debates about governance, pedagogy, and subject matter that concern relatively small numbers of specialists and interested parties. Our concern is with issues that spill over into the public forum or that come from public debates and are turned onto the academy.

Such issues have also attracted critics among alums – many with powerful financial and political clout – who view their alma mater both nostalgically as maintaining the cultural and social values of their youth and in terms of advancing their current vested interests. Alums have thus intervened in debates over curricula and canon, gender, free speech, and personal-safety issues. From the opposite perspective, faculty and student movements for greater transparency and justice have raised these issues before the public to new levels where challenge and change have become part of university life, altering institutional attitudes and administrative approaches. These challenges and changes have also been seized upon by American critics of higher education. To be sure, attention to scandals does demonstrate the continued importance of higher education in American society. Nevertheless, colleges and universities are seen less as a focus of authority than as a marketplace in which all sectors have their say, breaking down the separation and authority of the university and turning it into one more arena in the continued civil war of words, attitudes, and ideas currently dividing American society.

---

[1] Recent polemical summaries of such coverage include Sophia A. McClennen, "Enough with the Blue-baiting: The Biggest Threat on Campus Has Nothing to Do With Free Speech," *Salon* (Sept. 2, 2017), at www.salon.com/2017/09/02/enough-with-the-blue-baiting-the-biggest-threat-on-campus-has-nothing-to-do-with-free-speech; and Karin Fischer, "For a Dissatisfied Public, Colleges' Internal Affairs Become Fair Game," CHE (Feb. 18, 2019), at www.chronicle.com/interactives/Trend19-Intrusion-Main.

Second only to the high costs of higher education in the survey results discussed in Chapter 4 has been the issue of "what is taught and how." As we have seen, Democrats were moderately concerned about this issue.[2] But a growing majority of Republicans are opposed to current trends. Like the budgetary crisis covered in Chapter 6, the issues of curricula and methods have helped shape a growing public perception that the university was losing its moral center, focus, and authority. "What is taught" and how not only includes major differences in fields – humanities vs STEM or business for example – but most especially the subject matter and pedagogical approaches of certain humanities disciplines, especially in literature, cultural studies, and languages. Critics from the right wing also focus frequently on history curricula and new developments in the disciplines that include the sources and narratives of people of color, of the poor and marginalized that are perceived as challenging and negating a narrative of white exclusivity and triumphalism considered normative.

Second to the intellectual content of what is being taught, but often far more publicized and important to parents and students alike, are the gender issues around college life. What was once seen as "collegiate" life has become in the 2020s a contentious area of sexual difference, variation, and danger for many students: rape culture, sexual predation by faculty, coaches, and male athletes. The case studies presented below will trace the consistent presentation and mis-representation of this narrative in the pages of the *Chronicle of Higher Education, Inside Higher Education,* the *New York Times,* the *Atlantic,* the *New Republic,* Fox News, the *New York Post,* and other media.

*

According to the *Oxford Dictionaries,* a scandal is "an action or event regarded as morally or legally wrong and causing general public outrage." "Scandals" are nothing new to American academe and have long been part of Americans' deep respect for, and fascination with, college life. The public nature of academia's foibles is, ironically, part and parcel

---

[2] See Chapter 4, 91.

of its authority and separateness. As American society changed, so too did the nature of these scandals. As early as the 1740s, Harvard and Yale were scandalized by their undergraduates' attraction to the preachings of George Whitefield, the Great Awakener. Accusations, inquiries, condemnations, and expulsions followed as the colleges grappled with deviations from their core missions and beliefs.[3] The scandals were largely confined to the colleges themselves. But their impact was also public, given the intimate size of the communities that hosted them, the public aspect of much of early university governance in the colonies, and the colleges' role in bolstering religious and social authority. The pattern of academic scandals varied considerably over the history of American higher education. The colonial and early republican period thought of scandal in terms of belief and teaching. We have already briefly surveyed the strains of nineteenth-century anti-intellectualism and populism deeply ingrained in American society that cast higher education as frivolous or corrupting.[4] For elite critics of the early twentieth century, foibles included a lack of clear intellectual message, too strong a reliance on secondary-school curricula, or news of resignations among highly placed university officials.

As the twentieth century unfolded, "collegiate" life became one of America's core fascinations, and its relaxed and elite style a key element of new fashions.[5] Photojournalism, literature, theater, film, and radio brought various aspects of college life alive for a public eager to participate, if only vicariously. Americans might not have had need for or access to higher education, but its rarified atmosphere made it an object of both great respect and wary scrutiny. While the media focused on star athletes and their foibles from the 1920s through the end of the 1930s, reformers inside and outside academe addressed what they saw as the abuses of general college life: an over-reliance on leisure activities, on cliques, racial, gender, and class exclusion, many exemplified in "frat" culture. Their reforms included everything from curriculum changes, to new architecture, to inclusionary admissions policies. By the late 1940s and 1950s, the American obsession with Communist infiltration also targeted the nation's campuses; and scandals left the realm of lifestyle

---

[3] Hofstadter & Smith, I:62–82.   [4] Chapter 2, 45–49   [5] See Thelin, 155–259.

and learning to concentrate once again on beliefs and political loyalties. These scandals involved all segments of American society as campuses were scrutinized for unorthodox beliefs, curricula, and individual acts by members of Congress, state legislatures, and university administrations. In 1962, Nevitt Sanford and his colleagues released a report revealing widespread student discontent with campus life and bureaucratic indifference.[6] In chapters 2 and 3, we detailed the events of the late 1960s and the trauma that these produced both on university and college campuses and across all segments of American society. Chapter 5 has already examined the scandals affecting college administration and boards of directors, budgets, and spending priorities. What then are our contemporary "scandals of academia"?

ADMISSIONS

We should begin our detailed examination at the front door of higher education: in the scandals surrounding admissions policies, most especially at elite colleges and universities. In March 2019, US Federal prosecutors filed charges against dozens of elite figures including coaches, celebrities, admissions officers, and others. The admissions scandal involved up to $25 million in bribes to extend favorable treatment to forty-five children of wealthy – and prominent – American families to enroll these children under largely falsified athletic scholarships. The Federal investigation was named Operation Varsity Blues. The scandal involved eight schools, including Stanford, Yale, the University of Southern California, Georgetown, UCLA, Wake Forest, UT Austin, and the University of San Diego.[7] The investigations were widely reported across major media outlets, including CBS News, NBC News, CNN, *USA Today*, Associated Press, *ProPublica Illinois*, *People*, the *Wall Street Journal*, the *New York Times*, *Business Insider*, the *New York Post*, Fox News,

---

[6] Nevitt Sanford, *The American College: A Psychological and Social Interpretation of the Higher Learning* (New York: John Wiley).

[7] Sarah Brown, "8 Universities. Millions in Bribes. 10 Corrupt Coaches. What You Need to Know About the Admissions-Bribery Scandal," CHE (March 12, 2019), at www.chronicle.com/article/8-Universities-Millions-in/245873.

Bloomberg, Newsweek, the *Atlantic, Sports Illustrated,* the *Washington Post,* and others.[8] The *Los Angeles Times* reported in March 2019 that UCLA knew the details of the scandal in the making as early as its confidential report of 2014.[9]

Most reporting on the scandals focused less on the role of athletic directors and coaches, since it is common knowledge that they influence admissions. For example, according to a court affidavit, Georgetown gives its coaches about 158 admissions slots a year to fill as they like, regardless of academic or other qualifications.[10] More important for the press was what the scandal revealed about growing inequality in American educational opportunity.[11] In absolute numbers at the eight private universities involved in the scandal, more students came from the top 1 percent than from the bottom 40 percent of the US income scale. At Wake Forest, for example, 22 percent came from the top 1 percent ($630K+/year); 8 percent came from the bottom 40 percent (less than $38K/year). At the other end of the scale, at UCLA, 4 percent came from the top 1 percent and 19 percent from the bottom 40 percent. Overall, however, those in the top 20 percent of the income range (over $110K/year) accounted for an average of 64 percent of total enrollment, ranging from 72 percent at Wake Forest to 48 percent at UCLA. Those in the bottom 40 percent averaged about 11 percent. These are the kinds of schools where undergrads drink $100 bottles of "house wine." "If you walk around campus, you're most likely to get knocked down by a Range Rover or a high-end Audi," one faculty member noted.

---

[8] See, for example, https://en.wikipedia.org/wiki/2019_college_admissions_bribery_scandal.

[9] Nathan Fenno, "UCLA Knew of a Cash-for-Admissions Deal, Years before the Scandal" (April 12, 2019), at www.latimes.com/sports/la-sp-ucla-college-admissions-track-athlete-20190412-story.html; Jack Stripling, "The Origins of an Admissions-Bribery Mastermind Are Buried in a Confidential Report," CHE (May 29, 2019), at www.chronicle.com/article/The-Origins-of-an/246396.

[10] Andy Thomason, "In Bribery Scheme, Coaches Sold Their 'Admissions Slots' to Nonathletes. Wait, Coaches Influence Admissions?," CHE (March 13, 2019), at www.chronicle.com/article/In-Bribery-Scheme-Coaches/245891.

[11] Nell Gluckman, "How the Wealthy and Well Connected Have Learned to Game the Admissions Process," CHE (Aug. 2, 2019), at www.chronicle.com/article/How-the-WealthyWell/246872.

As Anthony P. Carnevale, a labor economist at Georgetown observed, "The thing people are getting mad about is that the meritocracy looks like it's locked in, so it's an aristocracy." "The whole system is a pay-for-play system," says Joseph A. Soares, a Wake Forest sociology professor who researches family income in admissions. "But that's America."[12]

Reactions and news analysis have varied widely. Within the academy, faculty at Yale and USC emphasized how the scandal highlighted the increasing lack of joint governance and called for a renewed role of faculty in the admissions process.[13] In March 2019, students filed suits against Stanford and the other schools involved in the scandal, citing an admissions system "warped and rigged by fraud."[14] Students at Tulane and Rutgers filed similar suits. In the US Senate both Democrats and Republicans introduced legislation calling for reform, including fines on colleges and universities that have the smallest proportion of low-income students.[15] Senator Elizabeth Warren called the scandal "just one more example of how the rich and powerful know how to take care of their own."[16]

---

[12] Jack Stripling, "'It's an Aristocracy': What the Admissions-Bribery Scandal Has Exposed About Class on Campus," CHE (April 17, 2019), at www.chronicle.com/article/It-s-an-Aristocracy-/246131; Tom Bartlett, "What the Admissions Scandal Reveals About Secrecy, Privilege, and the Nature of Merit," *Chronicle Review*, CHE (March 15, 2019), at www.chronicle.com/article/What-the-Admissions-Scandal/245901; Jerome Karabel, *The Chosen: The Hidden History of Admission and Exclusion at Harvard, Yale, and Princeton* (Boston: Houghton Mifflin, 2005).

[13] Wesley Jenkins, "The Bribery Scandal Revealed Holes in Admissions Oversight. Now Some Professors Want to Take Back That Role," CHE (Sept. 10, 2019), at www.chronicle.com/article/The-Bribery-Scandal-Revealed/247103.

[14] The text of the suit can be found in Lindsay Ellis, "Stanford Students Sue Elite Universities After Admissions Scandal," CHE (March 14, 2019), at www.chronicle.com/article/Stanford-Students-Sue-Elite/245896.

[15] Michelle Hackman, "College-Admission Scandal Draws Scrutiny in Washington," *Wall Street Journal* (March 15, 2019), at www.wsj.com/articles/college-admission-scandal-draws-scrutiny-in-washington-11552654841.

[16] Aaron Katersky, "Ringleader Pleads Guilty in $25 Million Nationwide College Admissions Cheating Scam," *ABC News* (March 12, 2019), at https://abcnews.go.com/US/hollywood-actors-ceos-charged-nationwide-college-admissions-cheating/story?id=61627873.

The reporting had its immediate effects on public opinion. In a September 2019 survey on higher education conducted by New America,[17] one major section was devoted to issues of college admissions:

> Americans want admissions at elite colleges and universities to change. In general, Americans do not like any admission preference that considers legacy status (63 percent opposed), athletic recruitment (57 percent opposed), or race/ethnicity (74 percent opposed).[18]

Of those responding to these questions, 62 percent of Democrats, 69 percent of Republicans, and 55 percent of Independents were opposed to legacy preferences.[19] Opposition to athletic preferences ranged from 54 percent for Democrats, 61 percent for Republicans, and 55 percent for Independents. As comparative data on New America's samplings, on the issue of affirmative action by race and ethnicity, 61 percent of Democrats polled by New America opposed special treatment, as did 89 percent of Republicans and 78 percent of Independents.

ATHLETICS

Athletics have been part of the education of "gentlemen" since antiquity. They were an essential element of the training and education of the chivalrous knight in the Middle Ages and of the courtier in the Italian Renaissance, and from such treatises as Castiglione's *Book of the Courtier* they entered the formal curriculum of English public schools and universities. The playing field was as essential to the education of a ruling class as was the classroom, and in many instances it gained far more attention and prestige. The Duke of Wellington probably did not say that "the battle of Waterloo was won on the playing-fields of Eton," but the sentiment expressed summed up the British elite's attitude toward the role of athletics in creating leaders.

From the first, American colleges made room for various forms of athletic activity. From the time of the University of Virginia's founding, a

[17] www.newamerica.org/education-policy/reports/varying-degrees-2019/findings.
[18] www.newamerica.org/education-policy/reports/varying-degrees-2019/executive-summary.
[19] www.newamerica.org/education-policy/reports/varying-degrees-2019/findings.

student culture that focused on leisure pursuits, including physical and athletic activities, existed almost parallel to and independent of academic life. The "honor" code of that campus remained by and large an extension of the old aristocratic ethic. "Campus life" focused less on subjects taught and increasingly on student organizations, of which teams were an integral part of the education of the "gentleman scholar." Such activities distinguished a college elite from those who needed to attend in order to develop skills for social mobility or professional advancement. By the 1870s memoirs and other descriptions of campus life emphasized the centrality of sports and other extracurricular activities in defining the collegiate experience.

By 1900 this extracurricular activity had come to include a standardized set of physical symbols: school colors, mascots, rings, school songs and anthems, athletic uniforms, varsity teams in every popular sport, and the fraternities and sororities that fed into them.[20] These activities drew participation from across the campus and followed regular annual rhythms and schedules that helped define the school both internally and to an increasingly fascinated American public. "Homecoming" became a central ritual both for the college and its alums and for an avid external audience who consumed magazine articles and photo spreads, novels, plays, and movies about the campus and its sporting life. Intercollegiate sports quickly became the chief focus of American interest in higher ed. The Harvard–Yale crew competitions, the Army–Navy or Princeton–Yale football games gained nationwide attention and could even commandeer large municipal stadiums like the Polo Grounds in New York.

By 1910 what had started out as student-run and managed intercollegiate sports had grown into professional organizations, with their own coaches, staffs, medical personnel, and publicity agents. These quickly developed independent structures from the rest of the college and university administration, since athletic directors were from the first paid by student organizations and then substantially funded by alum associations. The strength of these alliances made them impregnable to faculty and administration attempts at control and reform. From the 1890s the

---

[20] See Thelin, 159–62, 177–80, 208–11, 374–77 et passim.

theory that athletics drew alum attention and hence financial support to the university was used to bolster this independence and to lay the rationale for ever-increasing athletic program budgets. Coaches at schools like Yale and Chicago began drawing down salaries that far exceeded those of most faculty and administrators. They enhanced their positions and those of their teams and programs by contracting with Madison Avenue advertising agencies to bolster the appeal and raise the profile of their teams on the national level. Harvard, Princeton, and Yale became synonymous not with academic programs but with their "All American" teams; and they used this prestige to insure their independence from university control.

Between 1900 and 1925 American campuses saw a frenzy of stadium construction. The size and capacity of stadiums at UC Berkeley, Minnesota, Harvard, or Illinois matched that of ancient Rome's stadiums. By 1929 Harvard–Yale, Michigan–Ohio State, Stanford–UC, Texas–Texas A&M and USC–Notre Dame football games were drawing in excess of 100,000 fans from both the schools and the general public. Track and field and other sports also attracted admiring national audiences. By 1937, *Life Magazine* could report that intercollegiate football alone drew 20 million people into stadiums nationwide and brought in earnings of $30 million ($360 million in 2000 dollars). With independence, prestige, and vast new earnings, collegiate sports were also steeped in scandal. In 1929, the Carnegie Foundation issued a scathing report on abuses in collegiate sports that made headlines in papers across the nation. The foundation recommended that universities take back control over their varsity teams, but local and national businesses encouraged the independence and commercialization of these teams and made reform almost impossible. Even after the Great Crash of 1929 and the ensuing Great Depression of the 1930s, university boards of trustees continued to funnel badly needed funds away from academic programs and faculty salaries into stadiums and teams.

News and discussion of scandals were not restricted to educators or legislators but included many segments of the American public from the Carnegie Foundation to the daily press. Hollywood glamorized football heroes like Notre Dame player and coach Knute Rockne (in the 1940 film "Knute Rockne, All American," in which a young Ronald

Reagan had a leading role as star player George Gipp, the "Gipper"). But it could also produce the scathing satire of the Marx Brothers in the 1932 film "Horse Feathers," in which the new president of Huxley College, Quincy Adams Wagstaff (played by Groucho) actively courts and condones professional football players posing as college athletes. Both reflect a spectrum of genres in different media that delighted in campus life and magnified its scandals across America.

These trends continued throughout the 1940s and into the 1950s, despite the temporary decline in personnel and shifts in priorities caused by World War II. By the late 1950s, collegiate sports were an essential part of the return to normalcy of American life, as sports pageants and team competitions marked the seasons for many American households. Attendance at, and viewing televised programs from, the Rose Bowl, the Sugar Bowl, and Orange Bowl, among others, became favorite ritual activities during the holiday season. Even in the face of occasional scandal, Americans continued to support intercollegiate sports – as they continued to support higher education in general – throughout the post-war era and into the 1970s and 1980s. This support may, in fact, have remained steady not because of, but in spite of, the general American disillusionment with the university in the wake of the 1960s. Ironically, as Americans began to view faculty and their curricula with suspicion, collegiate sports remained the bedrock of their view of Americanness. Both alum loyalty and commercial interests maintained this idealized view into the new millennium. It was, after all, campus athletes who had confronted protestors at Columbia, Cornell, and other schools. It was athletes who continued to draw happy memories from alums and bring them back to campuses. It was athletes who most resembled the mythic virtues of authority, military uniformity, and victory; and it was athletes who were most effective in the endorsement of a wide variety of commercial products that increasingly helped define American consumer culture in the post-Vietnam era. If team practices were sometimes brutal, deals shady, or individual stars out of control or wildly overpaid in later careers, this matched the hyper-masculine and unbounded commercial culture espoused by critics of the 1960s counterculture.

*

Between 2000 and 2010, even after the effects of the Great Recession on school budgets and government financing, athletic programs saw increased spending across the nation.[21] The standard narrative of athletic departments and programs was that such expenditures brought the school high profile and increased revenues in the form of sponsorships and donations, largely from alums. But by 2010 only 17 of 300 NCAA Division I programs were even self-supporting; and many schools had to draw from general funds or from academic and building programs to support their teams. Most athletic programs, including varsity football, lost money annually. A 2015 study commissioned by the *Huffington Post* and the *Chronicle of Higher Education* found that subsidies paid by public universities alone for their athletic programs over the previous five years totaled $10.3 billion in mandatory athletics fees paid by all students and by other budget allocations.[22] Many students do not realize they are paying such fees; many never use the facilities or attend games. Students, parents, faculty, and legislators have raised vocal objections, but the spending remains untouched and rising, the justification being that sports bring in prestige and donations. Statistics gathered in the report, however, demonstrate the net loss to schools from their athletic programs, with subsidies as high as 90.6 percent of total expenditures.[23]

When in 2010 faculty at UC Berkeley protested against increased spending on athletics and the fact that the school's president was diverting $13 million annually from academic programs to athletics, the university reacted by cutting twenty-four varsity teams. Despite this, and negative reports from the Knight Foundation, coaches and their supporters among trustees and alums continued to demand high salaries and budgets with the claims that such sports provided the school with "intangibles." Athletes continued to receive preferential admissions

---

[21] See Thelin, 374–77.

[22] Brad Wolverton, Ben Hallman, Shane Shifflett, and Sandhya Kambhampati, "The $10-Billion Sports Tab: How College Students Are Funding the Athletics Arms Race," CHE (November 15, 2015), at www.chronicle.com/interactives/ncaa-subsidies-main?cid=rclink#id=table_2014.

[23] "Interactive Table: Who Foots the Bill in College Sports?" Source: NCAA Revenue and Expense Reports, 2010–2014; and the Department of Education's Integrated Postsecondary Education Data System (Ipeds), 2010–2014.

treatment and lucrative scholarships as coaches' salaries and new facilities continued to rise. The old "A&M" universities, which first rose as agriculture and mining schools, now transformed themselves into "Athletics and Medicine" schools to raise both their profile and their income base.[24]

But by the early years of the new millennium this ethos was drawing closer and closer into essential conflict with new sensibilities and social movements on campuses across the nation. Third-wave feminism, LGBTQ liberation, Title IX expansions, new cultural critiques, budget cuts, and new oversight caused by the Great Recession and shifting government financial aid drew new scrutiny of college athletics. Where audiences in the 1910s and 1920s might delight in the excesses of college athletes, those of the 2010s and 2020s were informed by new sensibilities, a new awareness of the place of gender, race, and class in the creation of the athletic mythos. They were ready and able to apply new standards to what appeared to remain an unmovable and unchanging collegiate athletic culture. The scandals of the 2010s were a whole new ball game.

*

By far the most notorious scandal to come out of these developments was the one that enveloped Penn State University. We have discussed this above in terms of governance and board actions, but here we will focus on athletics themselves.[25] In November 2011, Jerry Sandusky, an assistant football coach, was indicted on fifty-two counts of child molestation between 1994 and 2009.[26] He was convicted on forty-five counts in June 2012 and sentenced to between thirty and sixty years in prison. University president Graham Spanier, vice president Gary Schultz, and athletic director Tim Curley were charged with perjury, obstruction of justice, failure to report suspected child abuse, and related charges. The Penn State board of trustees commissioned an independent investigation from former FBI Director Louis Freeh. That report stated that Penn State's famed head football coach Joe Paterno – along with Spanier, Curley, and Schultz – knew about allegations of child abuse by

---

[24] Thelin, 381–85.   [25] See Chapter 5, 101–2.
[26] See https://en.wikipedia.org/wiki/Penn_State_child_sex_abuse_scandal.

Sandusky as early as 1998, had shown "total and consistent disregard . . . for the safety and welfare of Sandusky's child victims," and "empowered" Sandusky to continue his acts of abuse by failing to disclose them. Shortly after the scandal broke, Spanier resigned. The board of trustees fired Paterno and Curley.

The National Collegiate Athletic Association placed sanctions on Penn State's football program: a $60-million fine, a four-year post-season ban, scholarship reductions, and the voiding of its victories from 1998 to 2011. The Big Ten Conference imposed an additional $13 million fine. In March 2017, Curley, Schultz, and Spanier pleaded or were found guilty of misdemeanor charges of child endangerment. Conspiracy charges against Curley and Schultz were dropped, and Spanier was acquitted of conspiracy. In June 2017, all three were sentenced to jail terms, fines, and probation. Spanier was sentenced to four to twelve months in jail, a $7,500 fine, and two years of probation. His conviction was overturned on appeal.

The scandals attracted nationwide attention and were covered intensely in all media, including the *Pittsburgh Post-Gazette*, Associated Press, Reuters, Fox News, *USA Today*, the *Washington Post*, the *Chicago Tribune*, the *New York Times*, *Los Angeles Times*, *Sports Illustrated*, the *Huffington Post*, ESPN, ABC News, MSNBC, Yahoo Sports, Politico, BBC News, the *Wall Street Journal*, the *Chronicle of Higher Education*, and dozens of other outlets. Both the length of the scandal and its nature caused both left- and right-wing coverage to delve deeply into the role of college athletics in the education and support of young and vulnerable students, most especially in an age when Title IX was becoming more and more closely enforced to guarantee freedom and equality of access to athletics. Even Penn State's Aa1 bond rating was "placed on review for possible downgrade" by Moody's Investors Service because of the scandal's possible effects on the university's finances.

*

But Penn State was not alone. Baylor University, "a private Christian university" in Waco, Texas,[27] gained national attention for accusations

---

[27] See www.baylor.edu/about.

and later convictions for serial rape, gang rape, and non-sexual assaults by nearly twenty Baylor football players, by frat boys, and by others between 2012 and 2016.[28] The convictions resulted in long prison sentences for some of the players. In 2016, records revealed that university officials knew of, but failed to take action regarding, the assaults. As a result, university head coach Art Briles was fired in May 2016. University president Kenneth Starr, who had led the investigation into the sexual improprieties of former US President Bill Clinton, was forced to resign, as was Baylor athletic director Ian McCaw. The school's Title IX coordinator also resigned, claiming that the school's board of advisors was "a group of seniors that made sure that they were protecting the brand . . . instead of our students." The scandal resulted in several high-profile lawsuits by students, one of whom, a "Jane Doe," declared in a Federal lawsuit that Baylor was a "hunting ground for sexual predators." By the end of 2016 the university had reportedly lost $76 million in donations and other support due to the sexual-assault scandal. Projections saw a total loss of over $223 million. The damage done to the students, their families, and rest of the student body, faculty and alums, however, went far beyond money damages and lawsuits. Even with new attention from law enforcement, the courts, and the media, assaults continued into 2018, and lawsuits by women students into early 2019. Coverage appeared regularly in national media in everything from the *Wall Street Journal* to ABC News, CBS News, NBC Sports, *USA Today*, ESPN, and the *New York Post*.

In 2014, Michigan State University reported the first Title IX complaint against its women's gymnastics doctor Larry Nassar. No violation was found, and Nassar remained in his position. It was soon revealed, however, that he had been sexually abusing female gymnasts at the school since the 1990s, and that chief gymnastics coach Kathie Klages was aware of Nassar's actions from at least 1997 and had pressured the students to remain silent about their abuse. Once the internal MSU allegations were published by the *Indianapolis Star* in September 2016, however, Nassar was fired from his position and in February 2018 was sentenced to 40 to 175 years in prison on multiple counts. Coach Klages

---

[28] Wikipedia at https://en.wikipedia.org/wiki/Baylor_University_sexual_assault_scandal.

was suspended in February 2017 and resigned the next day. Nassar's supervisor, medical school dean William Strampel, was also forced to resign. In August 2019, he was sentenced to a year in prison for his failure to prevent Nassar's abuse.[29]

As the scandal unfolded, nearly 400 female students came forward as Nassar's victims. On January 24, 2018, revelations that MSU's president, Lou Anna Simon, was aware of the ongoing abuse but attempted a cover-up, led to Michigan's House of Representatives to call for MSU's board of trustees to fire her. She resigned the day of Nassar's convictions, followed by MSU athletic director Mark Hollis. On November 20, 2018, former president Simon was charged with two felonies and two misdemeanor counts for falsely telling police that she was unaware of the nature of the Title IX complaints against Nassar.[30] She retained her tenured position and in July 2019 retired from MSU to receive a $2.45-million payout over three years, as well as full benefits.[31]

Simon's position was handed to former Michigan Governor John Engler in January 2018. But the Republican politician was not able to heal the campus. In April 2018, he privately offered one accuser $250,000 to withdraw her case. He accused Nassar's first accuser of receiving "kickbacks" for her "manipulation" of other accusers. During the succeeding months he ignored the abused female students during meetings, demonstrating his disdain by shuffling papers during their presentations. In an interview with the *Detroit News* he portrayed the women accusers as "the ones who've been in the spotlight who are still enjoying that moment at times, you know, the awards and recognition."[32]

---

[29] Elizabeth Joseph and Jason Hanna, "Larry Nassar's Former Boss at MSU Gets a Year in Jail for Misconduct and Neglect of Duty," CNN (August 7, 2019), at https://edition.cnn .com/2019/08/07/us/msu-strampel-sentence-nassar/index.html.

[30] Fernanda Zamudio-Suaréz, "Former Michigan State President Is Charged with Lying to Police About Larry Nassar," CHE (Nov. 20, 2018), at www.chronicle.com/article/ Former-Michigan-State/245141.

[31] Sarah Brown, "Michigan State's Ex-President, Who Faces Criminal Charges, Will Retire with a $2.5-Million Payout," CHE (July 30, 2019), at www.chronicle.com/article/ Michigan-State-s/246820.

[32] Jack Stripling, "Engler's Michigan State U. Presidency Is as Imperiled as Ever. And that's Saying Something," CHE (Jan. 14, 2019), at www.chronicle.com/article/Engler-s-Michigan-State-U/245473; and Lily Jackson, "John Engler Is out at Michigan State. Here

In January 2019, the MSU board of trustees unanimously – Democrats and Republicans – called for Engler's immediate resignation, forbidding him to return to his office, an act that he portrayed as a Democratic political move.[33]

The scandal attracted national attention. In January 2018, ESPN reported that their investigation "found a pattern of widespread denial, inaction and information suppression of such allegations by officials ranging from campus police to the Spartan athletic department." It reported that at least sixteen football players had been accused of sexual assault or violence against women since 2007.[34] After a Congressional hearing into the MSU scandal, the bipartisan Protecting Young Victims from Sexual Abuse and Safe Sport Authorization Act of 2017 was signed into law by President Trump in February 2018. The Michigan attorney general's office and the United States Education Department both launched investigations. By 2018 abused students had filed about 150 law-suits against MSU, and by May 2018, MSU had agreed to pay $500 million in settlements to 332 female students. In September 2019, the Department of Education levied a $4.5 million fine against MSU, the largest ever such penalty for failing to report the abuse. According to then Education Secretary Betsy DeVos, "What happened at Michigan State was abhorrent." She called the crimes committed by Nassar and Strampel "disgusting and unimaginable" and "so too was the university's response ... This must not happen again."[35] Soon after DeVos' statement, MSU's new president, Samuel L. Stanley Jr., announced the

Are 3 Moments that Got Him Booted," CHE (Jan. 17, 2019), at www.chronicle.com/article/John-Engler-Is-Out-at-Michigan/245500.

[33] Jack Stripling, "Michigan State U. Forces out Engler Immediately," CHE (Jan. 17, 2019), at www.chronicle.com/article/Michigan-State-U-Forces-Out/245497.

[34] Paula Lavigne and Nicole Noren, "OTL: Michigan State Secrets Extend Far beyond Larry Nassar Case," ESPN.com (January 27, 2018), at www.espn.co.uk/espn/story/_/id/22214566/pattern-denial-inaction-information-suppression-michigan-state-goes-larry-nassar-case-espn.

[35] David Jesse, "Judge: It's 'Plausible' Michigan State Buried Sex Assault Claims against Athletes," USA Today (Aug 21, 2019), at https://eu.freep.com/story/news/education/2019/08/21/michigan-state-sexual-assault-lawsuit-bailey-kowalski/2071907001; Katherine Mangan, "Education Dept. Levies $4.5-Million Fine Against Michigan State Over Nassar Scandal," CHE (Sept. 5, 2019), at www.chronicle.com/article/Education-Dept-Levies/247079.

resignation of Provost June P. Youatt, whom the DoE had criticized for failing to take action against Strampel.

*

But these instances were not isolated. According to the *Conversation*,[36] 75 percent of the *US News & World Report* top 100 schools reported some form of sexual scandal between 2001 and 2013, with enrollments dropping by about 10 percent on average in the following year. Data, definitions, and methods of measurement vary widely, and assaults are often unreported. But the best consensus estimates are that about 20 percent of women are sexually assaulted during their college years.[37] Serial rapists accounted for 90 percent of campus assaults, with an average of six rapes per perpetrator.[38] Athletic males and males in fraternities are more likely to commit rapes.[39] Despite the waves of bad publicity around college sports, the mindset of administrators, trustees, alums, politicians, and media seems to be little changed, however. Even the coverage in the *Conversation* reflected an unthinking normalization of rape culture, akin to Americans' acceptance of gun deaths as "just another day." According to the *Conversation*, there is a "silver lining" to women being attacked and raped on campus. In a variation on "lightning never strikes twice," application rates drop for better chances of admission, and some reforms follow. But a silver lining for whom? According to the most recent figures released by the Association of American Universities in October 2019, 25.9 percent of undergraduate women, of the nearly 182,000 students on

---

[36] https://theconversation.com/should-you-apply-to-a-college-that-has-had-a-recent-scandal-114892.

[37] Charlene L. Muehlenhard, Zoë D. Peterson, Terry P. Humphreys, and Kristen N. Jozkowski, "Evaluating the One-in-Five Statistic: Women's Risk of Sexual Assault While in College," Annual Review of Sex Research, *Journal of Sex Research* 54.4–5 (2017), at https://doi.org/10.1080/00224499.2017.1295014.

[38] David Lisak, "Understanding the Predatory Nature of Sexual Violence," *Sexual Assault Report (SAR)* 14.4 (March–April 2011): 49–50, 55–57, at www.middlebury.edu/media/view/240951/original.

[39] Angela Carone, "Fraternities are Significantly Responsible for Campus Sexual Assault," in Jack Lasky, ed., *Sexual Assault on Campus* (Farmington Hills, MI: Greenhaven Press, 2016), 21.

all levels surveyed, experience some form of nonconsensual sexual contact. The figures ranged from 14 percent to 32 percent.[40]

*

In July 2019, Louisiana State University's flagship campus at Baton Rouge unveiled plans to renovate its 102,321-seat football stadium built in 2005.[41] The facility includes a locker room with lounging pods complete with iPad mounts, charging stations, and ventilated storage drawers. "This is why you come to LSU," boasted the team. The estimated cost would be $28 million paid for completely by funds generated by the team's Tiger Athletic Foundation. Meanwhile, LSU itself has been the object of a 50 percent slash in state support since 2008. Even after about $850,000 in repairs to the main campus library, it remains in "decrepit" condition, prone to regular flooding, with its basement inaccessible to staff and users. The entire campus has deferred $700 million in needed repairs and regular maintenance. LSU's athletic programs spent $137 million in 2018 alone. About 5.8 percent of those funds went into the LSU general budget. An LSU spokesman defended the athletic spending. Here the scandal, however, came from alums, former athletes, and sports commentators. Among the criticisms was that LSU's athletics programs were not paying their players like professionals.

TITLE IX

One cannot understand the sweeping, almost revolutionary, changes on college campuses around issues of gender and sexuality without some

---

[40] David Cantor, Bonnie Fisher, et al., "Report on the AAU Campus Climate Survey on Sexual Assault and Misconduct," The Association of American Universities (Oct. 15, 2019), at www.aau.edu/key-issues/campus-climate-and-safety/aau-campus-climate-survey-2019. See also Sarah Brown, "More Than 1 in 4 Undergraduate Women Experience Sexual Misconduct in College," CHE (Oct. 15, 2019), at www.chronicle.com/article/More-Than-1-in-4-Undergraduate/247345; Greta Anderson, "Top Universities Release Sexual Assault Reports," IHE (Oct. 16, 2019), at www.insidehighered.com/news/2019/10/16/universities-identify-campus-specific-sexual-assault-issues.

[41] Will Jarvis, "LSU Just Unveiled a $28-Million Football Facility. The Flood-Damaged Library Is still 'Decrepit'," CHE (July 22, 2019), at www.chronicle.com/article/LSU-Just-Unveiled-a/246750.

background in the federal legislation known as Title IX. This was part of the US Education Amendments Act of June 23, 1972 proposed by Republican President Richard M. Nixon to amend the Civil Rights Act of 1964. It applies to all schools receiving any form of Federal funding. Title IX states:

> No person in the United States shall, on the basis of sex, be excluded from participation in, be denied the benefits of, or be subjected to discrimination under any education program or activity receiving Federal financial assistance.[42]

Since then, Title IX has had a transformative effect on the equal status of women across a wide variety of issues, including access to all forms of educational opportunities and in protections against gender discrimination. While it was hardly the original intent of the act, perhaps its most visible achievement has been in women's athletics, opening opportunities and equal access to female competitors in all sports. The victory of the US Women's Soccer team in the 2019 World Cup competition amply demonstrates this. Beginning in the 1980s, the law began to be applied to cases of sexual assault. These, proponents argued successfully before the courts, constituted a prima facie case of sexual harassment and thus discrimination based on gender. In a landmark case in 2003 a Federal court ruled that a 1977 sexual assault by one Yale student of another constituted such harassment and thus fell under Title IX guidelines as gender discrimination.[43] As a result, Yale instituted its own grievance procedure, and other schools soon followed suit.

The purview of the law increased over the next two decades until in 2011 the Obama administration issued a "Dear Colleague" letter that updated guidelines for universities that finally made compliance with Title IX a matter of prime urgency. It called on colleges and universities to adhere to a standard of proof in cases of such accusations first set in 2002 based on the "preponderance of the evidence" (i.e., more

---

[42] Public Law No. 92-318, 86 Stat. 235 (June 23, 1972), codified at 20 U.S.C. §§ 1681–1688.

[43] The case was *Alexander v. Yale*, 631 F.2d 178 (2d Cir. 1980). See Robin Wilson, "Why Colleges Are on the Hook for Sexual Assault," CHE (June 6, 2014), at www.chronicle.com/article/Why-Colleges-Are-on-the-Hook/146943.

likely than not) used in civil cases, as opposed to the "beyond a reasonable doubt" standard required for criminal convictions. The Obama administration's expansion of Title IX recommendations for all institutions of higher learning were not mandatory. But given higher ed's concern for its students and its brands, the letter had several important effects, including the widespread opening of "Title IX" offices throughout higher education to insure understanding of and compliance with the law and its regulations. These called for prompt reporting, as well as internal measures to investigate and adjudicate complaints of sexual harassment, including accusations of assault and rape that might otherwise be within the purview of civil and criminal courts in the schools' jurisdiction areas. In a certain sense the law and the new requirements both punctured the traditional separation of the campus from civil society and, ironically, returned to a medieval practice of granting the universities their own tribunals and a large measure of almost clerical immunity from surrounding secular courts. With these came a sudden and substantial change in the culture of many campuses that appeared to throw many – left-wing and right-wing, feminists and traditionalists – off balance and calling for reforms.

*

Two of the best examples of these changes are the interrelated cases of Professors Laura Kipnis and Peter Ludlow of Northwestern University. Here the seismic shift from a culture of open student–faculty relationships to one of mutual distrust involved student protests, accusations of sexual harassment and rape, closed-door hearings before a Title IX tribunal, resignations, apparent recantations, and continued recriminations. These demonstrated the often awkward processes into which institutions of higher education have been placed by law and changing custom, the rise of student consciousness surrounding gender inequality and sexual predation embodied in the Me Too (or #MeToo) movement, and the unforgiving eye of critics of higher education who take all sides to task as the campus becomes the vicarious battleground around issues of equal rights and women's agency, personal freedom, and societal responsibility.

Laura Kipnis is a tenured professor of communication theory in the Department of Radio, Television, and Film at Northwestern. Over several months in 2015, she published a series of essays in the *Chronicle of Higher Education* detailing her reactions to the university's new codes of faculty–student behavior, which she labeled the "Great Prohibition," and reflected on similar developments across the nation's campuses.[44] As Kipnis explained, she grew up in a different time.[45] As students of art, she and her peers among the previous generation of feminists lived according to special rules of "mutual fascination" between faculty and students whose bodies blended with their minds and where asymmetrical equations of "power" were irrelevant, or at least helpful on occasion:

> When I was in college, hooking up with professors was more or less part of the curriculum. ... As Jane Gallop recalls in *Feminist Accused of Sexual Harassment* (1997), her own generational *cri de coeur*, sleeping with professors made her feel cocky, not taken advantage of. She admits to seducing more than one of them as a grad student – she wanted to see them naked, she says, as like other men. Lots of smart, ambitious women were doing the same thing, according to her, because it was a way to experience your own power. But somehow power seemed a lot less powerful back then. The gulf between students and faculty wasn't a shark-filled moat; a misstep wasn't fatal. We partied together, drank and got high together, slept together. The teachers may have been older and more accomplished, but you didn't feel they could take advantage of you because of it. How would they?

Later Kipnis had dated her own graduate students without any sense of being a "predator." But then came the Obama administration's enforcement of Title IX rules and their offices, their endless notices "peddling" guidelines to faculty, and a series of accusations by young women encouraged by the Me Too movement to file complaints against (mostly male) faculty. As Kipnis characterized her reaction to one famous incident:

---

[44] https://policies.northwestern.edu/docs/Consensual_Relations_011314.pdf.

[45] Laura Kipnis, "Sexual Paranoia Strikes Academe," *Chronicle Review*, CHE (Feb. 27, 2015), at www.chronicle.com/article/Sexual-Paranoia-Strikes/190351.

It's the fiction of the all-powerful professor embedded in the new campus codes that appalls me. ... To a cultural critic, the representation of emotion in all these documents plays to the gallery. The student charges that she "suffered and will continue to suffer humiliation, mental and emotional anguish, anxiety, and distress."

As a result of that article in the *Chronicle*, Kipnis became the target of well-publicized student protests, including the symbolic carrying of mattresses and pillows made famous by the Me Too movement. In the minds of many, she had indeed become, if not the predator, at the very least an apologist for predators. After an editorial in the student newspaper and a petition to the university's president, Kipnis found herself the object of one of the very Title IX "inquisitions" by the "Midwestern Torquemadas" she had mocked.[46] The article produced what one student called a "chilling effect" on her ability to report sexual harassment and what another termed a "hostile environment." Kipnis was again called before the Title IX tribunal, which she suggested might be called a "kangaroo court." No evidence was presented for the author to refute, and the Title IX "investigators doubled as judge and jury." After several weeks Kipnis was cleared of the accusations, and the charges were dropped.[47] The faculty senate then had its say, and Northwestern revised its procedures over such allegations.[48]

Kipnis next came to prominence as she detailed her experience of the Title IX proceeding against Prof. Peter Ludlow of Northwestern's Philosophy Department.[49] In early 2014, Ludlow had been accused of inappropriate sexual advances by an undergraduate student of his whom

[46] Laura Kipnis, "My Title IX Inquisition," *Chronicle Review*, CHE (May 29, 2015), at www.chronicle.com/article/My-Title-IX-Inquisition/230489.

[47] Brock Read, "Laura Kipnis Is Cleared of Wrongdoing in Title IX Complaints," CHE (May 31, 2015), at www.chronicle.com/blogs/ticker/laura-kipnis-is-cleared-of-wrongdoing-in-title-ix-complaints/99951.

[48] Peter Schmidt, "Northwestern U. Is Accused of Violating Academic Freedom," CHE (March 3, 2017), at www.chronicle.com/blogs/ticker/northwestern-u-is-accused-of-violating-academic-freedom/117184.

[49] Laura Kipnis, "Eyewitness to a Title IX Witch Trial," *Chronicle Review*, CHE (April 2, 2017), at www.chronicle.com/article/Eyewitness-to-a-Title-IX-Witch/239634; later included in Laura Kipnis, *Unwanted Advances: Sexual Paranoia Comes to Campus* (New York: HarperCollins, 2017).

he had allowed to sleep off a hangover on his bed and who went on to sue him and the university in civil court. A younger colleague, with whom he had had a three-month sexual affair, then accused him of nonconsensual sexual relations and rape. Neither accuser attended the Title IX trial, which was heavily staffed by university attorneys. As Kipnis recounts it, almost by default she was called upon to act as the ostracized Ludlow's faculty advisor. One of Ludlow's former female Ph.D. students also provided the defense with compelling expert and character witness. Despite reported ambiguities and contradictions in the accusers' cases and counter-evidence, the case dragged on. Ludlow eventually decided to tender his resignation rather than face continued courtroom conflict, protracted legal bills, and continued publicity and professional ostracism. He left the country without any form of financial settlement from the university. His first accuser later denounced the proceedings as benefiting no one but the university and its corporate public-relations image. Kipnis concluded, "high-flown terms like 'due process' now spout from my cynic's lips, as though democratic principles still matter and something should be done to save higher ed from its saviors."

Debate over these practices ultimately focused for both left and right on this issue of "due process."[50] In October 2014, for example, over two dozen Harvard law school professors led by Jeannie Suk Gersen, Elizabeth Bartholet, Janet Halley, and Nancy Gertner published an open letter condemning the Title IX system of "investigation and adjudication" used by the Obama administration as "so unfair as to be truly shocking" and "overwhelmingly stacked against the accused."[51] Gersen subsequently labeled the Title IX offices a "sex bureaucracy." As she put it, her and her colleague's action, "was not a conservative impulse. It was an impulse toward fairness and rules and in some ways a pushback against authoritarian university governance." That governance, many advocates for Title IX reform assert, is less about justice than about

---

[50] See, for example, Wesley Yang, "The Revolt of the Feminist Law Profs: Jeannie Suk Gersen and the Fight to Save Title IX from Itself," *Chronicle Review*, CHE (August 7, 2019), at www.chronicle.com/interactives/20190807-feminist-law-profs.

[51] "Rethink Harvard's Sexual Harassment Policy," *Boston Globe* (Oct. 14, 2014), at www.bostonglobe.com/opinion/2014/10/14/rethink-harvard-sexual-harassment-policy/HFDDiZN7nU2UwuUuWMnqbM/story.html.

protecting the "brand" against bad publicity and assuring consumer loyalty. Since 2011, Federal courts across the spectrum of jurisdictions and leanings decided in over 200 cases that Title IX tribunals have violated due process. More cases are pending; and by the summer of 2019 differing Federal district courts had issued conflicting opinions that could lead to a Supreme Court test.[52]

As with the medieval university, the public, civil, or criminal nature of faculty missteps or lack of professional judgment and ethics has given rise to serious conflict that involve both the university's image of authority and its insistence upon separateness from society at large. Are university-appointed panels and attorneys legally competent to adjudicate cases that may involve civil or criminal charges? Can they really provide such constitutionally guaranteed "due process"? Does not society have a right and obligation to protect all of its members, no matter what community they may temporarily belong to? And if so, what venue has final jurisdiction over such cases? The recent history of Title IX certainly makes the strong argument that society, represented by the Federal government, has both interest and standing in all such instances.

The tenure of Trump appointee Betsy DeVos as Education Secretary in 2017 further complicated the already fraught situation.[53] DeVos is a billionaire, Republican political operative, and Trump campaign contributor. While acknowledging the importance of Title IX protections, she launched a series of meetings with advocacy groups to investigate whether the Obama administration's 2011 guidelines constituted governmental "overreach." Those consulted included college and university administrators who welcomed clarifications and consistencies. They also included several men's-rights organizations. Discussions focused on the

---

[52] Jeremy Bauer-Wolf, "A Potential Title IX Supreme Court Case?," IHE (August 8, 2019), at www.insidehighered.com/news/2019/08/08/ruling-umass-amherst-title-ix-lawsuit-may-lead-supreme-court-case-experts-say.

[53] Andrew Kreighbaum, "DeVos Hints at Changes in Title IX Enforcement," IHE (July 14, 2017), at www.insidehighered.com/news/2017/07/14/after-full-day-meetings-title-ix-devos-says-improvements-needed; Laura Meckler, "Betsy DeVos Poised to Issue Sweeping Rules Governing Campus Sexual Assault," *Washington Post* (Nov. 25, 2019), at www.washingtonpost.com/local/education/betsy-devos-poised-to-issue-sweeping-rules-governing-campus-sexual-assault/2019/11/25/f9c21656-0f90-11ea-b0fc-62cc38411ebb_story.html.

thorny issue of "due process" and the rights of the accused. But the very nature of the men's groups set off strong criticisms from women's and survivors' groups expressing skepticism of DeVos' intentions and concerns that Title IX protections would be rolled back. Women's groups provided strong statistical data refuting claims that many rape charges were fabricated and casting doubt on the good faith of DeVos' efforts, which did result in the rollback of the Obama recommendations. Proposed changes included the "preponderance of the evidence" standard of proof, the sixty-day investigation period, and prohibition of mediation between the parties involved.

In July 2017, a further study documented the hitherto unrecognized extent of faculty sexual harassment of students.[54] Ten percent of women graduate students reported sexual harassment that went into administrative or public litigation. The study found that the majority of cases were not limited to verbal harassment and that they were the acts of serial harassers. In August 2019, Dartmouth College reached a $14 million settlement with nine women graduate students in psychology and brain science after their repeated complaints of sexual harassment and violence went unaddressed by university administrators. While Dartmouth eventually fired three tenured senior faculty after a Title IX investigation, the women's suit alleged a history of neglect in failing to protect their rights.[55]

Such harassers were overwhelmingly male, but some high-profile cases have included female faculty and charges of harassment leveled by male students. The charges against Professor Avital Ronell, of NYU's German and Comparative Literature Department, are a case in point. In August 2018, NYU's Title IX office found her guilty of the charges of sexual harassment against a male, and gay, graduate student, and NYU

---

[54] Nancy Chi Cantalupo and William Kidder, "A Systematic Look at a Serial Problem: Sexual Harassment of Students by University Faculty," *Utah Law Review* (June 30, 2018): 671–786. See also Colleen Flaherty, "Worse Than It Seems," IHE (July 18, 2017), at www.insidehighered.com/news/2017/07/18/study-finds-large-share-cases-involving-faculty-harassment-graduate-students-are.

[55] Nell Gluckman, "Dartmouth Women Reach Preliminary $14-Million Settlement With College," CHE (Aug. 6, 2019), at www.chronicle.com/article/Dartmouth-Women-Reach/246888.

suspended her for one year.[56] The case was further complicated by a letter signed by over fifty prominent academics defending Ronell and attacking the graduate student before many of the facts of the case had become public. Despite several signers' subsequent retraction of their support, the growing scandal attracted the attention of a wide audience both for the initial matter under accusation and subsequent litigation and for what appeared to be the academy's closing ranks around one of its prominent superstars at the expense – and future careers – of students and victims.[57]

New York Times and *New Yorker* articles shifted attention away from the immediate issues of sexual harassment by faculty members to apparent inconsistencies of the campus Me Too movement and of university Title IX procedures. Lisa Duggan, professor of social and cultural analysis at NYU, cast suspicion on the very notion of the corporate university's attempts to adjudicate such cases and the issue of "power relationships" within modern higher ed. In April, Andrea Long Chu, one of Ronell's graduate students who wrote of her experience in the *Chronicle,* called attention to a fall graduate course Ronell would teach entitled "Unsettled Scores."[58] In September 2019, NYU announced that Ronell would return to the classroom.[59] Her reinstatement sparked immediate protests from the graduate student union and from NYUtoo, a campus advocacy group. In an open letter they stated:

> NYU's decision to continue Ronell's employment constitutes an attack on survivors of sexual abuse and contributes to a hostile learning and working

[56] "What Happens to #MeToo When a Feminist Is the Accused?," *New York Times* (Aug. 13, 2018), at www.nytimes.com/2018/08/13/nyregion/sexual-harassment-nyu-female-professor.html.

[57] Masha Green, "An N.Y.U. Sexual-Harassment Case Has Spurred a Necessary Conversation About #MeToo," *New Yorker* (August 25, 2018), at www.newyorker.com/news/our-columnists/an-nyu-sexual-harassment-case-has-spurred-a-necessary-conversation-about-metoo.

[58] "I Worked With Avital Ronell. I Believe Her Accuser," *Chronicle Review,* CHE (Aug. 30, 2018), at www.chronicle.com/article/I-Worked-With-Avital-Ronell-I/244415.

[59] Emma Pettit, "Avital Ronell is Returning to the Classroom. Some Grad Students Want Her Gone," CHE (Sept. 5, 2019), at www.chronicle.com/article/Avital-Ronell-is-Returning-to/247084.

environment. The university already tacitly acknowledges this in making it a condition of Ronell's return that her future meetings with students be supervised. Moreover, Ronell's behavior is not isolated to this particular instance, but is part of a long-standing pattern of intimidation and misconduct, as testified by other students and faculty. We therefore call on NYU to enforce its policy "to maintain a safe learning, living, and working environment" and immediately terminate Avital Ronell's employment.[60]

Among other demands, the letter called for an annual report on all Title IX complaints, including the university's response to them, restorative-justice options for sexual misconduct, and in-person, rigorous trainings for faculty, staff, and students on "anti-harassment, sexual respect, racial sensitivity, and bystander intervention." But Ronell's reinstatement is not unique. Students at campuses across the country are now protesting against the reinstatement into the classroom of faculty already found guilty of Title IX infringements. At one campus, a graduate student noted that such behavior "created a culture in which some, maybe all, students viewed every interaction with [the offending faculty member] – and with faculty in general – as potentially sexualized."[61]

*

By September 2019, the pressures placed on Title IX itself had become the object of close scrutiny. As a result of the Obama administration's "Dear Colleague" letter of 2011, campuses scurried to establish formal Title IX offices. They staffed these with professionals with various levels of experience and expertise who immediately needed to balance the needs of the most vulnerable students who make accusations on the one hand, and the rights of the accused on the other. In addition, many faced pressure from their institutions – everyone from HR chiefs to deans and provosts – to protect the reputation of their schools and their

---

[60] "Hold NYU Accountable: Terminate Avital Ronell's Employment and Implement Institutional Reform #NYUtoo," at https://docs.google.com/document/d/105bUlMu2fD534Z211QZGk_Q8cN08Jy1s8hhUpXkqcGI/edit.

[61] Emma Pettit, "He Violated Sexual-Misconduct Policy. He's Back in the Classroom. What Should the University Do Now?," CHE (Nov. 15, 2019), at www.chronicle.com/article/He-Violated-Sexual-Misconduct/247558.

record of compliance with the law and with student safety. Title IX officers were thus both employees and individuals charged with being impartial and independent judges about campus compliance and culpability in protecting students. Recent statistics are telling. Survey data published in 2018 by the Association of Title IX Administrators reveal that 72 percent of Title IX officers are women.[62] Of these 74 percent are white. In 2018, only 46 percent reported directly to the president of the institution; and 62 percent of offices had separate budgets to do their mandated jobs. That meant that the majority of Title IX offices lacked access to the final campus decision-makers that their mandates required and that one-third of offices still had no separate budget.

Even more telling is the profile of the officers themselves: in 2018, only 21 percent of Title IX officers were full-time, and 61 percent held their positions part-time and were charged with other administrative responsibilities. The overwhelming majority (87 percent) of officers were in their jobs for less than five years, 64 percent for less than three years, and 20 percent for less than one year. Burnout and turnover were constant, and this lack of continuity translated into student unease in reporting cases, difficulty in assessing the fairness of accusations, and the isolation of officers from both students and faculty. Caught between student crises, student suspicions of inadequate concern and process, and administrative rigidity and wariness of Title IX's impact on their school's reputation, many officers resign or are forced out after relatively brief periods.[63] Meanwhile, student willingness to report sexual harassment and assault continues to rise. Colleges and universities continue simultaneously to comply with Title IX regulations, to establish working procedures, and to attempt to minimize negative reporting and public scrutiny.

*

But the final tribunal remains that of public opinion. As Eric Kelderman put it, the concept of "due process" has broadened in

---

[62] https://atixa.org/about.

[63] Sarah Brown, "Life Inside the Title IX Pressure Cooker," CHE (Sept. 5, 2019), at www.chronicle.com/interactives/20190905-titleix-pressure-cooker.

meaning from a basic legal principle to a rhetorical device invoked against a wide range of ills attributed to higher education and Title IX.[64]

A September 2018 poll conducted by public broadcasting station WGBH in Boston found that 77 percent of respondents supported the view that higher ed had a positive impact on American society.[65] But opinions went in the opposite direction when it came to higher ed's handling of issues. The poll found that 57 percent supported calls for more diversity of opinion and more protections of free-speech rights. Fifty-nine percent of respondents believed that faculty have a political slant, and 54 percent felt that schools are lax in protecting students from sexual attack and harassment. Half held that higher ed falls short in addressing students' mental-health concerns.

POLITICAL CORRECTNESS

According to the *Oxford Dictionaries*, political correctness is "the avoidance of forms of expression or action that are perceived to exclude, marginalize, or insult groups of people who are socially disadvantaged or discriminated against."[66] The right-wing catchall, "politically correct," is not a clever and original brickbat to use against liberals. It was first used in 1793 in the US Supreme Court case *Chisholm v. Georgia*.[67] It appeared occasionally throughout the nineteenth century. In 1934, the *New York Times* reported that Nazi Germany was granting reporting permits "only to pure 'Aryans' whose opinions are politically correct." Ironically, it began appearing in its current context among left-wing American groups after World War II to mock Stalinist, Maoist, and other Communist regimes' insistence on the ideological purity of the moment. This use continued through the 1960s and 1970s among progressive groups wary

---

[64] Erik Kelderman, "How Due Process Became a New Front in the Culture Wars," CHE (May 17, 2018), at www.chronicle.com/article/How-Due-Process-Became-a-New/243453.

[65] Scott Jaschik, "Positive View of Higher Ed, with Lots of Caveats," IHE (September 17, 2018), at www.insidehighered.com/news/2018/09/17/new-national-survey-finds-generally-positive-views-higher-education-weak-points-well; and also see Chapter 4, 85–92 and passim.

[66] www.lexico.com/en/definition/political_correctness.   [67] 2 US (2 Dall.) 419 (1793).

of ideologues. It had the largest impact on American thought, however, from the neo-Conservatives. In 1987, Allan Bloom's *The Closing of the American Mind* zeroed in on American higher education as a hotbed of a new "political correctness" among faculty.[68] An October 1990 *New York Times* article by China expert Richard Bernstein made the term standard among critics of higher ed. It soon became a potent political tool of the right-wing. Dinesh D'Souza's *Illiberal Education: The Politics of Race and Sex on Campus*, funded in large part by the right-wing John M. Olin Foundation, solidified the targeting of higher ed.[69]

In May 1991, at a University of Michigan graduation, President George H.W. Bush laid out the right-wing consensus:

> The notion of political correctness has ignited controversy across the land. And although the movement arises from the laudable desire to sweep away the debris of racism and sexism and hatred, it replaces old prejudice with new ones. It declares certain topics off-limits, certain expressions off-limits, even certain gestures off-limits. What began as a crusade for civility has soured into a cause of conflict and even censorship. Disputants treat sheer force – getting their foes punished or expelled, for instance – as a substitute for the power of ideas. Throughout history, attempts to micromanage casual conversation have only incited distrust. They have invited people to look for an insult in every word, gesture, action. And in their own Orwellian way, crusades that demand correct behavior crush diversity in the name of diversity.[70]

As the theory developed in the twenty-first century, it expanded not only to include the supposed liberal bias of most university and college faculty but also to characterize concerns about marginalization into an ideologically consistent attack on free speech. This attack allegedly originated in the leftist thought of the Frankfurt School in Germany. The theory of "Cultural Marxism" was proposed by Michael Minnicino in

---

[68] Bloom, *The Closing of the American Mind.*

[69] Dinesh D'Souza, *Illiberal Education: The Politics of Race and Sex on Campus* (New York: Vintage, 1992).

[70] Remarks at the University of Michigan Commencement Ceremony in Ann Arbor, 4 May 1991. George Bush Presidential Library, at https://bush41library.tamu.edu/archives/public-papers/2949.

1992 and gained wide traction among right-wingers.[71] In 2001, Patrick Buchanan wrote in *The Death of the West: How Dying Populations and Immigrant Invasions Imperil Our Culture and Civilization* that "political correctness is cultural Marxism . . . its trademark is intolerance."[72]

In October 2016 candidate Donald Trump stated,

> Political correctness – oh, what a terrible term – has transformed our institutions of higher education from ones that fostered spirited debate to a place of extreme censorship, where students are silenced for the smallest of things.[73]

FREE SPEECH

The political weaponization of this critique was quick in coming. In February 2017, Iowa State Senator Mark Chelgren, a conservative Republican, proposed a bill that would have set quotas on the faculty members at the state university system based on their political beliefs, so that neither Republicans nor Democrats had more than a 10 percent majority.[74] The law would have authorized state officials to check voter registration records of all applicants. As Chelgren put it, "I believe it is imperative that the students, the customers, have as much information as possible. . . . Students who are paying the bills – tuition at universities – should have an understanding of the political affiliations that professors are associated with, so when they ask a question, they can put it in context." Quickly denounced as "wackadoodle," the bill was still

---

[71] Michael Minnicino, "The New Dark Age: The Frankfurt School and 'Political Correctness'" (Washington, DC: Schiller Institute, 1992).

[72] Patrick Buchanan, *The Death of the West: How Dying Populations and Immigrant Invasions Imperil Our Culture and Civilization* (New York: St. Martin's Press, 2001), 89.

[73] Steven Johnson, "Conservatives Say," CHE (Aug. 20, 2019), at www.chronicle.com/article/Conservatives-Say/246981.

[74] Peter Schmidt, "Iowa Bill Would Force Universities to Consider Political Affiliation in Faculty Hiring," CHE (Feb. 22, 2017), at www.chronicle.com/article/Iowa-Bill-Would-Force/239261.

recognized as making it "much more difficult for Iowa State, the University of Iowa, and the University of Northern Iowa to recruit top faculty."

Simultaneously, Secretary of Education DeVos went further in the ideological attack on faculty as elitist ideologues. In a February 2017 speech before the Conservative Political Action Conference she told the college students in the group that:[75]

> The fight against the education establishment extends to you too. The faculty, from adjunct professors to deans, tell you what to do, what to say, and more ominously, what to think. They say that if you voted for Donald Trump, you're a threat to the university community. But the real threat is silencing the First Amendment rights of people with whom you disagree.

In September 2017, then-Attorney-General Jeff Sessions decried what he considered infringements of First Amendment rights on campus and pledged to lend the weight of the Justice Department to support lawsuits against colleges that were allegedly violating free-speech rights:

> "The American university was once the center of academic freedom, a place of robust debate, a forum for the competition of ideas," Sessions said. "But it is transforming into an echo chamber of political correctness and homogenous thought, a shelter for fragile egos."[76]

As with so much of the right-wing critique of higher ed, however, such charges do not stand up to scrutiny. A 2017 study by two Republican-voting political scientists who specialize in studies of free speech and "political correctness" found that right-wing rhetoric was inaccurate and exaggerated:

> We think the headline-grabbing episodes are in fact not typical of academe – and that things are better than the news coverage suggests. Not all is well with academe, but right-wing alarmism obscures the fact that the

---

[75] Scott Jaschik, "DeVos vs. the Faculty," IHE (Feb. 24, 2017), at www.insidehighered.com/news/2017/02/24/education-secretary-criticizes-professors-telling-students-what-think.

[76] Sadie Gurman, "Sessions says Free Speech 'Under Attack' on College Campuses," AP News (September 26, 2017), at https://apnews.com/d72c5252daf94f51867e2c8a0ea7e0a4.

left's stranglehold on campuses has less influence on college students than people think. As everyone in academe knows, there is a cottage industry on the right that spotlights the ideological tilt of colleges and accuses academe of brainwashing a generation of students. But most undergraduates are in fact not ideologically pliable. By the time they reach college, most students have developed a political point of view.[77]

As Jason Blakely noted in the *Atlantic*:

Such reports have in turn reinforced a longstanding political narrative, which seeks to demean America's universities as ideologically narrow, morally slack, hypersensitive, and out of touch. For example, commentators like the *New York Times* columnist Ross Douthat have argued that America's "university system" is "genuinely corrupt" in relying on "rote appeals to ... left-wing pieties to cloak its utter lack of higher purpose."[78]

But the war of words over free speech had concrete consequences. As administrators attempted to accommodate the new axis of opinion gripping the nation, students and many faculty reacted strongly against what they perceived as a marked increase in hate and other objectionable speech on campus. In February 2017, the Berkeley campus of the University of California – the birthplace of the campus Free Speech Movement in the 1960s – was thrust into national prominence again as students and faculty demonstrated against an invitation to Milo Yiannopoulos, then editor of the extreme right-wing *Breitbart News*.[79] In the traditional spirit of free expression of ideas on the college campus, the administration turned down numerous student requests to prevent Yiannopoulos' visit. As a result, nearly 1,500 students demonstrated

---

[77] Robert Maranto and Matthew Woessner, "Why Conservative Fears of Campus Indoctrination Are Overblown," *Chronicle Review*, CHE (July 31, 2017), at www.chronicle.com/article/Why-Conservative-Fears-of/240804.

[78] "Deconstructing the 'Liberal Campus' Cliché," *Atlantic* (Feb. 13, 2017), at www.theatlantic.com/education/archive/2017/02/deconstructing-the-liberal-campus-cliche/516336.

[79] Beth McMurtrie, "Mayhem at Berkeley Hardens New Battle Lines on Free Speech," CHE (Feb. 3, 2017), at www.chronicle.com/article/Mayhem-at-Berkeley-Hardens-New/239099.

peacefully against the talk and what they characterized as hate speech that had no place on a college campus. Meanwhile, however, about a hundred anarchists from the Bay Area – not associated with Berkeley – infiltrated the campus, set fires, and damaged buildings before their action was contained.

President Trump and the right-wing media, however, condemned the action as one of students themselves preventing freedom of speech. Trump tweeted: "If U.C. Berkeley does not allow free speech and practices violence on innocent people with a different point of view – NO FEDERAL FUNDS?" His lead was followed by the right-wing Heritage Foundation: "1964: Berkeley students march to demand free speech. 2017: Berkeley students riot to demand free speech be denied." The right-wing Young Americans for Liberty student organization claimed that 1,500 protestors threw smoke bombs, damaged property, and started fires, proving, the group asserted, that "even the most liberal, open-minded campuses in our country harbor intolerance for those that disagree with them." Without long delay the Goldwater Institute, a right-wing think-tank, released its prepared model legislation for state governments to punish students at public colleges who "shut down" speakers on campus.

Within three months of Trump's election the narrative of an American higher education hijacked by enemies of freedom had been codified and broadcast widely. In June 2017, the Republican-led legislature in Wisconsin, with the support of Governor Scott Walker, put forward precisely the legislation proposed by the Goldwater Institute.[80] The bill called for the suspension of students who are found twice to "interfere with the expressive rights of others" and for the state system to set up a reporting mechanism on such incidents. Similar legislation was already being introduced in Michigan, Texas, and California. In March 2019, Donald Trump signed an executive order mandating that colleges and universities "uphold free speech";[81] and by July 2019, legislation

[80] J. Clara Chan, "As a Free-Speech Bill Advances in Wisconsin, Some Fear a Chilling Effect," CHE (June 23, 2017), at www.chronicle.com/article/As-a-Free-Speech-Bill-Advances/240433.
[81] "Executive Order Improving Free Inquiry, Transparency, and Accountability at Colleges and Universities." See Andy Thomason, "Here's What Trump's Executive Order on Free

mandating "free speech" on campus and punishment for infractions had either passed or been proposed by Republican legislatures in nearly two dozen states.[82]

In February 2017, Middlebury College in Connecticut witnessed heated, and in one incident,[83] physical confrontation as students and faculty objected to plans to invite political scientist and eugenicist Charles A. Murray, co-author of the controversial "bell curve" theory that posits genetic reasons for frequent under-performance by black and other peoples of color in American society.[84] Both Murray and the faculty moderator Prof. Allison Stanger were heckled during and after the talk; and Stanger was injured by a student afterwards. Many senior faculty and administrators were unprepared for the confrontation, but other faculty had already warned about, and now joined students in rejecting, the presence of what many saw as a racist spreading his discredited ideas. The incident demonstrated the tensions between the classic separateness of the campus as a place devoted to open discussion and consideration of all forms of ideas and the pressures to reflect more the evolving consciousness of many young people about racial and social inequalities and injustices. It also reflected what many consider students' oversensitivity to difference and challenges to their world views, whether left- or right-wing. Faculty and administrators pondered what went wrong with preparations and their attempt to instill a sense of open-minded debate in a place apart. Some also mused on the impact that the incident would have for right-wing critics of higher education.

Two of the most highly covered and distorted controversies around campus free speech centered on Yale University. The first involved an incident in October 2015 around a Halloween celebration on campus

---

Speech Says," CHE (March 21, 2019), at www.chronicle.com/article/here-s-what-trump-s/245943.

[82] Katherine Mangan, "More States Are Passing Campus Free-Speech Laws. Are They Needed, or Is the Crisis Talk Overblown?," CHE (July 23, 2019), at www.chronicle.com/article/More-States-Are-Passing-Campus/246753.

[83] Fernanda Zamudio-Suaréz, "What Could Middlebury Have Done to Avoid a Free-Speech Fracas?," CHE (March 7, 2017), at www.chronicle.com/article/What-Could-Middlebury-Have/239421.

[84] Richard J. Herrnstein and Charles Murray, *The Bell Curve: Intelligence and Class Structure in American Life* (New York: Free Press, 1994).

and a professor's comments about appropriate costumes.[85] The original *Atlantic* treatment of the incident was quickly picked up and magnified by multiple sites, including RealClearPolitics, RealClearEducation, the fire.org, and medium.com. The second focused on the issue of monuments, institutional memory, and historical responsibility for past social and political evils. Students questioned the naming of one of Yale's most venerable residence halls, Calhoun College, after John C. Calhoun. A Yale graduate, US Senator, and the nation's seventh vice-president, Calhoun was an avowed white supremacist and apologist for slavery in the years leading up to the Civil War. Among the student demands were that the term "master" for hall moderators be changed since it evoked the culture of slavery. The controversy resulted in many student sit-ins and the arrest and later exoneration of a black custodian for smashing the hall's stained-glass window depicting black slaves at work on a plantation. In February 2017, the university reversed its decision to retain Calhoun's name and instead announced the hall's new naming after Grace Murray Hopper, a Yale Ph.D. who became a noted computer scientist and a US rear admiral. One new hall was to be named after Anna Pauline Murray, a Yale Law School graduate in 1965, a legal scholar, and a civil rights activist. But another was to be named after Benjamin Franklin who, many students noted, was also a slave owner. Student concerns also included the fact that the Franklin naming came at the urging of a wealthy businessman who had donated $250 million for both buildings. After further protests, that hall was also renamed. Students stressed that their symbolic demands were part of a far larger dynamic, in which many black professors were leaving Yale and in which less than 3 percent of its humanities faculty were black, while black enrollments totaled about 11 percent of the student body.

The true nature of the controversy, however, was largely ignored by the press, and the impression that the public received was that several spoiled (black) students, "the few activists willing to invest time and

---

[85] Connor Friedersdorf, "The New Intolerance of Student Activism: A Fight over Halloween Costumes at Yale has Devolved into an Effort to Censor Dissenting Views," *Atlantic* (Nov. 9, 2015), at www.theatlantic.com/politics/archive/2015/11/the-new-intolerance-of-student-activism-at-yale/414810.

energy into the game," backed by a permissive liberal faculty, had dictated arbitrary demands around a set of largely meaningless symbols:

> What [these incidents] had in common was an administration and student body coordinated around an ideology that continually mutated to ensure moral entrepreneurship and a continued supply of purges, as new forms of human behavior or commonplace descriptors became off-limits. Some of this energy was genuine, some cynical.[86]

*

Given the close attention America has always paid to higher education, and the heightened tension of the campus as a cockpit for social and intellectual innovation and experimentation, off-campus controversies tend to become both magnified and crystallized in the context of higher ed's devotion to deep scrutiny of issues. Faculty and students engage in a give-and-take of ideas and their criticism. But such on-campus scrutiny of controversies and events can have quite a negative impact on the image of a particular campus and of higher education in general. The consequences of such events on the University of Missouri's flagship campus at Columbia is another case in point.[87] Following the 2014 police killing of an unarmed black youth in Ferguson, MO in the fall of 2015, and in the face of racist slurs on campus, black students began a nonviolent protest by setting up a tent city on campus to call attention to widespread and institutional racism and what they saw as administrative indifference. A graduate student went on a hunger strike, and the school's football team refused to practice until the school's president resigned. The protests came both as a result of the Ferguson incident and as part of the rising Black Lives Matter movement. Racist and anti-Semitic posts followed on campus as the school won national attention for hindering free speech after a media-department professor

---

[86] Natalia Dashan, "The Real Problem at Yale Is Not Free Speech," *Palladium* (August 5, 2019), at https://palladiummag.com/2019/08/05/the-real-problem-at-yale-is-not-free-speech.

[87] Anemona Hartocollis, "Long After Protests, Students Shun the University of Missouri," *New York Times* (July 9, 2017), at www.nytimes.com/2017/07/09/us/university-of-missouri-enrollment-protests-fallout.html.

attempted to prevent media coverage of the protests. In the wake of the incidents the university president and chancellor resigned.

Alum and parent concerns were soon amplified by right-wing media as the core narrative became one of a campus out of control and in the hands of violent students and faculty. Both presidential candidates Hillary Clinton and Donald Trump cited the incidents, and Trump labeled black protestors "disgusting" and "disgraceful." Professor Melissa Click – who took the students' side – was fired after becoming a right-wing target.[88] What followed was a 35 percent decline in new enrollments, of which 42 percent of black students turned away from the school and 21 percent of white applicants sought other campuses and state systems. Overall black enrollments fell from 10 percent to 6 percent. Faculty and other job cuts, cancellation of building projects, a library without a book budget, and fundraising shortfalls followed. True to the nature of such negative narratives, students already enrolled almost all opted to complete their degrees at the school, a sign that those familiar with the disputes realized their largely nonviolent and free expression. Meanwhile, those remote from the incidents based their decisions on hearsay, negative reporting, and pre-judgments.

*

But not all controversy over free speech centered around students. In a Trump-era culture, where a new political orthodoxy viewed academic freedom with suspicion, individual professors and their public statements became the target of renewed right-wing hostility and outright threat. In 2017, Jessie Daniels and Arlene Stein reviewed a series of incidents and trends in a *Inside Higher Education* post.[89] These included a commencement speech at Hampshire College by Keeanga-Yamahtta Taylor, assistant professor of African-American studies at Princeton University, who called Trump a "racist, sexist megalomaniac." Her remarks were picked

[88] Tomi Obaro, "Before Syracuse, There Was Mizzou," *BuzzFeed News* (Nov. 26, 2019), at www.buzzfeednews.com/article/tomiobaro/mizzou-football-boycott-protests-2015-racism.

[89] "Protect Scholars against Attacks from the Right," IHE (June 26, 2017), at www.insidehighered.com/views/2017/06/26/why-institutions-should-shield-academics-who-are-being-attacked-conservative-groups.

up by Fox News, and she was immediately assailed by over four dozen threatening emails from right-wingers, some of which made threats of physical violence. Hampshire College immediately condemned the attacks and supported Taylor.

But not all faculty had the full or immediate support of their schools. Individual faculty members and departments have also had to reconsider offerings in everything ranging from courses on athletics, to gender studies,[90] to race as legislators, donors, religious leaders, and media continued to closely scrutinize "what's taught" on college campuses. In July 2017, Professor Johnny E. Williams of Connecticut's Trinity College Department of Sociology was targeted by the online Campus Reform and other right-wing media for supposedly inciting violence against "white" people for sharing an anonymous post in response to a shooting that targeted US Congresspeople. Trinity's campus was forced to close after threats of violence from right-wing trollers; and Williams and his family were forced into hiding. Trinity's president soon placed Williams on leave during a review of "the events concerning Professor Williams."

In early 2018, a classroom dispute at Indiana University of Pennsylvania over civil behavior in a religious studies class discussion on gender led to the expulsion of a right-wing student and the branding of his female professor as an enemy of free speech.[91] There followed right-wing media condemnations and personal threats of murder and rape against the professor and the lionizing of the student on Fox News and other media that critics have called the "internet outrage machine." Over the professor's and the faculty's objections, the university president, fearing bad publicity, allowed the student to return to class. But the public damage had been done. In a March 18, 2018 editorial, the *Pittsburgh Post-Gazette* stated:

> Colleges, universities, and the faculty and administrators who staff them have a sacred duty: To cherish, nourish, and protect free speech and

[90] J. Clara Chan, "Can a Single Course Jeopardize an Academic Department?," CHE (June 8, 2017), at www.chronicle.com/article/Can-a-Single-Course-Jeopardize/240299.

[91] Michael Vasquez, "How a Student Got Kicked Out of Class – and Became a Conservative Hero," CHE (May 31, 2018), at www.chronicle.com/article/How-a-Student-Got-Kicked-Out/243549.

academic freedom, and foster a love of these two great freedoms in the minds and hearts of students. . . . Indiana University of Pennsylvania and [the] professor have failed in this duty, by seeking to punish a student for expressing his views.

*

One of the most widely known cases is that of Steven Salaita.[92] A native of Bluefield, West Virginia, Salaita was an award-winning author who received tenure at Virginia Tech in 2006. In 2013, he published a *Salon* op-ed against the "support our troops" slogan in the wake of 9/11. Fellow faculty supported his free-speech rights, but the school's associate VP for PR stated:

> While our assistant professor may have a megaphone on Salon.com, his opinions not only do not reflect institutional position, we are confident they do not remotely reflect the collective opinion of the greater university community.[93]

Salaita was then hired as a tenured professor in the American Indian Studies Program at the University of Illinois at Urbana-Champaign. But in the summer of 2014 Salaita had tweeted very strong condemnations of both Israel's policy toward Palestine and against President Benjamin Netanyahu, which appeared to many to have crossed the line of acceptable academic discourse. At the urging of students, faculty, and donors who viewed his comments as anti-Semitic, in August 2014 Illinois' board of trustees voted eight to one to withdraw Salaita's job offer over the objection of faculty and forty-one department heads, chairs, and directors. The school's president stated that "Professor Salaita's approach indicates he would be incapable of fostering a classroom environment

---

[92] Steven Salaita, "My Life As a Cautionary Tale: Probing the Limits of Academic Freedom," *Chronicle Review*, CHE (Aug. 29, 2019), at www.chronicle.com/interactives/08282019-salaita-academic-freedom.

[93] Peter Schmidt, "Virginia Tech Professors Fault University over Tepid Defense of Colleague," CHE (November 20, 2013), at http://chronicle.com/article/Virginia-Tech-Professors-Fault/143171.

where conflicting viewpoints would be given equal consideration."[94]
A well-publicized scandal around freedom of speech followed. Articles
appeared in the *Nation,* the *Atlantic,* the *Chronicle,* and the *Huffington Post,*
as well as in the *Tablet,* the *Jewish Journal, Salon,* and other media outlets,
both left and right. Salaita sued the university, and eventually won his
case and a monetary award in excess of $800,000. As he puts it:

> More important, dozens of scholarly associations, various committees at
> the University of Illinois, labor unions, a federal judge, individual theorists
> of free speech, and the AAUP itself had already declared my case a clear-
> cut violation of academic freedom.

But Salaita's vindication meant little in academic terms. Even the
AAUP reacted suspiciously to his claims of free speech. He went on to
the Edward W. Said Chair of American Studies at the American
University of Beirut for one year but was not renewed. After failing to
find a position at any other American college, he eventually found
employment driving a school bus. As he summarized his situation:

> Why? Because academic freedom can do little to alter the fine-tuned cultures
> of obedience that govern nearly every campus. I cannot venture a
> comprehensive theory of freedom or know for certain in what spaces
> freedom may be possible, but it won't be in selective institutions possessed
> of wealthy donors, legislative overseers, defense contracts, and opulent
> endowments. ... It's important, then, to avoid treating academic freedom
> as sacrosanct and view it instead as a participant in material politics.
> Academic freedom cannot function without tenure, worker solidarity, and
> an adequate job market, which are all in decline. "Can academic freedom be
> saved?" is a less pertinent question than, "Is there any longer a marketplace
> for academic freedom?" The corporate university is disarming academic
> freedom by diminishing the circumstances in which it can be effective.

Similar, if less spectacular, incidents of criticism of faculty speech on
social media and other fora, mostly from the right, but also sometimes

---

[94] Christine Des Garennes and Julie Wurth, "Updated: UI Trustees Reject Salaita," *News-Gazette* (Sept. 11, 2014), at www.news-gazette.com/news/updated-ui-trustees-reject-salaita/article_d38feb38-4f68-50ea-b748-4a7a87cb27bb.html.

from the left, have prompted administrations to silence, investigate, or warn faculty at CUNY's John Jay College, Grand Canyon University, the University of Tampa, Dartmouth College, the University of Delaware, New Jersey's Essex Community College, Texas A&M, California State at Fresno, Drexel University, and others.[95] In August 2019,[96] Marquette University saw over a hundred faculty signing an open letter to protest new speech regulations.[97] These were drawn up during the summer recess without faculty or student participation by the school's policy-review committee, which is limited to Marquette's chief of staff to the provost, assistant VP for human resources, assistant general counsel, and senior associate VP for finance. The group focuses on "operational efficiency," according to faculty members. To protect "free speech" the new rules would prohibit demonstrations of any kind without prior permission of the dean's and provost's offices. The new rules also warned faculty and students that they

> should expect university personnel [i.e., campus police] to be present for all or part [of demonstrations] ... to ensure organizers' own rights are protected and the university's regular operations and activities are not interrupted. Accordingly, university representatives may film, photograph, or record [demonstrations].

Faculty and students expressed suspicions that the regulations were specifically aimed at preventing unionization drives and to otherwise protect the brand. The faculty letter stated in part:

> Marquette's new anti-demonstration policy is an affront to the culture of civic engagement and democratic participation that institutions of higher education should seek to promote. As opposed to the US Constitution and Bill of Rights – which put limits on the government and enumerate

---

[95] "Professors in the Political Cross Hairs," Special Report, CHE (July 26, 2017), at www .chronicle.com/specialreport/Professors-in-the-Political/129.

[96] Megan Zahneis, "'I Don't Think We Should Be Afraid of Protests': Marquette Faculty Members Speak out against Policy Requiring Approval for Demonstrations," CHE (Aug. 29, 2019), at www.chronicle.com/article/I-Don-t-Think-We-Should/247050.

[97] https://docs.google.com/forms/d/e/1FAIpQLSfHy1yZQezIRNLMgbdIg_ feO3QP28lbZHFGBYBn0vNfd8VYYOg/viewform.

citizens' rights – this document puts limits on community members and enumerates the powers and authority of the university and its police. This is inconsistent with this university's tradition of promoting free expression.

TRIGGER WARNINGS

While academics' rights to free speech and inquiry were being scrutinized from outside the walls of the campus, within the campus a new controversy arose in the mid 2010s over students' demands for what have come to be known as "trigger warnings." According to the *Merriam-Webster Dictionary*, a trigger warning is "a statement cautioning that content (as in a text, video, or class) may be disturbing or upsetting."[98] Such meanings grew out of the "triggers" for those suffering post-traumatic stress disorder (PTSD) from battlefield experience, sexual and other attacks, or other forms of bodily or psychological harm. According to a book-length collection of essays and studies published in 2017 and edited by Emily J.M. Knox,[99] opinions about the origins, purposes and efficacy of such warnings vary across the political spectrum but are on the whole, student-, not faculty-, driven. Most faculty who teach in sensitive areas likely to be effected, including gender studies, media, literature, or historical and cultural studies, have accepted the validity of such warnings for a variety of reasons, ranging from the pragmatic to the theoretical, from whatever makes students comfortable in a learning environment to basic steps in dismantling patriarchal systems of oppression. Opposition has risen from attempts to make such warnings mandatory. As early as 2014, the AAUP issued a statement opposing such requirements. It began:

A current threat to academic freedom in the classroom comes from a demand that teachers provide warnings in advance if assigned material contains anything that might trigger difficult emotional

---

[98] www.merriam-webster.com/dictionary/trigger%20warning.

[99] Emily J. M. Knox, *Trigger Warnings: History, Theory, Context* (Lanham, MD: Rowman & Littlefield).

responses for students. This follows from earlier calls not to offend students' sensibilities by introducing material that challenges their values and beliefs.[100]

Despite their acceptance within academia – and higher ed's opposition to mandatory implementation – the national media have, by and large, trivialized, dismissed, or condemned them as yet another example of how higher education has turned future citizens into coddled consumers,[101] asserting that such warnings were diminishing the public forum and restricting open and free speech.

*

In the end the controversy over free speech has affected all three elements of academic life: authority, innovation, and separateness. As Daniels and Stein put it:

> Colleges and universities hire scholars to teach and to produce knowledge. For many years, being a professor was a job where you got paid to read and think, insulated to some extent from the rough and tumble of the rest of society. ... Now, "we can no longer hold a position of splendid isolation," University of California, Berkeley, sociologist Michael Burawoy has said. As the cloistered ivory tower goes the way of the card catalog, we have to rethink what it means to be a professor.

Many of today's academic humanists pride themselves on being the heirs of Petrarch, Erasmus, or Valla. But would Petrarch's attacks on the medical profession, Erasmus' on the Church, or Valla's on the papacy and its political underpinnings be protected in today's academia? Or would the majority of academics conclude that such figures were better off in their historical status as "independent scholars"?

---

[100] "On Trigger Warnings," *AAUP Reports and Publications* (August 2014), at www.aaup.org/report/trigger-warnings.

[101] Jenny Jarvie, "Trigger Happy: The 'Trigger Warning' Has Spread from Blogs to College Classes. Can it Be Stopped?," *New Republic* (March 4, 2014), at https://newrepublic.com/article/116842/trigger-warnings-have-spread-blogs-college-classes-thats-bad.

CANONS

A "canon" is defined by the *Oxford Dictionaries* as "a general law, rule, principle, or criterion by which something is judged."[102] In this sense the historically accepted books of the Bible are judged "canonical." But such canons can be applied to any collection of books, music, or any cultural production.

As Randal Johnson summarized it in his introduction to Pierre Bourdieu's *The Field of Cultural Production*:

> During the 1980s the question of the formation and perpetuation of canons [came] increasingly to the fore in Anglo-American literary and cultural criticism. Discussions of the canon inevitably impinge on broader questions of aesthetic, literary and cultural value as well as on the constitution, preservation and reproduction of authority and symbolic power in the field. The literary canon has explicitly become both the site and the stake of contention as different groups have argued for its rearrangement along lines more favorable to their divergent interests and agendas.[103]

Canons gain their greatest force through a process of credentialing, but institutions insure their standardization and endurance. Of these the academy has been most prominent. Just like the medieval monastery and its preservation of the works of antiquity and its production of new works, the modern academy exerts its authority in defining, preserving, and passing on "the process of canonization" to what it deems to have authority and to bolster its own authority.[104] Like the medieval monastery, it innovates by creating new work that then becomes part of the accepted canon. As Bourdieu notes, the modern academic institution that creates canons is "much like the priesthood in the religious order."[105] Like medieval monasteries, "academies ... are obliged to combine tradition and tempered innovation."[106]

---

[102] www.lexico.com/en/definition/canon.

[103] Pierre Bourdieu, *The Field of Cultural Production* (New York: Columbia University Press, 1993), 19–20.

[104] Bourdieu, *Field*, 123.   [105] Bourdieu, *Field*, 243.   [106] Bourdieu, *Field*, 123.

Among the most prominent of curricula and syllabi that teach, analyze, critique, and reformulate canon are Columbia University's Core Curriculum, St. John's College of Maryland's Great Books, and Reed College's Humanities 110. All three began as traditional canonical collections of readings, largely in the Western tradition. But over the decades they have reexamined what the canon means in changing social and political contexts where the student body, faculty, and culture have changed dramatically with new global awarenesses and new perspectives on race, gender, and class.

At Columbia, for example, the core curriculum was launched in 1919 as "Contemporary Civilization" and concentrates on an intellectual tradition beginning with the ancient Hebrews, Greeks, and Romans, progressing through Muslim thought and including early modern and modern thinkers including Kant, Adam Smith, Mary Wollstonecraft, and other feminist thinkers, French and American revolutionary writings, Arendt, Woolf, Gandhi, Marx, Fanon, and Foucault. As its description notes:

> The Core Curriculum is the set of common courses required of all undergraduates and considered the necessary general education for students, irrespective of their choice in major. The communal learning – with all students encountering the same texts and issues at the same time – and the critical dialogue experienced in small seminars are the distinctive features of the Core.[107]

The core was constantly reexamined, revised, and expanded.[108] With the 1960s, first women authors, and then the great works of other global civilizations were added to the core. The courses now undergo a review of content and approach every three years to insure that they remain current and that they reflect the changing outlooks and requirements of various student and faculty constituencies. Columbia University Press published a corresponding series entitled Classics of Civilization, at first focused on Western thinkers, edited by some of the most prominent

---

[107] www.college.columbia.edu/core/core.
[108] www.college.columbia.edu/core/timeline.

(Columbia) intellectuals of the time. It has since morphed into a global series.

St. John's, on the other hand, continues to require its Great Books curriculum, launched in 1937, which remains focused on "Western" civilization. As the college describes it,

> While the list of books has evolved over the last century, the tradition of all students reading foundational texts of Western civilization remains. The books read at St. John's include classic works in philosophy, literature, political science, psychology, history, religion, economics, math, chemistry, physics, biology, astronomy, music, language, and more.[109]

That list has changed over the decades to insure that one's view of that civilization remains "diverse, complex, multifaceted and multicultural." As college president Peter Kanelos noted,

> The works that form our program of study have been in conversation with one another for millennia and represent a radical diversity of experience and perspective. ... There is little consensus or agreement between the texts we encounter. What we learn is the myriad ways that arguments are made, that truth is sought or rejected, that beauty is defined or denied. We understand that the four years studying these texts does not represent the end point of education, but rather the beginning.

Reed College has offered its Humanities (Hum) 110 since the 1940s as a core requirement. The college describes it thus:

> Humanities 110 introduces students to humanistic inquiry by considering a range of artistic, intellectual, political, and religious strategies that emerged in different geographical and temporal contexts. The course examines how varieties of human thought interact to produce distinctive ways of life. Recognizing that no community is self-contained, we seek also to interpret texts as artifacts of cultural exchange, influence, and differentiation.[110]

---

[109] www.sjc.edu/academic-programs/undergraduate/great-books-reading-list.
[110] www.reed.edu/humanities/hum110.

It is intended as an introduction to the humanities in general and the issues of authorship, transmission, reception, and for essential skills in reading, interpretation, criticism, and intellectual discourse. Texts come from far-ranging sources, including ancient Egypt and the Middle East to Europe, and now Central America, and Harlem. The course is generally reviewed and modified every ten years.

Lucía Martínez Valdivia, assistant professor of English and Humanities, teaches a section of the Reed course and describes herself as "female, mixed race, American and Peruvian, gay, atheist and relatively young." As she puts it,

> Everything that is now canonical was once innovative. ... This doesn't mean that we can't acknowledge problems, weaknesses, inaccuracies, that we can't question these works; rather, it means that we should do so productively, in good faith.[111]

In September 2017, a group of students belonging to the group Reedies Against Racism staged nonviolent sit-ins during Hum 110 lectures. Students claimed that the course was too white, male, and Eurocentric. While the college has a policy of open debate and compromise, instructors and many students objected to what gradually became disruptions and demands for specific changes, and instructors walked out of lecture rooms.

Reed, like Columbia and St. John's, has been able to change its canon over time and in response to such challenges. Nevertheless, the right-wing media has taken such events as yet further examples of the disarray of higher education. Disregarding the work of faculty, administration, and students in both addressing such grievances and expanding the canon, *Business Insider* ignored the wall of separateness and authority conservatives themselves insist on for higher ed.[112] It adopted the stance

---

[111] Colleen Flaherty, "Occupation of Hum 110," IHE (September 11, 2017), at www.insidehighered.com/news/2017/09/11/reed-college-course-lectures-canceled-after-student-protesters-interrupt-class.

[112] Daniella Greenbaum, "The Latest Example of Political Correctness Run Amok: A Misguided Revolt at One of the Most Liberal Colleges in America," *Business Insider* (April 18, 2018), at www.businessinsider.com/reed-college-humanities-110-course-controversy-2018-4?r=US&IR=T.

of many right-wing media outlets that academia was incapable either of recognizing the problem with student challenges or of adequately responding while preserving their own missions and identities. It editorialized:

> Identity politics do not belong in the classroom. Reed College is making a mistake by allowing the unfair charge of racism to govern the creation of university curricula ... if the process at Reed is repeated elsewhere, they may be subverted to the wave of political correctness sweeping campuses across the country.

CULTURE WARS

The dynamic between authority and innovation within higher education is often lost or misinterpreted among its critics. We cannot here fully review the history of the Culture Wars and battles over canon formation that characterized conflicts in the 1970s through the 1990s. The term "culture war" itself was born in 1870s Germany to describe the conflict (*Kulturkampf*) between the Catholic Church and the secularizing government of Chancellor Otto von Bismarck. Contemporary American newspapers anglicized the term into "culture war." In the 1960s, Richard Hofstadter established that America had a long history of conflict between progressive and conservative forces that often manifested itself as anti-intellectualism. We have already noted Allan Bloom's 1987 *The Closing of the American Mind* and its attack on higher ed. But it was not until the 1991 book *Culture Wars: The Struggle to Define America* by James Davison Hunter, professor of Religion, Culture, and Social Theory at the University of Virginia, that the term was applied to American politics to describe a spectrum of areas that the right wing saw as betraying "traditional" American values.[113] During the 1992 presidential campaign, conservative candidate Patrick Buchanan declared that, "There is a religious war going on in our country for the soul of America. It is a cultural

---

[113] James Davison Hunter, *Culture Wars: The Struggle to Define America* (New York: Basic Books, 1991).

war, as critical to the kind of nation we will one day be as was the Cold War itself."[114]

That war raged furiously through the 1990s as many academic disciplines in the humanities adopted new theoretical models, many borrowed from French and German schools; and historians began to incorporate the voices and movements of marginalized American groups, pitting adherents of traditional subject approaches and literary canons against those who would innovate to incorporate new insights and methods. These insights and methods were often explained, analyzed, and debated in professional terms that made them indecipherable to most Americans.

In a blog post on academic jargon from February 2017, Maximillian Alvarez usefully made the distinction between the "job" academics in the humanities perform and their "role" within the broader society.[115] Professional jargon is as necessary in the humanities as it is in the hard sciences for communicating easily and effectively to colleagues in the same fields for "advancing human knowledge, shaping the minds of tomorrow," and imparting "wisdom." Yet the language used in the academy both to produce innovation and to enhance authority can often overemphasize the separateness of the profession and its disciplines and sub-disciplines in ways that seem intentionally to exclude the general public – professional and non-specialist – from a clear understanding of what the academy does and the role that it plays in society. As Michael Clune recently noted:

> How can we distinguish mere authoritarianism from valid professional judgment, judgment that seeks to counter the prejudices and blindnesses of individual experts? How can we know that when an expert tells us Emily Dickinson or Zora Neale Hurston are great writers, she isn't simply expressing her subjective opinion? One way to assure people of the validity of expert judgments is by making the reasoning behind them transparent. Yet expertise isn't generally compatible with the capacity to show just anyone the evidence for our judgment. The opposite is more often the case.[116]

---

[114] https://buchanan.org/blog/1992-republican-national-convention-speech-148.

[115] Maximillian Alvarez, "The Poverty of Theory," in *Baffler* (February 22, 2017), at https://thebaffler.com/latest/accidental-elitism-alvarez.

[116] "The Humanities' Fear of Judgment," CHE (August 26, 2019), at www.chronicle.com/interactives/20190826-CluneJudgement.

We have already noted how the distinction between Church authority and individual revelation often reinforced much of American anti-intellectualism and its egalitarian disdain for expertise.[117] In contemporary America this disdain and antagonism has been secularized and most frequently focuses on what many, inside and outside academia, dismiss as "theory" and its impact on "what's taught." It has become part of a narrative, originally constructed by right-wing writers like George Will, that academia has deliberately seceded from the American consensus by adopting foreign ways of analysis and closed, often esoteric, discussion that serve few but intellectual and cultural bi-coastal elites. In the false narrative constructed by Charlie Kirk, founder of the right-wing Turning Point USA, Marx and Engels' *Communist Manifesto* is the most assigned book on college campuses.[118] The accusation of left-wing bias among faculty, and of the ideological bias of humanistic disciplines, has become a standard rallying cry among the right-wing.[119]

This criticism is especially aimed at the catch-all term "postmodernism" and a skewed understanding of its origins, elements, and intent.[120] "Foucault" has become symbolic of a wave of foreign – mostly French – thinking that supposedly took over academia in the 1970s and 1980s. This movement, it is asserted, set out deliberately to undermine the foundations of knowledge and truth with a series of relativisms based on subjective theories of language and understanding. In the 1980s the criticisms of power structures leveled by postmodern theory and those inspired by identity-based perspectives were conflated in the eyes of conservative academics and public critics. The result was a narrative that caricatured higher education as awash in the denial of

---

[117] See Chapter 2, 46–48.

[118] Matthew Boedy, "Debunking Charlie Kirk on the Uselessness of the Humanities," Medium (April 9, 2018), at https://medium.com/@mboedy/debunking-charlie-kirk-on-the-uselessness-of-the-humanities-35337f8890b8.

[119] Aaron Hanlon, "Lies About the Humanities – and the Lying Liars Who Tell Them," CHE (Dec. 7, 2018), at www.chronicle.com/article/Lies-About-the-Humanities-/245261.

[120] See Andrew J. Perrin, "Stop Blaming Postmodernism for Post-Truth Politics," *Chronicle Review*, CHE (Aug. 4, 2017), at www.chronicle.com/article/Stop-Blaming-Postmodernism-for/240845.

facts and of permanent truths and that undermined the rational, scientific basis for both knowledge and the institutions that are based on such fundamentals. Thus the academy's intellectual innovations were seen as undermining its own authority.

*

Controversy and debate are fundamental to all intellectual progress and innovation. So too are the experimentation and many of the false starts that inform students' lives and their learning to discern and judge in a time and space apart. Human institutions grow, mature, and fail with time; and failure is a natural, if unwanted, part of the human condition. The authority of all human institutions rises and falls with the integrity, proper governance, and reform of their constituent parts. Yet the varieties of scandals that have beset higher education over the recent past – and their increased scrutiny, much of it by hostile parties – have led to the creation of a narrative of an irredeemably failed institution that lacks focus, has lost authority, and has abandoned its mission to preserve and protect both historical traditions and the future – its students – from neglect and abuse.

While the sciences, technologies, medicine, and business were largely exempt from such scrutiny, the humanities – especially literature and language departments, cultural and various other studies and history – have borne the brunt of this criticism. Such attacks fit closely the agendas of powerful right-wing foundations, such as the Olin and Koch, which have seen such studies as inimicable to the values of capitalism. After the election of Trump in late 2016, critics on the left and right saw his new "alternative facts" and Republican "post-truth" politics as the natural result either of leftist intellectuals' demolition of all certainties or of American populism's long-held disdain for expertise and elite opinion. Both represented a significant challenge to long-held orthodoxies of intellectual authority nurtured by the academy. In the next chapter we will examine these changes in belief systems.

CHAPTER 8

Exchanging Beliefs: The Anti-Enlightenment. From Humanities to Technologies

INTRODUCTION

O NE OF THE MAJOR SHIFTS THAT underlay Henry VIII's Dissolution of the Monasteries was his validation of the Protestant Reformation and the exchange of belief systems that it involved. The most important modern studies of this process vary in their interpretations. David Knowles, whose *The Religious Orders in England* was the standard for decades, saw "the great enterprise of the suppression of the monasteries" as a premeditated plan drawn up for the king by Thomas Cromwell.[1] More recently, Diarmaid MacCulloch's *Thomas Cromwell* traced a series of unplanned events and unforeseen personal motives culminating in essentially the same result. On the other hand, in his *The Stripping of the Altars* Eamon Duffy concentrated on the radical change in belief and practice during, and in the wake of, the Dissolution. His masterwork is as detailed as MacCulloch's but in a far different way. Where MacCulloch saw the contingent elements of causality, Duffy saw the random, but often planned, results of the same processes. Taken together, however, all three masterworks point in the same direction and afford us valuable insights into changes of belief systems. Over the course of the half century that they studied, England went from a deeply Catholic country, where medieval beliefs and practices permeated every aspect of life, to a fundamentally Protestant one, in which the religious goals of the Reformers and their new practices took the place of the old dispensation. Change was often swift and helped by many willing

---

[1] See Knowles, *Religious Orders* III:198–205, 291–303, 367.

hands. It was often haphazard, and the result of many differing agendas. And it was often slow, uncertain, stalled, reversed, and long fought, as many local centers resisted passively, actively fought back, and ultimately required persuasion, incentives, and compulsion to change completely.

Again, we are not here attempting to use the sixteenth-century Dissolution as a rigid analogy or blueprint for current changes in higher education. But we are attempting to illustrate how various forces, motives, and unintended consequences greatly change the ways in which the world and its people are perceived. Such historical insights can lend some deep background into how a society comes to devalue older ways of thought and practice – and the institutions that preserve them – and embrace alternate and new ones, even over the course of a single generation.

This chapter discusses such general changes in public discourse about advanced learning. Over the past generation this discourse has changed from a humanist mode of enshrining historic traditions, educating future citizens, and maintaining rigorous research to one that privileges the immediate benefits of technology and commerce. We will review how this has been reflected in program shifts: from the heyday of liberal-arts and sciences curricula, enrollments, publications, and public authority in the years following World War II into the early 1970s and their almost precipitous replacement by STEM, business, technology, health-care, and service-industry programs, degrees, and prestige in the decades since.

Essential to this transformation are the negative narratives surrounding it. These include well-worn tropes that the liberal arts and humanities are dead-ends both to finding first jobs and later careers; that the liberal arts curricula lack any social authority and provide little more than diversion or "rounding" for the more important exertions toward obtaining a pragmatic college or professional degree; that the pure sciences are both too costly and too essential to leave to open-ended research without clear outcomes; and that society and individual communities demand practical training and answers to pressing problems. We will also explore these narratives specifically as an example of changing modes of thought for interpreting the world. They represent an exchange of societal belief systems: a turning and shift so fundamental as to equal the rejection of the monastic world-view and the embrace of secularization that characterized the early modern and the Enlightenment.

THE ANTI-ENLIGHTENMENT

In 1962, Richard Hofstadter's *Anti-Intellectualism in American Life* laid out the deep currents in American society that run counter to the Enlightenment. We have followed this historical development in chapters 2 and 4. Hofstadter traced this to the evangelical revolt against authority and modernity, to a Jacksonian rejection of expertise, to a business culture's disdain for "pure" research, and to Americans' faith in practical education to create citizens and economic opportunity. First we will examine quickly the Enlightenment tradition that emerged from classical sources, medieval scholastic thought, and early modern humanism. These traditions and sources premised a transparent and open universe subject to rational human inquiry and understanding, research, and the accumulation of knowledge. These, in turn, were underscored by a psychology of rational humanity, and the direct and intrinsic connection between the life of the mind and the life of society. In this both the arts and sciences emerging from the early modern university and individual research played an essential role and soon adopted the same methodologies of predicating research questions, determining correct and consistent methodologies, testing hypotheses, and building upon the accumulated findings of the past.

The Enlightenment grew out of both Renaissance humanism and the Scientific Revolution of the sixteenth and seventeenth centuries.[2] It focused on the intellectual and ethical progress of humanity through a new understanding of the natural, personal, and cultural world. Deriving in large part from the thought of Hobbes, Locke, Descartes, Bayle, Leibniz, and Spinoza, it was best expressed by such French *Philosophes* as Voltaire, d'Alembert, Diderot, and Montesquieu; through German

---

[2] William Bristow, "Enlightenment," *The Stanford Encyclopedia of Philosophy* (Fall 2017 Edition), Edward N. Zalta (ed.), at https://plato.stanford.edu/archives/fall2017/entries/enlightenment.

thinkers like Lessing and Kant; and through British figures like Hutcheson, Smith, and Hume. In America the Enlightenment heavily influenced the thought of Jefferson, Franklin, Madison, and other political leaders of the Founders' generation and shaped the Deism that marked the early American republic's official attitude toward religious toleration.

The Enlightenment enterprise, as embodied in Diderot's and d'Alembert's *Encyclopedia,* saw human activity and society as guided by reason and the quest for knowledge as liberating humanity from various forms of ignorance and from social, economic, and political oppression. Fully developed Enlightenment thought of the eighteenth century came to embody the True, the Good, and the Beautiful as categories of inquiry, analysis, and aesthetic discernment and taste. Universalism, internationalism and cosmopolitanism, rationalism, empiricism, and a skepticism toward received beliefs were its key characteristics. In the minds of Diderot and other *Philosophes* obscurantism, ignorance, and blind belief – often associated with the organized religion of priests and monks – were the foundations and cornerstones of such oppression. Their gradual removal would therefore be a continuous process of both enlightenment and freedom, but only if its proponents maintained their own integrity and replaced vertical, oppressive authorities of power with the lateral, liberating authorities of knowledge and informed culture. Both the American and French revolutions have been taken as key political outcomes of the movement. Overall, the Enlightenment was conceived as a movement of, by, and for elites who could lead society to perfection. In this regard it was also the outcome of the humanist belief that careful understanding of all forms of cultural artifacts could produce a ruling elite devoted to the common good. This elite could, however, be expanded through careful intellectual and ethical education, and through political renewal.

From the start of Judeo-Christian intellectual life this enterprise had many critics and opponents. It continued in the medieval debate between rationalism and belief in both methodologies and basic approaches to fundamentally shared positions on human nature, perception, and belief systems. These went hand-in-hand with the Enlightenment. Recent historical debates focus on Rousseau's insistence on individual, subjective experience and emotion, his "religion of the heart," rather than of the intellect, for example.[3] In Germany and in Britain, opposition gained strength as a reaction to the excesses of the French Revolution and the imposition of sweeping new changes by the revolutionaries, by Napoleon, and by Frederick II of Prussia and other absolutist monarchs whose authoritarian rule were bolstered by Enlightenment principles.

In the twentieth century, research by Isaiah Berlin, Darrin McMahon, Max Horkheimer, Theodor Adorno, and others portrayed the rise of radical ideologies in the nineteenth century as culminating in the disasters of Fascism, Nazism, and Communism in the twentieth.[4] They saw these as fundamental to the Enlightenment's emphasis on authority and a universalism that abstracts human thought and action away from the particular and the different. Their thought has become central to what has come to be called the "Counter-Enlightenment,"[5] which more recently has been proposed by such influential thinkers as Michel Foucault[6] and Graeme Garrard.[7]

*

In the early American Republic the Enlightenment remained influential through the writings and political activities of the Founders. As early as 1822, however, Thomas Jefferson was bewailing currents of religious anti-intellectualism and their effects on higher education. In his letter of November 2 of that year to Thomas Cooper, later president of South Carolina College, Jefferson wrote about the situation at his University of

---

[3] Arthur M. Melzer, "The Origin of the Counter-Enlightenment: Rousseau and the New Religion of Sincerity," *American Political Science Review* 90.2 (1996): 344–60.

[4] In Max Horkheimer and Theodor Adorno, *Dialect of Enlightenment,* Edmund Jephcott, trans., Gunzelin Schmid Noerr, ed. (Stanford: Stanford University Press, 2002).

[5] See "Counter-Enlightenment," *Wikipedia,* at https://en.wikipedia.org/wiki/Counter-Enlightenment.

[6] As in his debate with Jürgen Habermas, in the essay, "What is Enlightenment?," in Paul Rabinow, ed., *The Foucault Reader* (New York: Pantheon Books, 1984), 32–50.

[7] Graeme Garrard, *Counter-Enlightenments: From the Eighteenth Century to the Present* (Abingdon: Routledge, 2006); Graeme Garrard, *Rousseau's Counter-Enlightenment: A Republican Critique of the Philosophes* (Buffalo: State University of New York Press, 2003).

Virginia.[8] A Deist and an admirer of the French Enlightenment, sharing its disdain for religious denominations, the former US president was not sparing in his criticisms:

> The atmosphere in our country is unquestionably charged with a threatening cloud of fanaticism, lighter in some parts, denser in others, but too heavy in all. I had no idea, however, that in Pennsylvania, the cradle of toleration and freedom of religion, it could have arisen to the height you describe. Systematical in grasping at an ascendancy over all other sects they [Presbyterians and Calvinists] aim, like the Jesuits, at engrossing the education of the country, are hostile to every institution which they do not direct, and jealous at seeing others begin to attend at all to that object. The diffusion of instruction, to which there is now so growing an attention, will be the remote remedy to this fever of fanaticism.

Things appeared to be worse the further west on the frontier one went. The Connecticut-born and Yale-educated Julian Monson Sturtevant was a mathematician and natural scientist. He married into the famed New England Fayerweather family and in 1829 moved to the Illinois frontier. He was later president of Illinois College. He recorded this Sunday service in Jacksonville, Illinois:

> The community was perpetually agitated by sectarian prejudices and rivalries. ... The speaker was not "apt to teach." He was without even average intelligence or culture, and commenced his sermon with much hesitation and evident uncertainty. After speaking fifteen minutes, without any trace of connected thought, so far as I was able to perceive, certainly with no distinct propositions, he suddenly began to rant. His words were spoken so rapidly and in so high a key that few could be understood. Nothing seemed clear but the frequent repetition of cant words and phrases void of connection, all accompanied by a vehemence of tone and gesture that astonished and distressed me. ... To my amazement I was assured on the way home by a lady of our own congregation, from whom I had hope for better things, that we had heard a most excellent sermon. My cup was full! Was this woman a fair type of the people among

[8] Excerpted in Hofstadter & Smith I:395–96.

whom my future life was to be spent? Was sect so strong that in order to prevent our community from being further divided religiously we must listen on Sabbath morning to such a shower of emptiness and stupidity?[9]

As in the United States in the 1960s and 2010s, "stupidity" and lack of "intelligence" were the most damning epithets that intellectual elites and progressives could hurl. In this the academy remained wedded to the principles of the Enlightenment: that proper information, properly disseminated, would bring about proper social and cultural change. Distress at populists and movements unregulated by higher elites remained a keynote of criticism. Countercharges of "deplorables" and "love of the uneducated" would continue to characterize controversy over enlightenment into the present day. We have already noted Hofstadter's analysis of key elements of this populist criticism of America's educated elites and how seamlessly they could meld with political populism. The preaching style witnessed on the Illinois frontier in the 1830s remained key to such criticism: emotional, indifferent to the rhetorical rules of argumentation taught at the nation's universities, unintelligible to the educated, but extremely moving and encouraging to the average citizen.

Nor was such perceived anti-intellectualism confined to the frontier or a simple matter of cultural differences and attitudes. Andrew D. White, raised a Quaker, a self-described self-made man (in the new telegraph industry), and first president of Cornell University, described the attacks upon his new school in the 1870s:

Beside these financial and other troubles, another class of difficulties beset us, which were, at times, almost as vexatious. These were the continued attacks made by good men in various parts of the State and Nation, who thought they saw in Cornell a stronghold – first of ideas in religion antagonistic to their own; and secondly, of ideas in education likely to injure their sectarian colleges. From the day when our charter was under consideration at Albany they never relented, and at times they were violent ... far and wide was spread the story that Mr. Cornell and myself were attempting to establish an institution for the propagation of "atheism" and "infidelity."... Everything that we could do in the way of

---

[9] Excerpted from Sturtevant's *An Autobiography*, 161–63, in Hofstadter & Smith I:417–18.

reasoning with our assailants was in vain. In talking with students from time to time, I learned that, in many cases, their pastors had earnestly besought them to go to any other institution than to Cornell.[10]

What we broadly consider "anti-intellectualism" was not confined to the populists and "uneducated." In the 1930s, Robert Maynard Hutchins, president of the University of Chicago from 1929 to 1945, set off an uproar with his ideas for the reform of higher education.[11] Many of his specific proposals were criticized on a case-by-case basis. One of the most insightful analyses came from John Dewey (d.1952), progressive educational theorist and philosopher. Dewey focused on the authoritarian nature of Hutchins' view of higher education and its essential anti-enlightenment nature. Working within the triad of separateness, authority, and innovation, Hutchins had argued that reform would come to higher education only when schools turned less to the "vulgar" pursuit of money and professionalism, "a misconception of democracy," the innovations of science and research, and an erroneous "doctrine of progress." Instead, he argued, the academy should reject the tradition of "Descartes, Hume and Rousseau" and return more to the time-tested authority of the classic liberal education, of received wisdom, and unified principles.

Dewey focused on the self-contradictory elements of Hutchins' critique: his call for "the pursuit of truth for its own sake" and an elitist defense of the liberal arts that necessitated narrowing the scope of university research and teaching. Dewey wrote in 1937, foreshadowing the criticisms of Foucault and others on the determinative nature of power in forms of discourse:

> There are indications that Mr. Hutchins would not take kindly to labelling the other phase of his remedial plan "authoritarian." But any scheme based on the existence of ultimate first principles, with their dependent hierarchy of subsidiary principles, does not escape authoritarianism by

---

[10] From Andrew D. White, *Autobiography*, I:422–26, excerpted from Hofstadter & Smith II:557–58.

[11] *The Higher Learning in America* (New Haven: Yale University Press, 1936), excerpted in Hofstadter & Smith II:924–40.

calling the principles "truths." I would not intimate that the author has any sympathy with fascism. But basically his idea as to the proper course to be taken is akin to the distrust of freedom and the consequent appeal to some fixed authority that is now overtaking the world. There is implicit in every assertion of fixed and eternal first truths the necessity of some human authority to decide, in this world of conflicts, just what those truths are and how they shall be taught. This problem is conveniently ignored. Doubtless much may be said for selecting Aristotle and St. Thomas as competent promulgators of first truths. But it took the authority of powerful ecclesiastic organization to secure their wide recognition. Others may prefer Hegel, or Karl Marx, or even Mussolini as the seers of first truths; and there are those who prefer Nazism. As far as I can see, President Hutchins has completely evaded the problem of who is to determine the definite truths that constitute the hierarchy.[12]

*

The 1960s have been seen as both profoundly liberating, as an extension of the Enlightenment's program of freedom and knowledge; and alternatively as profoundly anti-enlightenment in their anti-authoritarian tendencies. Both these strains have influenced American society since the 1960s and have had a deep impact on our politics and on higher education in recent years. Hofstadter wrote too soon to take account of another aspect of higher education. Since the 1970s in academia itself the Enlightenment enterprise has been soundly critiqued by students of French and other European thought in literature, history, and specialized program departments. Time-tested assertions of empirical fact and standardized truths, of Rankean reality "as it really is," have engendered fierce debates across humanities disciplines. Einstein's revolution, for example, has been interpreted as introducing basic doubt to the empirical, rationally discernible universe. Such debates, often inadequately distilled for popular consumption, have fueled grave doubts over the mission, goals, and competence of higher education to guide and inform

---

[12] John Dewey, "President Hutchins' Proposals to Remake Higher Education," *Social Frontier* 3 (January 1937): 103–4.

American society and have de-authorized the expertise of many aspects of American academia. As one expert put it:

> The bigger concern today is that Americans have reached a point where ignorance – at least regarding what is generally considered established knowledge in public policy – is seen as an actual virtue. To reject the advice of experts is to assert autonomy, a way for Americans to demonstrate their independence from nefarious elites – and insulate their increasingly fragile egos from ever being told they're wrong.[13]

At the same time, the humanist educational agenda, essentially the creation of a highly educated elite in the liberal arts, designed to produce a class of civic leaders, came under harsh attack first in the wake of the student movement of the 1960s and then in the Culture Wars of the 1980s and 1990s. Debate ranged among traditionalists of a perceived "Western" civilization like Allan Bloom and George Wills, and theorists on the intellectual left who saw the humanist enterprise both for what it was (the creation of a cultural and political elite designed to rule) and as the negation of other voices and intellectual traditions. Rebecca Bushnell has summarized the debate over this pedagogy.[14] O. B. Hardison, Jr., professor of English at the University of North Carolina at Chapel Hill and at Georgetown University and director of the Folger Shakespeare Library in Washington DC, stated the traditionalist position that was then current among most university, institute, and foundation leaders:

> Liberal education is an ideal that has dominated Western thought about the aims of education for almost three millennia. The term "liberal" (from Latin *liberus*, meaning free man) is apt because it emphasizes the fact that the individual and political concerns of liberal education are two sides of the same coin. According to Socrates in Plato's *Republic*, education is the process of learning truth. It frees the individual from bondage to illusions – from the myriad superstitions, mythologies, and prejudices

---

[13] Tom Nichols, "How America Lost Faith in Expertise, And Why That's a Giant Problem," *Foreign Affairs* (March/April 2017), at www.foreignaffairs.com/articles/united-states/2017-02-13/how-america-lost-faith-expertise.

[14] See Bushnell, *Culture of Teaching*, 3–4 for both these quotes.

that imprison the ignorant. The result is wisdom, which is a combination of self-confidence and humility.

Debate focused on how widely this humanist culture could – or should – be diffused and over what the very term "free" meant in the twentieth century. Historians are quick to remind readers that Hardison's "free" man was a male authoritarian who with his elite peers dominated a society in which slavery or its variations in serfdom or other forms of peonage was the norm for over 90 percent of the population. Women, people of color, workers of all types, and students were not free in this or any other sense. According to the new critics, such "freedom" was not part of the natural order of things but a carefully and long-lasting construction that enabled the few and deracinated and oppressed the many. These thinkers were heavily influenced by European theoretical frames most closely associated with Michel Foucault, Pierre Bourdieu, and Jean-Claude Passeron, and by the Latin American Liberation theorists that included Paulo Freire. As Mas'ud Zavarzadeh and Donald Morton put it, in an alternative model of education,

> The teacher makes it possible for the student to become aware of his position, of his own relations to power/knowledge formations. Such a teacher often has an adversarial role in relation to the student: the teacher is a deconstructor, not a mere supporter in the traditional sense of the word. She helps reveal the student to himself by showing him how his ideas and positions are the effects of larger discourses (of class, race and gender, for example) rather than simple, natural manifestations of his consciousness or mind.

Stanley Aronowitz and Henry A. Giroux summarized the agenda of such pedagogy as:

> refusing forms of knowledge and pedagogy wrapped in the legitimizing discourse of the sacred and the priestly, its rejection of universal reason as a foundation of human affairs, its claim that all narratives are partial, and its call to perform critical readings on all scientific, cultural and social texts as historical and political constructions.[15]

---

[15] Stanley Aronowitz and Henry A. Giroux, *Postmodern Education: Politics, Culture, and Social Criticism* (Minneapolis: University of Minnesota Press, 1991), 82.

Was the humanist agenda and its heirs in the European Enlightenment the most reliable and time-tested method of expanding civic engagement and equality, of forging a common culture of shared belief and practice? Or was it instead the tool of a hegemonic state and culture aimed at producing numbing conformity to a canon of works and a political agenda of a smaller and smaller elite of white European males? As Jonathan Dollimore characterized it, humanism was a "residual metaphysic within secularist thought" that has enabled "the classic ideological effect: a specific cultural identity is universalized or naturalized ... activated in defense of one cultural formation, one conception of what it is to be truly human, to the corresponding exclusion of others."[16] Emmanuel Chukwudi Eze[17] and Susan Strickland,[18] for example, have brought together research that demonstrates how the Enlightenment marginalized people of color, women, and other oppressed groups.

Could therefore the avant-garde of pre-modern Europe translate to the twentieth century, and was an early modern intellectual movement born out of the declining freedom of the Italian city-states, and then embraced by the absolutist monarchies of Europe, transferable to North America and its officially democratic, multi-cultural, multi-ethnic, and multi-religious society?[19] Was a shared belief system even desirable in the midst of so many cultural influences, new directions, and focal points? As Dewey had asked in the 1930s, who would decide what was to be shared, and among whom? What of the decidedly second-class status that the historical humanists assigned to women in early modern Italy? What of the almost solely white European source of such "shared" beliefs? Did these assumptions not enshrine and normalize the use of these same texts and methods in an American society officially devoted to the

---

[16] Jonathan Dollimore, *Radical Tragedy: Religion, Ideology, and Power in the Drama of Shakespeare and his Contemporaries* (Chicago: University of Chicago Press, 1984), 258.

[17] Emmanuel Chukwudi Eze, *Race and the Enlightenment: A Reader* (Malden, MA: Wiley-Blackwell, 1997).

[18] Susan Strickland, "Feminism, Postmodernism and Difference," in Kathleen Lennon and Margaret Whitford, eds., *Knowing the Difference: Feminist Perspectives in Epistemology* (New York: Routledge, 1994), 265–74.

[19] On this transformation, see Grafton and Jardine, *From Humanism to the Humanities*, esp. xi–xvi.

historic elimination of all forms of inequality and oppression? Was not the American university and its liberal-arts curriculum the tap root and well source of this hegemonist application of cultural force?

*

As we have seen in Chapter 7, these debates focused on the most tangible manifestation of these stances: books used in the classroom and the "canon formation" around them. The debate over which texts are the most useful and necessary for the education of both citizens and future professionals is as old as the first ancient treatises on education. Which authors or authorities should be used in the classroom and for research was one of the most fundamental debates of medieval intellectual life; and the changing nature of the canon truly demarked shifts in medieval culture. The humanists' revolt and their later dominance was nothing else if not a continued part of the debate over what books are to be used and taught, and how they should be read and interpreted. By the sixteenth century, humanist educators like Erasmus, Vives, Elyot, and Ascham debated intensely the selection of books to be used for one's own research (broad) and for teaching (narrow).[20] The changes in the English universities during the Protestant Reformation also focused on what books, in what editions and interpretations, ought to be taught at the university, and by further extension what disciplines and what texts constituted a true Christian education. One need remember again that all early American colleges and universities were founded as essentially religious schools to educate a class of Christian leaders to preach, teach, and to take up the necessary civic professions. The texts from Jefferson and Sturtevant that we have excerpted above were written within this context. It was only in the twentieth century that most of these universities and colleges turned away from these official religious affiliations, even if they retained deep – and largely unspoken – cultural affinities and outlooks into the twenty-first. The religious right's condemnations of godlessness on university campuses therefore has as much to do with deep historical traditions in American higher ed as with new curricula.

[20] See Bushnell, *Culture of Teaching*, 117–43.

Which histories, and whose, matter in the pluralistic society and culture of twenty-first-century America? Was higher education in the liberal arts to be dominated by the same curriculum and canon that even Erasmus and his contemporaries found ambivalent at best and problematic of social and cultural rigidification? To what tradition did a United States – in which "whites" were soon to become a minority of the population – really belong? What of the wisdom of the Middle East and of Asia, or Latin America, and of Africa, of its texts and traditions? Columnist and author George Will summed up the challenge for the right-wing of the debate who saw the critics of the traditional canon as "delegitimizing Western civilization by discrediting the books and ideas that gave birth to it."[21]

*

Many on the religious right equated these historical humanities – the venerable liberal-arts education – as vector carriers for the disease of "secular humanism," a common association throughout modern industrial societies. This equation was nothing new, and as Hofstadter demonstrated, it derived from strains in American culture that went back to the Puritans and other radical reformers in the seventeenth century.[22] But in America this secular humanism was seen as the equivalent of Communist nihilism, a movement designed to insidiously penetrate all levels of education to remove both God and morality from the education of youth and to substitute virtue with moral ambivalence and relativism, to put Marx in the place of Jesus. Right-wing theorists saw it as an attempt to inculcate a numb conformity to the intellectual snobbery of a remote and indifferent coastal elite who drew their inspiration not from American values but from corrupted European systems of thought and politics. The liberal arts extolled by humanist elites was also seen as arrogant and anti-religious, dismissing those who considered themselves religious traditionalists, in O. B. Hardison's words quoted above, as "superstitious," "ignorant," "in bondage to" "mythologies" and "prejudices." While Hardison called for "humility" as well, such remarks were

---

[21] George Will, in "Literary Politics," *Newsweek* (April 22, 1991): 72.
[22] See Chapter 2, 34–36, 45–48.

seen to characterize an elite apology for the secular liberal arts as espoused during the Enlightenment, an association that would have a devastating impact on subsequent attempts to defend the humanities.

Criticism also came from within the ranks of the most prestigious scholars of early modern humanism themselves. As early as 1939, the towering Renaissance scholar Douglas Bush had observed that "in spite of our long subservience to secular liberalism, the climate of opinion in some quarters has changed a good deal. Voices can be heard declaring that the Renaissance, so far as it involved a secular revolt, was more of a calamity than a triumph."[23] In 1954, the famed literary scholar and author C. S. Lewis had criticized early modern humanism as "stillborn" and sterile, driven by personal ambition for patronage and position, falsely rejecting the dynamic culture of the late Middle Ages.[24]

We have already reviewed the essential political conservatism of English humanism and its mission to provide loyal civil servants and courtiers.[25] In their 1986 study, *From Humanism to the Humanities,* Anthony Grafton and Lisa Jardine took aim at assumptions that humanist pedagogy offered something fresh and liberating and saw instead numbing routine and memorization designed to create a loyal elite. They were not alone, or the first, to focus on the disciplinary elements of humanist education or the dynamics of societal power that such education reinforced.

Pierre Bourdieu and Jean-Claude Passeron had critiqued the "symbolic violence" of such education that,

> contributes by reproducing the cultural arbitrary which it inculcates, toward reproducing the power relations which are the basis of its power of arbitrary imposition (the social reproduction function of cultural reproduction).[26]

---

[23] In Bush, *The Renaissance and English Humanism,* 32.

[24] In C. S. Lewis, *English Literature in the Sixteenth Century* (Oxford: Oxford University Press, 1954), 20–21.

[25] See Chapter 1, 31–32.

[26] Pierre Bourdieu and Jean-Claude Passeron, *Reproduction in Education, Society and Culture,* Richard Nice, trans. (London: Sage, 1977), 5, 10.

In 1991, Richard Halpern analyzed early modern English education in the humanist tradition with Foucault's critique:

> the ideological function of Tudor schooling must ... be understood to include not only the transmission of doctrine or governing representations, but also the imposition of certain productive or disciplinary practices. The schools hammered in ideological content and also laid down economics of recreation and labor, punishment and reward. They thus participated in the disciplinary "accumulation of men" which, according to Foucault, complemented, and reinforced the accumulation of capital.[27]

The solution for some left-wing theorists was to dismantle the structures of authority embodied in the university as a space and time apart. According to Michael Ryan,

> To accept academic freedom as a rallying cry is tantamount to accepting a definition of the academy as a separable realm from the social world ... instead of emphasizing the fact that the social world is constructed and that therefore it could be constructed in a different form, the liberal philosophy of academic freedom would make that world appear natural.[28]

By the late 1980s Allan Bloom, George Will, William J. Bennett, Roger Kimball, Dinesh D'Souza, and others – several funded by the right-wing Olin Foundation – were presenting a unified critique of what they saw as the attack by feminist, multiculturalists, and leftists on the venerable humanist and Enlightenment tradition.[29] They called for resistance to this new criticism, which they saw as altering the curriculum beyond repair and turning the campus into a political arena. For these men the abandonment of innovation was a worthy price for restoring the authority and separateness of higher education. They asserted that only

---

[27] Richard Halperin, *The Poetics of Primitive Accumulation: English Renaissance Culture and the Genealogy of Capital* (Ithaca, NY: Cornell University Press, 1991), 26.

[28] Michael Ryan, "Deconstruction and Radical Teaching," in Barbara Johnson, ed., *The Pedagogical Imperative: Teaching as a Literary Genre*, Yale French Studies 63 (New Haven: Yale University Press, 1982), 45–58, at 58.

[29] See Chapter 3, 69–70; Chapter 7, 180–82.

by staying within a received canon of wisdom inherited from the Enlightenment could the humanities retain their value in society.[30]

*

The flight from Enlightenment authority has been hastened by a widespread cultural illiteracy toward the digital. We will examine the impact of the digital in Chapter 9, but here we should note that "digital literacy" is a broad concept.[31] It includes the skill set required to discern the quality and truth claims of the myriad sources of information – and disinformation – now available online. Everything from learning how to navigate computer systems and websites, to distinguishing reliable sources of reference (Google or Wikipedia, or the Stanford Encyclopedia of Philosophy?), to a new appreciation of online grammar and semantics, to the ability to judge quality have become essential to navigating digital culture. Yet few standard curricula exist on any level to acculturate digital readers and writers. In the short term this leads to a great deal of misinformation and in the long term to the further undermining of authority and expertise: every question from climate change, to inoculation, to Shakespeare's authorship is now open to individual interpretation in a way that the Bible and the authority of the Catholic Church became open to questioning and interpretation by new masses of laity through the media of the printing press and Reformation preaching. As Danah Boyd has noted:

> Because of my privilege as a scholar, I get to see how expert knowledge and information is produced and have a deep respect for the strengths and limitations of scientific inquiry. Surrounded by journalists and people working to distribute information, I get to see how incentives shape information production and dissemination and the fault lines of that

---

[30] See the summary in Bushnell, *Culture of Teaching*, 1–9.

[31] See Eileen Gardiner and Ronald G. Musto, *The Digital Humanities: A Primer for Students and Scholars* (New York: Cambridge University Press, 2015), 117–19; Alison J. Head and Michael B. Eisenberg, "Project Information Literacy Progress Report: Lessons Learned. How College Students Seek Information in the Digital Age," The Information School, University of Washington (Dec. 1, 2009), at http://ctl.yale.edu/sites/default/files/basic-page-supplementary-materials-files/how_students_seek_information_in_the_digital_age.pdf.

process. I believe that information intermediaries are important, that honed expertise matters, and that no one can ever be fully informed. As a result, I have long believed that we have to outsource certain matters and to trust others to do right by us as individuals and society as a whole. This is what it means to live in a democracy, but, more importantly, it's what it means to live in a society. In the United States, we're moving towards tribalism, and we're undoing the social fabric of our country through polarization, distrust, and self-segregation. And whether we like it or not, our culture of doubt and critique, experience over expertise, and personal responsibility is pushing us further down this path.[32]

Simultaneously, new political movements on the right have again raised the specter of fascist and Nazi disregard for fact and truth. These have subjected all public debate to the impact of power and will in ways that recall John Dewey's warnings and that have become frighteningly real in the current political environment and structures of the nation. Facts and those who discover, analyze, and propound them have rarely been so distrusted and marginalized. The impact of this on higher education has been profound, most especially when it attempts to inform public policy and legislation. Academia as a whole has focused on the ramifications of this de-authorization in the classroom but has so far failed to act accordingly to reassert its place in society.

*

Steven B. Gerrard, a professor of Philosophy at Williams College, offers a compelling example of this debate in the interaction of students, faculty, and administration around the values of free inquiry and speech, cultural hegemony, power relationships, and Enlightenment values in the liberal-arts college of today.[33] According to Gerrard,

---

[32] "Did Media Literacy Backfire?," *Points: Data & Society* (Jan. 5, 2017), at https://points
.datasociety.net/did-media-literacy-backfire-7418c084d88d.

[33] Steven B. Gerrard, "The Rise of the Comfort College: At American Universities, Personal
Grievances Are What Everyone's Talking," *Bloomberg.com* (Sept. 9, 2019), at www
.bloomberg.com/opinion/articles/2019-09-09/free-speech-is-no-longer-safe-speech-at-
today-s-elite-colleges; and Steven B. Gerrard, "How Comfort Conquered College,"
Bloomberg.com (Sept. 10, 2019), at www.bloomberg.com/opinion/articles/2019-09-10/
how-comfort-college-dogma-conquered-reason-and-evidence.

The liberal Enlightenment is being threatened all over the globe, mostly from the right. In American elite colleges, however, the threat is coming from the left – as the "consumer's college" gives way to the "comfort college." The aim of the consumer's college was to train a broad range of students for different forms of success. The primary goal of the comfort college? Diversity and inclusion. While these, and the accompanying call for social justice, are noble aspirations, what happens when they eclipse critical inquiry and the pursuit of knowledge? What happens when they outweigh everything else?

Gerrard goes on to discuss shifts in curricula and canons demanded by student groups, and the college's attempts to accommodate these:

When a Williams College department is given permission to create a new teaching position, the dean of the faculty assigns the search committee to read, among other works, "'We Are All for Diversity, But . . .' How Faculty Hiring Committees Reproduce Whiteness and Practical Suggestions for How They Can Change."[34] The authors say:

"Another unnamed logic of Whiteness is the presumed neutrality of White European enlightenment epistemology. The modern university – in its knowledge generation, research, and social and material sciences and with its 'experts' and its privileging of particular forms of knowledge over others (e.g., written over oral, history over memory, rationalism over wisdom) – has played a key role in the spreading of colonial empire. In this way, the university has validated and elevated positivistic, White Eurocentric knowledge over non-White, Indigenous, and non-European knowledges."

In November 2019, Williams students launched a well-publicized boycott campaign against their English department to redress issues of the canon that they contend have not included peoples of color and

[34] Özlem Sensoy and Robin DiAngelo, "'We Are All for Diversity, But . . .': How Faculty Hiring Committees Reproduce Whiteness and Practical Suggestions for How They Can Change," *Harvard Educational Review* (Winter 2017), at www.hepg.org/HER-Home/Issues/Harvard-Educational-Review-Volume-87-Number-4/HerArticle/We-Are-All-for-Diversity,-but-".

discussions of race.[35] Gerrard focuses on the key role of authority and separateness in higher education and the impact of innovation on both:

> Some of the power and authority of a university stems from the belief in its truth-seeking mission. When that dissolves, the elitist gatekeeping function will remain (at least for a while and at least for some), but its deliberative role in American democracy will be diminished.

FROM HUMANITIES TO TECHNOLOGIES

One must recall that the humanist movement that formed the basis of the modern liberal arts was a reaction to, and an intended reform of, the professional training that was then prevalent in Italian universities. Law, medicine, and the service activities of the notary were the most highly prized skills that the universities of Bologna, Naples, or Salerno produced, often in direct response to the political requirements of rulers. Even in the age of humanism, Italian universities like Bologna, Padua, Rome, Pisa, and Ferrara remained strong in professional education in law and medicine, in the natural sciences and mathematics, and in practical subject matter that would serve a largely civil society.[36] With the shift in the Italian political landscape away from the civic chancellory and toward the princely court, the curriculum of the humanists gained wider traction and influence throughout Europe. It was this courtly humanism that dominated English education, both inside and outside the university, and that inspired the first American colleges. Nevertheless, the practical goals and structures of Italian universities remained key to European higher education into the nineteenth century. We have already traced the roots of the American university from the English tradition of the liberal arts and the creation of the gentleman scholar, an elite educated to lead civil society. By the early years of the American republic, however, the curriculum at many colleges was

[35] Colleen Flaherty, "The Williams English Boycott," IHE (Nov. 9, 2019), at www .insidehighered.com/news/2019/11/06/students-williams-call-boycott-english-department.

[36] See Grendler, *Universities*, 267–352, 408–73.

already reflecting the new realities of life in America and the need for practical skills more suited to the frontier than to the courts of Europe.

In 1795, William R. Davie's plan for the University of North Carolina offered a full range of arts, sciences, and practical fields.[37] These included professorships and syllabi in moral and political philosophy and history, civil government and political constitutions, international law, astronomy, physics, hydraulics, pneumatics, optics and electricity, mathematics, chemistry, medicine, agricultural and mechanical arts, English literature, and classics. In January 1800, Jefferson's plan for the University of Virginia stated:

> I will venture even to sketch the sciences which seem useful and practicable for us, as they occur to me while holding my pen. Botany, Chemistry, Zoology, Anatomy, Surgery, Medicine, Natural Philosophy [science], Agriculture, Mathematics, Astronomy, Geology, Geography, Politics, Commerce, History, Ethics, Law, Arts, Fine Arts.[38]

By 1828, the faculty and corporation of Yale University found it necessary to issue a report defending the traditional humanities curriculum against a growing chorus of critics who called for more "practical" subject matters and the elimination of the classics. The report addressed the interrelated issues of the subject matter taught and of elitism and populism in higher education. The document is of primary importance for the history of American higher education, since Yale, along with Princeton, then educated the largest number of presidents and faculty members for the new colleges of the South and West:

> The expediency of retaining the ancient languages, as an essential part of our course of instruction, is so obviously connected with the object and plan of education in the college, that justice could not be done to the particular subject of inquiry in the resolution, without a brief statement of the nature and arrangement of the various branches of the whole system. . . . The guardians of the college appear to have ever acted upon the principle, that it ought not to be stationary, but continually advancing.

---

[37] Hofstadter & Smith, I:167–69.

[38] Letter to Joseph Priestley, January 18, 1800, in Hofstadter & Smith, I:175–76.

Some alternation has accordingly been proposed, almost every year, from its first establishment. . . . Not only the course of studies, and the modes of instruction, have been greatly varied; but whole sciences have, for the first time, been introduced; chemistry, mineralogy, geology, political economy, etc. . . . In laying the foundation of a thorough education, it is necessary that *all* the important mental faculties be brought into exercise. . . . In the course of instruction in this college, it has been an object to maintain such a proportion between the different branches of literature and science, as to form in the student a proper *balance* of character. . . . Our republican form of government renders it highly important, that great numbers should enjoy the advantage of a thorough education. On the Eastern continent, the *few* who are destined to particular departments in political life, may be educated for the purpose; while the mass of people are left in comparative ignorance. But in this country, where offices are accessible to all who are qualified for them, superior intellectual attainments ought not to be confined to any description of persons. *Merchants, manufacturers*, and *farmers*, as well as professional gentlemen, take their place in our public councils. A thorough education ought therefore to be extended to all these classes.[39]

With the later nineteenth century, the German model of "learning for its own sake" and "pure research" slowly became the norm for American higher ed.[40] New schools founded on the German model, like Johns Hopkins, focused increasingly on science, medicine, and applied technologies, what today we call STEM. American foundations, such as the Carnegie, enthusiastically embraced this German research university over the Oxbridge model. Their influence was welcomed by American corporate elites, who also saw the shift from the traditional liberal-arts college to research as an aid to business and to a form of governance familiar to their class. Efficiency of governance and a contempt for "faculty values" quickly overcame faculty resistance. Schools like Stanford, for example, actively undertook purges of older faculty who did not cooperate in the new research model of the entrepreneurial

---

[39] Hofstadter & Smith, I:275–91.   [40] See Chapter 2, 44–45.

university.[41] Toward the end of the nineteenth century, the liberal arts, which remained strong among the nation's small independent colleges, were incorporated into the new research universities as separate schools, largely for undergraduates, and as preparatory studies for the professional schools that slowly developed by the early twentieth century. But their appeal was often class- and region-based, with the strongest concentration of traditional liberal-arts colleges in New England and in the Midwestern communities founded by New Englanders.

Over the history of American higher education, the humanities have remained key to this undergraduate experience, but never did they predominate as the major draw for most students. By the end of World War II, higher education's participation in defense research had dramatically shifted both public and foundation support toward a handful of "Research 1" universities. Meanwhile, the practical goals of returning veterans participating in the GI Bill bolstered attempts at equality but further moved curricula away from the humanities toward business and engineering, with an accompanying shift in gender predominance as campuses again became "masculinized."[42] President Truman's Commission on Higher Education of 1946 enshrined these changes as national policy.[43] With the clarion call that education "should not get lost in the past," the Commission recommended the replacement of "liberal education" with a "general education" that would democratize the old humanistic goal of educating elites to one of preparing citizens for a technological and industrial future:

> Colleges must find a right relationship between specialized training on the one hand, aiming at a thousand different careers, and the transmission of a common cultural heritage toward a common citizenship on the other.[44]

Nevertheless, the prosperity, and the political and cultural consensus of the post-war period made it the golden age of the liberal arts and humanities. With the development of both technical colleges, land-grant universities, and professional schools for law, medicine, nursing, and

---

[41] Thelin, 238–45. [42] Thelin, 262–68.

[43] For a summation of the Commission report, Hofstadter & Smith, II:970–90.

[44] Hofstadter & Smith, II:989.

engineering, American higher ed demonstrated the versatility of its corporate model and its ability to adapt to changing social and cultural needs and priorities. The restructuring of higher education with the incorporation of the liberal-arts college into a broader research university made the liberal arts the ideal preparation for the professional schools and degrees now on offer. By 1964, however, the drift away from the humanities was already worrying many in higher education. That year the Commission on the Humanities, co-sponsored by the American Council of Learned Societies (ACLS), the Council of Graduate Schools in the United States, and the United Chapters of Phi Beta Kappa issued its report and recommendations.

The report encapsulates the state, impact, and self-image of the academic humanities in the USA at mid century. After a foreword that offers the proposition that "the humanities are in the national interest," on which proposition "there is no room for debate,"[45] the report then incorporates statements from twenty-four major learned societies then under the aegis of the ACLS. One of the most explicit statements was contributed by the American Historical Association. After offering a comprehensive definition of the humanities, it goes on to note that:

> history (and this is most important) has become one of the central disciplines and indispensable experiences of liberal education. ... It is no accident that history and English literature are the two most powerful major studies in many of our leading universities and colleges.

Yet, it continues, the worldview of the humanities is already under threat:

> Paradoxically the world is now moving so fast that history of the knowable past seems to Americans more than ever irrelevant, out of date and useless. ... American civilization is becoming increasingly unbalanced. The humanities – conceived for the individual, his [sic] culture, and all his values – have been slighted by the federal government, persistently underestimated by the public.[46]

---

[45] American Council of Learned Societies et al., *Report of the Commission on the Humanities*, v.
[46] American Council of Learned Societies et al., *Report*, 119.

In a sense the report repeated nearly five hundred years of humanists laments at the world's under-appreciation of their cultural treasures and of their claims to authority. But it also reflected some real changes in the public's outlook toward the purposes of higher education and in the cultural values embodied in the research university. The post-Vietnam university accelerated these changes. With what John Thelin noted as the "new vocationalism,"[47] students reflected an obsession with preprofessional study – medicine, business, accounting, law – any field that would give an advantage over the overcrowded cohort of graduates in a society still reeling from political and cultural divisions and now facing stagflation and recession. By the 1980s this sense of urgency was supplemented by the breaking down of the barriers of separateness among students as popular culture absorbed both student life and the research concerns of many traditional humanist scholars. An oversupply of fresh Ph.D.s and continued corporatization of governance also contributed to the weakening of faculty control over the curriculum. The gradual penetration of neoliberal ideology around the "marketplace of ideas" also transformed the role of the university from a separate time and place to study and evaluate long-held values to a consumer supermarket of ideas, skills, and career opportunities. Finally, the hi-tech revolution of the 1980s radically began to change methods of scholarly communication, pedagogy, and the cultural assumptions and expectations of students.

By the 2010s, 40 percent of undergraduates in the United States were majoring in business- and management-related subjects. According to Richard Arum and Jarip Roksa, the percentage of students who study more than twenty hours a week had fallen from 67 percent in 1961 to 20 percent in 2010. Math and science majors studied an average of 14.7 hours a week, business majors 9.6 hours, education and social work 10.6, and communication majors 10.5 hours. The majority of these students read only textbooks and short articles, and rarely wrote papers longer than three pages. By contrast, 88 percent of humanities majors were expected to read at least 40 pages a week – largely in primary sources, including fiction, history, philosophy, and other liberal arts – and to devote far longer hours to study. The more selective the school, the

[47] Thelin, 327.

greater the expectation of such requirements. At the most selective colleges, 92 percent of students were required to read over forty pages a week.[48]

*

With 2.5 *quintillion* bytes of data created daily by the 2010s, the accumulated learning and wisdom of the past two millennia could no longer make any claims to centrality or to student energies.[49] Both authority and separateness were further eroded by a constant stream of innovations.[50] From the 1980s on, the deployment of computer technologies to age-old questions and research agendas in the humanities accompanied attempts to accommodate traditional humanities fields to the impact of the digital. Much of this was embodied in digital humanities methodologies, "DH" theory and discourse, centers, and professorships. This turn has, however paradoxically, contributed to the movement toward technology as the determinative factor in cultural discourse.[51] This has seen a divergence between the digital as a tool, and a publishing and communication platform – "the digital in the humanities" – and the digital as a fundamental transformation of the humanities. DH theory as expounded by such notable critics as Franco Moretti in his "distant reading," Stephen Ramsay's "algorithmic criticism," Lev Manovich's "cultural analytics," and N. Katherine Hayles' "posthuman" "writing machines" has moved from humanities discourse aided by computers to the humanities themselves as an object of computational analysis. Thus the types of questions asked, the methods used, the predominance of quantitative approaches, data-mining, and big-data studies have deepened the shift toward hi-tech and the public perception that technology holds the key to solutions even in the liberal arts and humanities.

---

[48] Richard Arum and Jarip Roksa, *Academically Adrift: Limited Learning on College Campuses* (Chicago: University of Chicago Press, 2011), 4, 69–80.

[49] Peter Marber, "The Most Forward-thinking, Future-proof College in America Teaches Every Student the Exact Same Stuff," *Quartz* (June 21, 2017), at https://qz.com/994810/the-most-forward-thinking-future-proof-college-in-america-teaches-every-student-the-exact-same-things.

[50] Thelin, 326–44.

[51] See Gardiner and Musto, *Digital Humanities*, 142–45 for a brief summation.

As one critic has asserted, DH "confuses more information for more knowledge."[52]

Rens Bod's *A New History of the Humanities* is indicative of parallel trends in the historical analysis of the humanities.[53] His subtitle, *The Search for Principles and Patterns from Antiquity to the Present*, presents the emerging attitude in what he claims to be the "first overarching history of the humanities in the English language."[54] Bod emphasizes a theory that only by their ability to see patterns, rules, laws, general principles, group-ings, and commonalities can the humanities continue to have any value. This contradicts centuries of the humanities' emphasis on the unique and the exceptional, rather than on the group or the general rule examined by the social and physical sciences, and again points to the general trend to value quantification and classification – the keystones of STEM – as the only valid form of intellectual inquiry. Such analysis is the obverse of critiques that view traditional humanistic inquiry as essentially "non-cognitive."[55] To disprove this biased assumption, Bod therefore touts the humanities' value as the forerunners to modern science.[56] Although there is certainly historical validity to this claim, his emphasis is to justify the traditional humanities precisely because of their contri-bution to science and technology, a common meme among contempor-ary apologists, but one that continues to devalue the humanities.

Bod's work reflects a broad debate among humanists and specialists in the liberal arts. At a 2014 conference at St. John's College in Sante Fe, NM, John Agresto, past president of St. John's and former deputy chair-man of the National Endowment for the Humanities, noted the tiny percentage of humanities majors on American campuses. He warned that the liberal arts are "dying," but that this was "less a murder than a suicide." He blamed much of the public's disenchantment on the sup-posed preponderance of critical theory and a turning away from

---

[52] Timothy Brennan, "The Digital-Humanities Bust: After a Decade of Investment and Hype, What Has the Field Accomplished? Not Much," CHE (Oct. 15, 2017), at www .chronicle.com/article/The-Digital-Humanities-Bust/241424.

[53] Bod, *New History.*   [54] Bod, *New History*, 1.

[55] Hanlon, "Lies About the Humanities," www.chronicle.com/article/Lies-About-the-Humanities-/245261.

[56] See for example, Bod, *New History*, 240–49.

traditional texts and themes that would serve a consensus view of social utility. But Andrew Delbanco, director of American studies and Julian Clarence Levi Professor in the Humanities at Columbia University, stressed, instead, a post-1968 hermetic view of the humanities: "You cannot explain the value of a liberal education to those who have not had one."

*

Larger trends both in degrees awarded and fields transformed reinforce such anecdotal examples. Recent data gathered from the Graduate Records Examination Program and the Council of Graduate Schools,[57] and the Humanities Indicators Project of the American Academy of Arts and Sciences confirms a general picture that higher degrees (both master's and doctorate) in the humanities continue to decline.[58] Meanwhile, such fields as health sciences and education have shown robust growth. The best indicator of continued faith in the vigor of humanities fields might be the overall percentages and numbers of graduates going on to doctorates in any particular field. While master's programs continue to show strong growth across many arts and sciences programs, the doctorate now accounts for only 11.3 percent of post-graduate degrees. In 2015–16 health sciences accounted for 19.6 percent of doctoral degrees awarded, engineering 13.6 percent, education 12.4 percent, social and behavioral sciences 12.4 percent, and biological and agricultural sciences 11.9 percent.[59] Arts and humanities accounted for 7.4 percent. Masters' degrees in business and education made up for 21.2 percent and 18.9 percent, respectively. Humanities students made up about 10.9 percent of all those pursuing a graduate degree.

[57] Hironao Okahana and Enyu Zhou, "Graduate Enrollment and Degrees: 2006 to 2016," in *Graduate Enrollment and Degrees, 2006–2016* (Washington, DC: Council of Graduate Schools, September 2017), at https://cgsnet.org/ckfinder/userfiles/files/CGS_GED16_Report_Final.pdf. See also Vimal Patel, "Amid Professors' 'Doom-and-Gloom Talk,'" Humanities Ph.D. Applications Drop," CHE (Sept. 28, 2017), at www.chronicle.com/article/Amid-Professors-/241311.

[58] "Bachelor's Degrees in the Humanities" (updated May 2017), at www.amacad.org/humanities-indicators/higher-education/bachelors-degrees-humanities.

[59] Okahana and Zhou, "Graduate Enrollment and Degrees," 11–12 and Fig. 3.

In terms of applications for graduate study, the year 2015–16 saw a continuation of recent trends: mathematics and computer sciences showed an increase of 5.5 percent, physical and earth sciences of 5.0 percent, business of 3.2 percent, and biological and agricultural sciences of 3.1 percent. In the opposite direction, the arts and humanities showed the biggest decline, of 6.2 percent. From 2011 to 2016 the average annual decline for the arts and humanities was about 3 percent.[60] In 2016, arts and humanities represented only 8.6 percent of all doctorate applications.[61] They totaled 5 percent of all graduate school admissions,[62] 8.2 percent of doctorate enrollments,[63] and 7.4 percent of doctorates granted.[64] Tracking the success – in or out of academe – of those who do complete doctorates in the humanities has only begun to take on rigorous reporting.[65]

The latest statistics compiled by the Humanities Indicators initiative paints a similar picture and is particularly valuable for tracking the changes in undergraduate humanities enrollments over the long term.[66] From 1949 to 2015, for example, bachelor's degrees in the humanities ranged from about 9.75 percent of all BA's in 1949, to a historical high of about 17 percent in 1967, and back down to just over 5 percent in 2015. From 2011 to 2017, on the other hand, fields like history have seen a decline of nearly 34 percent, English languages and literatures and philosophy of about 20 percent. Over the same period computer-science degrees have seen a net increase of nearly 75 percent; nursing, health, and medical of about 70 percent; engineering of about 50 percent; and math and statistics of over 30 percent.[67] In 2015, bachelors' degrees in all

---

[60] Okahana and Zhou, "Graduate Enrollment and Degrees," 46, Table C.2.

[61] Okahana and Zhou, "Graduate Enrollment and Degrees," 26, Table B.2.

[62] Okahana and Zhou, "Graduate Enrollment and Degrees," 28, Table B.4.

[63] Okahana and Zhou, "Graduate Enrollment and Degrees," 35, Table B.15.

[64] Okahana and Zhou, "Graduate Enrollment and Degrees," 40, Table B.22.

[65] Audrey Williams June, "Want to Know where Ph.D.s in English Get Jobs? This Is What Grad Programs Will Tell You," CHE (Sept. 25, 2019), at www.chronicle.com/article/ Want-to-Know-Where-PhDs-in/247220.

[66] www.humanitiesindicators.org/content/indicatordoc.aspx?i=197.

[67] Benjamin M. Schmidt, "The History BA Since the Great Recession: The 2018 AHA Majors Report," *AHA Perspectives* (Nov 26, 2018), at www.historians.org/publications-and-directories/perspectives-on-history/december-2018/the-history-ba-since-the-great-recession-the-2018-aha-majors-report.

the humanities made up just under 12 percent of total undergraduate degrees. This was less than a third of the 37 percent for the sciences (health and medical, natural, and behavioral and social combined). The humanities' share was less than two-thirds the size of that for business and management, which took 19 percent of bachelors' degrees.

The impact on the infrastructure of the humanities – and of higher education in general – was no less severe. Between 2007 and 2012, an average of 6 percent of humanities departments had ceased to grant degrees. For languages and literature departments that number was 12 percent. At public colleges and universities it had reached 18 percent.[68] In the three years prior to January 2019, according to data compiled by the Modern Language Association (MLA),[69] foreign languages and literatures alone had lost 651 programs across the nation, reflecting a decline in enrollments of just over 15 percent since 2009,[70] what one commentator has called an "extinction event."[71]

Meanwhile, however, increased Federal spending was making science and technology programs more responsive to public pressures and support. The separateness that university faculty and administrators vaunted as sacred to their authority and ability to innovate lay in tatters in the face of ever-increasing cooperation with corporate- and government-supported research.

INNOVATION AND TECH

By 2018, Columbia University was reflecting back on the fiftieth anniversary of the '68 takeover,[72] offering its own version of remote events

---

[68] Table HDS2-S3 at www.amacad.org/humanities-indicators/higher-education/bachelors-degrees-humanities.

[69] Dennis Looney and Natalia Lusin, "Enrollments in Languages Other Than English in United States Institutions of Higher Education, Summer 2016 and Fall 2016: Preliminary Report," (New York: MLA, February 2018), at www.mla.org/content/download/83540/2197676/2016-Enrollments-Short-Report.pdf.

[70] Steven Johnson, "Colleges Lose a 'Stunning' 651 Foreign-Language Programs in 3 Years," CHE (Jan. 22, 2019), at www.chronicle.com/article/Colleges-Lose-a-Stunning-/245526.

[71] Andrew Kay, "Academe's Extinction Event," *Chronicle Review*, CHE (May 10, 2019), at www.chronicle.com/interactives/20190510-academes-extinction-event.

[72] See Thomas Vinciguerra, "A Provost's Reflections: David P. Truman and the Bust of '68," *Columbia Magazine* (Fall 2017), at https://magazine.columbia.edu/article/provosts-

surrounding the protests unleashed by the combination of campus participation in government research, the Vietnam war, and the university's
aggressive plans to expand into the Morningside Heights neighborhood.[73] Meanwhile the university – using its authority in the name of
innovation to break down its separateness – had finally accomplished
what it had set out to do in 1968. It had moved beyond its walled-in
campus to take over the surrounding neighborhood by eliminating the
last traces of the Harlem Valley district to the north with a dazzling new
sci-tech campus of glass and steel devoted to research in neuroscience
and business. Dubbed the Manhattanville Campus, the new expansion
would cover seventeen acres.[74] According to Columbia, "the campus will
provide innovative spaces for teaching, pioneering research, artistic
expression and the shared human experiences of a great city defined
by openness and diversity."[75]

New York, like a few other world capitals, was quickly becoming a
meeting ground of higher ed, the corporate world, and the shift toward
the technical university. As Columbia was completing its Harlem Valley
campus, Cornell University was creating a new $2 billion, fourteen-acre
campus on Roosevelt Island in the middle of New York's East River. The
goal of the campus was to actively cooperate with business, "marking [a]
transformational milestone for tech in NYC."[76] Here Cornell, with the
top-down cooperation of New York State, took over land largely derelict
for decades but which the local community had envisioned as more
housing and recreation space for the city's dwindling middle-class.

Opposite it across the East River, Rockefeller University was also
expanding its campus by building over the existing FDR Drive to create
the new sci-tech Stavros Niarchos Foundation–David Rockefeller River

reflections; and Phillip Lopate, "Confessions of a Reluctant Revolutionary," *Columbia
Magazine* (Winter 2017–18), at https://magazine.columbia.edu/article/confessions-
reluctant-revolutionary.

[73] See above, Chapter 3, 60–66.
[74] "Welcome to a New Urban Campus for the 21st Century," at https://manhattanville
.columbia.edu/about.
[75] https://manhattanville.columbia.edu.
[76] https://tech.cornell.edu/news/cornell-tech-campus-opens-on-roosevelt-island-marking-
transformational-mile.

Campus devoted to "the betterment of humanity."[77] Further downtown in New York and Brooklyn, New York University was gaining an unwelcome reputation for buying up large tracts of real estate to expand its many programs in STEM and its business-related programs and to house an ever-increasing student population. In the Boston Area, Harvard paints a picture of "a sun-bright future" for a "new innovation cluster" as it finally unveils plans for its over 100 acres in the neighboring community of Allston to build its John A. Paulson School of Engineering and Applied Sciences (SEAS). The plan includes three "innovation labs" – the i-lab, Launch Lab, and Life Lab – and requires the services of a new "head of enterprise real estate [to] oversee private development aligned with the University's strengths."[78] According to spokespeople for all these expansions, such "innovation" would aid local neighborhoods, cities, and the globe via the spillover and trickle-down from the billions invested and spent.

These are not isolated cases.[79] In the early 1970s, the National Science Foundation funded the first series of "University Innovation Centers." These morphed into technology-transfer offices at such schools as Yale, and then, in the wake of a 2014 Brookings Institute report, into "innovation districts." By the early years of the twenty-first century, "innovation campuses" had begun sprouting across the nation. In June 2019, Virginia Tech announced a $1-billion innovation campus initiative to become partners with the planned Amazon.com HQ2 initiative. It joined Stanford University's CS+X project, the University of Pennsylvania's 2016 Pennovation Center (a "distinctive blend of offices, labs, and production space" aimed at "advancing knowledge and generating economic development"), MIT's Stephen A. Schwarzman College of Computing, announced late in 2018, and the University of Toronto plans for a similar center.

---

[77] https://snf-dr-rivercampus.rockefeller.edu.

[78] "A Sun-Bright Future in Allston," *Harvard Gazette* (May 26, 2016), at https://news .harvard.edu/gazette/story/2016/05/a-sun-bright-future-in-allston.

[79] See Matthew Wisnioski and Lee Vinsel, "The Campus Innovation Myth: A Half-Century of Occasional Breakthroughs – and Many Disappointments," *Chronicle Review*, CHE (June 11, 2019), at www.chronicle.com/interactives/20190611-vinsel.

Despite a 2013 statistical analysis that indicated that 87 percent of such campuses and centers lost money over the previous twenty years,[80] administrators continue to steer their campuses away from the humanities and liberal arts and toward tech. The trade-offs of the dynamic are explicit: the surrender of separateness and some authority in exchange for the benefits of innovation. Virginia Tech boasted that its Innovation Campus would not be:

> a walled and ivy-covered fortress, ... [but] an open urban community anchoring a vibrant neighborhood where growing companies and start-ups will co-locate, and students, staff, and faculty will reside, study, and collaborate.

CURRICULAR CHANGES

But the majority of US colleges and universities witnesses far less dramatic, but equally important shifts in curricula. While the statistics are clear, individual cases offer a more nuanced picture of change. At Wellesley College, for example, the paradigmatic image of the refined liberal-arts college of the early twentieth century has been giving way to more complex changes.[81] From 2008 and 2016, Wellesley saw a 14 percent drop in humanities enrollments and an 8 percent decline in the social sciences. Meanwhile, enrollments in math and the sciences rose by 29 percent. Over the same period, arts and humanities majors dropped from 27 percent to 23 percent. Social-sciences majors remained fairly steady, from 44 percent to 42 percent, and math and science majors rose from 18 percent to 23 percent. The overall trend at such a key liberal arts college was the shift from humanities to STEM majors. The trends are similar across broader samplings. In 1995, for example, English was the most popular major in nine out of the top twenty

---

[80] Walter D. Valdivia, "University Start-Ups: Critical for Improving Technology Transfer," Center for Technology Innovation at Brookings (November 2013), at www.brookings .edu/wp-content/uploads/2016/06/Valdivia_Tech-Transfer_v29_No-Embargo.pdf.

[81] Colleen Flaherty, "Liberal Arts College Students Are Getting Less Artsy," IHE (Feb. 21, 2017), at www.insidehighered.com/news/2017/02/21/liberal-arts-students-fears-about-job-market-upon-graduation-are-increasingly?

liberal-arts colleges. By 2013 that number had fallen to one out of twenty. As a new "credentialism" sweeps elite schools, economics has risen to number one at four out of the top ten liberal-arts schools.[82] Schools like Williams College have made up for the shortfalls by offering students double majors, allowing them to study both what they enjoy and what they think will land them jobs. Schools like Carleton College and George Washington University have witnessed the same shifts from humanities to STEM fields.[83]

Various analyses have attempted to explain this dramatic shift, and we have already discussed many cultural and intellectual ones. But there are political ones as well. One of the constant themes of right-wing propagandists like Charlie Kirk, founder and executive director of Turning Point USA, has been the alleged left-wing ideology of university faculty, especially in the humanities, and the uselessness and "ornamental" status of the humanities themselves.[84] In a tweet from April 7, 2018, Kirk laid out what he claimed to be the connection:

> 80 percent of humanities papers in higher education are not cited once. No wonder: they are filled with anti-science, anti-western, and anti-American ideas.[85]

There have also been attempts to offer marketplace justifications that question the very notion of the liberal arts as having little if any valence in American society today. Such approaches focus on issues of market branding, citing the very words "liberal" and "arts" as taboo in today's

---

[82] William Deresiewicz, *Excellent Sheep: The Miseducation of the American Elite and the Way to a Meaningful Life* (New York: Free Press, 2014), 16–17.

[83] Steven Johnson, "'Better, Not Bigger': As Private Colleges Hunger for Students, One University Slims Down," CHE (July 17, 2019), at www.chronicle.com/article/Better-Not-Bigger-As/246716; Jared Gans, "Faculty Sign Petition Demanding Information about LeBlanc's Proposed Enrollment Cut," *GW Hatchet* (Oct. 16, 2019), at www.gwhatchet.com/2019/10/16/faculty-sign-petition-demanding-information-about-leblancs-proposed-enrollment-cut.

[84] Hanlon, "Lies About the Humanities," www.chronicle.com/article/Lies-About-the-Humanities-/245261.

[85] Matthew Boedy, "Debunking Charlie Kirk on the Uselessness of the Humanities," *Medium* (April 9, 2018), at https://medium.com/@mboedy/debunking-charlie-kirk-on-the-uselessness-of-the-humanities-35337f8890b8.

political climate of right-wing critique and zealous career pursuit.[86] These come hand-in-hand with a neoliberal emphasis on metrics as the key to valuing every aspect of contemporary society, including higher ed.[87] Such marketplace approaches echo and reinforce political pressures to eliminate humanities and liberal-arts majors and to meet the needs of corporate employers. In 2011, Republican Governor Rick Scott of Florida announced a plan to shift state support toward STEM education and away from the liberal arts and social sciences. As he claimed in a radio interview,

> You know, we don't need a lot more anthropologists in the state. It's a great degree if people want to get it, but we don't need them here. I want to spend our dollars giving people science, technology, engineering, math degrees ... so when they get out of school, they can get a job.[88]

In 2017, Republican Kentucky governor Matt Bevin urged his state's universities to

> find entire parts of your campus ... that don't need to be there ... either physically as programs, degrees that you're offering, buildings that ... shouldn't be there because you're maintaining something that's not an asset of any value, that's not helping to produce that 21st century educated workforce. ... If you're studying interpretive dance, God bless you, but there's not a lot of jobs right now in America looking for people with that as a skill set.[89]

---

[86] "What's in a Name? College-Bound Students Weigh in on the 'Liberal Arts,'" *Arts & Science Group, Student Poll* 13.1 (September 2017), at www.artsci.com/insights/studentpoll/volume-13-issue-1. See also Liam Adams, "Liberal-Arts Colleges Should Take Initiative in Defining Themselves, Survey Suggests," CHE (Sept. 11, 2017), at www.chronicle.com/article/Liberal-Arts-Colleges-Should/241149.

[87] See Jerry Z. Muller, *The Tyranny of Metrics* (Princeton: Princeton University Press, 2018), esp. 67–87.

[88] Caitlin Zaloom, "STEM Is Overrated: College is Not Just Job Prep, and the Job Market Changes Constantly," *Atlantic* (Sept. 9, 2019), at www.theatlantic.com/ideas/archive/2019/09/college-not-job-prep/597487.

[89] Bruce Schreiner, "Bevin Implores Universities to Cut Programs That Don't Produce Money-making Grads," *Lexington Herald Leader* (Sept. 14, 2017), at www.kentucky.com/news/local/education/article172961586.html.

Bevin went on to encourage state campuses to produce four times as many engineers than current numbers. His call was greeted by University of Louisville's interim president as a "natural fit" for the system's plans.

Even after the defeat of Republican governor Scott Walker in Wisconsin and the election of a pro-education Democratic governor, the state has witnessed a push to substitute the "Wisconsin Idea" as the search for truth in the service of the public with vocational training in the service of corporate job requirements. In March 2018, the administration of the Stevens Point campus of the university announced plans to eliminate majors in English, philosophy, political science, and history among thirteen majors slated. The reason given: budget readjustment in the face of "some changing enrollment behaviors." According to the provost and vice chancellor, "students are far more cost-conscious than they used to be." Despite much opposition from students, faculty, alums, and the public, and calls for both the chancellor and provost to resign, that November the administration announced plans to eliminate six liberal arts majors, including geography, geology, French, German, two- and three-dimensional art, and history.[90] The cuts in the arts and humanities reflected "a national move among students towards career pathways," administrators argued. Meanwhile, the school planned to add majors in chemical engineering, computer-information systems, conservation, law enforcement, finance, fire science, graphic design, management, and marketing. According to the school's provost, "We need to make sure that knowledge is relevant, and it's applied." Echoing the mantra of austerity in higher education, he added, "The reality is that we just can't be everything to everyone, regardless of the public-good value of some of the coursework."

In April 2019, the University of Tulsa (UT) – which then had an endowment of $1.1 billion for just 4,000 students – announced that it was cutting dozens of programs including majors, minors, and graduate

---

[90] Adam Harris, "The Liberal Arts May Not Survive the 21st Century," *Atlantic* (Dec. 13, 2018), at www.theatlantic.com/education/archive/2018/12/the-liberal-arts-may-not-survive-the-21st-century/577876.

offerings, largely in the liberal arts.[91] The plan, dubbed "True Commitment," was developed in great secrecy and came largely at the behest of oil magnate George Kaiser, owner of the Bank of Oklahoma. According to Jacob Howland, McFarlin Professor of Philosophy and past chair of the Department of Philosophy and Religion, the procedure flew in the face of AAUP guidelines for shared governance:

> It included no one from the humanities or the natural sciences and was chaired by an accounting professor (who was just appointed to the newly created position of senior vice-provost for academic initiatives). All committee members were furthermore required to sign blanket non-disclosure agreements.

In 2018, Frederic Dorwart, president of the George Kaiser Family Foundation, was appointed chair of the UT board.[92] In May 2013, *Bloomberg* disclosed that "at least $1.25 billion of the charity's $3.4 billion in assets is invested in ways that benefit Kaiser's for-profit endeavors."[93] The foundation's senior staff also populate many of the city's boardrooms, while Kaiser's bank served as the corporate trustee of the university's $1.1 billion endowment. The university's president, a former legal counsel for the US Central Intelligence Agency with no previous academic experience, was appointed to the Kaiser bank's board in 2018; and the wife of Kaiser Foundation's executive director served as the university's provost and executive vice-president for academic affairs. Two Kaiser bank directors also sat on the university's board.

---

[91] Beckie Supiano, "U. of Tulsa Has a Billion-Dollar Endowment for Just 4,000 Students. Why Is It Cutting Programs?" CHE (April 15, 2019), at www.chronicle.com/article/U-of-Tulsa-Has-a/246117.

[92] Liam Knox, "U. of Tulsa Faculty to Ask Oklahoma's Attorney General to Halt Controversial Restructuring Plan," CHE (Aug. 22, 2019), at www.chronicle.com/article/U-of-Tulsa-Faculty-to-Ask/246997; Jacob Howland, "Corporate Wolves in Academic Sheepskins, or, a Billionaire's Raid on the University of Tulsa," *Nation* (June 18, 2019), at www.thenation.com/article/higher-education-corporate-takeover-kaiser-university-of-tulsa.

[93] Brendan Coffey, "Billionaire George Kaiser's Friendly Foundation: George Kaiser's Charity Puts a Lot of Money Where He Does," *Bloomberg* (May 10, 2013), www.bloomberg.com/news/articles/2013-05-09/billionaire-george-kaisers-friendly-foundation.

There would be cuts in physics and chemistry and some business offerings. The school also planned to eliminate all of its theater degrees, majors in philosophy and religion, Russian and Chinese studies, and an M.A. in history. All fifteen departments in Tulsa's College of Arts and Sciences would be consolidated into three "interdisciplinary" divisions, and the sixty-eight degree programs would be reduced to thirty-six. The plan raised teaching requirements across the university from five to eight courses a year. The goal was to shift funding, faculty, and priorities into the creation of a "professional super college" combining business, health sciences, and law. Tulsa's provost Levit offered the standard mantra for the changes: "For too long, we have tried to be everything to everyone." She described the university as "a high-touch undergraduate institution ... that is STEM-heavy with a professional, practical focus." University president Clancy announced plans for a

> Tulsa Enterprise for Cyber Innovation, Talent and Entrepreneurship, which will allow industry, federal agencies and TU to work together to defend information systems, [including] four cyber centers of excellence: an engineering research center, a multi-federal agency cybersecurity center for excellence, a cybersecurity insurance institute and a consortium of business sectors.

According to Jacob Howland, "Tulsa is essentially becoming a sort of pre-professional school. ... The writing's on the wall – they're just destroying the liberal arts, natural sciences and humanities at TU."[94] The university's president dismissed complaints from faculty, students, and alums, including an August 2019 appeal to the state's attorney general joined by one-third of the faculty, as "inflammatory rumors." In November 2019, Tulsa's board of trustees voted to reject faculty efforts at compromise and to endorse the restructuring plan, which would cut 40 percent of academic programs in favor of STEM concentrations. According to Tulsa's president after the vote, "there will be no 'repeal'

---

[94] Nick Hazelrigg, "Reorganizing away the Liberal Arts: Professors Fear University of Tulsa Abandoning its Historic Commitment to Education beyond Job Training," IHE (June 6, 2019), at www.insidehighered.com/news/2019/06/06/cuts-leave-concerns-liberal-arts-tulsa.

or 'rollback' of True Commitment."[95] On November 13, amid administration efforts to muzzle continued protests by filing ethics complaints against individual faculty as "bullies," the faculty senate overwhelmingly approved a vote of no-confidence in the school's president and provost. "True Commitment to who?" protested students.[96]

Tulsa's transformation was aided by such educational consulting firms as EAB,[97] which specializes in restructuring plans for higher ed and which targets presidents, provosts, and trustees and offers consultations on how to "illuminate your underutilized instructional resources":

> universities commonly offer more sections than are needed to meet student demand, with under-enrolled sections representing a suboptimal use of faculty time and effort. Academic Performance Solutions research revealed that as many as 28% of seats on campus go unfilled each semester. With just a few smart scheduling checks, university leaders can spotlight opportunities to free up capacity and redirect resources to the priorities they care about most.[98]

That is to say, they offer blueprints on how to restructure faculties, departments, disciplines, and programs. EAB promotes replacing "evidence of disciplinary excellence" as a basic criterion in evaluating promotion and tenure. It even furnishes "Guidance and Resources for Transitioning from Siloed Departments to a Collaborative Academic Governance Model" and a pamphlet called "Divisional Reorganization Talking Points" for high-level administrators.[99] According to EAB, in 2017 it served over 1,500 schools, colleges and universities as diverse as the University of Denver, Georgia State, Augustan College, and

---

[95] Lauren Fisher, "Tulsa Trustees Override Faculty to Uphold Academic-Restructuring Plan with Sweeping Cuts," CHE (Nov. 7, 2019), at www.chronicle.com/article/Tulsa-Trustees-Override/247504.

[96] Lauren Fisher, "How a Radical Restructuring Plan Fractured a Campus and Fueled a No-Confidence Vote," CHE (Nov. 14, 2019), at www.chronicle.com/article/How-a-Radical-Restructuring/247542.

[97] https://eab.com/about.

[98] (August 9, 2017), at https://eab.com/technology/infographic/operations/illuminate-your-underutilized-instructional-resources.

[99] https://eab.com/research/academic-affairs/toolkit/the-multidisciplinary-reorganization-toolkit.

Arapahoe Community College. But EAB remains an opaque entity to outsiders. Its website provides no information about its officers, board, or history. By April 2017, EAB was working its magic at McDaniel College in Maryland with its "McDaniel Commitment" plan that called for a similar hollowing-out of the liberal arts.

But not all shifts have been explicitly motivated by politics or monied interests. Also in Maryland, the University of Maryland's main campus at College Park has seen the number of English majors decline by 40 percent between 2012 and 2015. Analysts see various causes for the dramatic fall. One was internal, as changes in curriculum, overwhelmingly supported by the faculty, eliminated core requirements in favor of a more broad-based general-education program that no longer required key English courses. But many see the major issue as the uncertainty over career prospects in the wake of the 2008 recession and the steady chorus that has undervalued the humanities as preparing students for the marketplace. Bonnie Thornton Dill, dean of the College of Arts and Humanities, reflected the findings of several recent polls in noting that:

> people are looking at higher education more as a personal good than a social good and therefore don't fully understand the economic value of the arts and humanities. As a result, people are moving in a careerist direction at the undergraduate level.[100]

At Southern Illinois University at Carbondale, the school's new chancellor announced a new "synergy" plan in November 2017 that would also replace all disciplinary departments with schools of the humanities, allied health, art and design, and architecture.[101] According to the chancellor, the solution to financial problems

> is to eliminate the primary obstacles for multidisciplinary interaction – the financial structure associated with departments. By eliminating departments, we coarsen the delivery of resources to support innovative thinking.

---

[100] Colleen Flaherty, "Major Exodus," IHE (Jan. 26, 2015), at www.insidehighered.com/news/2015/01/26/where-have-all-english-majors-gone.

[101] Colleen Flaherty, "Doing Away with Departments," IHE (Nov. 17, 2017), at www.insidehighered.com/news/2017/11/17/southern-illinois-u-carbondale-wants-dissolve-academic-departments-all-them.

The plan to "coarsen" things would also increase faculty work loads and eliminate departmental operating papers written under shared governance rules by faculty. Such papers outline policy for hiring, tenure, and promotion.

At the University of Central Missouri rapid changes have been underway without much faculty input. Under a plan called "Strategic Governance for Student Success," programs in health studies would be merged with the College of Health Sciences and Technology. The College of Arts, Humanities, and Social Sciences would be eliminated.[102] Many more individual examples could be brought to bear from across the United States. But the Maryland dean's comments bring us back to the origins of the humanist revolt from the medieval Italian university: from higher education as a path toward professional career opportunity to one designed to educate citizens and leaders through a comprehensive grounding in the liberal arts and sciences. As we shall see in our final chapter, we may again be at a decisive juncture in the history of higher education.

---

[102] Eric Kelderman, "Can Closing a Humanities College Save a University?," CHE (April 13, 2018), at www.chronicle.com/article/Can-Closing-a-Humanities/243113.

CHAPTER 9

Transformations, Takeovers, Closings

INTRODUCTION

T
HE WALLS THAT SEPARATED THE MONASTERY from the secular world in the sixteenth century were of brick, stone, and mortar. But in the twenty-first century neither the walls of separation, not their dissolution, need be physical or at all visible. Political and cultural conflict, corporatization, commodification, the ubiquitousness of the digital that makes physical place irrelevant have all dissolved separateness by bringing the external world into the campus and by extending the role of the university into close partnerships with government, business, and community. All, in a sense, dissolve the cytoplasm of the university into the world surrounding it.

The Dissolution of the Monasteries in the late 1530s came quickly and from several directions, and it was completed just as rapidly. But it is important to remember that it came as the culmination of decades of critique by humanist thinkers, of attack by religious reformers, and of political maneuver by newly emerging states.[1] The resulting Reformation wrought enormous ideological and physical changes. It was the result of the strenuous efforts of some for, and the various responses of the many against, fundamental change. Speeches and sermons, letters, books and pamphlets, public debates and closed-door meetings, apologetics and attacks, defenses and counterattacks, petitions, legal cases, and trials, marches and processions, demonstrations, altercations and revolts, book

---

[1] See Chapter 1, 15–20.

lists, bannings, and burnings, dismissals from university positions, violent confrontations and peaceful retreats, business schemes and deals, official royal legislation, and local ordinances all preceded the Dissolution. In the end, however, the wholesale transformations, closings, and dissolutions of the English monasteries ultimately followed the political directive and will of the English Crown and would not have been possible without the centralized power of the state. Equally important to note are the results.

The Dissolution saw the vast majority of religious houses abandoned, their communities dissolved and scattered, their physical plants left for sale, pillage, and ruin. Yet many institutions were saved to be transformed into hospitals, grammar schools, cathedral and parish churches, university residential colleges, rural estates, and homes. From the time of Cardinal Wolsey and Thomas Cromwell's original vision for the revitalization of a declining English monasticism, such plans envisioned the closing of some houses, the reform of others, and the transformation of yet others to what the reformers considered more social purposes. Not every act of the Dissolution was committed in the spirit of greed or religious zeal. A few prominent institutions survived. Canterbury, Norwich, Durham, Westminster, Gloucester, Chester, Oxford, Bath, and Bristol are among the sixteen monasteries that continued to thrive but with their fabrics and missions realigned to the English Reformation and the royal will.[2]

In the previous chapters we discussed many of the causes of our modern dissolution: the collapse of academic authority both on campus and within society at large, the driving need for innovation in the post-war American research university, and the political, social, and economic pressures encouraging the walls of separation to come tumbling down. In this final chapter we will address some of the results and key elements of these transformations: corporatization, the accompanying commodification and monetization of research, their effects on scholarly communication, the impact of the digital, and the repurposing and physical closings of institutions of higher education.

---

[2] Knowles, *Religious Orders*, III:389–92.

THE NEOLIBERAL MARKETPLACE: THE CORPORATE
UNIVERSITY

The medieval university was among the earliest corporations in history. As we have seen, the name *universitas* meant any collective, or "corporate," body. In the medieval Kingdom of Naples, for example, the civic governments of southern Italy were generally called *universitates.* Chapter 2 reviewed how the first colonial American colleges and universities received their charters as corporations and how their governing boards were already known as boards of trustees.[3] The shift toward the modern corporate model manifests itself in several forms: within traditional universities and colleges, through newly established for-profit schools, and via higher-education curricula within mega-corporations.

Contrasting the triad of authority, separateness, and innovation of the historical university, Noam Chomsky offers one definition of this corporatization:

> converting schools and universities into facilities that produce commodities for the job market, abandoning the traditional ideal of the universities: [which is] fostering creative and independent thought and inquiry, challenging perceived beliefs, exploring new horizons and forgetting external constraints.[4]

Such conversion contains two key elements. The first is a shift away from the humanist tradition of treating students both as responsible young adults in the process of becoming citizens and as charges in need of acculturation in a whole array of cognitive, ethical, professional, and social skills. Corporatization has instead turned them into "customers" who pay for professional training and career preparation.[5] The second element is the shift in the role of faculty away from those who employ their intellectual and moral authority to guide this humanistic educational process and into employees of a corporate-administrative entity

---

[3] See Chapter 2, 33–42.

[4] Noam Chomsky, "Academic Freedom and the Corporatization of Universities," University of Toronto, Scarborough, April 6, 2011, at https://chomsky.info/20110406.

[5] Stanley Aronowitz, *The Knowledge Factory: Dismantling the Corporate University and Creating True Higher Learning* (Boston: Beacon Press, 2005).

whose function is to guarantee both the satisfaction of their customers and the monetization of their "human and capital resources."

These trends are the result of several causes, including what many critics see as the neoliberal drive to turn every public institution into a market. Even thinkers like Michel Foucault at first saw this marketplace as a haven from the "normative-disciplinary system" of the nation-state and a platform for "personal insurrections," an idea that has influenced many academic critical theorists.[6] As we have seen above, they are also due to concurrent and interrelated changes in the make-up of college and university boards, in the backgrounds of administrators, and in faculty surrender of authority and self-governance.[7] Vast sums of federal and corporate research money bring concomitant regulation and control of university administration in areas of basic research, laboratories, and staff both in the sciences and business and increasingly in humanities departments and centers.

The propagation of neoliberalism as an ideological movement on America's campuses had been the explicit mission goal of the Olin Foundation.[8] In the spring of 2017, controversy erupted at Wake Forest University over a $3.7 million Koch Foundation grant to finance the school's Eudaimonia Institute, devoted to studying "human flourishing and well-being."[9] Critics focused on the university's establishing the institute without input or oversight from the faculty senate. They argue that Eudaimonia's classical allusions are less about humanistic tradition than about studies of entrepreneurship, capitalism, corporations, and trade. Wake Forest does have a history of founding institutes for various humanities and social-science studies. But faculty have objected to the general lack of oversight as to how such foundations are able to penetrate the university's walls of shared governance and oversight. The faculty senate's resolution stated that the Koch Foundation sought "to

[6] Kévin Boucaud-Victoire, "How Michel Foucault Got Neoliberalism So Wrong: An Interview with Daniel Zamora," *Jacobin Magazine* (Sept. 6, 2019), at https://jacobinmag.com/2019/09/michel-foucault-neoliberalism-friedrich-hayek-milton-friedman-gary-becker-minoritarian-governments.

[7] Chapters 3 and 5.   [8] See Chapter 3, 68–70.

[9] Peter Schmidt, "Koch Money Brings Distress Over a University's Well-Being Institute," CHE (April 4, 2017), at www.chronicle.com/article/Koch-Money-Brings-Distress/239686.

co-opt higher education for its ideological, political, and financial ends" through such infiltration, a charge very much in accordance with the Olin and Koch strategies from their inception. In keeping with the foundations' agenda, the chairman of the school's economics department has labeled faculty opposition "part of a neo-Marxist ideological agenda." Similar Koch efforts[10] – and faculty protests – have taken place at schools as diverse as Amherst, Yale, Western Carolina University, and George Mason University.

*

The corporatization of existing institutions has gone hand-in-hand with the rapid growth of for-profit education companies. Phoenix, Trump, Coursera, Corinthian, and ITT Technical have combined elements of new board governance, digital technologies, high-level investment, and monetization to offer a model of higher education that is purely the exchange of money for credentialing. Such entities make no effort to disguise their commercial functions and goals to attract customers and gain market share. Many have met the fate of non-educational start-ups and have faced rapid declines and closures, and their short-lived successes challenge and undermine the authority of the traditional university.

But aside from the corporatization of university administration, values, and the interchange of personnel and faculty, corporatization also has a far more direct and challenging aspect: the creation of the university within the mega-corporation as the "corporate university." According to one recent definition:

> the phrase "corporate university" can be defined as a "centralized strategic umbrella for the education and development of employees … [which] is the chief vehicle for disseminating an organization's culture and fostering

---

[10] Peter Schmidt, "George Mason Faculty Demands Review of University's Agreements with Donors," CHE (May 5, 2016), at www.chronicle.com/article/George-Mason-Faculty-Demands/236365; Schmidt, "How One College Quelled Controversy over a Koch-Financed Center," CHE (Oct. 4, 2016), at www.chronicle.com/article/How-One-College-Quelled/237984.

the development of not only job skills, but also such core workplace skills as learning-to-learn, leadership, creative thinking, and problem solving."[11]

The corporate university has its roots in post-war business culture. GE's Crotonville campus was founded in 1956. MacDonald's Hamburger [sic] University was created in 1962.[12] Founded in 1974, the American Council on Education's Program on Noncollegiate Sponsored Instruction (ACE/PONSI) evaluates "instructional courses and programs offered by business and industry, labor unions, professional and voluntary associations, and government agencies and makes recommendations for college credit based upon such instruction." One goal fostered by participating corporations is "eliminating fragmentation and redundancy in education programs."[13] By 2000, ACE/PONSI recommended that courses from over 250 companies receive college credit. These companies include Apple, Amazon, Bell Telephone, Walt Disney, Boeing, Motorola, McDonald's, J.P. Morgan Chase, General Electric, Pixar, Shell, Mars, United Health, Ford, IKEA, and thousands of others that have established "corporate universities" or "corporate academies" on the European and Asian model of offering in-house, high-level curricula.[14] According to one analysis,

> In 1993, corporate universities existed in only 400 companies. In 2001, this number jumped to 2,000 ... according to Corporate University Xchange, this number will grow to exceed 3,700 by 2010, which is more than the number of private United States universities (2000).[15]

[11] Denise R. Hearn, "Education in the Workplace: An Examination of Corporate University Models (edited version, Nov. 19, 2018)," at www.newfoundations.com/OrgTheory/ Hearn721.html.

[12] Doug Guthrie, "Corporate Universities: An Emerging Threat to Graduate Business Education," *Forbes* (Jan. 22, 2013), at www.forbes.com/sites/dougguthrie/2013/01/22/ corporate-universities-an-emerging-threat-to-graduate-business-education.

[13] Lisa Tanner, "Corporate University Approach Taking Hold," *Dallas Business Journal* (July 27, 2003), at www.bizjournals.com/dallas/stories/2003/07/28/focus2.html.

[14] "Why Winning Organizations Have Corporate Universities," Center for Strategy and Leadership (Feb. 4, 2015), at www.c4sl.eu/why-winning-organizations-have-corporate-universities.

[15] Hearn, "Education in the Workplace."

These are not isolated instances of businesses deciding on their individual agendas, but theorized fields with larger associations that coordinate and promote the achievements of business-created schools of higher learning.[16] In July 2019, Amazon.com announced that it was spending $700 million on education for 100,000 employees, including its Amazon's Machine Learning University with sixty "on-ground" facilities. Dan Ayoub, general manager of education for Microsoft, told *Inside Higher Ed*:

> When 65 percent of the jobs that today's students will hold don't even exist yet, it's clear that the fourth Industrial Revolution is driving demand for skills at a level that is outpacing our current credentialing models. In this atmosphere, universities and businesses who choose to embrace and invest in helping people build the necessary skills for the jobs of the future stand to reap great benefits.[17]

Andrea Backman, "chief employability officer" of Strategic Education, added:

> Gone are the days of higher learning institutions operating in separate silos from employers. The blending of education and work, highlighted by Amazon's announcement, will intensify, and higher learning institutions that are nimble and innovative enough to adapt to a fast-changing economy and work force will be able to keep pace.

As Peter P. Smith, UMUC Orkand Endowed Chair, University of Maryland Global Campus, put it: "Amazon's approach exposes multiple weaknesses in the traditional academic delivery model."

Further, about 16 percent of these universities have forged partnerships with traditional colleges and universities. For example,

---

[16] In addition to the Corporate University Xchange, see, for example, the Global Council of Corporate Universities, at www.globalccu.com. See also Mark Allen, ed., *The Corporate University Handbook: Designing, Managing and Growing a Successful Program* (New York: American Management Association, 2002); and Martyn Rademakers, *Corporate Universities: Drivers of the Learning Organization* (London: Routledge, 2015).

[17] Doug Lederman, "Is Amazon Training Its Workers or Creating a College Alternative?," IHE (July 17, 2019), at www.insidehighered.com/digital-learning/article/2019/07/17/perspectives-field-amazons-big-dollar-entry-training-workers.

Intel offers employees the opportunity to enroll in an MBA program at Babson College, which offers a degree that focuses on Intel case studies. Valencia Community College earns between $1.5 and $2 million annually by offering college-level courses to Walt Disney World and Universal Studio employees. Such large corporations now create partnerships with schools for cyberinfrastructure, brick and mortar dormitories, and classrooms and curricula. In the middle of budget tightening at the University of Maryland, which would soon result in the elimination of many liberal-arts programs,[18] administrators have signed an agreement with Siemens for infrastructure support and with defense contractor Northrup Grumman to construct a new campus unit devoted to programs in cybersecurity. SUNY has decided to develop a separate nanotechnology division with the aid of corporate curricula. Ohio State has joined with IBM to design courses for the same.[19]

Despite numerous failures and closings,[20] a growing number of universities continue to offer "boot-camps,"[21] intensive programs designed with and for corporate employers and run by online program managers (OPMs), such as 2U. The University of Virginia's School of Continuing and Professional Studies, Yale's Flatiron School, and Dominican University's Make School are among recent examples. All these offer a conscious rejection of the thousand-year university tradition of what corporate spokespeople now call "coagulated knowledge." According to analyst Jeanne Meister, teaching the wisdom of past ages is no longer the goal of the corporate university: "the chief concern for knowledge workers in nearly every industry and occupation is the short shelf life of their knowledge, causing them to have to constantly retool their skills." As Apple president Tim Cook has remarked, "I don't think a four-year

---

[18] See Chapter 8, 243.

[19] Doug Belkin and Caroline Porter, "Corporate Cash Alters University Curricula," *Wall Street Journal* (April 7, 2014), at www.wsj.com/articles/corporations-join-up-with-colleges-to-1396914967.

[20] Steve Lohr, "As Coding Boot Camps Close, the Field Faces a Reality Check," *New York Times* (Aug. 24, 2017), at www.nytimes.com/2017/08/24/technology/coding-boot-camps-close.html.

[21] Goldie Blumenstyk, "Tech-Skills Boot Camps Are on the March," CHE (Oct. 9, 2019), at www.chronicle.com/article/Tech-Skills-Boot-Camps-Are-on/247314.

degree is necessary to be proficient in coding. I think that is an old, traditional view."[22] This was echoed by Apple marketing executive Phil Schiller when asked about creating an Apple museum: "We are focused on inventing the future, not celebrating the past."[23]

COMMODIFICATION, MEASUREMENT, AND MONETIZATION OF RESEARCH

One of the first steps in the process of the Dissolution of the Monasteries under Henry VIII and Thomas Cromwell was the drawing up in 1535 of a minutely detailed list of the assets and properties of all the religious establishments of the realm, including monastic houses, and the careful evaluation of their value to the Crown and to the broader elite. The evaluation was nothing new.[24] Since 1306 the kingdom had been subject to just such an annual survey, the *annates*, requiring a payment of the "first fruits" of all episcopal sees to the papal treasury in Rome. After Henry VIII's break with the papacy in 1533, the payments were diverted to the royal treasury. But new circumstances required new analysis. The process of drawing up this new tax record, the *Valor Ecclesiasticus*, entailed a careful visitation carried out in each shire with detailed information supplied by the clergy, supported by their property registers and account books. By early 1536, the final figures were in the hands of royal officials. The motives of the survey may have varied: from a genuine desire to assess the importance of the house and its contribution to the realm to a desire to locate assets for confiscation. It formed the factual basis for the examination of monastic life carried out by royal officials in the Visitation of 1535/6.

The result encapsulated an era. If *Domesday Book*, commissioned by William the Conqueror in 1085, marked the end of Anglo-Saxon England and the opening inventory of the Norman kingdom, the *Valor*

---

[22] Aseem Thapliyal, "Apple CEO Tim Cook Says 4-year Degree Not Necessary for Coding," *Business Today* (May 11, 2019), at www.businesstoday.in/latest/trends/tim-cook-apple-ceo-says-4-year-degree-not-necessary-coding/story/345666.html.

[23] https://news.softpedia.com/news/Apple-s-Phil-Schiller-Says-No-to-Corporate-Museum-263427.shtml.

[24] See Knowles, *Religious Orders*, III:241–59, 268–90.

Ecclesiasticus was in some ways a final inventory of past achievement and the accumulations of culture, both physical and immaterial, that medieval monasticism had created. In this it was like Isidore of Seville's *Etymologies*, the encyclopedia summarizing late antiquity and providing a basis for later medieval thought. Similarly, the eighteenth-century *Encyclopedia* by Diderot and his colleagues created both the summary of the *ancien regime* and a base text for modernity. Like the index at the end of a book, such measurement is both a final summation in tabular form of what had proceeded it and a platform for future work.

Critics may argue that such measurement and counting has been part of the day-to-day reality of social and political units for centuries and that such isolated cultural objects are simply symbolic and thus empty of any real valence. Yet, recent US presidential debates and the failure of candidates like Al Gore and Hillary Clinton to persuade against their opponents' simple and often simplistic deployment of slogan and symbol has demonstrated that people tend to think not in terms of charts and tables but in terms of symbols; and in creating and conveying such symbols the right-wing has excelled over the past generation. Right-wingers may display disdain for the careful exposition of facts and figures that measurement offers, but they relish the opportunity to encapsulate such findings via slogan and logo. The end of things may compel careful counts and measurements, but it is perceived in simple symbols.

*

This section will summarize twenty-first century trends in both the sciences and the humanities to commodify, measure, and monetize teaching and research. University cooperation with government and private entities has long been an essential part of the American research university; and such cooperation has greatly benefited society at large.[25] The post-war research university, spurred by the national defense demands of World War II, soon became central to public policy. Both the demographic pressures on higher education brought about by the GI Bill and Federal access policies and the government's funding of vast new

---

[25] See Thelin, 260–80.

science research through the National Institutes of Health, the National Science Foundation, and the Department of Defense – the "big science" that Vannevar Bush christened the "endless frontier" – made the university a willing partner with government policy. This came as a welcome change from seeking support from industrialists and their foundations. But Federal research agendas also came with a price: practical project goals supplanted pure research on many campuses. By the late 1950s, UC President Clark Kerr could praise the "federal grant university" as the crowning achievement of American higher education. But what pleased administrators and trustees caused rising anxiety among faculty and students as the authority that came with separation began to wither in the face of government agendas for innovation.

Yet the research university as a universal ideal was not an evenly distributed phenomenon. By 1960, 79 percent of all Federal funds went to twenty major research universities, and 57 percent went to six. By the early 1960s, Federal funds were accounting for larger and larger shares of major university budgets. The results on the ground were profound: research, especially in the hard sciences, took greater and greater priority over teaching. It also established new hierarchies among faculty researchers more or less adept at grantsmanship. What John Thelin has called "gilt by association" shifted the emphasis of American university life further from its liberal arts and sciences origins and more toward both professionalization and research. By the late 1960s, the traditional liberal-arts college had increasingly been subsumed into the research model as part of the "university college": an undergraduate prep school for professional degrees. We have already seen how by the mid 1960s this model of the "knowledge industry" was being critiqued by both faculty and students.[26] By the early 1970s the student revolt and widespread social and political conflicts in American society had forced the Federal government to largely abandon its close ties to higher ed, first with defense contracts, and then across many forms of sci-tech research.

In response, many major universities began to establish offices of "technology transfer," working either with select departments and researchers on campus or in active partnerships with large corporations

---

[26] See Chapter 2, 57–58.

to develop patentable processes and products. By the 1980s and 1990s this trend toward large-scale investment in, and profit from, technological and scientific research had taken monetization in new directions for the hard and natural sciences. According to the 2016 Science & Engineering Indicators from the National Science Board, 65.2 percent of funding of university research came from business, with 26.7 percent of research funding coming from government sources.[27] During the intervening decades many campuses, with the cooperation of state legislatures, established working partnerships to create "innovation zones" and "economic incubators" near their campuses. Stanford, Berkeley, and Silicon Valley; Harvard, Boston University, and Tufts near Route 128; Duke, NC State at Raleigh, and UNC at the Research Triangle of North Carolina; the University of Michigan and Pfizer's biomedical research in Ann Arbor are among the best-known examples from this period.[28] In 2015, Penn State launched a $30-million program to open "innovation hubs" across the state.[29] More recent examples include Yale in biomedical research, Cornell-Technion in technology start-ups, Miami in life sciences, Stanford in computer engineering and business apps, Columbia in neuroscience, Rockefeller in bioscience, and Harvard in engineering and applied sciences. The web pages announcing these costly expansions demonstrate a consistent corporate framing and an ability to obfuscate intent.

Elsewhere, many older agriculture and mining schools, the old land-grant state universities, began a rebranding of their A&M roots as "Athletics and Medicine" schools. The University of Maryland, Texas, and many UC schools began investing heavily in hospitals and medical research as a path to both prestige and financial health. Stanford has been called the "best college in America" for its major corporate start-ups.[30] In October 2019, the University of Michigan at Ann Arbor announced a $50 million Center for Academic Innovation to further

[27] At www.nsf.gov/statistics/2016/nsb20161.   [28] Thelin, 341–42.

[29] Lindsay Ellis, "How the Great Recession Reshaped American Higher Education," CHE (Sept. 14, 2018), at www.chronicle.com/article/How-the-Great-Recession/244527.

[30] Madeline Stone, "9 Incredibly Successful Startups that Were Born at Stanford," *Business Insider* (Sept. 22, 2014), at www.businessinsider.com/9-successful-startups-to-come-out-of-stanford-2014-9.

online initiatives and off-site learning. According to James DeVaney, the center's founding executive director, "There's a great deal of blurring between our activities in the online, hybrid and residential domains." "Ecosystems," "innovation cycles," and "social learning experience" mark the new language of higher ed.

Other STEM fields have also seen a radical shift in outlook. One of the major recent examples is Boeing's successful attempt to create what it labeled a "peaceful revolution" in engineering education.[31] By the 1990s Boeing's top management began to worry that both its model and the skill sets of its chief engineers were becoming stale. In addition, they felt that colleges and universities were overemphasizing theory and pure research over practice. The company therefore began to influence schools and departments to radically revamp their engineering curricula to focus on "outputs, not inputs" and to teach "skills" over "rote knowledge." To accomplish this, Boeing funded an effort to rewrite the engineering field's accreditation standards, to establish a series of "fellowships" to bring faculty into Boeing facilities to see their practical work and its results, to actively recruit faculty members into their workforce, and to encourage an array of alliances between corporations and higher education to establish "innovation" centers. Iowa State's Virtual Reality Applications Center, for example, began partnering with Boeing in 2004. More recently Boeing contributed $6 million to Iowa State's Student Innovation Center.

According to Lindsay Ellis:

> Boeing's little-known quest had widespread reverberations on American college campuses, helping entrench a core assumption: employers are higher education's customers – and new hires need to meet their standards.

In 2017, it was reported that Amazon.com had hired 500 newly minted and senior Ph.D.s for its applied-science and research-science units. That number was greater than the multi-year hiring plans of many

---

[31] Lindsay Ellis, "The Boeing Blueprint: What Happens When a Corporate Giant Sets its Sights on Higher Education?," CHE (Sept. 26, 2019), at www.chronicle.com/interactives/20190926-Boeing.

state university campuses, including those in Florida, California, and Connecticut.[32] Meanwhile, individual science faculty are expected both to fund their own research and to contribute to the university's bottom line. In addition, faculty are increasingly tempted or directed into their own ventures, using the university and its resources as incubators for privatization.

In some cases, corporate money has also directly funded and suggested research agendas. In July 2017, it was disclosed that Google had cherry-picked many academics to pursue research agendas and findings that could be favorable to its corporate interests.[33] Over 300 academics were identified as receiving Google money and pursuing its interests in a range of privacy, antitrust, copyright and patent, internet, advertising, first amendment, and other issues. According to the *Wall Street Journal*, Google paid $5,000 to $400,000 "for research supporting business practices that face regulatory scrutiny" in a "wish list" of topics. Most of the researchers never disclosed their connections to Google. In response, Verizon and AT&T have funded various research papers aimed against Google. Monsanto and Merck have done the same to bolster their own products.[34] According to David Michaels, former head of the Occupational Safety and Health Administration and professor of environmental and occupational health at George Washington University,

> It has become standard operating procedure for corporations to attempt to manufacture scientific uncertainty when they're faced with allegations that their products or their activities cause harm. Rather than saying, "Let's get to the bottom of this. Let's have an independent and unconflicted evaluation," the instinct is to hire corrupt scientists and to blow smoke ... this is done so widely now.[35]

---

[32] Audrey Williams June, "Amazon Is Hiring Ph.D.s – Hundreds This Year," CHE (Oct. 24, 2017), at www.chronicle.com/article/Amazon-Is-Hiring-PhDs-/241544.

[33] Brody Mullins and Jack Nicas, "Paying Professors: Inside Google's Academic Influence Campaign," *Wall Street Journal* (July 14, 2017), at www.wsj.com/articles/paying-professors-inside-googles-academic-influence-campaign-1499785286.

[34] Kent Anderson, "Trust Falls – Are We in a New Phase of Corporate Research?," *Scholarly Kitchen* (Aug. 15, 2017), at https://scholarlykitchen.sspnet.org/2017/08/15/trust-falls-new-phase-corporate-research.

[35] Francie Diep, "Why Scientists Defend Dangerous Industries," CHE (Nov. 24, 2019), at www.chronicle.com/article/Why-Scientists-Defend/247598.

Hand-in-hand with this trend is higher ed's recruitment of industry personnel, often with advanced research degrees, into prominent administrative positions as vice-provosts or vice-presidents for research and the corresponding influence of corporate members on university boards. The growing concentration of power in such offices and the vast sums of research monies pouring in from patents and from corporate partnerships further skew the perspective of the university into the direction of STEM and away from liberal arts agendas, funding, and faculties. Prestigious schools do continue to vaunt their liberal-arts offerings and star faculty, and many such schools excel at the task of teaching the arts and humanities. Yet it was becoming increasingly clear both from declining enrollments in these fields and from administrative attitudes and actions (amply treated in our preceding chapters) that such gestures were largely designed for marketing purposes.[36] Schools recruit a few charismatic and highly paid faculty to attract students and to maintain the schools' historic brands.

The humanities too are increasingly being forced by corporate universities to conform to the science model of self-funded research and institutional support, most especially in the age of the digital and large-scale projects. "Big data" and 3-D and virtual-reality renderings in the digital humanities require vast computer power, human expertise, and financial resources. Its chief proponents are therefore turning increasingly to the values and methods of monetization, often establishing their own labs and firms to attract funding for this work. Research centers in the humanities facing program eliminations and budget cuts seek independent sources of finance and support both for ongoing projects and to meet day-to-day administrative costs. In the 2010s, "DH" became code for attempts to attract research and admin money with digital humanities initiatives.

The "ivy-covered walls" that once separated the research and teaching of the university from the more pressing concerns of business, industry, and financial returns are breached. What then will remain of the distinct character of higher education as a time and space apart?

---

[36] See Chapter 8, 223–33 and passim.

SCHOLARLY COMMUNICATION

Such trends have affected more than faculties, students, and tuitions. Universities – among them the largest and best endowed – have also been reevaluating their spending priorities in some of the most traditional areas long associated with higher education, including their university presses and their place in scholarly communication. Since the foundation of a printing press in Cambridge, MA in 1638, and its formal evolution into Harvard University Press in 1913, the publishing arm of the university has served both to evaluate and disseminate the work of faculty within the world of scholarly communication to advance knowledge and to familiarize the broader public with academics' examination of issues of concern to society. In these capacities it has been essential to the American system of higher education.

In 1869, the president of Cornell University, Andrew D. White, opened the first American university press to operate in the name of the university itself.[37] The oldest continuously operating university press is Johns Hopkins, founded in 1878. Others followed in quick succession and were founded and conceived as indispensable components of the modern research university. As such, their mission was to disseminate knowledge outside of the classroom without the commercial constraints of making profit to sustain operations. Endowments and outright budget allocations relieved the burden of signing titles for their market appeal, and instead allowed scholars to publish deep and original research.

But by 1935, Harvard University Press had realized the potential for expanding out the readership and market for scholarly monographs and other books by creating "scholarship plus," what came to be known as the "Harvard Model."[38] Such titles "cross-over" the line between strictly

---

[37] Gene R. Hawes, *To Advance Knowledge: A Handbook on American University Press Publishing* (New York: American Association of University Presses, 1967); Peter Givler, "University Press Publishing in the United States," in Richard E. Abel and Lyman W. Newman, eds., *Scholarly Publishing: Books, Journals, Publishers and Libraries in the Twentieth Century* (New York: Wiley, 2002), at www.aupresses.org/about-aaup/about-university-presses/history-of-university-presses.

[38] "A Brief History of Harvard University Press," at www.hup.harvard.edu/about/history.html.

academic topics and those of interest to an educated, general lay audience. They could range across the fields of the liberal arts, humanities, social sciences, and physical sciences (where fewer books are the norm), most especially as such titles and topics touched on current affairs and cultural concerns. The model swept the university-press world so that by the 1970s most university presses had followed Harvard's model and had at least some series aimed at this general audience. The reasons for the initiative were several: to increase the presses' bottom line, to further the reach of scholarly research and discourse, to enhance the brand of both the press and its parent university, and to attract new generations of authors and readers.

In 1937, the Association of American University Presses was founded to accommodate the shared interests and issues of a growing number of scholarly publishers. With the passage of the National Defense Education Act (NDEA) in 1957, the university presses entered a golden age of public support and interest. Lists, programs, and readership expanded accordingly, making the publication of many highly specialized monographs economically viable, with average sales into the low thousands. But the end of the 1960s and of America's love affair with higher education also had a dramatic effect on scholarly publishing. As Peter Givler, past president of the AAUP noted:

> From 1920 to 1970, new university presses continued to open at a rate of about one a year. Between 1970 and 1974, ten more new presses were founded, but only five more were started between 1975 and 2000. The year 1970 also marked the beginning of a slow decline in purchases by libraries of scholarly monographs, particularly in the humanities and social sciences, a decline that continues to this day and that has had a profound impact on university presses.

As Federal funding for research and higher education began to dry up, so did library-acquisition budgets. By 1960 university presses could expect to sell an average of about 5,000 copies of a scholarly monograph. But between 1980 and 2000 that number had plummeted in its key market, the library, to about 2,000 copies in 1980; to 1,000 by the late 1980s; to 500 by 1990; and to 200 by the year 2000. Sales numbers continue to plummet. Prices of scholarly titles also shifted radically from the 1960s, when they often matched those of trade books, to well over $200 a copy by the 2020s. Even at these prices the sales generated were often not enough to cover editorial, production, printing, advertising, and distribution costs without continued and ever-higher subsidies from host institutions, donors, and foundations.[39]

By 2015, university-press publishing had moved decisively into the Harvard cross-over model and away from the scholarly monograph, most especially in the humanities. But at their core the 140 university presses in North America continue to service the needs of some 4,200 institutions of higher education, acquiring, editing, peer-reviewing, publishing, and distributing the work of tens of thousands of scholars and faculty. They continue to provide the decisions about quality and impact that are essential to higher education's processes of hiring, tenure, and promotion (HTP).[40] According to a 2017 survey conducted with support from the Mellon Foundation,[41] the total books published by an extrapolated sum for just over 100 university presses was 76,000 or 15,000/year from 2009 to 2013. Of these, primary monographs totaled 19,000 or 4,000/year, and of that total humanities monographs numbered 15,000 or 3,000/year, or 19.7 percent. This number is startling in that the humanities have traditionally been the key monograph subject area, as the hard sciences and technology fields publish final research in book form far less regularly.

A follow-up study was conducted by Joseph Esposito and colleagues through Ithaka S+R to attempt to determine the buying patterns of

---

[39] See Gardiner and Musto, *Digital Humanities*, 159–60; John Thompson, *Books in the Digital Age: The Transformation of Academic and Higher Education Publishing in Britain and the United States* (Cambridge: Polity Press, 2005).

[40] See Mark Edington in "What is the Biggest Challenge in University-press Publishing?," CHE (June 4, 2017), at www.chronicle.com/article/What-is-the-biggest-challenge/240210.

[41] Joseph J. Esposito and Karen Barch, "Monograph Output of American University Presses, 2009–2013: A Report Prepared for the Andrew W. Mellon Foundation" (Feb. 10, 2017), at https://scholarlykitchen.sspnet.org/wp-content/uploads/2017/02/Monograph-Output-of-University-Presses.pdf; summary in *Scholarly Kitchen* (Feb. 14, 2017), at https://scholarlykitchen.sspnet.org/2017/02/14/monograph-output-american-university-presses-2009-2013.

research libraries.[42] Although the study's data remains incomplete and its authors advise caution, they did find some interesting trends. Roughly 178,000 monograph copies were purchased by the 54 research libraries surveyed in FY 2017. These represented roughly the entire range of about 140 university presses or an average of about 3,300 purchases a year per library and about 1,271 copies across all titles sold per press.[43] The study seems to confirm that the barriers to library acquisitions remain low and that traditional acquisitions channels remain open and have even expanded with the entry of Amazon.com into library sales. But the general downward trend in university press sales remains real.

*

At the same time commercial presses – which often include the two university-press giants, Oxford and Cambridge – have taken up much of the cross-over market from the UPs and have done so with resources far beyond the reach of the scholarly presses. HarperCollins, Allen Lane, Viking, and Penguin-Random House, Pearson in its many subsidiaries, and other world-spanning media conglomerates, can offer authors attractive resources, advances and royalties, and worldwide access. They can underprice and over-distribute far beyond the university presses, and their access to online distributors like Amazon.com and independent and chain bookstores remains far-reaching. What had once been the specialized content of scholarly communication is now the commercial-ized and commodified tie-in to television and video, reaching wide audiences keyed to the rapid turnover of issues and cultural personal-ities, the "thought leaders" who appropriate the research and termin-ology of professional scholars to claim insights as their own in the public

[42] Katherine Daniel, Joseph J. Esposito, and Roger C. Schonfeld, "Library Acquisition Patterns: Preliminary Findings," Ithaka S+R (July 19, 2018), at https://sr.ithaka.org/publications/library-acquisition-patterns-preliminary-findings. See also Katherine Daniel, "Library Acquisition Patterns: A Preliminary Report with Data from OCLC's WorldShare Management Services," Ithaka S+R (July 19, 2018), at https://sr.ithaka.org/blog/library-acquisition-patterns; and Joseph Esposito, "Good Data, Bad Data, You Know I've Had My Share: Library Book Acquisition Patterns," *Scholarly Kitchen* (July 23, 2018), at https://scholarlykitchen.sspnet.org/2018/07/23/good-data-bad-data-know-ive-share-library-book-acquisition-patterns.

[43] Private correspondence with Joseph J. Esposito, October 11, 2019.

forum. The university presses and their authors are all too often marginalized in this process, further increasing the motivation of well-known and respected scholars to seek commercial contracts with large firms.

Many academic authors remain indifferent to these dynamics, since their real market remains the small circle of internal academic experts, their colleagues, administrators, and peer reviewers. Their rewards remain less in royalties and public acclaim than in the returns of the academic gift economy: lines on CVs, hiring, tenure, and promotion; university perks and emoluments; conference invitations and paid travel; awards and offices in learned societies; journal, book, and series editorships; the ability to attract and retain the best undergrads and graduate students; and the recognition and the deserved respect of colleagues for their long and deeply developed expertise. This internalization, a marked characteristic of academia since the late 1960s,[44] has thus contributed to the declining presence of higher education in American civil discourse and has hindered higher ed's ability to attract and retain loyalty and support. As so many aspects of American culture, ranging from the digital to the political, have torn down walls of separation, academic publishing has retained them in an ever-tightening circle of authority and influence.

Despite the efforts of the Mellon Foundation, ACLS, and a few other foundations to bolster the university presses, the situation continues to deteriorate. As colleges and universities cut back and realign their programs, departments, and budgets,[45] and as fewer and fewer faculty emerge as tenured with the time and resources to publish, budgets and research agendas shrink.[46] The university presses are not immune from the austerity programs recently put into effect across the spectrum of colleges and universities. This has resulted in severe cuts to university support for publications, programs, and presses, and to an increasing series of university press closures. We will offer a few examples here.

*

[44] See Chapter 3, 70–80.   [45] See Chapter 6, 111–39; Chapter 8, 233–44.
[46] See Chapter 6, 139–50.

In March 2017, Duquesne University announced that it was closing its 90-year-old university press, one of the leading publishers of Milton studies. Dismissing faculty protests and the press' own attempts to present a restructuring plan that would have cut its budget by two-thirds, a university spokesperson declared that the school could no longer afford its $200,000 annual subsidy. Keeping the press alive "would take away funds necessary for programs that directly benefit Duquesne students and other academic programs."[47] The assumption that a university press does not "directly benefit" students and programs reflects a generation of change in the thinking of college and university administrators.

Duquesne was a small university press, publishing about ten titles a year with a staff of three editors. But on the other end of the scale, the prestigious Stanford University Press (SUP) has faced the same budgetary rationale. SUP publishes 140 titles a year, with a backlist of almost 3,000 titles across the liberal arts, social and natural sciences, law, and business in both print and digital forms.[48] In April 2019, Stanford University announced that it would not continue its $1.7 million annual subsidy to the press, citing budget constraints. Stanford holds a $26.5 billion endowment,[49] and the subsidy amounts to 0.027 percent of Stanford's $6.3-billion 2017–18 budget. But as former press director Grant Barnes noted:[50]

> The near-execution of Stanford University Press is no surprise. For years it has been on death row. A five-year plan, another five-year plan, an execution date, a reprieve ... death by a thousand cuts. ... Stanford's commitment to the humanities has, at least in recent decades, been a matter of debate. Its great reputation was earned in the sciences and in engineering and medicine. Its schools of business and law were similarly

---

[47] Lindsay McKenzie, "Duquesne U. Rejects Last-Ditch Proposals to Save Its Press," CHE (March 30, 2017), at www.chronicle.com/article/Duquesne-U-Rejects-Last-Ditch/ 239639.

[48] www.sup.org/books.

[49] Samuel Cohen, "And I was Worried about Kentucky," (April 26, 2019), at https:// samuelscohen.com/2019/04/26/and-i-was-worried-about-kentucky.

[50] Grant Barnes, "What Really Happened at Stanford University Press: An Insider's Account," CHE (May 10, 2019), at www.chronicle.com/article/What-Really-Happened- at/246276.

favored. ... To be a great university, the humanities and social sciences were needed but not necessarily central.

After vigorous criticism from across academia and publishing, Stanford walked back its decision with a promise of one additional year's subsidy, with more a possibility.[51] But, as Barnes noted, publishers cannot attract authors, editors, reviewers, library sales, buyers, or classroom-reading use if their existence remains in doubt. For their continued survival, a good number of presses, like SUP, have been subsumed into the administrative structures of their campus libraries, with press direct-ors either sharing a library position or reporting to the library dean or provost, sometimes through joint entities like offices of digital scholarly publishing.[52] Examples include the University of Michigan Press, the University of Utah Press, Pennsylvania State University Press, NYU Press, and Purdue University Press.

In June 2017, the *Chronicle of Higher Education* asked press directors what university presses would look like twenty years from then.[53] Their responses varied considerably. Some replied, "much the same." Peter J. Dougherty, then director of Princeton University Press, however, pre-dicted that:

> There will be 20 to 25 big university presses serving global markets, while many of the smaller state-university presses will be absorbed by their host-university libraries, doing mainly digital publishing.

Niko Pfund, president and academic publisher at Oxford University Press, replied similarly:

---

[51] Alexander C. Kafka, "Facing Blowback, Stanford Partly Reverses Course and Pledges Press Subsidy for One More Year," CHE (April 30, 2019), at www.chronicle.com/article/ Facing-Blowback-Stanford/246211; Cathy N. Davidson, "Shame on Stanford: The University's Plan to Cut Subsidies to its Scholarly Press is Dystopian," CHE (April 30, 2019), at www.chronicle.com/article/Shame-on-Stanford/246210.

[52] Joseph J. Esposito and Rick Anderson, "Revisiting Two Perspectives on Library-based University Presses," *Scholarly Kitchen* (July 19, 2017), at https://scholarlykitchen.sspnet .org/2017/07/19/revisiting-two-perspectives-library-based-university-presses.

[53] "How Will University Presses Look 20 Years from Now?," *Chronicle Review*, CHE (June 4, 2017), at www.chronicle.com/article/How-will-university-presses/240230.

Much of what we publish is not immersive reading but "extractable" research, meaning that readers often dip into our books (and journals and online products) looking for specific information rather than reading from acknowledgments to epilogue. This baseline utility will remain the same, with presses serving as a filter and as an agent of improvement and effective dissemination.

Beatrice Rehl, humanities publishing director at Cambridge University Press, New York, neatly summarized the situation:

> The real question is: What is the university going to look like 20 years from now? Scholarly publishing is highly dependent on what happens in the university. Changes in curriculum, research/scholarly outputs, and credentialing norms, among other variables, will affect university presses. Watch this space.

THE IMPACT OF THE DIGITAL

In our book *The Digital Humanities*,[54] Eileen Gardiner and I investigated the role of the digital in scholarly and academic life. We acknowledged the great advantages that the digital brings in discovery, research, writing, publishing, and pedagogy; in the accessibility and sustainability of large archival and monographic collections; and in organizing and disseminating knowledge on all levels. The digital is changing every discipline of the verbal, visual, and aural, both in the conference room and the classroom, and transforming scholarly peer review and credentialing.

However, elements of the digital have negatively disrupted many aspects of higher education. Among these are the decentering nature of the digital that moves the locus of education away from the physical department, institute, classroom, and campus. Websites and distance education, podcasts, MOOCs, VR, Zoom, and other technologies both expand porosity and break down the walls of the physical institutions of knowledge and learning. Digital libraries and publishing also decenter vital aspects of the traditional campus. All diffuse the expertise and

---

[54] Gardiner and Musto, *Digital Humanities.*

authority of the academy. In April 2017, Purdue University announced that it would purchase the for-profit distance educator Kaplan University, founded in 2000 as a division of the Washington Post Company.[55] The move was spearheaded by university president Mitch Daniels, the former Republican governor of Indiana. The purchase, approved by state legislators that August, called for Kaplan's 32,000 students, its programs, 15 campuses and learning centers, and academic staff of about 3,000 to be absorbed by Purdue. For Kaplan, being part of a nonprofit "is a huge marketing benefit." It also returns a profit to Kaplan that is less transparent to the public.[56] However conceived and presented to the public, the purchase, and several others like Western Governor's and Southern New Hampshire University's, represent the further blurring of the separation between the university and the business world.

Many campuses must now cope with the financial realities behind the myth of digital access and pedagogy. A recent study of nearly two hundred administrators indicates that distance education in whatever form does not cut costs for either students or campuses but in the majority of cases can actually increase them for both constituencies.[57] It burdens already-overstretched school budgets and raises costs for those most likely to take advantage of distance and online instruction: the part-time, the working, and the marginalized.

Does the digital also threaten to further de-authorize academia by removing the essential physical foundations of separateness? Distance education dissolves the sense of the campus as a separate place and has the potential to break down associations to unique places and times, to special physical environments of learning and social experience. The campus, institute, and center are now potentially little more than

---

[55] Goldie Blumenstyk, "Purdue's Purchase of Kaplan Is a Big Bet – and a Sign of the Times," CHE (April 28, 2017), at www.chronicle.com/article/Purdue-s-Purchase-of-Kaplan/239931; Goldie Blumenstyk, "Purdue Wins State Approval for Controversial Deal with Kaplan U." (Aug. 10, 2017), at www.chronicle.com/article/Purdue-Wins-State-Approval-for/240900.

[56] Kevin Carey, "The Creeping Capitalist Takeover of American Higher Education: The Corporations Devouring American Colleges," *Huffington Post* (April 1, 2019), at www.huffpost.com/highline/article/capitalist-takeover-college/.

[57] Carl Straumsheim, "Online Education Costs More, Not Less," IHE (Feb. 17, 2017), at www.insidehighered.com/news/2017/02/17/study-challenges-cost-and-price-myths-online-education.

a series of URLs. Will students and parents therefore experience higher education like they do digital and other media? Will the rapidly and easily accessed world of information and knowledge become merely another passing experience? As important, are such ephemeral experiences breaking down the loyalties of born-digital students and future alums to their alma mater as a real time and place, a real stage in their development toward becoming mature adults and citizens?

One major example of this dissolution is the progress of MOOCs (Massive Open Online Courses) over the past decade.[58] Originally conceived in 2006 as a quantum leap over traditional distance education, including computer-aided study, the first impetus came from MIT's OpenCourseWare project. MOOCs were originally hosted almost exclusively by universities seeking to expand their outreach via self-paced instruction of largely traditional course syllabi. By the early 2010s, the movement had gained increasing support and momentum and was generally applauded as the next wave in higher education. By 2012, however,[59] most MOOC services were migrating from universities to not-for-profit and for-profit corporate providers including Coursera, Udacity, and to not-for-profits, including Khan Academy and edX. These MOOC companies are often financed by venture capital through companies like Google and the mega-publisher Pearson. They work in alliance with major universities, including Stanford, Harvard, Yale, Georgetown, NYU, MIT, the University of Pennsylvania, Caltech, the University of Texas at Austin, the University of California at Berkeley, San Jose State University, Brown, UNC, Syracuse, Northwestern, Rice, Georgia Tech, USC, and dozens of others. By the end of the 2010s, they had attracted millions of students, all accessing top-quality course content through major universities in everything from astronomy to medicine to statistics, to physiotherapy and literature. But according to higher-ed expert Kevin Carey,[60]

---

[58] Cathy Sandeen, "MOOCs Moving on, Moving up," IHE (June 22, 2017), at www
.insidehighered.com/views/2017/06/22/essay-looking-back-predictions-about-moocs.

[59] Laura Pappano, "The Year of the MOOC," *New York Times* (Nov. 2, 2012), at www.nytimes
.com/2012/11/04/education/edlife/massive-open-online-courses-are-multiplying-at-a-
rapid-pace.html.

[60] Carey, "The Creeping Capitalist Takeover," www.huffpost.com/highline/article/
capitalist-takeover-college/.

many colleges don't actually run online programs themselves. They outsource much of the work to an obscure species of for-profit company ... These companies are called online program managers, or OPMs ... like 2U, HotChalk and iDesign. As the founder of 2U puts it, "The more invisible we are, the better." But OPMs are transforming both the economics and the practice of higher learning. They help a growing number of America's most-lauded colleges provide online degrees ... The schools often omit any mention of these companies on their course pages, but OPMs typically take a 60% cut of tuition, sometimes more.

They were doing so with the full cooperation of the Trump administration. As Carey noted:

The person in charge of higher education at the Department of Education is Diane Auer Jones ... who worked for some of the most powerful operators in the previous for-profit scandals. Soon after starting at the department, Jones promptly threw out all of the regulatory work that her predecessors and career staff had been developing and began rushing through new versions that she wrote all on her own ... "The political staff are writing the regulations in secret and the policy staff are kept in the dark," [a] staffer says. Jones' proposed rules, released in January, amount to a sweeping deregulation of higher education. They include abolishing a rule that prevents colleges from outsourcing more than half of a program to outside companies – for example, OPMs – and a rule that bans federal aid to programs where students don't interact with an instructor.

But by the end of the 2010s, MOOCs had developed in ways that many could not have predicted. By 2017, Harvard, MIT, and Stanford had completed detailed studies of MOOCs' performance and impact. Completion rates have fallen far below initial expectations, anywhere from 7 percent to 15 percent on average. Most courses provided no transferable college credit, and the majority of courses were beginning to charge fees for completion certificates. Ironically, charging fees has resulted in far higher completion rates, of up to 70 percent. MOOC providers now offer alternatives to college degrees with certificates, nano-degrees, micro-masters, often sponsored by corporations like AT&T. Computer and data science, programming, and software development make up the majority of courses. While faculties at such schools as Duke and Amherst have objected to the pedagogical deficiencies of the courses, MOOCs have become part of the permanent landscape of American education. Schools like Arizona State University have maintained their MOOCs' commitment to broader undergraduate education, but meanwhile millions enroll in what amounts to professional development courses, with no connection to traditional campuses or forms of instruction. By the end of the 2010s, academia's authority and walls of separation were giving way to another wave of innovation that demonstrated the digital's ability to dissolve walls and institutions.

THE LIBRARY

Digital innovations have been felt and seen most acutely at the college and university library. The history of the great libraries of the world, their conceptualization, accumulation, standardization, and systemization, their destructions, dispersals, and renewals has itself filled volumes and bookshelves. Histories of the book, of reading, and of transmission have studied these themes intensely over the past generation. The fate of the large and important book collections in England's monasteries after the Dissolution has also been the object of intense study. These issues need not detain us here except to note that they all point to the intimate connection between the physical institution of the monastery and then of the university as the focus of authority, learning, and innovation precisely because it housed the intellectual resources of their cultures. But such libraries and collections were never simply the passive repositories of books. Their central purpose has always been the dissemination of the knowledge and information that they stored for society at large and the development of expertise and knowledge in the cumulative process of preservation, research, writing, teaching, and the innovation that accompanies them.

It may be impossible to determine the total sizes of English monastic, episcopal, royal, or university libraries before the Dissolution of the 1530s. Recent British scholarship continues an aversion to synthesizing detailed research or providing global estimates.[61] Some numbers garnered from various sources will therefore have to give an impression of relative size. In 1331, for example, the library at Canterbury's Christ Church, the largest in England and Wales, held 1,850 volumes. By comparison, in 1338, the library of the University of Paris contained about 1,722.[62] By 1400, the library of New College, Cambridge held about 300 books. Merton had about 500.[63] Circa 1500, the papal library in Rome owned about 4,000.[64] After 1500 the effects of the print revolution began to increase these numbers dramatically; and libraries based on hundreds of manuscripts soon hosted thousands of additional print volumes. The dispersal of the monastic libraries after the Dissolution has removed most evidence of the final size of these libraries. Royal seizures, purchases, theft, and disappearance make any estimates and reconstructions difficult.[65] But overall, it is safe to say that numbers of volumes in individual institutions rarely exceeded the high thousands.[66]

*

The development of American colleges also spurred the concomitant growth of their libraries. The earliest records of colonial colleges stress the importance of books. As Cambridge graduate John Eliot wrote in 1631 in favor of founding the college that would soon become Harvard:

---

[61] See David N. Bell, "The Libraries of Religious Houses in the Late Middle Ages," in Leedham-Green and Webber, *The Cambridge History*, I:126–51.

[62] David N. Bell, "Libraries in England and Wales," *Oxford Bibliographies* (March 2016), at www.oxfordbibliographies.com/view/document/obo-9780195396584/obo-9780195396584-0193.xml.

[63] Roger Lovatt, "College and University Book Collections and Libraries," in Leedham-Green and Webber, *The Cambridge History* I:152–77, at 156.

[64] Andrew Pettegree, *The Book in the Renaissance* (New Haven: Yale University Press, 2011), 19–20.

[65] See N. R. Ker, *Medieval Libraries of Great Britain: A List of Surviving Books*, 2nd ed. (London: Royal Historical Society, 1964). For recent synthesis of research, see "Introduction," in Leedham-Green and Webber, *The Cambridge History*, 1–10; and James P. Carley, "The Dispersal of the Monastic Libraries and the Salvaging of the Spoils," in Leedham-Green and Webber, *The Cambridge History*, 265–91.

[66] See Pettegree, *The Book in the Renaissance*, 319–32.

I beseech you let me be bould to make one motion, for the furtheranc of Larning among us... for a library, & a place for the exercize of Larning[67]

In 1643, the anonymous author of one of Harvard's first fundraising appeals wrote:

it pleased God to stir up the heart of one Mr. Harvard ... to give the one halfe of his Estate ... towards the erecting of a College; and all his Library ... the College was, by common consent appointed to be at Cambridge ... and is called ... Harvard College. The Edifice is very faire and comely within and without, having in it a spacious Hall ... and a large Library with some Bookes to it, the gifts of diverse of our friends.[68]

In 1693, the charter of William & Mary College assured that the school's endowments would be used,

for defraying the Charges that shall be laid out in Erecting and Fitting the Edifices of the said intended College, and furnishing them with Books.[69]

Article 5 of Yale's Charter of 1745 specified that the general meeting of the President and Fellows be held in the "college's library"; and Chapter 11 of its 1745 Laws was devoted to the administration and function of that library.[70] By 1816, George Ticknor had experienced the collections of books in libraries at the emerging German research university and wrote to his friend Stephen Higginson:

I cannot, however, shut my eyes on the fact, that one very important and principal cause of the difference between our University and the one here is the different value we affix to a good library, and the different ideas we have of what a good library is.[71]

With the rise of the American research university toward the end of the nineteenth century, the vast expansion of campus library facilities saw the creation of immense collections in quantum leaps of collection size. By 1865, Andrew D. White's dream of a great American research university included "libraries as rich as the Bodleian."[72] In 1930,

---

[67] Hofstadter & Smith, I:5.   [68] Hofstadter & Smith, I:6–7.
[69] Hofstadter & Smith, I:35.   [70] Hofstadter & Smith, I:51, 61.
[71] Hofstadter & Smith, I:256.   [72] Hofstadter & Smith, II:549.

Abraham Flexner, former secretary to the Carnegie Foundation and then-president of the Institute for Advanced Study at Princeton, could note that:

> university libraries have been so woven into the texture of university life and activity, that as far as physical arrangements go, work at every legitimate level is relieved of drudgery, inconvenience and delay. Sound educational ideals have been embodied in steel and stone.[73]

Steel and stone marked the great era of research-library construction. Harper Memorial at the University of Chicago (1912), Widener at Harvard (1915), Green at Stanford (1919), Sterling Memorial at Yale (1931), and Butler at Columbia (1934) came to symbolize the concentrated authority of these schools and the traditions that they preserved and built upon, the names of the great (male) thinkers of the past engraved large upon their facades. Whether neo-Classical, neo-Gothic, or neo-Romanesque, their solid and imposing structures summoned up tradition, authority, and the separateness that comes with the protection of past knowledge in the service of modern research.

By late 2018, the largest collections of titles held in university libraries in North America numbered in the millions of volumes. Among the top ten were Harvard with 21.2 million volumes in all forms, with over 2 million "e-books"; Michigan with 15.7 volumes and 3.9 million e-books; Toronto with 15.1 million volumes and 2.5 million e-books; UCLA with 13 million volumes and 2.5 million e-books; and Texas with 11.7 volumes and 1.5 million e-books.[74] Only the Library of Congress with 167 million items and the New York Public Library's research division with 25.3 million were larger. Measurements differ according to the organization counting, the number of items or titles, cataloged or uncatalogued, aggregated or individual, single sale or subscription, and the like. The total for the largest 116 schools listed in the 2018 Association of Research Libraries (ARL) statistics was 673.5 million volumes as opposed to 165.7 million e-books.

These numbers need further refining, for the number of hard-copy items – whether manuscripts, books, journals, maps, etc., is vastly

---

[73] Hofstadter & Smith, II:910.   [74] ARL figures, 2018.

outnumbered by digital holdings. Harvard's library, for example, is the largest academic library in the world. According to its website, it includes 18.9 million print volumes, 174,000 serial titles, about 400 million manuscript items, 10 million photographs, 56 million archived web pages, and 5.4 terabytes of born-digital archives and manuscripts.[75] At the number five spot, Columbia holds 13 million print volumes in 14.4 million records, over 160,000 journals and serials, 2.8 million e-books, as well as over 9 million "items" accessed through its CLIO online catalog, 1,500 databases, and 507 million articles.[76] But in the digital realm such numbers are constantly changing and largely meaningless. According to Christopher Cronin, Associate University Librarian for Collections at Columbia:

> Large research libraries no longer think of a library catalog as being a traditional inventory of what we have purchased, own, and hold in book stacks – it is now an access portal. As such, counting the number of "holdings" a library has is becoming less and less relevant within the library community; we increasingly talk more about content to which our users have access – including materials to which there is open access. Coordinated collecting with key library partners, complemented by extensive resource sharing networks, will continue to redefine the landscape of what we refer to as "our collection."[77]

The digital has changed the uses and the make-up of the traditional library quickly and decisively.[78] Digital cataloging, on-site computer consultations, digitization of existing collections, off-campus and remote access, consortial "holdings" however defined and accessed, new digital aggregations and born-digital collections, digitized and born-digital publications of journals, monographs, reference sources, primary-source materials and archives, even ancient scrolls, medieval manuscripts, and early modern print have now made it possible to access much of even the

---

[75] https://gsas.harvard.edu/student-life/harvard-resources/harvard-libraries.

[76] https://library.columbia.edu/about.html; https://clio.columbia.edu/articles.

[77] Email correspondence with author, Nov. 20, 2019.

[78] James J. O'Donnell, *Avatars of the Word: From Papyrus to Cyberspace* (Cambridge, MA: Harvard University Press, 1998), 64–70 et passim.

highest-level research online and off campus, from any number and variety of library partnerships, from any location.

The 1990s saw the launch of major digitization projects, such as Humanities E-Book of the American Council of Learned Societies, JSTOR, ProQuest, Ebsco, Project Gutenberg, the Internet Archive, Google Books, the Hathi Trust, and others. Several were sponsored by various consortia of university presses with the support of the Mellon Foundation and the National Endowment for the Humanities. Their missions ranged from digitizing existing collections from prize-winning monographs, to series and collections, to publishers' backlists, and complete library collections, to the creation of new born-digital work. These tens of millions of titles, and hundreds of billions of pages,[79] were in turn distributed to libraries and researchers through a variety of models ranging from open-access to subscription and purchase to institutional membership.[80] The net effect was that many libraries began replacing subject specialists and acquisition librarians with tech-savvy and digital-collection managers. Library discourse turned from specific subject matter and carefully curated collection development to the ingestion of tens and hundreds of thousands of digital items aggregated through external vendors, often the digital arms of large publishing conglomerates.[81]

With the development of these large digital collections and other resources, the nature of university and college library collections began to change. Physical book acquisition first went hand-in-hand with digital copies or versions, then shifted toward models like patron-driven acquisition in which physical books were purchased only when library staff or digital algorithms determined that digital usage and accompanying fees might warrant it; to a point when print acquisitions was becoming a smaller and smaller element in collection development and budgets. Between 2009 and 2015, total initial circulations of print books in ARL libraries fell by almost half, from 36 million to 19 million. As Rick

---

[79] In November 2019, the Internet Archive alone hosted over 330 billion web pages and 20 million books. See https://archive.org/about.

[80] See Gardiner and Musto, *Digital Humanities*, 19–23.

[81] As at the 18th Fiesole Collection Development Retreat in April 2016.

Anderson has noted, "a library that offers an increasing proportion of its information resources online should naturally expect to see a decline in the circulation of printed books – especially if there's significant overlap in content across formats."[82]

With new digital collections and cataloging now available, the physical uses of the library have begun to radically shift as well. Deaccessioning of physical books and journals has become a reality of the university library. In November 2019, a Google search for "deaccessioning of library books" brought up 202,000 items. These ranged from regular deaccessioning policies at Pepperdine[83] and Dartmouth[84] to experiments in deaccessioning rare books[85] and archival materials.[86] These in turn have led to changes in the physical form and uses of traditional campus libraries as administrators theorize that increased digital usage is being reflected in decreased foot traffic. Both substantial renovations and new library buildings have therefore begun to accommodate the new library as information center, collaborative environment, study lounge, and digital training point. The University of Arizona provides an excellent example of these trends. In March 2017, ASU's president and library provost, both innovators of large-scale digital initiatives, announced plans for a $100 million remake of the university's library system. According to library chief, James O'Donnell:

> It's time to realize that all of our users are primarily online users of our collections. [This] means changing your service model, your staffing structure and organization, and bringing in a bunch of new people. .... Libraries have and manage access to the best-quality learning and research resources, and we have the wizards to help you find what you need. We can take you to lots and lots of places that the open internet just can't plain take you, and we can show you how to get there.[87]

---

[82] Rick Anderson, "Less than Meets the Eye: Print Book Use Is Falling Faster in Research Libraries," *Scholarly Kitchen* (Aug. 21, 2017), at https://scholarlykitchen.sspnet.org/2017/08/21/less-meets-eye-print-book-use-falling-faster-research-libraries.

[83] https://library.pepperdine.edu/collections/deaccessioning.htm.

[84] https://researchguides.dartmouth.edu/deaccessioning.

[85] https://rbml.acrl.org/index.php/rbml/article/viewFile/139/139.

[86] https://americanarchivist.org/doi/pdf/10.17723/aarc.64.2.2221602x5k72812u.

[87] Carl Straumsheim, "'The Library Has Never Been More Important'," IHE (March 24, 2017), at www.insidehighered.com/news/2017/03/24/arizona-state-u-library-reorganization-plan-moves-ahead.

This also meant removing most of the print books in the library's collection to off-site storage, what university president Michael M. Crow called a "fulfillment center," similar to Amazon.com's Prime service. The library envisioned EdPlus, ASU's innovation unit, as an essential partner in this new information-focused model.

The Georgia Institute of Technology also launched a similar plan to remove almost all its print collections offsite to share a facility with Emory University. According to Irene M. H. Herold, president of the Association of College & Research Libraries (ACRL), this is a major trend among member institutions:

> Our focus is where it has been all along. ... We're not just knowledge preservers and information-literacy, critical-thinking instructors. We're also engaged in knowledge creation. It's just that the knowledge that's being created is able to be accessed and shaped and shared in such different ways than in the past.[88]

The schools around the San Francisco Bay area have also seen rapid transformations. Instead of places used to "warehouse knowledge, they're places where it's created now," according to a recent report.[89] Lounges, virtual-reality stations, 3-D printing, and mini-conference and collaboration spaces have taken the place of stacks of books as a consortium of libraries in the California State University system has now moved books to "centralized storage spaces." Much of this change has been instigated by neighboring corporations like Cisco and Google. "They told us they need our students to be able to work in interdisciplinary teams," said one library dean. As UC Santa Cruz's librarian Elizabeth Cowell stated, "No one has the funds to build new buildings, especially just to warehouse materials that people aren't using."

A 2017 summary of a survey of research librarians conducted by Ithaka S+R,[90] a spinoff of the Mellon Foundation, reinforced this trend:

---

[88] Straumsheim, "'The Library Has Never Been More Important'."

[89] Emily Deruy, "Virtual Reality and Smoothie Bars: What's in at Bay Area University Libraries?," *Mercury News* (July 10, 2017), at www.mercurynews.com/2017/07/10/virtual-reality-and-smoothie-bars-the-modern-university-library.

[90] Christine Wolff-Eisenberg, "US Library Survey 2016," Ithaka S+R (April 3, 2017), at https://sr.ithaka.org/publications/us-library-survey-2016.

so too are research libraries looking to pivot away from what Rick Anderson once called an identity as providers of "commodity" collections and toward new roles. Many are investing in acquiring distinctive collections and providing staffing to enable access to and preservation of these materials, as Anderson foresaw. Many also report that they are reshaping their staffing to provide a variety of new data and digital scholarship services.[91]

Among the survey's conclusions is that:

The 2016 cycle of the Library Survey demonstrates a number of ways in which libraries and library leaders have changed over the past three years. Academic libraries are in transition away from serving principally as collection builders and content providers, where size is a metric of success.

Borrowing the American corporate penchant for calling things by any other name than what they are, books have become "commodities," discarding them "deaccessioning," librarians "critical-thinking instructors," and the remnants of libraries "learning centers."

*

As important as the digital's breaking down the physical boundaries of separation is its tendency to break down the boundaries of authority and expertise. We have already noted this in our discussion of changing belief systems in Chapter 8, but here it is worthwhile to reiterate Dana Boyd's warnings about the failing state of media, and most especially digital literacy and its education. In a society that has long disdained expertise and elitism the academy's hold on authority and truth becomes more fragile with every source of information, opinion, rumor, and falsehood available to anyone with a few mouse clicks. The social, cultural, and economic disruptions caused by the Covid-19 pandemic and the elections of 2020 demonstrated both the effectiveness of digital access and the challenges to university authority and separateness posed by remote technologies. If the campus no longer serves as the focus of

---

[91] Roger C. Schonfeld, "The Strategic Direction of Research Library Leaders: Findings from the Latest Ithaka S+R Survey," *Scholarly Kitchen* (April 4, 2017), at https://scholarlykitchen.sspnet.org/2017/04/04/the-strategic-direction-of-research-library-leaders-findings-from-the-latest-ithaka-sr-survey.

either separateness or authority, and its functions of innovation have largely been usurped by corporate leviathans, what distinct role does the college and university play in the digital age?

PRIVATIZATION

In Chapter 8 we discussed at some length the transformations taking place at the University of Tulsa and other colleges. Observers see this process not only as a shift from humanities, arts, and sciences to STEM and business but also as the external manifestation of the privatization of colleges and universities on several levels. On the first, Tulsa model, a school that began as a private university has been absorbed into the business empire of an Oklahoma oil magnate. But other changes are more systemic and threatening to the nation's public higher education. As austerity budget cuts, shifting belief systems, outright political pressure, and student and family demand continue to take their toll on state universities, many systems now receive less than 20 percent of their revenues from the public. Many have therefore begun relying increasingly on a spectrum of private resources, many of which we have discussed in Chapter 6. This has paved the way to what Richard Vedder, director of the Center for College Affordability and Productivity at Ohio University, and Adjunct Scholar at the American Enterprise Institute, has called the "stealth privatization of one important American public sector institution underway – the state university."[92] Vedder, an opponent of big government and such programs as ObamaCare, identified three flagship campuses prime for privatization, including the University of Michigan, the University of Virginia, and the University of Colorado, as well as entire systems, including the University of New Hampshire.

Matthew T. Lambert, vice president for university advancement at the College of William & Mary, argues that a good dose of privatization – a "public–private model" – might be beneficial to ailing state systems and a sound method of preserving the very concept of public higher education. He too focuses on several large state systems, including Virginia,

---

[92] "Are State Universities Being Privatized?," *Forbes* (Jan. 26, 2012), at www.forbes.com/sites/ccap/2012/01/26/are-state-universities-being-privatized.

North Carolina, and California, as candidates for significant transformation.[93] In an interview with *Inside Higher Ed,* Lambert noted that "privatization need not represent a departure from public mission."[94] But he also summons up the potential threat if higher ed does not respond to growing challenges. He quotes Sebastian Thrun, founder of Udacity, as saying "in 50 years there will only be 10 institutions of higher education." That number just about matches the number of great abbeys left untouched by Henry VIII's Dissolution.

CLOSINGS

This brings us to our final topic, the increasing number of closings or consolidations of private colleges and public universities over the past three decades. In previous chapters, we have offered a small but increasing number of examples of the collapse of venerable institutions of higher learning. These range from majors and specializations, to departments and programs, and from small liberal-arts colleges to substantive threats to state university systems. Most of the schools affected have been for-profits or small not-for-profit liberal-arts schools. But reports indicate that the numbers have begun a slowly increasing cascade: a few percentage points a year that, like compound interest, have resulted in significant numbers over the past decade.[95] The 2018–19 school year marked the largest decline in two decades, as the number of colleges and universities that received Federal aid fell by 5.6 percent.[96] More than

---

[93] Matthew T. Lambert, *Privatization and the Public Good: Public Universities in the Balance* (Cambridge, MA: Harvard Education Press, 2014).

[94] Doug Lederman, "'Privatization and the Public Good'," IHE (December 8, 2014), at www .insidehighered.com/news/2014/12/08/does-privatizing-public-higher-education-necessarily-undermine-public-good.

[95] Doug Lederman, "The Culling of Higher Ed Begins," IHE (July 19, 2017), at www .insidehighered.com/news/2017/07/19/number-colleges-and-universities-drops-sharply-amid-economic-turmoil; Rick Seltzer, "Days of Reckoning," IHE (Nov. 13, 2017), at www.insidehighered.com/news/2017/11/13/spate-recent-college-closures-has-some-seeing-long-predicted-consolidation-taking.

[96] Doug Lederman, "The Incredible Shrinking Higher Ed Industry," IHE (Oct. 14, 2019), at www.insidehighered.com/news/2019/10/14/higher-ed-shrinks-number-colleges-falls-lowest-point-two-decades.

1,200 colleges closed between 2014 and 2018.[97] Nearly 90 percent of these were for-profits. This dissolution has left half a million students without schools, financial aid, degrees, or job prospects, and thousands of families without livelihoods.[98] The Federal government keeps an online database of "Closed School Weekly/Monthly Reports," "the official lists that guaranty agencies may use to discharge loans for students."[99]

An August 2017 analysis of 559 small schools by the Council of Independent Colleges (CIC) was based on fourteen years of financial data and was generally positive about prospects. It found that "two-thirds (67 percent) of small and mid-sized private colleges and universities had achieved a level of financial health at or above the 3.0 CIC threshold of viability by 2013–2014, the most recent year studied." That, however, means that 33 percent of those examined failed to meet the minimum requirement for resource sufficiency, operating results, financial assets, and debt management.[100] According to innovation and organizational experts Clayton M. Christensen and Michael B. Horn, closings will continue to increase:

> We've admittedly played with those predictions over time – from suggesting that 25 percent of colleges would fail in *The New York Times* in 2013 to one of us, Clay Christensen, making more casual predictions in front of audiences where he has said that 50 percent of colleges would fail. The predictions have predictably generated some animosity and rolling of eyes. But it's also prompted some college and university presidents to tell

---

[97] Dan Bauman and Brian O'Leary, "Data: College Closures, 2014–18," CHE (April 4, 2019), at www.chronicle.com/interactives/college-closures. See also Kristin Stowe and David Komasara, "An Analysis of Closed Colleges and Universities," *Planning for Higher Education* 44.4 (July–Sept., 2016): 79–89.

[98] Michael Vasquez and Dan Bauman, "How America's College-Closure Crisis Leaves Families Devastated," CHE (April 4, 2019), at www.chronicle.com/interactives/ 20190404; Jon Nichols, "I Lost My Dream Job in a Rural Town – But Telling Me to Move Doesn't Help," *Guardian* (June 23, 2017), at www.theguardian.com/us-news/2017/jun/ 23/dream-job-rural-town-rensselaer-indiana.

[99] www2.ed.gov/offices/OSFAP/PEPS/closedschools.html.

[100] Hollie M. Chessman et al., "The Financial Resilience of Independent Colleges and Universities," CIC-TIAA Institute_Financial Resilience of Independent Colleges_August 2017.pdf.

us in public and private settings that they think the 50 percent failure prediction is conservative – that is, the number of failures will be far higher.[101]

Much of this trend can be traced back to the recession of 2008 and resulting economic distress for states, schools, and most especially families struggling to maintain or aspire to middle-class status and send their children to college. The main impetus toward college for most families remained social mobility and increased skill sets, which in almost all cases was measured in rising salaries.[102] As Sue Desmond-Hellman, chief executive officer of the Bill & Melinda Gates Foundation and co-chair of its Commission on the Value of Postsecondary Education, stated:

> As the cost of a credential rises, and student debt goes to record levels, people are actually asking a question I never thought I'd hear: "Is going to college a reliable path to economic opportunity?" This question of value needs to be addressed, and we feel that it needs to be addressed urgently.[103]

But with the proliferation of online courses, private for-profit schools, and corporate outreach and academies that we have discussed above, the pathway to these income brackets has been viewed increasingly as outside the walls of the campus and the pathway of traditional degrees. This has resulted in the perfect storm of what observers are calling the "great enrollment crash."[104] In November 2017, for example, a Moody's tuition survey projected enrollment growth

---

[101] Clayton M. Christensen and Michael B. Horn, "Perilous Times," IHE (April 1, 2019), at www.insidehighered.com/views/2019/04/01/many-private-colleges-remain-danger-opinion.

[102] See surveys on attitudes towards higher ed and its benefits in Chapter 4, 87–91.

[103] Katherine Mangan, "Everyone Wants to Measure the Value of College. Now the Gates Foundation Wants a Say," CHE (May 16, 2019), at www.chronicle.com/article/Everyone-Wants-to-Measure-the/246301.

[104] Bill Conley, "The Great Enrollment Crash: Students Aren't Showing up. And It's Only Going to Get Worse," CHE (Sept. 6, 2019), at www.chronicle.com/interactives/20190906-Conley; "; Bill Conley, Where Did All the Students Go? Five Views on the Great Enrollment Crash," CHE (Oct. 2, 2019), at www.chronicle.com/interactives/20191006-A-Crisis-in-Enrollment.

nationwide of less than 1 percent across public and private univer-sities.[105] But 61 percent of Midwestern schools reported enrollment drops. For the rest of the nation, Moody's projected decreases of about 40 percent. In 2017, it changed its overall assessment of higher ed's health from "stable" to "negative," and it did so again for 2019.[106] In May 2019, it was calculated that many private liberal-arts colleges would miss their enrollment goals that fall.[107]

In August 2018, the New England Association of Schools and Colleges alone listed over ninety member institutions merged, closed, or no longer accredited since the 1970s. These range from Andover College in Maine, to Andover Newton Theological Seminary in Lexington, MA; to Boston State College; the College of the Sacred Heart in Fall River, RI; to Mount Ida College in Dedham, MA; and Wheelock College in Boston.[108] Like the small, underpopulated houses planned for closure or merger under Cardinal Wolsey, or those with total assets of under £200 dissolved under Cromwell, these marginal schools that demon-strated financial failings or no longer served vital constituencies or social purposes, have been the first to disappear.[109] But they also presage far more sweeping and dramatic changes in the coming years. Now, according to Moody's Investor Service, "closure rates of small colleges and universities will triple in the coming years, and mergers will double."[110] As Bill Conley, vice president for enrollment management at Bucknell University, warns:

---

[105] Rick Seltzer, "Public Colleges Expected to Feel Tuition Pressure," IHE (Nov. 10, 2017), at www.insidehighered.com/quicktakes/2017/11/10/public-colleges-expected-feel-tuition-pressure.

[106] Adam Harris, "Moody's Downgrades Higher Ed's Outlook from 'Stable' to 'Negative'," CHE (Dec. 5, 2017), at www.chronicle.com/article/Moody-s-Downgrades-Higher/241983; Cailin Crowe, "Moody's Gives Higher Ed a Negative Outlook, Again," CHE (Dec. 4, 2018), at www.chronicle.com/article/Moody-s-Gives-Higher-Ed-a/245258.

[107] Eric Kelderman, "Enrollment Shortfalls Spread to More Colleges," CHE (May 20, 2019), at www.chronicle.com/article/enrollment-shortfalls-spread/246341.

[108] "Merged, Closed, or Previously Accredited," at www.neche.org/for-the-public/merged-closed-or-previously-accredited.

[109] See Chapter 1, 17–18.

[110] Kellie Woodhouse, "Closures to Triple," IHE (Sept. 28, 2015), at www.insidehighered.com/news/2015/09/28/moodys-predicts-college-closures-triple-2017.

This is my summer of 2019 takeaway: Higher education has fully entered a new structural reality. You'd be naïve to believe that most colleges will be able to ride out this unexpected wave as we have previous swells.[111]

Many state systems not facing imminent closure are still grappling with substantial financial crises, in part because of the lingering effects of the 2008 recession, and in part because of the nationwide collapse in enrollments. "Merger" is the operative word for such systems.[112] Since 2011, Georgia has merged eighteen campuses into nine. The Pennsylvania State System of Higher Education has been in crisis mode since the early 2010s, with plans for mergers or campus closings brought about by legislative budget cuts, rising debt, staff and faculty layoffs, and enrollment drops.[113] Wisconsin,[114] Vermont,[115] Maine, Minnesota, New Hampshire, Connecticut,[116] and New York have pursued similar strategies, with varied outcomes.[117] According to the University of Connecticut's president, "Doing nothing is not an option. Our system as it is will not survive."

Among other vulnerable state systems are those designated as "Midwestern" by research organizations, including the National Science Foundation.[118] They include Illinois, Indiana, Iowa, Michigan,

[111] Conley, "The Great Enrollment Crash," www.chronicle.com/interactives/20190906-Conley.

[112] Robert Witt and Kevin P. Coyne, "A Merger Won't Save Your College," CHE (Sept. 22, 2019), at www.chronicle.com/article/A-Merger-Won-t-Save-Your/247194.

[113] Rick Seltzer, "Are Mergers in Pennsylvania Higher Ed's Future?," IHE (March 27, 2017), at www.insidehighered.com/news/2017/03/27/mergers-havent-been-part-pennsylvania-public-higher-eds-past-might-future-be.

[114] Eric Kelderman, "With an Ambitious Merger Proposal, Wisconsin Charts Its Own Course for Change," CHE (Oct. 12, 2017), at www.chronicle.com/article/With-an-Ambitious-Merger/241440; Rick Seltzer, "Whittling Down Wisconsin's Colleges," IHE (Oct. 13, 2017), at www.insidehighered.com/news/2017/10/13/wisconsin-merger-plan-stokes-controversy-some-see-upside.

[115] Rick Seltzer, "Vermont's Merger Map," IHE (July 27, 2016), at www.insidehighered.com/news/2016/07/27/vermont-pushes-combine-public-colleges-administrations.

[116] Rick Seltzer, "Consolidating Community Colleges," IHE (April 4, 2017), at www.insidehighered.com/news/2017/04/04/president-proposes-consolidation-connecticut-state-system.

[117] Seltzer, "Vermont's Merger Map."

[118] Jon Marchus, "The Looming Decline of the Public Research University," *Washington Monthly* (Sept./Oct. 2017), at https://washingtonmonthly.com/magazine/septemberoctober-2017/the-looming-decline-of-the-public-research-university.

Minnesota, Ohio, and Wisconsin. Here state budget cuts, declines in Federal research funding and grants, and enrollment drops have resulted in declines in rankings, flight of faculty and doctoral students, and cuts in programs and salaries for those remaining. Some observers have seen the beginnings of a substantial brain drain.[119] As early as 2012 the National Science Board announced that it was "concerned about the continued ability [of public universities] to conduct the basic science and engineering research that leads to innovations."

*

Over the 2010s, the media have covered school closings on a monthly, often a weekly, basis. We will offer a few examples here. In May 2014, Virginia Intermont College,[120] a 130-year-old liberal arts college in Bristol, VA, held its last commencement exercise and prepared to shutter its windows and close down. Persistent debt had forced the delay of salaries and a policy that required approval for any expense over $10. Finally, the school's main debt-holding bank announced that it would foreclose on the campus, offering up its thirty acres and dozens of properties for sale to the best available bidder. To make the transition smooth, terminate staff, sell off assets, to "teach-out" students to neighboring schools, and to turn off the lights, the college hired Arthur J. Rebrovick Jr., the head of an executive consulting firm, as its interim – and last – president. According to Rebrovick, "Except for the emotional tug of not being able to find a buyer for the campus, this has been an enjoyable piece of work."

Rebrovick is not alone as a hired agent for closings. Some firms, long known for their work in shuttering failed retail outlets, now also specialize in closing down campuses and selling off their assets. "Everything must go! No reasonable offer refused!" proclaims Eaton Hudson College Liquidators. As one of their officers recently noted:

[119] See, for example, Scott T. Gibson "Why New Humanities Ph.D.s Should Leave the Country," CHE (May 19, 2016), at www.chronicle.com/article/Why-New-Humanities-PhDs/236528.

[120] Lawrence Biemiller, "Meet the Guy Who Turns Off the Lights When a College Closes," CHE (Feb. 12, 2017), at www.chronicle.com/article/Meet-the-Guy-Who-Turns-Off-the/239164.

For colleges, we have desks, chairs, computers, book cases, file cabinets, everything you would think of in a regular office. Everything in a college you'll find in either any business environment or a call center or an operations center. This is a whole different group of people who come in to buy these. We had a ton of people coming in just to buy the Mac computers, which we sold out in two days. They were completely gone. . . . Unfortunately, this is a trend. Our pipeline has gotten a little bit busy – not necessarily saying we'll get every one of these opportunities, or these colleges will all close.[121]

For many of the colleges, the Trump Department of Education expected "the receiver, who has control of the institutions and their finances, to resolve this situation."[122]

One of the most famous – and controversial – cases was that of Sweet Briar College, a private women's liberal-arts college founded in 1901. In March 2015, the college's board abruptly announced the school's closing due to "insurmountable financial challenges."[123] Faculty received termination notices for that June 30 and promptly approved a vote of no-confidence in the president and board. The response of faculty, alums, students, and other supporters, including the local Commonwealth attorney, gained national attention as they formed the nonprofit Saving Sweet Briar to reverse the board's decision. The case went to Virginia's supreme court, which blocked the decision. After the mediation of the state's attorney general, the school sacked its board and president and rescinded its closing decision.[124] But Sweet Briar's salvation came at a

---

[121] Lindsay Ellis, "'Everything Must Go!': A Rash of College Closures Keeps This Liquidation Firm Busy," CHE (June 17, 2019), at www.chronicle.com/article/everything-must-go-a/246514.

[122] Bauman and O'Leary, "Data: College Closures," www.chronicle.com/interactives/college-closures.

[123] Nick Anderson and Susan Svrluga, "Sweet Briar College to Close Because of Financial Challenges," *Washington Post* (March 3, 2015), at www.washingtonpost.com/news/grade-point/wp/2015/03/03/sweet-briar-college-to-close-because-of-financial-challenges.

[124] Jessie Pounds, "Transfer of Power Complete at Sweet Briar College," *Roanoke Times* (July 2, 2015). See also Steve Kolowich, "How to Bring a College Back to Life," CHE (April 1, 2017), at www.chronicle.com/article/How-to-Bring-a-College-Back-to/239663.

price, one already borne by many other schools.[125] Beginning with the fall 2018 semester, the college restructured all of its academic departments and replaced them with three new "centers": Engineering, Science and Technology in Society; Human and Environmental Sustainability; and Creativity, Design and the Arts.[126]

The list continues to grow. Marian Court College was closed in 2015.[127] In July 2016, St. Catharine College in Kentucky closed its doors.[128] December 2016, Dowling College in New York filed for Chapter 11 bankruptcy protection, selling its two campuses due to financial shortfalls. The sale liquidated its assets, including substantial real estate on Long Island valued as high as $50 million.[129] In February 2017, St. Joseph's College in Indiana announced that it was suspending operations at least for the 2017–18 academic year in the hopes of a viable restructuring plan.[130] After an internal probe uncovered more than $31 million in unreported debt and unpaid payroll taxes, in September 2019, the 115-year-old College of New Rochelle announced its final graduation and closure. A&G Realty Partners and B6 Real Estate Advisors planned to auction off all the college's property and other possessions. CNR's controller was to serve three years in prison and to pay restitution. Its 2,700 students would be "taught-out" to other schools.[131]

[125] See Chapter 6, 129–39.

[126] Josh Moody, "Sweet Briar College Releases Details on New Core Curriculum," *News Advance* (Dec. 15, 2017), at www.newsadvance.com/news/local/sweet-briar-college-releases-details-on-new-core-curriculum/article_74f8b092-e1d4-11e7-90f1-176841c28d06.html.

[127] Kellie Woodhouse, "No Choice But to Close?," IHE (June 18, 2015), at www.insidehighered.com/news/2015/06/18/enrollment-declines-drove-closure-marian-court-college.

[128] Paul Fain, "The Department and St. Catharine," IHE (June 2, 2016), at www.insidehighered.com/news/2016/06/02/small-private-college-closes-blames-education-department-sanction.

[129] Rick Seltzer, "Dowling Files for Bankruptcy Protection," IHE (Dec. 1, 2016), at www.insidehighered.com/quicktakes/2016/12/01/dowling-files-bankruptcy-protection.

[130] Scott Jaschik, "College Will Suspend Operations," IHE (Feb. 6, 2017), at www.insidehighered.com/news/2017/02/06/saint-josephs-indiana-will-suspend-operations.

[131] Mark Lungariello, "College of New Rochelle Files for Bankruptcy, Campus to be Sold at Auction," *Rockland/Westchester Journal News* (Sept. 23, 2019), at https://eu.lohud.com/story/news/education/2019/09/20/college-of-new-rochelle-bankruptcy-closing-campus-sold-auction/2376019001.

In July 2017, the evangelical Fuller Theological Seminary, based largely in California, announced that it was closing several of its locations. The school was "retooling for a different world" because of the growing demand for, and increases in, online education. According to Fuller's provost:

> the significant increase in online enrollment has been matched by a decrease in enrollment on our geophysical campuses. To offer one snapshot, while winter quarter online enrollment has increased by almost 50% from 2013–17, enrollment on our regional campuses has decreased by about 30% during the same period.[132]

In April 2019, the president of Hampshire College resigned in the face of mounting deficits, declining enrollments, and failed attempts to merge with another school. Hampshire faced closure or the drastic elimination of staff and faculty positions (110 to 60 full-time faculty) and of its founding principles of self-governance. Many humanities positions were cut as the trustees decided to add four visiting faculty positions in high-demand areas: game design and animation; film, photo and video; anthropology; and critical dance.[133] The school also went the way of many of its peers: eliminating departments and majors in favor of task- and project-centered learning, aimed at greater preparation for the marketplace.[134] By November 2019, Hampshire had made enough adjustments that the New England Commission of Higher Education announced that it would continue the school's accreditation.[135]

---

[132] Joseph Hartropp, "Fuller Theological Seminary Closes Some Campuses," *Christian Today* (July 19, 2017), at www.christiantoday.com/article/fuller-theological-seminary-closing-some-campuses-welcome-online-shift/110932.htm.

[133] Scott Jaschik, "Hampshire President Quits; Board Votes to Try to Stay Independent," IHE (April 8, 2019), at www.insidehighered.com/news/2019/04/08/hampshire-college-president-quits-and-board-votes-raise-money-try-stay-independent; Vimal Patel, "Hampshire Faces Questions About Its Survival: This Is How It's Charting a Path Forward," CHE (May 1, 2019), at www.chronicle.com/article/Hampshire-Faces-Questions/246220.

[134] Jacquelyn Voghel, "'No Majors, No Departments': Hampshire College Votes to Shape Academics around Modern Challenges," *Daily Hampshire Gazette* (Oct. 16, 2019), at www.gazettenet.com/HampshireUpdate-hg-101719-29359892.

[135] www.neche.org/wp-content/uploads/2019/11/Hampshire-Press-Release-11.23.2019.pdf.

At Wheeling Jesuit University in West Virginia the board sold its campus in 2017 to the local diocese to help pay down the school's mounting debt. In March 2019, it declared a "financial exigency" and moved to terminate twenty of its fifty-two full-time faculty and other staff; to encourage its students to enroll in Jesuit schools outside the state; to eliminate most liberal-arts majors, including theology, philosophy, history, and literature, as well as engineering, and to replace them with a new emphasis on pre-professional programs and athletics, including its football team.[136] In June 2019, the Jesuit Province of Maryland severed its ties with the school, and Wheeling's Jesuit board president stepped down amid sex and financial scandals involving the school and the diocese.[137]

By July 2019, Cincinnati Christian University was facing bankruptcy and closure for millions of dollars of debt. This comes after a failed attempt to realign the school's failing finances by shifting its priorities from academics to athletics and spending millions on its losing football team. Revelations soon surfaced that the board – without public disclosure or record of its deliberations – had appointed as its new president a fellow board member. That new appointment was a local businessman with financial interests in the bank that holds the university's debt and who himself had been fined and penalized $150,000 by the Securities and Exchange Commission for lying on financial statements and who owes $300,000 in back state taxes.[138]

The response of the Federal government to such mismanagement has been mixed: from the Trump administration's laissez-faire approach to recent Congressional legislation requiring greater transparency in

---

[136] Greg Toppo, "Wheeling Jesuit Declares Financial Exigency," IHE (March 12, 2019), at www.insidehighered.com/quicktakes/2019/03/12/wheeling-jesuit-declares-financial-exigency. Greg Toppo, "A Jesuit University without History or Philosophy?," IHE (April 5, 2019), at www.insidehighered.com/news/2019/04/05/two-years-after-rescue-wheeling-jesuit-guts-faculty-programs.

[137] Rick Seltzer, "When Should the Board Have Known?," IHE (June 11, 2019), at www.insidehighered.com/news/2019/06/11/tied-bishop-scandal-wheeling-jesuit-chairman-steps-down-months-after-exigency.

[138] Eric Kelderman and Dan Bauman, "'Dire Financial Straits': A Portrait of a Desperate University That Made All the Wrong Bets," CHE (July 19, 2019), at www.chronicle.com/article/Dire-Financial-Straits-/246735.

financial reporting.[139] In New Jersey Thomas H. Kean, former state governor who then went on to become president of Drew University in Madison, noted:

> I fear for the future of liberal arts colleges in general. . . . Small ones that do not have major endowments to back them up, that's a large number of places. And yet, like Drew, there are a lot of very good places, and their loss would be dramatic for the country, and the country would be a much poorer place without them.[140]

Kean had himself rescued the school from financial problems during his tenure and has seen them return as Moody's downgraded Drew's bonds rating in March 2017 for the second time in two years. The Covid-19 pandemic now makes all enrollment and closure predictions uncertain.

*

Many reasons – social, economic, devotional – led to the choice of monasteries to be dissolved first by Wolsey and then by Cromwell and Henry VIII. But as Eamon Duffy has demonstrated in great detail, by the time the Dissolution was completed, the predominant cause for monasticism's permanent disappearance from the British landscape was ideological, enshrined in the most rigid thought of English Protestantism and backed up by the Crown.[141] Aside from the social and economic forces that have contributed to this acceleration of American campus closings, there is also an ideology underpinning the manner in which such decimations of higher education can be justified and normalized, and that is based on a marketplace survival of the fittest. By 2020, social utility and research results ("mobility-boosters or know-ledge-creators") – both defined in economic returns – have become the

---

[139] Chris Lisinski, "College Campuses Face Penalties under Closure Bill Approved by House," *Daily Hampshire Gazette* (Oct. 2, 2019), at www.gazettenet.com/college-closure-bill-29002727.

[140] Rick Seltzer, "Drew's Downgrade," IHE (March 31, 2017), at www.insidehighered.com/news/2017/03/31/drew-university-after-spending-attract-more-students-faces-large-deficits.

[141] Introduction, 19–20; Chapter 8, 204–5.

chief criteria for evaluating higher education. According to a recent Brookings Institution report:

> universities act as ladders for social mobility, which makes for a more dynamic and fairer society. They are also laboratories for research, expanding our knowledge in directions that can improve the welfare of the broader population. A good case can be made for public support for institutions that act in one or both of these ways: as what we label either ladders or labs. But there are some institutions that cannot claim to be either mobility-boosters or knowledge-creators: these are the laggards. These institutions have a weaker claim on the public purse.[142]

---

[142] Dimitrios Halikias and Richard V. Reeves, "Ladders, Labs, or Laggards? Which Public Universities Contribute Most," *Brookings Report* (July 11, 2017), at www.brookings.edu/research/ladders-labs-or-laggards-which-public-universities-contribute-most.

CHAPTER 10

Conclusions: New Directions?

INTRODUCTION

THE DISSOLUTION OF THE MONASTERIES DID not mean that they were totally eradicated. Although many were simply abandoned, substantial numbers became parish churches, cathedrals, hospitals, schools, and university colleges. They thus preserved some functions, even if different from their original founding purpose. Many monastic complexes became stately homes for wealthy friends and servants of the king.

But what were the consequences for the monasteries in terms of the triad of institutional qualities that we have posed as essential to the survival and growth of any institutional system: authority, separateness, and innovation? We have surveyed briefly the contributions of medieval monasticism to these three qualities in Chapter 1. We observed that the loss of monastic authority in the late Middle Ages and its assumption by the university was one of the chief causes contributing to the social consensus that their time had passed. The dissolution of the physical and intellectual separateness of the monastery as a place and time apart is embodied in the ruins dotting the British Isles and many other parts of Europe. This lost authority and separateness had disappeared hand-in-hand with the monastery's other chief quality: its ability to innovate for medieval society in everything from architecture to health care and sanitation, to farming and forestry, to intellectual life and book production, to liturgies and music. By 1535 most of these innovations had been absorbed and adapted either into the learning of the university or into the arts and technologies of secular society. The monastery as a vital institution had already passed into history long before its physical walls came tumbling down.

*

But how far can we stretch metaphors and historical analogies? Has the original idea of this book been borne out by our preceding chapters? How far has the history and fate of the American college and university matched that of medieval cloister? How closely are the societies, economies, political systems, and mental universe of the sixteenth century aligned with those of the twenty-first? Can the historian really claim that history repeats itself in such literal terms? Our ready answer would be that throughout this book we have attempted to avoid such simple comparisons, even while drawing attention to institutional structures and patterns of growth, maturity, and decline. If history does not repeat itself, human social and intellectual organization, and the institutions that embody them, do have certain rhyming patterns. These patterns make such broad metaphorical comparisons of some use to the historian. Throughout this book we have attempted to demonstrate that much of the peril facing American higher education today is the construction of a narrative of decline, abuse, and irrelevance similar to the one deployed by the Tudor monarchy of the sixteenth century. We have attempted to track the elements of this modern narrative. How valid are our observations, and what sense can we make of future directions deriving from them?

As recent poll results, news reports, voting patterns, and legislative agendas indicate, Americans are increasingly hostile to the current shape of higher education. They believe that it no longer serves the interests of society or of personal mobility and economic advantage. They decry what are reported as the athletic, sexual, fiscal, and intellectual scandals of academe. A growing and vocal group claim that professors brainwash students and prevent free inquiry; or they perceive higher ed as serving only the elite and employing only those who share a contempt for American values. If such current trends continue, and if closings and transformations mount as enrollments plummet, how far will Americans continue to support our colleges and universities when politicians attack and condemn them, oligarchs and corporations absorb and transform their mission, and governments and legislatures refuse to support them? By the year 1500 monasticism had grown, thrived, and survived for about 1,000 years. By the year 2000 the university will have grown, thrived, and survived for another millennium. What grounds will we have for optimism about the condition of our colleges and universities fifteen years from now when we reach the year 2036, the 500th anniversary of the Dissolution of the Monasteries?

NEW DIRECTIONS?

Higher education has taken many forms historically. The monastic and cathedral masters of novices evolved into the university professors of the later Middle Ages. The private- and public-school masters of the Italian Renaissance were joined by humanist essayists, orators, and tutors of princes. Court artists and intellectuals joined the new educators of the *ancien régime*. In the Catholic lands of early modern Europe older monasticism gave way to new orders like the Jesuits or the reformed mendicants.[1] Only in the past century has higher education been concentrated into a strict and exclusive system of degree-granting universities and colleges with the goal of certifying professional status across a broad spectrum of socially useful and creative fields of endeavor. There is no guarantee that this short-lived, highly concentrated, complex, and expensive system of education will or should remain unchanged.

Across the board, the American system of higher education has seen dramatic shifts in emphasis in both subject matter and degrees earned. We have already discussed the growing trend toward business, health, and service-industry specialties, and the increasingly rapid decline of humanities, arts, and sciences curricula. Here Stephen Jaeger's distinction between "charismatic" and "intellectual" cultures in regard to the cathedral schools of the Middle Ages may bear scrutiny for our conclusions. For instead of lamenting the shift in university education away from strict disciplinary approaches to subject matter, pedagogy,

---

[1] See John W. O'Malley, SJ, *The First Jesuits* (Cambridge, MA: Harvard University Press, 1993), esp. 200–83 for schools and intellectual culture; and Paul Grendler, *Jesuit Schools and Universities in Europe, 1548–1773* (Boston: Brill, 2018).

professional development, and reward – what Jaeger would term an "intellectual" culture of education – we may be seeing the shift, demanded by the public, toward his "charismatic" educational culture where knowledge per se is not the ultimate goal but where moral education for citizens takes a predominant role.

Such a turn would mark a decided return to our understanding of the humanities and liberal arts as the core subjects in the development of knowledgeable citizens and wise leaders, one made canonical by the Renaissance humanists and their critiques of scholastic scholarship. This concentrates on the world of higher education for what social historian Norbert Elias called the "civilizing effect" of education and may point to a fruitful mission for the university that is less new than reiterative.

We can gain yet another insight from Jaeger's paradigms: that by the twelfth century the cathedral-school education of the eleventh century had become outdated as the universities took their place and the training in disciplines replaced a moral education. Yet in the very process of losing their institutional setting, these eleventh-century practices became "widely admired social values" for the twelfth century. That is, as their institutional walls dissolved, they permeated society at large. The same may be said of the thousands of clerics affected by what medievalists call the Gregorian Reform of the eleventh and twelfth centuries focused around the conflicting claims of the Church and State to control spiritual matters. These educated and literate clerics, expelled from their institutions for failings, including clerical marriage and newly illegal bonds to secular rulers, then went on to create a new class of officials, the *magisteriales*, who filled the courts, chancellories, and schools of the emperor and high aristocracy. They formed the backbone of the new intellectualism that historians call the Twelfth-Century Renaissance. In the sixteenth century, nuns and monks expelled from the monasteries under Henry VIII would form an equally large, skilled, and literate class that diffused throughout a newly secularizing Reformation society.

There are now thousands of Ph.D.s in both the arts and sciences who will never gain permanent employment within US academe. What outlets are available to them? As a class they are not without precedent or impact. The new Ph.D.s already enrich government, corporate, and foundation work. But their loss to higher education constitutes a grand interruption of long traditions of knowledge, authority, and institutional memory at a perilous time. Who will be left to stand guard?

We have already reviewed the three distinct forms of the corporate university and what challenges these present to the survival of traditional higher education. But are there other alternatives, once again formed and governed by faculty and students? Do models like the New School in New York and St. John's College in Annapolis offer some possibilities and cautions? The New School was founded in 1919 as the New School for Social Research on the principles of faculty governance and close bonds between faculty and students, nurturing open inquiry and progressive social ideals.[2] In the 1930s it served as a refuge for European intellectuals fleeing the Nazi and other right-wing regimes. Since then it has developed along the lines of many other colleges, slowly acquiring more and diverse schools and disciplinary concentrations, until today it is "The New School, A University." By the 2000s it was beset by a range of conflicts and scandals common to academe, including a 2008 senior-faculty vote of no confidence in its president. St. John's College has been discussed above[3] and is now in danger of following the same path. Can their original models be replicated and scaled today in a manner that minimizes costs and maximizes the impact of technology to enhance both the authority of faculty and the experience of higher education as a time and space apart?

REIMAGINING THE ACADEMY

There are several alternatives for the future of higher education; and this book does not claim to offer any original visions. Experts on higher education and those with a wealth of experience on the highest levels of college and university administration have offered many different views over the past decade. We will cite and summarize briefly some of the more recent perspectives.

[2] https://en.wikipedia.org/wiki/The_New_School; and https://www.newschool.edu/about.
[3] See Chapter 5, 108–9; Chapter 7, 198.

297

Among the first is the attitude, largely expressed by highly placed insiders at prestigious institutions, that all is essentially fine and that the many critiques of higher ed are exaggerated and alarmist. They reassure us that the system will survive as it is, despite ups and downs, as has happened so many times across the history of America. In *Higher Education in America* the former president of Harvard University, Derek Bok, reviews the spectrum of higher education, considers criticisms, finds some problems, and makes recommendations for some improvement. His focus is largely institutional, and it concludes that the future is bright for higher education, essentially as it is. "Of all the problems discussed in previous chapters, only two are in urgent need of improvement," he notes. He continues:

> In the end, the key ingredients of progress will be a determination on the part of academic leaders to concentrate on raising graduate rates *and* improving the quality of education coupled with a willingness on the part of public officials, foundations, and other donors to support the research and experimentation required before embarking on expensive reforms of unproven value. . . . It is impossible to predict just how vigorous and successful universities will be in exploiting . . . new possibilities. But there is no sign of any decline in their entrepreneurial zeal or their capacity for innovation . . . the next twenty-five years will eventually take their place . . . as another of the great creative periods in the history of American higher education.[4]

A variation on this theme, from a similarly privileged vantage point, is by William G. Bowen, former president of Princeton University and then of the Andrew W. Mellon Foundation, with co-author Michael S. McPherson. The latter is former president of Macalester College, dean of faculty at Williams College, fellow of the Institute for Advanced Research, and senior fellow at the Mellon Foundation. An expert on higher ed's economics, he co-chaired the American Academy of Arts and Sciences Commission on the Future of Undergraduate Education that released its 2017 report, *The Future of Undergraduate Education, The Future*

---

[4] Derek Bok, *Higher Education in America* (Princeton: Princeton University Press, 2015), 407, 408, 411–12.

of America. Bowen and McPherson's *Lesson Plan: An Agenda for Change in American Higher Education* also concedes that there are problems, but that they are exaggerated and "lend themselves to hyperbole."[5] The real issue is higher ed's failure to meet a spectrum of important public needs. These include completion rates, affordability and government funding, especially for the "disadvantaged," increasing efficiency, bringing sports programs under control, and better harnessing technology. Their approach is a "re-engineering of essential elements" for necessary reforms.

Then there are neoliberal visions, according to which everything, including higher education, is a marketplace, with all the dangers and opportunities of any other monetized transaction. Such approaches include Ryan Craig's *College Disrupted: The Great Unbundling of Higher Education*,[6] which offers a journalistic prospectus for higher education as a hi-tech research and investment opportunity; Jon McGee's *Breakpoint: The Changing Marketplace for Higher Education*,[7] which views higher education as a dynamic marketplace in a period of flux; Charles J. Sykes' *Fail U.: The False Promise of Higher Education*,[8] where "value for money" is being lost on college costs and student debt that buy only contingent faculty, misplaced capital spending, and a campus culture of "alleged traumas." Within this neoliberal discourse, but from a critical point of view, Jon Nixon's *Higher Education and the Public Good: Imagining the University*[9] focuses on the need to rescue higher ed from commodification and to restore it as a force for the public good. So too, Henry A. Giroux's *Neoliberalism's War on Higher Education* argues that corporate forces are in the process of destroying higher education, but that global youth and public intellectuals can and do resist.[10]

---

[5] William G. Bowen and Michael S. McPherson, *Lesson Plan: An Agenda for Change in American Higher Education* (Princeton: Princeton University Press, 2016).

[6] Ryan Craig, *College Disrupted: The Great Unbundling of Higher Education* (New York: Palgrave Macmillan Trade, 2015).

[7] Jon McGee, *Breakpoint: The Changing Marketplace for Higher Education* (Baltimore: Johns Hopkins University Press, 2015).

[8] Charles J. Sykes, *Fail U.: The False Promise of Higher Education* (New York: St. Martin's Press, 2016).

[9] Jon Nixon, *Higher Education and the Public Good: Imagining the University* (London: Continuum, 2012).

[10] Henry A. Giroux, *Neoliberalism's War on Higher Education* (Chicago: Haymarket Books, 2014).

A third alternative is laid out by such visionaries as Michael M. Crow, president of Arizona State University and a pioneer in the application of digital solutions to higher ed. Crow plots a future for American academe somewhere between Bok and Bowen's confidence in the continued authority of the academy – with the necessary reforms – and neoliberal scenarios.[11] The future of higher ed lies in heeding the "imperative of innovation" in order to meet both internal institutional needs for sustainability and the needs of American society at large.[12] Only through massive application of new technologies can the academy both keep up with worldwide trends and maintain its record of excellence. Such an imperative can be met by overcoming resistance to new models. This is accomplished by embracing the breakthroughs of the digital era and through active collaboration "with leading venture capitalists and investment advisors to source, fund, pilot and credential higher education technology companies." It is apparent that such partnering breaks down walls of separation in the interests of needed innovation. At the same time, Crow's model of the new technology-driven university appears to maintain its authority through a dynamic balance of clear mission and historical perspectives on the history of higher ed to preserve, create, and disseminate knowledge. How that precarious balance will play itself out over the next several decades remains to be seen.

Such works project several essential visions of the future of American higher ed: the first of the amelioration of an essentially sound situation, the second of existential threat to survival, the third an embrace of realities on the ground to transform and maintain the place of higher education in American society. Which is the more accurate? It most likely depends on where the authors sit; and on what side of the growing divide of inequality – social, economic, technological, and cultural – in America. The well-endowed, Research 1 universities from which the

---

[11] See Michael M. Crow, "Wave 5: Launching the Next Wave in Higher Education," ASU GSV Summit April 20, 2016, at https://president.asu.edu/sites/default/files/asu_gsv_final_branded_041516.pdf. Crow elaborates on these ideas in *The Fifth Wave: The Evolution of American Higher Education* (Baltimore: Johns Hopkins University Press, 2020).

[12] See Chapter 8, 223–36; and "The Innovation Imperative," CHE (Sept. 2019), at https://store.chronicle.com/products/the-innovation-imperative.

optimistic authors come will, no doubt, continue to survive and thrive. But the small, liberal-arts colleges and many public universities could well face extinction or cooptation, most especially if the future lies in the massive application of new technologies controlled by corporate elites. Again, such a divide reflects and may replicate the ultimate fate of England's monasteries. The vast majority ended in bare ruins, the select few that had received royal favor and reprieve survived and thrived anew as the new cathedrals and royal abbeys of the realm.

Some of the analyses above present a version of re-engineering reform, with the best, brightest, and largest focusing their attention and energies on re-invigorating a venerable institution. Some proponents of market forces endorse replacing the current system with far more skills-focused schools, especially at the community-college level or with the continued privatization of state institutions to form robust, if differently focused and funded large-scale institutions. Some see neoliberalism destroying the current fabric of higher ed. Some continue to trust in the promise of technology to solve social, economic, and cultural problems. But altogether such treatments – by acknowledged and knowledgeable experts – envision our system of higher education as remaining essentially the same in its general form, extent, and purposes. Reform, even radical reform, will keep the system – and its institutions – intact for the foreseeable future.

REINVENTING THE UNIVERSITY

But other futures are also imaginable – and if many of the trends discussed in the previous chapters continue – possible and perhaps probable. What might they be? We have already discussed the continued growth of corporate universities, both in-house and by extension into existing campuses, breaking down walls of separation, coopting both higher education's authority and its history of innovation. Are America's corporations the twenty-first century version of Tudor England's great barons who enriched themselves on the ruin of the monasteries and who directed the realignment of their resources and societal mission? Are distance education and other manifestations of the digital making physical campuses – and their time and place

———. "On Trigger Warnings," *AAUP Reports and Publications* (Aug. 2014), at www.aaup.org/report/trigger-warnings.

———. "Trends in the Academic Labor Force, 1975–2015," at www.aaup .org/sites/default/files/Academic_Labor_Force_Trends_1975-2015.pdf.

———. "Visualizing Change: The Annual Report on the Economic Status of the Profession, 2016–17," at www.aaup.org/file/FCS_2016-17.pdf.

American Council of Learned Societies et al., *Report of the Commission on the Humanities* (New York: ACLS, 1964).

Anderson, Kent, "Trust Falls – Are We in a New Phase of Corporate Research?" *Scholarly Kitchen* (Aug. 15, 2017), at https://scholarlykitchen .sspnet.org/2017/08/15/trust-falls-new-phase-corporate-research.

Anderson, Rick, "Less than Meets the Eye: Print Book Use Is Falling Faster in Research Libraries," *Scholarly Kitchen* (Aug. 21, 2017), at https:// scholarlykitchen.sspnet.org/2017/08/21/less-meets-eye-print-book-use-falling-faster-research-libraries.

Anderson, Robert D., *European Universities from the Enlightenment to 1914* (Oxford: Oxford University Press, 2010).

André, Bernard, *The Life of Henry VII*, Daniel Hobbins, ed. and trans. (New York: Italica Press, 2011).

Aronowitz, Stanley, *The Knowledge Factory: Dismantling the Corporate University and Creating True Higher Learning* (Boston: Beacon Press, 2005).

———, and Henry A. Giroux. *Postmodern Education: Politics, Culture, and Social Criticism* (Minneapolis: University of Minnesota Press, 1991).

Arum, Richard, and Jarip Roksa, *Academically Adrift: Limited Learning on College Campuses* (Chicago: University of Chicago Press, 2011).

Association of Governing Boards of Universities and Colleges, *Public Confidence in Higher Education* (2018), at https://agb.org/sites/default/ files/report_2018_guardians_public_confidence.pdf.

Bäuml, Franz H., "Varieties and Consequences of Medieval Literacy and Illiteracy," *Speculum* 55.2 (1980): 237–65.

Beach, Alison I., and Isabelle Cochelin, eds., *The Cambridge History of Medieval Monasticism in the Latin World*, 2 vols. (Cambridge: Cambridge University Press, 2020).

Bell, David N., "Libraries in England and Wales," *Oxford Bibliographies* (March 2016), at www.oxfordbibliographies.com/view/document/obo-9780195396584/obo-9780195396584-0193.xml.

Bell, Daniel, *The Reforming of General Education: The Columbia College Experience in its National Setting* (New York: Columbia University Press, 1966).

D'Souza, Dinesh, *Illiberal Education: The Politics of Race and Sex on Campus* (New York: Vintage, 1992).

Duffy, Eamon, *The Stripping of the Altars: Traditional Religion in England, 1400–1580* (New Haven: Yale University Press, 1992; 2nd, rev. ed., 2005).

Ehrenreich, Barbara, *Fear of Falling: The Inner Life of the Middle Class* (New York: HarperCollins, 1989).

Erasmus, Desiderius, *Ten Colloquies*, Craig R. Thompson, ed. and trans. (Indianapolis: Bobs-Merrill, 1957).

Esposito, Joseph J., "Good Data, Bad Data, You Know I've Had My Share: Library Book Acquisition Patterns," *Scholarly Kitchen* (July 23, 2018), at https://scholarlykitchen.sspnet.org/2018/07/23/good-data-bad-data-know-ive-share-library-book-acquisition-patterns.

—— and Karen Barch, "Monograph Output of American University Presses, 2009–2013: A Report Prepared for the Andrew W. Mellon Foundation" (Feb. 10, 2017), at https://scholarlykitchen.sspnet.org/wp-content/uploads/2017/02/Monograph-Output-of-University-Presses.pdf.

——, Karen Barch, and Rick Anderson, "Revisiting Two Perspectives on Library-based University Presses," *Scholarly Kitchen* (July 19, 2017), at https://scholarlykitchen.sspnet.org/2017/07/19/revisiting-two-perspectives-library-based-university-presses.

Fitzmaurice, Andrew, *Humanism and America: An Intellectual History of English Colonisation, 1500–1625* (Cambridge: Cambridge University Press, 2004).

Fletcher, J. M., "The Faculty of Arts," in J. I. Catto and Ralph Evans, eds. *The History of the University of Oxford* I *The Early Oxford Schools* (Oxford: Oxford University Press, 1984), 369–99.

Foucault, Michel, "What is Enlightenment?," in Paul Rabinow, ed., *The Foucault Reader* (New York: Pantheon Books, 1984), 32–50.

Gardiner, Eileen, and Ronald G. Musto, *The Digital Humanities: A Primer for Students and Scholars* (New York: Cambridge University Press, 2015).

Garrard, Graeme, *Counter-Enlightenments: From the Eighteenth Century to the Present* (Abingdon: Routledge, 2006).

——. *Rousseau's Counter-Enlightenment: A Republican Critique of the Philosophes* (Buffalo: State University of New York Press, 2003).

Georgetown University Center on Education and the Workforce, "A First Try at ROI" (November 2019), at https://cew.georgetown.edu/cew-reports/CollegeROI.

Ginder, S. A., J. E. Kelly-Reid, and F. B. Mann, *Enrollment and Employees in Postsecondary Institutions, Fall 2017; and Financial Statistics and Academic*

difficulties of maintaining it have informed the history of the AAUP and other professional organizations. How likely is it then for a faculty or a disciplinary group to pull up stakes and leave a university for some still-undiscovered shores of self-governance? American faculties of the twenty-first century are not like the English masters who left Paris in 1165, or the Oxford masters who seceded to move to Cambridge in 1209. Twelfth-century scholars could easily change location to found or enlarge their own schools because, after all, they had no physical university to speak of. There were no classroom buildings, dorms, dining halls, libraries, or laboratories, or administrators other than themselves and what they could carry away with them. Is such a secession possible or even worth contemplating for twenty-first century American academics?

On the other end of the spectrum of possibilities or projections, does the digital now make it possible for groups of faculty scattered across a landscape of now-dissolved college and university walls – but sharing common disciplinary interests and methods – to avail themselves of central "service portals" like university libraries and other facilities? Could a humanities faculty based in rented or newly purchased halls draw remotely on the vast digital holdings of a Columbia, Stanford, or Harvard to provide teaching and research materials for a new kind of student experience: one based physically in satellites but connected to the larger world of learning via digital networks? Could our massive Research 1 universities – already decisively moving into hi-tech and STEM research and innovation centers allied with business – make themselves available as high-powered service centers for decentered clusters of liberal-arts and science faculties? Many state systems are already deploying such a model for existing satellite campuses. Can the same model now used by many European universities to house students in independent residence halls also be deployed? What use will be made of the now-emptying halls, libraries, gyms, and common rooms of our many smaller colleges?

The recent case of Marlboro College in Vermont offers an interesting scenario. In November 2019, the college announced that it was closing its doors – the usual financial and enrollment issues were the top causes – and that it would merge with Emerson College in Boston, transferring to it its $30-million endowment and $10 million in real estate.[13] The move was hailed by many as a sensible salvation, but some alums soon objected to the hasty decision. One group of alums proposed an innovative alternative: that alums themselves would save the college by buying it for a bargain price, $5 million. Many alums were, in fact, well-placed faculty themselves, and the plan offered a new variation on faculty–student governance. The plan was ultimately rejected, but it did highlight the lost element in discussions of higher ed. Amid all the talk, planning, and initiatives of administrators drawn largely from the corporate world or sharing its ideology, faculty and students remain the silenced core of higher education. It is they who will need to formulate and implement any new vision of a dissolved university.

But would alums' resistance to the threatened closing of their alma maters soon become another example of the fetishization of the unique physical object that we have seen at work in the digital age? Forty-five percent of Marlboro alums polled, in fact, wanted to preserve their historical memories by "working to retain the campus for cultural purposes." On some college campuses today, underused or unused buildings are already being converted into various forms of offices and housing, some newly constructed in clusters for retirees attracted by the surviving life or cultural memories of college campuses.[14] Will the campus become as sentimental but as unnecessary a throwback as the now-fetishized LP and turntable, the cahier and ink pen, the film camera, and the brick-factory-turned-museum? Will the university as a separate time and place, of personal and collective experience and memory, join a bygone but irretrievably abandoned past accessible only to a knowing and refined elite? If so, what will become of the constituencies of higher education as campuses, their resources, and special values face closure and dissolution? Who will defend a distant but unimportant cultural memory at a time of existential threat?

[13] Megan Zahneis, "A College Prepares to Close Its Doors as Students and Alumni Mourn – and Scheme," CHE (Nov. 18, 2019), at www.chronicle.com/article/A-College-Prepares-to-Close/247567.

[14] Anemona Hartocollis, "At Colleges, What's Old Is New: Retirees Living on Campus," *New York Times* (Sept. 10, 2019), at www.nytimes.com/2019/09/10/us/college-university-retirement-communities.html.

Cobban, A. B., *The Medieval English Universities: Oxford and Cambridge to c. 1500* (Aldershot: Scolar Press, 1988).

——. *The Medieval Universities: Their Development and Organization* (London: Methuen, 1975).

College Board, "Trends in Higher Education: Average Published Undergraduate Charges by Sector and by Carnegie Classification, 2018–19," at https://trends.collegeboard.org/college-pricing/figures-tables/average-published-undergraduate-charges-sector-2018-19.

"Counter-Enlightenment," *Wikipedia*, at https://en.wikipedia.org/wiki/Counter-Enlightenment.

Cox, Archibald, et al., *Crisis at Columbia: Report of the Fact-Finding Commission Appointed to Investigate the Disturbance at Columbia University in April and May 1968* (New York: Vintage Books, 1968).

Craig, Ryan, *College Disrupted: The Great Unbundling of Higher Education* (New York: Palgrave Macmillan Trade, 2015).

Crow, Michael M., *The Fifth Wave: The Evolution of American Higher Education* (Baltimore, MD: Johns Hopkins University Press, 2020).

——. "Wave 5: Launching the Next Wave in Higher Education," ASU GSV Summit April 20, (2016), at https://president.asu.edu/sites/default/files/asu_gsv_final_branded_041516.pdf.

Daniel, Katherine, "Library Acquisition Patterns: A Preliminary Report with Data from OCLC's WorldShare Management Services." Ithaka S+R (July 19, 2018), at https://sr.ithaka.org/blog/library-acquisition-patterns.

——, Joseph J. Esposito, and Roger C. Schonfeld, "Library Acquisition Patterns: Preliminary Findings," Ithaka S+R (July 19, 2018), at https://sr.ithaka.org/publications/library-acquisition-patterns-preliminary-findings.

Davison Hunter, James, *Culture Wars: The Struggle to Define America* (New York: Basic Books, 1991).

Davis, Angela, *An Autobiography* (New York: Random House, 1974).

Deresiewicz, William, *Excellent Sheep: The Miseducation of the American Elite and the Way to a Meaningful Life* (New York: Free Press, 2014).

De Vries, Jan, *European Urbanisation, 1500–1800* (London: Methuen, 1984, reprt., Routledge, 2013).

Dewey, John, "President Hutchins' Proposals to Remake Higher Education," *Social Frontier* 3 (Jan. 1937): 103–4.

Dollimore, Jonathan, *Radical Tragedy: Religion, Ideology, and Power in the Drama of Shakespeare and His Contemporaries* (Chicago: University of Chicago Press, 1984).

Bernard, G. W., "The Dissolution of the Monasteries," *History* 96.324 (2011): 390–409.

——. *The King's Reformation: Henry VIII and the Remaking of the English Church* (New Haven: Yale University Press, 2005).

Black, Robert, "Literacy in Florence, 1427," in Daniel E. Bornstein and David Spencer Peterson, eds., *Florence and Beyond: Culture, Society and Politics in Renaissance Italy* (Toronto: Centre for Reformation and Renaissance Studies, 2008), 195–210.

Bloom, Allan, *The Closing of the American Mind: How Higher Education Has Failed Democracy and Impoverished the Souls of Today's Students* (New York: Simon and Schuster, 1987).

Blumenthal, Joseph, *The Printed Book in America* (Boston: David R. Godine and Dartmouth College Library, 1977).

Bod, Rens, *A New History of the Humanities* (Oxford: Oxford University Press, 2013).

Bok, Derek, *Higher Education in America* (Princeton: Princeton University Press, 2015).

Boucaud-Victoire, Kévin, "How Michel Foucault Got Neoliberalism so Wrong: An Interview with Daniel Zamora," *Jacobin Magazine* (Sept. 6, 2019), at https://jacobinmag.com/2019/09/michel-foucault-neoliberalism-friedrich-hayek-milton-friedman-gary-becker-minoritarian-governments.

Bound, John, Breno Braga, Gaurav Khanna, and Sarah Turner, *Public Universities: The Supply Side of Building a Skilled Workforce*. National Bureau of Economic Research Working Paper No. 25945 (June 2019), at www.nber.org/papers/w25945.

Bourdieu, Pierre, *The Field of Cultural Production* (New York: Columbia University Press, 1993).

——, and Jean-Claude Passeron. *Reproduction in Education, Society and Culture*, Richard Nice, trans. (London: Sage, 1977).

Bousma, William, "Learning and the Problem of Undergraduate Education," in John Voss and Paul L. Ward, eds., *Confrontation and Learned Societies* (New York: New York University Press, 1970), 70–103.

Bowen, William G., and Michael S. McPherson, *Lesson Plan: An Agenda for Change in American Higher Education* (Princeton: Princeton University Press, 2016).

Boyd, Danah, "Did Media Literacy Backfire?" *Points: Data & Society* (Jan. 5, 2017), at https://points.datasociety.net/did-media-literacy-backfire-7418c084d88d.

Briggs, Charles F., "Literacy, Reading, and Writing in the Medieval West," *Journal of Medieval History*, 26:4 (2000): 397–420.

Depending on how one frames and answers this question today about the universities, one might be able to foresee a second life of the liberal arts and sciences at least without the major infrastructure it now requires. But how? Will the ten or a dozen or the very few dozen major research universities that survive serve the same social purpose as the great abbeys that survived the Dissolution? Will the Harvards, Yales, and Stanfords suffice for the survival of advanced research, much as the survival of a few great abbeys, however converted and reused, managed for England after the Dissolution? Or will these, like those formerly great abbeys, also slip into cultural and social irrelevance and other, newer institutions take their place? This book has posed such questions repeatedly and offered a good number of modern examples to illustrate the issues they pose. If, in the end, it has not offered many answers, it has at least attempted to set these questions within their proper historical and contemporary contexts.

*

In 1523, the abbot Richard Kidderminster (*c.*1462–*c.*1532) surveyed his small part of the monastic landscape at Winchcombe Abbey, founded in 798. He wrote with delight about his life of learning and collegiality:

> It was a fine sight to see how the brethren devoted themselves to sacred learning, how they made use of Latin even in their familiar conversations, and how the cloister at Winchcombe at that time had all the appearance of a young university, though on a minute scale. Added to this, regular observance was so ardently observed among us, and brotherly charity was so honoured, that you would have said that there could not possibly be another such family, so united, so harmonious, and yet so small, in the whole of England. The good God alone knows what a joy it was then for me to be immersed in sacred studies with my brethren in the cloister. There day and night I passed the time at my books in a little study I had constructed; would that I had allowed it to stand till the present day! My industry was such that practically all the learning I have in Scripture and divinity was gained there in the cloister. I have written all this that those who come after may learn that theology may be as fruitfully studied in the cloister as at the university.[15]

---

[15] Quoted in Knowles, *Religious Orders*, III:92.

From such a perspective how could Richard Kidderminster have known that there would be none who would come after him, or envisioned the disastrous ruin of his world in just ten years? How could he have foreseen that the university to which he so confidently drew comparison would replace his cloistered world so quickly and so utterly? But again, one might ask, as an intelligent, observant, and learned man of his times, how could he not have seen what was coming?

Cobban, A. B., *The Medieval English Universities: Oxford and Cambridge to c. 1500* (Aldershot: Scolar Press, 1988).

——. *The Medieval Universities: Their Development and Organization* (London: Methuen, 1975).

College Board, "Trends in Higher Education: Average Published Undergraduate Charges by Sector and by Carnegie Classification, 2018–19," at https://trends.collegeboard.org/college-pricing/figures-tables/average-published-undergraduate-charges-sector-2018-19.

"Counter-Enlightenment," *Wikipedia*, at https://en.wikipedia.org/wiki/Counter-Enlightenment.

Cox, Archibald, et al., *Crisis at Columbia: Report of the Fact-Finding Commission Appointed to Investigate the Disturbance at Columbia University in April and May 1968* (New York: Vintage Books, 1968).

Craig, Ryan, *College Disrupted: The Great Unbundling of Higher Education* (New York: Palgrave Macmillan Trade, 2015).

Crow, Michael M., *The Fifth Wave: The Evolution of American Higher Education* (Baltimore, MD: Johns Hopkins University Press, 2020).

——. "Wave 5: Launching the Next Wave in Higher Education," ASU GSV Summit April 20, (2016), at https://president.asu.edu/sites/default/files/asu_gsv_final_branded_041516.pdf.

Daniel, Katherine, "Library Acquisition Patterns: A Preliminary Report with Data from OCLC's WorldShare Management Services." Ithaka S+R (July 19, 2018), at https://sr.ithaka.org/blog/library-acquisition-patterns.

——, Joseph J. Esposito, and Roger C. Schonfeld, "Library Acquisition Patterns: Preliminary Findings," Ithaka S+R (July 19, 2018), at https://sr.ithaka.org/publications/library-acquisition-patterns-preliminary-findings.

Davison Hunter, James, *Culture Wars: The Struggle to Define America* (New York: Basic Books, 1991).

Davis, Angela, *An Autobiography* (New York: Random House, 1974).

Deresiewicz, William, *Excellent Sheep: The Miseducation of the American Elite and the Way to a Meaningful Life* (New York: Free Press, 2014).

De Vries, Jan, *European Urbanisation, 1500–1800* (London: Methuen, 1984, reprt., Routledge, 2013).

Dewey, John, "President Hutchins' Proposals to Remake Higher Education," *Social Frontier* 3 (Jan. 1937): 103–4.

Dollimore, Jonathan, *Radical Tragedy: Religion, Ideology, and Power in the Drama of Shakespeare and His Contemporaries* (Chicago: University of Chicago Press, 1984).

Bernard, G. W., "The Dissolution of the Monasteries," *History* 96.324 (2011): 390–409.

——. *The King's Reformation: Henry VIII and the Remaking of the English Church* (New Haven: Yale University Press, 2005).

Black, Robert, "Literacy in Florence, 1427," in Daniel E. Bornstein and David Spencer Peterson, eds., *Florence and Beyond: Culture, Society and Politics in Renaissance Italy* (Toronto: Centre for Reformation and Renaissance Studies, 2008), 195–210.

Bloom, Allan, *The Closing of the American Mind: How Higher Education Has Failed Democracy and Impoverished the Souls of Today's Students* (New York: Simon and Schuster, 1987).

Blumenthal, Joseph, *The Printed Book in America* (Boston: David R. Godine and Dartmouth College Library, 1977).

Bod, Rens, *A New History of the Humanities* (Oxford: Oxford University Press, 2013).

Bok, Derek, *Higher Education in America* (Princeton: Princeton University Press, 2015).

Boucaud-Victoire, Kévin, "How Michel Foucault Got Neoliberalism so Wrong: An Interview with Daniel Zamora," *Jacobin Magazine* (Sept. 6, 2019), at https://jacobinmag.com/2019/09/michel-foucault-neoliberalism-friedrich-hayek-milton-friedman-gary-becker-minoritarian-governments.

Bound, John, Breno Braga, Gaurav Khanna, and Sarah Turner, *Public Universities: The Supply Side of Building a Skilled Workforce*. National Bureau of Economic Research Working Paper No. 25945 (June 2019), at www.nber .org/papers/w25945.

Bourdieu, Pierre, *The Field of Cultural Production* (New York: Columbia University Press, 1993).

——, and Jean-Claude Passeron. *Reproduction in Education, Society and Culture*, Richard Nice, trans. (London: Sage, 1977).

Bousma, William, "Learning and the Problem of Undergraduate Education," in John Voss and Paul L. Ward, eds., *Confrontation and Learned Societies* (New York: New York University Press, 1970), 70–103.

Bowen, William G., and Michael S. McPherson, *Lesson Plan: An Agenda for Change in American Higher Education* (Princeton: Princeton University Press, 2016).

Boyd, Danah, "Did Media Literacy Backfire?" *Points: Data & Society* (Jan. 5, 2017), at https://points.datasociety.net/did-media-literacy-backfire-7418c084d88d.

Briggs, Charles F., "Literacy, Reading, and Writing in the Medieval West," *Journal of Medieval History*, 26:4 (2000): 397–420.

higher education, processing the tuition fees of "customers" while protecting not their young charges but their own corporate brands. Campus
after campus and system after system – adopting nineteenth-century
corporate immunity strategies – force students to return to physical
classrooms and dorms while also coercing them to sign liability waivers
for illness or death if infected by Covid-19. By August 2020, university and
college boards of trustees, who have insisted that students return to
campuses, were responsible for over 26,000 cases of Covid-19 at over
750 schools and for sixty-four student deaths. By September 2020, thousands more had been infected. On campus after campus faculty-shared
governance could now be safely ignored or crushed. Graduate student
unions and rights could be swept aside: all in the name of responding
to – or exploiting – the national crisis.

We could easily add dozens of examples of such actions across the
spectrum of American colleges and universities from the daily press and
from a growing body of hastily assembled studies. Coverage in the *New
York Times*, the *Washington Post*, the *Chronicle of Higher Education*, and
Inside Higher Education, among many others, records the daily traumas
visited upon campuses, faculty rights, and student well-being. Our aim
here, however, is not to begin another book about the effects of the
pandemic on higher ed – dozens are no doubt already on the way – but
to point out how the deeply embedded structural changes discussed in
the chapters above have only been aggravated and hastened by the
current crisis. No one can safely predict – and it is not the job of the
historian to do so – how Covid-19 will affect higher education in the long
run. Nor can we speculate on what changes the 2020 elections will bring.
This book has been built upon a historical metaphor and a fundamentally historical outlook. It is neither current journalism nor futurist
prediction. But it is clear that the pandemic has only hastened the
processes that we have laid out in the pages above.

*

But not all on the horizon need be negative. While the pandemic has
disrupted normal social forms and structures – everything from the
performing arts, to athletics, to office culture, to the classroom – much
has also come to the fore that has already been in the works as nascent

and innovative in American culture. Advanced digital technology has been rapidly deployed for everything from remote learning, conferencing, and instruction to small-scale social gatherings, cultural events, and performances. The necessary social isolation and distancing that came with the pandemic have thrust large portions of the American – and the world – population unto their own resources and devices as neoliberal governments foster profits and leave citizens to live or die. Ironically or not, this has left open, interstitial spaces – a new iteration of Jürgen Habermas' public sphere – for quiet, individual reflection and the organization of small groups of culture workers to attempt to reconceive what social interaction on every level – from the concert hall, to the conference center, to the lecture room – might be in the wake of the serious disruption of the old accepted forms of our mass, capitalist, and consumerist society. While governments and their enablers have tried every means to force populations back into old molds, into whatever definition of the nineteenth-century factory suits local cultures and institutions – the people themselves – especially in the Anglo-Saxon world – have decided to take their own paths, at least for now and tentatively and uncertainly.

How will such incipient structures and forms of social life begin to emerge within the world of higher education? In our last chapter we already began to offer some concepts of how academics, most especially in the humanities, might reconceive what the "college" and "campus" might look like. As negative as the forces of government and corporations have been in pushing through their own crisis plans, the pandemic has allowed entirely new thinking about a broad array of social and institutional settings and structures. Will higher education – by which I mean here chiefly its faculties and their collegial organizations – be able to use the crisis to rebuild an academy governed by its own intellectual agendas and the immediate needs of students for instruction and enlightenment? Will scholars and teachers be able to sink deep institutional roots for innovative structures and organizations that become independent of the predominant higher-education corporation? Can humanists, in particular, use this crisis to re-imagine their own roles and their relationships with their colleagues and students and with society at large?

——. "On Trigger Warnings," *AAUP Reports and Publications* (Aug. 2014), at www.aaup.org/report/trigger-warnings.

——. "Trends in the Academic Labor Force, 1975–2015," at www.aaup .org/sites/default/files/Academic_Labor_Force_Trends_1975-2015.pdf.

——. "Visualizing Change: The Annual Report on the Economic Status of the Profession, 2016–17," at www.aaup.org/file/FCS_2016-17.pdf.

American Council of Learned Societies et al., *Report of the Commission on the Humanities* (New York: ACLS, 1964).

Anderson, Kent, "Trust Falls – Are We in a New Phase of Corporate Research?" *Scholarly Kitchen* (Aug. 15, 2017), at https://scholarlykitchen .sspnet.org/2017/08/15/trust-falls-new-phase-corporate-research.

Anderson, Rick, "Less than Meets the Eye: Print Book Use Is Falling Faster in Research Libraries," *Scholarly Kitchen* (Aug. 21, 2017), at https:// scholarlykitchen.sspnet.org/2017/08/21/less-meets-eye-print-book-use-falling-faster-research-libraries.

Anderson, Robert D., *European Universities from the Enlightenment to 1914* (Oxford: Oxford University Press, 2010).

André, Bernard, *The Life of Henry VII*, Daniel Hobbins, ed. and trans. (New York: Italica Press, 2011).

Aronowitz, Stanley, *The Knowledge Factory: Dismantling the Corporate University and Creating True Higher Learning* (Boston: Beacon Press, 2005).

——, and Henry A. Giroux. *Postmodern Education: Politics, Culture, and Social Criticism* (Minneapolis: University of Minnesota Press, 1991).

Arum, Richard, and Jarip Roksa, *Academically Adrift: Limited Learning on College Campuses* (Chicago: University of Chicago Press, 2011).

Association of Governing Boards of Universities and Colleges, *Public Confidence in Higher Education* (2018), at https://agb.org/sites/default/ files/report_2018_guardians_public_confidence.pdf.

Bäuml, Franz H., "Varieties and Consequences of Medieval Literacy and Illiteracy," *Speculum* 55.2 (1980): 237–65.

Beach, Alison I., and Isabelle Cochelin, eds., *The Cambridge History of Medieval Monasticism in the Latin World*, 2 vols. (Cambridge: Cambridge University Press, 2020).

Bell, David N., "Libraries in England and Wales," *Oxford Bibliographies* (March 2016), at www.oxfordbibliographies.com/view/document/obo-9780195396584/obo-9780195396584-0193.xml.

Bell, Daniel, *The Reforming of General Education: The Columbia College Experience in its National Setting* (New York: Columbia University Press, 1966).

D'Souza, Dinesh, *Illiberal Education: The Politics of Race and Sex on Campus* (New York: Vintage, 1992).

Duffy, Eamon, *The Stripping of the Altars: Traditional Religion in England, 1400–1580* (New Haven: Yale University Press, 1992; 2nd, rev. ed., 2005).

Ehrenreich, Barbara, *Fear of Falling: The Inner Life of the Middle Class* (New York: HarperCollins, 1989).

Erasmus, Desiderius, *Ten Colloquies*, Craig R. Thompson, ed. and trans. (Indianapolis: Bobs-Merrill, 1957).

Esposito, Joseph J., "Good Data, Bad Data, You Know I've Had My Share: Library Book Acquisition Patterns," *Scholarly Kitchen* (July 23, 2018), at https://scholarlykitchen.sspnet.org/2018/07/23/good-data-bad-data-know-ive-share-library-book-acquisition-patterns.

—— and Karen Barch, "Monograph Output of American University Presses, 2009–2013: A Report Prepared for the Andrew W. Mellon Foundation" (Feb. 10, 2017), at https://scholarlykitchen.sspnet.org/wp-content/uploads/2017/02/Monograph-Output-of-University-Presses.pdf.

——, Karen Barch, and Rick Anderson, "Revisiting Two Perspectives on Library-based University Presses," *Scholarly Kitchen* (July 19, 2017), at https://scholarlykitchen.sspnet.org/2017/07/19/revisiting-two-perspectives-library-based-university-presses.

Fitzmaurice, Andrew, *Humanism and America: An Intellectual History of English Colonisation, 1500–1625* (Cambridge: Cambridge University Press, 2004).

Fletcher, J. M., "The Faculty of Arts," in J. I. Catto and Ralph Evans, eds. *The History of the University of Oxford* I *The Early Oxford Schools* (Oxford: Oxford University Press, 1984), 369–99.

Foucault, Michel, "What is Enlightenment?," in Paul Rabinow, ed., *The Foucault Reader* (New York: Pantheon Books, 1984), 32–50.

Gardiner, Eileen, and Ronald G. Musto, *The Digital Humanities: A Primer for Students and Scholars* (New York: Cambridge University Press, 2015).

Garrard, Graeme, *Counter-Enlightenments: From the Eighteenth Century to the Present* (Abingdon: Routledge, 2006).

——. *Rousseau's Counter-Enlightenment: A Republican Critique of the Philosophes* (Buffalo: State University of New York Press, 2003).

Georgetown University Center on Education and the Workforce, "A First Try at ROI" (November 2019), at https://cew.georgetown.edu/cew-reports/CollegeROI.

Ginder, S. A., J. E. Kelly-Reid, and F. B. Mann, *Enrollment and Employees in Postsecondary Institutions, Fall 2017; and Financial Statistics and Academic*

5 Strengthen Title IX offices and make Title IX regulations more consistent and transparent.

Why? *See Chapter 7.*

6 Reform admissions standards by strengthening affirmative action and class-based admissions and by increasing oversight of admissions policies and offices.

Why? *See Chapter 7.*

7 Encourage direct taxation of athletic programs' independent revenues and increase legislative oversight of college athletics' independent ventures.

Why? *See Chapter 7.*

8 Strengthen the National Endowments for the Humanities and the Arts, the National Science Foundation, and other Federal agencies to include more direct aid to researchers.

Why? *See Chapter 8.*

9 Tighten regulation and oversight of for-profit colleges and universities.

Why? *See Chapter 9.*

10 Launch a new, digital-age version of the National Defense Education Act of 1957 to increase aid to scholarly publishers, libraries, and other institutions of scholarly communication.

Why? *See Chapter 9.*

Select Bibliography

The following select bibliography provides all primary and secondary works used in this book. While it also includes edited volumes, most individual chapters within these volumes are found in the footnotes. It contains feature articles in weekly and monthly news media, but it does not contain the numerous news reports from daily coverage in the *Chronicle of Higher Education* and *Inside Higher Education*, and such sources as AOL, *Bloomberg*, *Forbes*, the *Guardian*, the *LA Times*, the *Nation*, the *New York Times*, *Politico*, *Slate*, the *Wall Street Journal*, and the like. Full citations to these sources appear in the footnotes. URLs to online resources and publications are current as of February 2020.

AAM Columns, "Medieval Literacy." Sewanee Medieval Colloquium (Sept. 19, 2015), at http://medievalcolloquium.sewanee.edu/ask-a-medievalist/aam-columns/literacy.php.

Allen, Mark, ed., *The Corporate University Handbook: Designing, Managing and Growing a Successful Program* (New York: American Management Association, 2002).

American Academy of Arts and Science, Humanities Indicators Project, "Bachelor's Degrees in the Humanities," updated May 2017, at www.amacad.org/humanities-indicators/higher-education/bachelors-degrees-humanities.

——. "Trends in the Demographics of Humanities Faculty: Key Findings from the 2012–13 Humanities Departmental Survey," at www.humanitiesindicators.org.

American Association of University Professors, "Background Facts on Contingent Faculty Positions [1975–2015]," at www.aaup.org/issues/contingency/background-facts.

apart – quaint relics of a bygone era? Will continued Federal and state austerity measures hasten the rate of closure, first of America's smaller and marginal schools, then of its state systems, and then of the majority of its renowned private liberal-arts colleges? How many major research universities and liberal-arts colleges will have survived over the next twenty-odd years? Will Moody's projections match the most pessimistic, if still not widely publicized, visions of higher ed's collapse? Whatever the next few years see in significant political realignments, will current trends in American public opinion that have cast doubt on higher-ed's mission, methods, and impact accelerate politicians' drive to dismantle our colleges and universities? Such perfect-storm scenarios may be fanciful "hyperbole," or they may become a harsh reality. This book has presented enough hard fact, study, survey, and expressed opinion to admit that real possibility.

*

Within these scenarios, what would survive of what we have consistently emphasized as the essence of higher education? Based on the historical liberal arts and sciences, our system has not only educated students for their roles in society and governance but has also prepared them as individuals to evaluate the present on the basis of past experience and wisdom. Can this form of humanistic education survive in the face of increasing emphasis on STEM and credentialing? What alternative visions, however utopian, might we conjure in these final pages? What futures might lay ahead for higher education outside, and without our current system, of colleges and universities?

The original monastic impulse did not emerge from a void or a society in collapse. Its founders walked away from thriving cities and markets, lucrative careers, and well-established social networks, centuries of cultural achievements and institutions. They set off into their wilderness individually and in small groups to rebuild a world, "to make the desert a city." Could higher ed's remaining corps of highly skilled and professional humanists regroup today without the support of departments, faculties, grants and rewards, salaries, tenured positions, and rigorous forms of communication to form their own academies? Like the first humanists in Renaissance Italy, could individuals or groups find space

Will the liberal arts and sciences have to go their separate ways as science and technology become increasingly too expensive to house and support and the humanities become increasingly marginalized in American society? Will the next two decades see a new series of independent research centers in the humanities, of corporate training programs in advanced humanities and business skills, and of corporate-funded and directed research in high-end science and technology? What will be left for our universities and colleges to do?

Can the American public itself be persuaded once again to pick up the burden of universal, egalitarian higher education that had once propelled the nation to world leadership? Even as progressive political forces retake majorities in Federal, state, and local elections, it is estimated today that it will take another generation to repair the damage currently already done to America's cultural and political system. Does higher education have another generation of grace?

2036

The lessons of the Protestant transformation of Britain's spiritual life after the Dissolution might offer some final lessons and patterns. How did the spiritual life of the English survive the wholesale destruction of abbeys, their libraries, cloisters, refectories, hospitals, mills, and granges? How did the medieval life of the mind and the culture that supported it survive without the accompanying liturgies, rituals, and rites, the symbolic social acts embodied in the monasteries? Did the simplified and non-material devotions of Protestantism leave a permanent impoverishment of spiritual life? Or were they the beginning of a new period of growth?

If one were to ask the educated British layperson today about the history of the Dissolution, they are likely to respond that it was, after all, a good thing, since it abolished an older, outworn system that depended on superstitious and wrongheaded thinking, on the squandering of resources, and on the forced devotion and abuse of thousands of individuals. Life after the Dissolution and the Reformation, they would argue, was a necessary step in the evolution of a nation and of a modern world that was more rational, secular, and scientific, more egalitarian, and less dependent on the past and on alien forms of thought and life.

Bristow, William, "Enlightenment," *The Stanford Encyclopedia of Philosophy* (Fall 2017 edition), Edward N. Zalta, ed., at https://plato.stanford.edu/archives/fall2017/entries/enlightenment.

British National Archives, "Dissolution of the Monasteries," at www.nationalarchives.gov.uk/help-with-your-research/research-guides/dissolution-monasteries-1536-1540/#4-the-dissolution-and-the-build-up-to-it-1524-1540-key-records.

Brockliss, Laurence W. B., *The University of Oxford: A History* (Oxford: Oxford University Press, 2016.)

Brooke, Christopher N. L., ed., *A History of the University of Cambridge*, 4 vols. (Cambridge: Cambridge University Press, 1988–2004.)

——. "Cambridge in the Age of the Puritan Revolution," in Victor Morgan, *History of the University of Cambridge* II. *1546–1750* (Cambridge: Cambridge University Press, 2004), 464–82.

Brown, Peter Robert Lamont, *The Cult of Saints: Its Rise and Function in Latin Christianity* (Chicago: University of Chicago, 1980).

Brustein, Robert, "Whose University: The Case for Professionalism," *The Bulletin of the Midwest Modern Language Association* 2.2 (Autumn 1969): 31–36.

Buchanan, James M., and Nicos E. Devletoglou, *Academia in Anarchy: An Economic Diagnosis* (New York: Basic Books, 1979).

Buchanan, Patrick, *The Death of the West: How Dying Populations and Immigrant Invasions Imperil Our Culture and Civilization* (New York: St. Martin's Press, 2001).

——. "Speech to the 1992 Republican National Convention," at https://buchanan.org/blog/1992-republican-national-convention-speech-148.

Buckley, William F. Jr., *God and Man at Yale: The Superstitions of "Academic Freedom"* (Washington, DC: Regnery, 1951).

Buringh, E., and J. Van Zanden, "Charting the 'Rise of the West': Manuscripts and Printed Books in Europe. A Long-Term Perspective from the Sixth through Eighteenth Centuries," *Journal of Economic History* 69.2 (2009): 409–45.

Bush, Douglas, *The Renaissance and English Humanism* (Toronto: University of Toronto Press, 1939, repr., 2016.)

Bush, George H. W., "Remarks at the University of Michigan Commencement Ceremony in Ann Arbor, 4 May 1991," George Bush Presidential Library, at https://bush41library.tamu.edu/archives/public-papers/2949.

Bushnell, Rebecca W., *A Culture of Teaching: Early Modern Humanism in Theory and Practice* (Ithaca, NY: Cornell University Press, 1996).

Cantalupo, Nancy Chi, and William Kidder, "A Systematic Look at a Serial Problem: Sexual Harassment of Students by University Faculty," *Utah Law Review* (June 30, 2018): 671–786.

Canterbury Psalter, University of Cambridge, Trinity College Library, MS R.17.1.

Cantor, David, Bonnie Fisher, et al., "Report on the AAU Campus Climate Survey on Sexual Assault and Misconduct," The Association of American Universities (Oct. 15, 2019), at www.aau.edu/key-issues/campus-climate-and-safety/aau-campus-climate-survey-2019.

Carlson, David R., *English Humanist Books: Writers and Patrons, Manuscript and Print, 1475–1525* (Toronto: University of Toronto Press, 1993).

Carnegie Foundation, *Control of the Campus: A Report on the Governance of Higher Education* (Princeton, NJ: Carnegie Foundation, 1982).

Carone, Angela, "Fraternities are Significantly Responsible for Campus Sexual Assault," in Jack Lasky, ed., *Sexual Assault on Campus* (Farmington Hills, MI: Greenhaven Press, 2016).

Caspar, Scott E., and Joan Shelly Rubin, "The History of the Book in America," in Michael F. Suarez S. J. and H. R. Woudhuysen, eds., *The Book: A Global History* (Oxford: Oxford University Press, 2013), 682–709.

Caspari, Fritz, *Humanism and the Social Order in Tudor England* (New York: Columbia University Teacher's College Press, 1968).

Cassirer, Ernst, Paul Oskar Kristeller, and John Herman Randall, Jr., eds. *The Renaissance Philosophy of Man* (Chicago: University of Chicago Press 1969).

Catto, J. I., and Ralph Evans, eds., *The History of the University of Oxford*, I. *The Early Oxford Schools* (Oxford: Oxford University Press, 1984).

Celenza, Christopher S. *The Intellectual World of the Italian Renaissance: Language, Philosophy, and the Search for Meaning* (New York: Cambridge University Press, 2020).

Chessman, Hollie M., et al., "The Financial Resilience of Independent Colleges and Universities," CIC-TIAA Institute_Financial Resilience of Independent Colleges_August 2017.pdf.

Childress, Herb, *The Adjunct Underclass: How America's Colleges Betrayed Their Faculty, Their Students, and Their Mission* (Chicago: University of Chicago Press, 2019).

Chomsky, Noam, "Academic Freedom and the Corporatization of Universities." University of Toronto, Scarborough (April 6, 2011), at https://chomsky.info/20110406.

Clark, James, *The Benedictines in the Middle Ages* (Woodbridge: Boydell, 2014).

Epilogue

I N HER 2007 BOOK, *THE SHOCK DOCTRINE: The Rise of Disaster Capitalism*, Naomi Klein examined the late stages of an oligarchic system that depends not on its alleged adherence to markets and economic supply-and-demand but on opportunism and the brute force of circumstances to further control work forces and resources. This control, she observed, is accomplished through taking advantage of "disasters" – crisis points in society, nature, and economic and belief systems – to force through rapid and highly unpopular change, consolidation of power, and further erosion of economic and political equality. We can find historical precedent in many cases across time, but here, at the end of our examination of the dissolution of the American university, let us return to our original metaphor, or historical analogy, to cast more light on this phenomenon.

We have made the point across these chapters that the original Dissolution of the Monasteries under Henry VIII and his chief minister Thomas Cromwell was not a well thought-out, strategic plan implemented through stealth, but a series of opportunistic acts enabled by a wide variety of individuals and social and cultural forces. By the time of the final monastic closures in 1540, no one in England was yet certain that this was an irreversible upheaval, but the results certainly put the final seal on momentous currents of change. We have also observed that the causes for King Henry's alignment with the English reformers were both intellectual and moral persuasion and the weight of circumstances: two "shocks," one domestic and one foreign. The first was domestic: the revolt known as the Pilgrimage of Grace in October 1536, which nearly toppled the Tudor

Appendix: Ten Steps for Restoring American Higher Education

The preceding Chapter 10 and Epilogue envisioned possible futures for higher education in some unconventional settings and ways, even if still based on the historical precedents of higher learning and the university. But what can we do now to strengthen and reform our existing institutions of higher learning? The Ten Steps below recommend some very specific ways to reform and revitalize our current colleges and universities. They draw on existing structures, precedent, policy, and legislation. Each is followed by a "Why?" and a reference to the appropriate chapter in Part II above, where these issues are discussed at length.

1 Tighten regulation and oversight of the corporate boards of universities for membership, qualifications, and general oversight policies. Use existing corporate legislation and statutory authority.
   Why? *See Chapter 5.*
2 Tax university endowments. Thomas Piketty's 1 percent tax and recent Senate recommendations point to the need to increase accountability and draw-downs for use in financial aid and faculty salaries.
   Why? *See Chapter 6.*
3 Strengthen faculty and contingent-faculty unions and encourage the NLRB to recognize more faculty unions through simpler and more transparent processes.
   Why? *See Chapter 6.*
4 Increase Federal student-loan programs, direct student grants (Pell, etc.), and loan forgiveness. Replace private, for-profit loan programs and firms with Federal funding.
   Why? *See Chapter 6.*

Libraries, Fiscal Year 2017: First Look (Provisional Data) January 2019, at https://nces.ed.gov/pubs2019/2019021REV.

Giroux, Henry A., "Liberal Arts Education and the Struggle for Public Life: Dreaming about Democracy," in Darryl J. Gless and Barbara Herrnstein Smith, eds., *The Politics of Liberal Education* (Durham, NC: Duke University Press, 1992), 119–44.

———. *Neoliberalism's War on Higher Education* (Chicago: Haymarket Books, 2014).

Givler, Peter, "University Press Publishing in the United States," in Richard E. Abel and Lyman W. Newman, eds., *Scholarly Publishing: Books, Journals, Publishers and Libraries in the Twentieth Century* (New York: Wiley, 2002), at www.aupresses.org/about-aaup/about-university-presses/history-of-university-presses.

Graff, Gerald, "Teach the Conflicts," in Darryl J. Gless and Barbara Herrnstein Smith, eds., *The Politics of Liberal Education* (Durham, NC: Duke University Press, 1992).

Grafton, Anthony, and Lisa Jardine, *From Humanism to the Humanities* (Cambridge, MA: Harvard University Press, 1986).

Green, Ian M., *Humanism and Protestantism in Early Modern English Education* (Farnham: Ashgate, 2009; 2nd ed. New York: Routledge, 2016).

Green, Masha, "An N.Y.U. Sexual-Harassment Case Has Spurred a Necessary Conversation About #MeToo," *New Yorker* (August 25, 2018), at www.newyorker.com/news/our-columnists/an-nyu-sexual-harassment-case-has-spurred-a-necessary-conversation-about-metoo.

Green, V. H. H., *A History of Oxford University* (London: B. T. Batsford, 1974).

Grendler, Paul F., *Jesuit Schools and Universities in Europe, 1548–1773* (Boston: Brill, 2018).

———. *Schooling in Renaissance Italy: Literacy and Learning, 1300–1600* (Baltimore: Johns Hopkins University Press, 1989).

———. *The Universities of the Italian Renaissance* (Baltimore: Johns Hopkins University Press, 2002).

Habermas, Jürgen, *The Structural Transformation of the Public Sphere: An Inquiry into a Category of Bourgeois Society*, Thomas Burger and Frederick Lawrence, trans. (Cambridge, MA: The MIT Press, 1989).

Halikias, Dimitrios, and Richard V. Reeves, "Ladders, Labs, or Laggards? Which Public Universities Contribute Most," *Brookings Report* (July 11, 2017), at www.brookings.edu/research/ladders-labs-or-laggards-which-public-universities-contribute-most.

Hall, David D., *A History of the Book in America*, 5 vols. (Chapel Hill: University of North Carolina Press, 2000–2010).

Halperin, Richard, *The Poetics of Primitive Accumulation: English Renaissance Culture and the Genealogy of Capital* (Ithaca, NY: Cornell University Press, 1991).

Hartman, Geoffrey, *Criticism in the Wilderness: The Study of Literature Today* (New Haven: Yale University Press, 1980).

Harvard University Press, "A Brief History of Harvard University Press," at www.hup.harvard.edu/about/history.html.

Hawes, Gene R., *To Advance Knowledge: A Handbook on American University Press Publishing* (New York: American Association of University Presses, 1967).

Head, Alison J., and Michael B. Eisenberg, "Project Information Literacy Progress Report: Lessons Learned. How College Students Seek Information in the Digital Age," The Information School, University of Washington (Dec. 1, 2009), at http://ctl.yale.edu/sites/default/files/basic-page-supplementary-materials-files/how_students_seek_information_in_the_digital_age.pdf.

Hearn, Denise R., "Education in the Workplace: An Examination of Corporate University Models (edited version, Nov. 19, 2018)," at www.newfoundations.com/OrgTheory/Hearn721.html.

Herrnstein, Richard J., and Charles Murray, *The Bell Curve: Intelligence and Class Structure in American Life* (New York: Free Press, 1994).

Highfield, J. R. L., "The Early Colleges," in J. I. Catto and Ralph Evans, *The History of the University of Oxford* I. *The Early Oxford Schools* (Oxford: Oxford University Press, 1984), 369–99.

Hodges, George, *The Project Gutenberg EBook of Fountains Abbey*. Project Gutenberg, 2016, at www.gutenberg.org/files/52581/52581-h/52581-h.htm.

Hofstadter, Richard, *Anti-Intellectualism in American Life* (New York: Vintage Books, 1962).

———. *The Paranoid Style in American Politics* (New York: Vintage Books, 1965; rev. ed., with new foreword by Sean Wilentz, 2008).

——— and Wilson Smith, eds., *American Higher Education: A Documentary History*, 2 vols. (Chicago: University of Chicago Press, 1961).

Horkheimer, Max, and Theodor Adorno, *Dialect of Enlightenment*, Edmund Jephcott, trans., Gunzelin Schmid Noerr, ed. (Stanford: Stanford University Press, 2002).

Horn, Walter, and Ernest Born, *The Plan of St Gall*, 3 vols. (Berkeley: University of California Press, 1979).

Hurlburt, Steven, and Michael McGarrah, *The Shifting Academic Workforce: Where Are the Contingent Faculty?* TIAA-CREF Delta Cost Project (November 2016), at www.air.org/sites/default/files/downloads/report/Shifting-Academic-Workforce-November-2016.pdf.

Hutcheson, Philo A., *A People's History of American Higher Education* (New York: Routledge, 2019.)

Jaeger, C. Stephen, *The Envy of Angels: Cathedral Schools and Social Ideals in Medieval Europe, 950–1200* (Philadelphia: University of Pennsylvania Press, 1994).

Kallendorf, Craig W., trans., *Humanist Educational Treatises* (Cambridge, MA: Harvard University Press, 2002).

Kapur, Ajay, Niall Macleod, and Narendra Singh, "Plutonomy: Buying Luxury, Explaining Global Imbalances," *Citigroup, Equity Strategy, Industry Note* (Oct. 16, 2005), at https://delong.typepad.com/plutonomy-1.pdf.

Karabel, Jerome, *The Chosen: The Hidden History of Admission and Exclusion at Harvard, Yale, and Princeton* (Boston: Houghton Mifflin, 2005).

Ker, N. R., *Medieval Libraries of Great Britain: A List of Surviving Books*, 2nd ed. (London: Royal Historical Society, 1964).

Kerr, Clark, *The Uses of the University* (Cambridge, MA: Harvard University Press, 1964).

Kezar, Adrianna, Tom DePaola, and Daniel T. Scott, *The Gig Academy: Mapping Labor in the Neoliberal University* (Baltimore: Johns Hopkins University Press, 2019).

Kipnis, Laura, *Unwanted Advances: Sexual Paranoia Comes to Campus* (New York: HarperCollins, 2017).

Kittellson, J. M., and P. J. Transue, eds., *Rebirth, Reform and Resilience: Universities in Transition, 1300–1700* (Columbus: Ohio State University Press, 1984).

Klein, Naomi, *The Shock Doctrine: The Rise of Disaster Capitalism* (New York: Henry Holt, 2007).

Knapp, L. G., J. E. Kelly-Reid, and S. A. Ginder, *Employees in Postsecondary Institutions, Fall 2010, and Salaries of Full-Time Instructional Staff, 2010–11* (NCES 2012-276), U.S. Department of Education (Washington, DC: National Center for Education Statistics), retrieved [Jul. 22, 2019] from http://nces.ed.gov/pubsearch at https://nces.ed.gov/pubs2012/2012276.pdf.

Knowles, David, *Christian Monasticism* (New York: McGraw Hill, 1969).

———. *The Religious Orders in England* III. *The Tudor Age* (Cambridge: Cambridge University Press, 1959, repr. 2004).

—— and R. Neville Hadcock, *Medieval Religious Houses: England and Wales* (London: Longman, 1971).

Knox, Emily J. M., *Trigger Warnings: History, Theory, Context* (Lanham, MD: Rowman & Littlefield, 2017).

Krieger, Leonard, *Ranke: The Meaning of History* (Chicago: University of Chicago Press, 1977).

Kuhn, Thomas, "The Essential Tension: Tradition and Innovation in Scientific Research," in *The Third (1959) University of Utah Research Conference on the Identification of Scientific Talent*, C. Taylor, ed. (Salt Lake City: University of Utah Press, 1959), 162–74.

Lambert, Matthew T., *Privatization and the Public Good: Public Universities in the Balance* (Cambridge, MA: Harvard Education Press, 2014).

Lawrence, C. H., *Medieval Monasticism*, 4th ed. (London: Routledge, 2015).

Leedham-Green, Elisabeth, and Teresa Webber, *The Cambridge History of Libraries in Britain and Ireland* I. *To 1640* (Cambridge: Cambridge University Press, 2013).

Levy, Peter B., "Spiro Agnew, the Forgotten Americans and the Rise of the New Right," *Historian* 75 (Winter 2013): 719.

Lewis, C. S., *English Literature in the Sixteenth Century* (Oxford: Oxford University Press, 1954).

Lewry, P. Osmund, "Grammar, Logic and Rhetoric," in J. I. Catto and Ralph Evans, *The History of the University of Oxford* I. *The Early Oxford Schools*, 401–33.

Lisak, David, "Understanding the Predatory Nature of Sexual Violence," *Sexual Assault Report (SAR)* 14.4 (March – April 2011), at www.middlebury .edu/media/view/240951/original.

Looney, Dennis, and Natalia Lusin, "Enrollments in Languages Other than English in United States Institutions of Higher Education, Summer 2016 and Fall 2016: Preliminary Report" (New York: Modern Language Association, 2018), at www.mla.org/content/download/83540/2197676/ 2016-Enrollments-Short-Report.pdf.

Lopate, Phillip, "Confessions of a Reluctant Revolutionary," *Columbia Magazine* (Winter 2017–18), at https://magazine.columbia.edu/article/ confessions-reluctant-revolutionary.

Lynch, Sarah B., *Medieval Pedagogical Writings: An Epitome* (Leeds: Kismet Press, 2018).

MacCulloch, Diarmaid, *Thomas Cromwell: A Revolutionary Life* (London: Allen Lane, 2018).

MacLean, Nancy, *Democracy in Chains: The Deep History of the Radical Right's Stealth Plan for America* (New York: Viking, 2017).

MacMullen, Ramsey, "The Place of the Holy Man in the Later Roman Empire," *Harvard Theological Review* 112.1 (Jan. 2019): 1–32.

Marchus, Jon, "The Looming Decline of the Public Research University," *Washington Monthly* (Sept./Oct. 2017), at https://washingtonmonthly .com/magazine/septemberoctober-2017/the-looming-decline-of-the-public-research-university.

McGee, Jon, *Breakpoint: The Changing Marketplace for Higher Education,* (Baltimore: Johns Hopkins University Press, 2015).

Melville, Gert, *The World of Medieval Monasticism: Its History and Forms of Life* (Athens, OH: Cistercian Publications, 2016).

Melzer, Arthur M., "The Origin of the Counter-Enlightenment: Rousseau and the New Religion of Sincerity," *American Political Science Review* 90.2 (1996): 344–60.

Minnicino, Michael J., "The New Dark Age: The Frankfurt School and 'Political Correctness'" (Washington, DC: Schiller Institute, 1992).

Moulton, Ian F., ed., *Reading and Literacy in the Middle Ages and Renaissance* (Turnhout: Brepols, 2004).

Muehlenhard, Zoë, D. Peterson, Terry P. Humphreys, and Kristen N. Jozkowski, "Evaluating the One-in-Five Statistic: Women's Risk of Sexual Assault while in College," Annual Review of Sex Research, *Journal of Sex Research* 54.4–5 (2017), at https://doi.org/10.1080/00224499.2017 .1295014.

Muller, Jerry Z., *The Tyranny of Metrics* (Princeton: Princeton University Press, 2018).

Munro, John, "Medieval Population Dynamics to 1500" (University of Toronto, September 2013), at www.economics.utoronto.ca/munro5/ L02MedievalPopulationC.pdf.

National Student Clearinghouse Research Center, "Completing College: A National View of Student Completion Rates, Fall 2012 Cohort," at https://nscresearchcenter.org/wp-content/uploads/SignatureReport16 .pdf.

NCAA Revenue and Expense Reports, 2010–2014.

New America, "Varying Degrees [2018]," at www.newamerica.org/ education-policy/reports/varying-degrees-2018.

New England Association of Schools and Colleges, "Merged, Closed, or Previously Accredited" (Aug. 2018), at www.neche.org/for-the-public/ merged-closed-or-previously-accredited.

Newman, John Henry, *The Idea of a University Defined and Illustrated: In Nine Discourses Delivered to the Catholics of Dublin* (Dublin: J. Duffy, 1852), in

Project Gutenberg, 2008, at www.gutenberg.org/files/24526/24526-pdf .pdf.

Nixon, Jon, *Higher Education and the Public Good: Imagining the University* (London: Continuum, 2012).

O'Donnell, James J., *Avatars of the Word: From Papyrus to Cyberspace* (Cambridge, MA: Harvard University Press, 1998).

Okahana, Hironao, and Enyu Zhou, "Graduate Enrollment and Degrees: 2006 to 2016," in *Graduate Enrollment and Degrees, 2006–2016* (Washington, DC: Council of Graduate Schools, September 2017), at https://cgsnet .org/ckfinder/userfiles/files/CGS_GED16_Report_Final.pdf.

O'Malley, John W., S. J., *The First Jesuits* (Cambridge, MA: Harvard University Press, 1993).

Petrarca, Francesco, *Invectives*, David Marsh, trans. (Cambridge, MA: Harvard University Press, 2003).

Pettegree, Andrew, *The Book in the Renaissance* (New Haven: Yale University Press 2011).

Piketty, Thomas, *Capital in the Twenty-First Century*, Arthur Goldhammer, trans. (Cambridge, MA: Harvard University Press, 2013).

Plan of St Gall, at www.stgallplan.org/en/index_plan.html.

Price, Lorna, *The Plan of St Gall in Brief* (Berkeley: University of California Press, 1982).

Rademakers, Martyn, *Corporate Universities: Drivers of the Learning Organization* (London: Routledge, 2015).

Randall, H., *The Universities of Europe in the Middle Ages*, 3 vols. (Oxford: Oxford University Press, 1988).

Reynolds, E. E., *Thomas More and Erasmus* (New York: Fordham University Press, 1965).

Ridder-Symoens, Hilde, ed., *A History of the European University* I. *Universities in the Middle Ages* (Cambridge: Cambridge University Press, 1991).

Riehl Leader, Damian, *The University to 1546*, (1988), vol. I of Christopher N. L. Brooke, ed., *A History of the University of Cambridge*, 4 vols. (Cambridge: Cambridge University Press, 1988–2004).

Ryan, Michael, "Deconstruction and Radical Teaching," in *The Pedagogical Imperative: Teaching as a Literary Genre*, Barbara Johnson, ed., Yale French Studies 63 (New Haven: Yale University Press, 1982), 45–58.

Sanford, Nevitt, *The American College: A Psychological and Social Interpretation of the Higher Learning* (New York: John Wiley, 1962).

Schmidt, Benjamin M., "The History BA Since the Great Recession: The 2018 AHA Majors Report," *AHA Perspectives* (Nov. 26, 2018), at www

.historians.org/publications-and-directories/perspectives-on-history/
december-2018/the-history-ba-since-the-great-recession-the-2018-aha-
majors-report.

Schonfeld, Roger C., "The Strategic Direction of Research Library Leaders:
Findings from the Latest Ithaka S+R Survey," *Scholarly Kitchen* (April 4,
2017), at https://scholarlykitchen.sspnet.org/2017/04/04/the-strategic-
direction-of-research-library-leaders-findings-from-the-latest-ithaka-sr-
survey.

Schrecker, Ellen, *No Ivory Tower: McCarthyism and the Universities* (New York:
Oxford University Press, 1986).

Simon, Joan, *Education and Society in Tudor England* (Cambridge:
Cambridge University Press, 1966).

Smith, Wilson, and Thomas Bender, eds., *American Higher Education
Transformed, 1940–2005: Documenting the National Discourse* (Baltimore:
Johns Hopkins University Press, 2008).

Stark, Jack, "The Wisconsin Idea: The University's Service to the State," in
Wisconsin Legislative Reference Bureau, ed., *State of Wisconsin 1995–1996
Blue Book* (Madison: Wisconsin Legislature Joint Committee on Legislative
Organization, 1995), 100–179.

Stevenson, John James, "University Control," *Popular Science Monthly* 61
(September, 1902): 396–406.

Stone, Lawrence, ed., *The University in Society* I. *Oxford and Cambridge from the
14th to the Early 19th Century* (Princeton: Princeton University Press, 1974,
repr. 2019).

Stowe, Kristin, and David Komasara, "An Analysis of Closed Colleges and
Universities," *Planning for Higher Education* 44.4 (July–Sept. 2016): 79–89.

Strickland, Susan, "Feminism, Postmodernism and Difference," in
Kathleen Lennon and Margaret Whitford, eds., *Knowing the
Difference: Feminist Perspectives in Epistemology* (New York: Routledge, 1994),
265–74.

Students for a Democratic Society, "Port Huron Statement (1962)," at
www2.iath.virginia.edu/sixties/HTML_docs/Resources/Primary/
Manifestos/SDS_Port_Huron.html.

Sykes, Charles J., *Fail U.: The False Promise of Higher Education* (New York:
St. Martin's Press, 2016).

Tanner, J. R., *Tudor Constitutional Documents* (Cambridge: Cambridge
University Press, 1922).

Thelin, John R., *A History of American Higher Education*, 2nd ed. (Baltimore:
Johns Hopkins University Press, 2011).

Thompson, John, *Books in the Digital Age: The Transformation of Academic and Higher Education Publishing in Britain and the United States* (Cambridge: Polity Press, 2005).

Tobriner, Marian Leona, *Vives' Introduction to Wisdom* (New York: Columbia University Teacher's College Press, 1968).

Trilling, Diana, "On the Steps of Low Library," in Diana Trilling, *We Must March My Darlings: A Critical Decade* (New York: Harcourt Brace Jovanovich, 1977), 76–153.

UC Berkeley Labor Center, "The High Public Cost of Low Wages," at http://laborcenter.berkeley.edu/pdf/2015/the-high-public-cost-of-low-wages.pdf.

US Bureau of Labor Statistics, Consumer Price Index, at www.in2013dollars.com/2000-dollars-in-2018.

US Congressional Research Service, "College and University Endowments: Overview and Tax Policy Options," (May 4, 2018), at https://fas.org/sgp/crs/misc/R44293.pdf.

US Department of Education, National Center for Education Statistics (2018), *Digest of Education Statistics, 2016* (NCES 2017-094), at https://nces.ed.gov/programs/digest/d16/ch_3.asp.

——. Integrated Postsecondary Education Data System (Ipeds), 2010–2014.

Valdivia, Walter D., "University Start-Ups: Critical for Improving Technology Transfer," Center for Technology Innovation at Brookings (November 2013), at www.brookings.edu/wp-content/uploads/2016/06/Valdivia_Tech-Transfer_v29_No-Embargo.pdf.

Vinciguerra, Thomas, "A Provost's Reflections: David P. Truman and the Bust of '68," *Columbia Magazine* (Fall 2017), at https://magazine.columbia.edu/article/provosts-reflections.

Wallerstein, Immanuel, and Paul Starr, eds., *The University Crisis Reader: The Liberal University Under Attack* (New York: Vintage Books, 1971).

Weber, Max, "Politics as a Vocation," in Tony Waters and Dagmar Waters, eds. and trans., *Weber's Rationalism and Modern Society* (New York: Palgrave Macmillan, 2015), 129–98.

Wilk, Jocelyn, curator, "1968: Columbia in Crisis," Columbia University Libraries, at https://exhibitions.library.columbia.edu/exhibits/show/1968.

Wolff-Eisenberg, Christine, "US Library Survey 2016." Ithaka S+R (April 3, 2017), at https://sr.ithaka.org/publications/us-library-survey-2016.

Woodward, G. W. O., *The Dissolution of the Monasteries* (London: Pitkin, 1974).

Woodward, William Harrison, *Desiderius Erasmus Concerning the Aim and Method of Education* (New York: Columbia University Teacher's College Press, 1964).

———. *Studies in Education during the Age of the Renaissance, 1400–1600* (New York: Columbia University Teacher's College Press, 1967).

———. *Vittorino da Feltre and Other Humanist Educators* (New York: Columbia University Teacher's College Press, 1963).

Index

Sandeen, Cathy, 138
Sandusky, Jerry, 101, 163
Sanford, Nevitt, 57, 155
San Jose State University, 269
Santayana, George, 8
scandals
    definitions, 153
    See also admissions; athletics; boards of
        trustees; canons; Culture Wars; free
        speech; political correctness; sexual
        assault and harassment; Title IX;
        trigger warnings
Schalin, Jay, 104
Schiller, Phil, 253
scholarly communication, 45, 228, 246,
    260–67
Scholasticism, 23
Schultz, Gary, 101–2, 163–64
sciences, 49, 60
    ancient, 40
    decline, 280
    funding, 205, 248, 255
    future, 303
    monographs, 262
    Ph.D.s, 296
    physical, 230
    publishing, 265
    See also liberal arts and sciences
Scientific Revolution, 206
Scopes Trial, 49
Scott, Rick, 238
Scranton Report, 71
Scranton, William, 63
SDS. *See* Students for a Democratic Society
separateness, 6
    1970s, 86
    authority, 7–9
    balance, 97
    British schools, 29
    budget struggles, 150
    canons, 199, 222
    Chomsky, 247
    colonial, 37–38
    Columbia, 66, 234
    decline, 259, 264
    definitions, 7–8
    digital turn, 229, 245, 264, 268, 271, 279,
        301
    Enlightenment, 211
    free speech, 186, 195
    future, 303
    German model, 44
    governance, 99
    illusion, 70
    jargon, 201
    legal implications, 171
    libraries, 274

loss, 10, 45, 75–76, 86, 148, 219, 228, 233,
    236
medieval, 24, 67
monastic, 11, 245, 293
Nixon, 80
public opinion, 111
research university, 72
scandals, 154
Title IX, 175
World War II, 52
    See also institutional triad
Service Employees International Union, 148
Serviceman's Readjustment Act of 1944. *See*
    GI Bill
Sessions, Jeff, 183
Seven Sisters, 51
sexual assault and harassment, 145, 163–69,
    170–71, 173, 176, 179
Sidney, Philip, 32
Silicon Valley, 256
Silliman, Benjamin, 96
Simon, Lou Anna K., 105, 166
Simon, William, 68
Slosson, Edward, 49
Smith, Adam, 207
Smith, Peter P., 251
Soares, Joseph A., 157
Society for African American Students, 62
Sorbon, Robert de, 27
Southern New Hampshire University, 268
Spanier, Graham, 101–2, 163–64
Spinoza, Baruch, 206
Sputnik, 53
St. Catharine College, 288
St Gall Plan, 11–14, 303
St. John's College, Maryland, 108
    board overreach, 108–9
    canons, 199
    founding, 39
    governance, 297
    Great Books, 197–98
    model, 69
St. John's College, Santa Fe, 230
St. Joseph's College, Indiana, 288
Stanford University
    AAU, 49
    admissions scandal, 155, 157
    endowment, 49, 113, 122–23
    faculty purges, 225
    Green Library, 274
    innovation incubators and zones, 256
    library collections, 304
    MOOCs, 269–70
    Press, 265–66
Stanford, Leland, 49
Stanger, Allison, 186
Stanley, Samuel L., Jr, 135, 167–68